5

Dictionary of
BRITAIN

ADRIAN ROOM

Oxford University Press
1986

Alphabet illustrations by
Robert Kettell

Photographs by:

Nicky Dixon, Rob Judges, Julian
Prentis

The publishers would like to
thank the following for their
permission to use photographs:

Animal Photography Partnership
Associated Press
The Automobile Association
BBC Hulton Picture Library
Birmingham City Council
British Tourist Authority
E J Brooks & Son
Camera Press
J Allan Cash Photo Library
Colorsport
Eagle Alexander Communications
Mary Evans Picture Library
The Guide Dogs for the Blind
Association
Marc Henrie
Kobal Collection
Frank Lane Picture Agency Ltd
Liberty
Mansell Collection
Merit Games
Network
City of Nottingham
Oxford & County Newspapers
Pacemaker Press
The Photo Source
Press Association
Royal Doulton
Royal Mint
The Salvation Army
Scottish Tourist Board
Brian and Sal Shuel
Sotheby's

The publishers would like to
thank the following for their time
and assistance:

British Standards Institute
Paul Goodson
Ideal Bakers
London Transport
News of the World
Derek Roberts

© Maps copyright Oxford
University Press

Oxford University Press
Walton Street, Oxford OX2 6DP

Oxford New York Toronto Delhi
Bombay Calcutta Madras Karachi
Petaling Jaya Singapore
Hong Kong Tokyo Nairobi
Dar es Salaam Cape Town
Melbourne Auckland

and associated companies in
Beirut Berlin Ibadan Nicosia

OXFORD is a trade mark of
Oxford University Press

ISBN 0 19 211662 2

ISBN 0 19 283056 2 Pbk.

© Oxford University Press 1986

Filmset in Palatino

Printed in Great Britain
at the University Press, Cambridge

Contents

Introduction

The *Dictionary of Britain* gives up-to-date information on all aspects of British life and institutions. It explains everything that other nationalities find interesting, amusing, puzzling or even frustrating about Britain and the British. Important public events, major government posts and well-known organizations of all kinds are described. Also included are events, institutions and people that show a typically British set of values or an important facet of British life. Entries on regional foods shed light on the culinary variety within Britain, while descriptions of sports, crafts and societies show what the British do in their spare time.

Extensive cross-references and a thematically arranged index make the dictionary easy to use. Finally, information that can most usefully be summarized in list or map form is included towards the back of the book and cross-referred to from the main text.

Adrian Room
Petersfield, Hampshire

Key to phonetic symbols

Vowels and diphthongs

1	iː	*as in*	see /siː/	11	ɜː	*as in*	fur /fɜː(r)/
2	ɪ	*as in*	sit /sɪt/	12	ə	*as in*	ago /ə'gəʊ/
3	e	*as in*	ten /ten/	13	eɪ	*as in*	page /peɪdʒ/
4	æ	*as in*	hat /hæt/	14	əʊ	*as in*	home /həʊm/
5	ɑː	*as in*	arm /ɑːm/	15	aɪ	*as in*	five /faɪv/
6	ɒ	*as in*	got /gɒt/	16	aʊ	*as in*	now /naʊ/
7	ɔː	*as in*	saw /sɔː/	17	ɔɪ	*as in*	join /dʒɔɪn/
8	ʊ	*as in*	put /pʊt/	18	ɪə	*as in*	near /nɪə(r)/
9	uː	*as in*	too /tuː/	19	eə	*as in*	hair /heə(r)/
10	ʌ	*as in*	cup /kʌp/	20	ʊə	*as in*	pure /pjʊə(r)/

Consonants

1	p	*as in*	pen /pen/	13	s	*as in*	so /səʊ/
2	b	*as in*	bad /bæd/	14	z	*as in*	zoo /zuː/
3	t	*as in*	tea /tiː/	15	ʃ	*as in*	she /ʃiː/
4	d	*as in*	did /dɪd/	16	ʒ	*as in*	vision /'vɪʒn/
5	k	*as in*	cat /kæt/	17	h	*as in*	how /haʊ/
6	g	*as in*	got /gɒt/	18	m	*as in*	man /mæn/
7	tʃ	*as in*	chin /tʃɪn/	19	n	*as in*	no /nəʊ/
8	dʒ	*as in*	June /dʒuːn/	20	ŋ	*as in*	sing /sɪŋ/
9	f	*as in*	fall /fɔːl/	21	l	*as in*	leg /leg/
10	v	*as in*	voice /vɔɪs/	22	r	*as in*	red /red/
11	θ	*as in*	thin /θɪn/	23	j	*as in*	yes /jes/
12	ð	*as in*	then /ðen/	24	w	*as in*	wet /wet/

Pronunciation

For each entry a recommended pronunciation is given. The model followed is RP, a non-regional accent of British English. In this accent *r* is sounded only before vowels. Final *r* in the spelling is silent unless the word is followed by one beginning with a vowel. This 'linking r' is shown in brackets as in *welfare officer* /ɒfɪsə(r)/: the *r* is to be sounded only when the next word begins with a vowel. When a linking *r* is possible within a headphrase, it is shown as at the end of *welfare*. Thus /ˈwelfeər ˌɒfɪsə(r)/. The high mark /ˈ/ shows the main stress in the phrase, and the low mark /ˌ/ shows the secondary stress. Sometimes the stress changes when a word is added to a headphrase. In such cases the pronunciation for the expanded phrase is shown in full in brackets. For example, *trilby (hat)* /ˈtrɪlbɪ (ˌtrɪlbɪ ˈhæt)/. When the addition of a word does not affect the position of the main stress, the additional word alone is shown in brackets. For example, *bring-and-buy (sale)* /ˌbrɪŋ ən ˈbaɪ (seɪl)/. The style of pronunciation shown is a careful one. For instance, *first class* is given as /ˌfɜːst ˈklɑːs/, although in fluent colloquial speech the /t/ is very likely to be omitted. A /t/ is also shown in *hot cross bun* where native speakers of English are likely to say /ˌhɒk krɒs ˈbʌn/. Users of the dictionary who want systematic information on such features are referred to *An English Pronunciation Companion* by A C Gimson and S M Ramsaran (OUP 1982).

Susan Ramsaran
University College, London

The Lion and the Unicorn
were fighting for the Crown;
The Lion Beat the Unicorn
all round about the town.

Some gave them white bread,
and some gave them brown;
Some gave them plum-cake,
and sent them out of town.

Traditional English nursery rhyme

'A' level /ˈeɪ ˌlevl/ **(Advanced level)** (education) A higher-level examination of the *GCE*, normally taken at the age of 17 or 18, two years after the *'O' level* examination. It is the standard for entrance to university and other higher education, and to many forms of professional training.

A N Other /ˌeɪ ˌen ˈʌðə(r)/ (language) A way of giving the name of a member of a sports team when his or her name is not yet known or when the member has not yet been selected. Also used as a specimen name in other circumstances, such as on a form, to show how it should be completed. [from 'another']

A to Z /ˌeɪ tə ˈzed/ (daily life) A general title for a street directory of a town or city, especially one of London.

AA /ˌeɪ ˈeɪ/**, the (Automobile Association, the)** (transport) One of the two leading British clubs for motorists, which offers its members practical advice and assistance, legal aid and a range of specialized services. Compare *RAC*.

Abdication /ˌæbdɪˈkeɪʃn/**, the** (history) The formal giving up of the throne in 1936 by King Edward VIII, so that he could marry an American divorcee, Mrs Wallis Simpson.

Aberdeen Angus /ˌæbədiːn ˈæŋgəs/ (animal world) A breed of black, hornless, beef cattle, originally reared in the Scottish counties of Aberdeen and Angus.

Aberdonian /ˌæbəˈdəʊnɪən/ (geography) Someone born or living in Aberdeen or the former county of Aberdeenshire, *Scotland*.

academic year /ˌækədemɪk ˈjɪə(r)/ (education) The year beginning in October in universities and establishments of *further education* or *higher education*, and September in schools (see *school year*), and ending in late June or early July. The year, which is usually divided into three *terms*[1], ends with important examinations, such as *GCE* and *CSE* in schools or a *first degree* in a university.

academy /əˈkædəmɪ/ (education) The name of certain schools and *colleges*[3], in particular some private secondary schools and a number of *public schools*[1] in *Scotland* (eg, *Edinburgh Academy*).

Academy /əˈkædəmɪ/, **the** (arts) The short title of a famous *academy*, especially the *Royal Academy* (*of Arts*) or the *British Academy*.

Academy of St Martin-in-the-Fields /əˌkædəmɪ əv snt ˌmɑːtɪn ɪn ðə ˈfiːldz/, **the** (arts) A leading *London* chamber orchestra, whose first concerts in the 1960s were held in the church of *St Martin-in-the-Fields*.

ACAS /ˈeɪkæs/ **(Advisory, Conciliation and Arbitration Service, the)** (work) An organization set up by the government in 1975 to provide mediation and arbitration as a means of avoiding or ending strikes or other industrial disputes. The Service also advises on industrial relations and encourages *collective bargaining*.

Access (card) /ˈækses (kɑːd)/ (finance) A major type of credit card issued by a group of banks including *Lloyds*, *Midland*, *National Westminster*, the *Clydesdale Bank* and the *Royal Bank of Scotland*. Compare *Barclaycard*.

Accession Day /ækˈseʃn deɪ/ (history) The day (6 February 1952) when *Queen Elizabeth* II acceded to the throne, marked annually by the flying of the *Union Jack* on government buildings. It is not a *bank holiday*.

accumulator /əˈkjuːmjʊleɪtə(r)/ (sport and leisure) A progressive bet in horse racing, especially on four or more races, in which the bet and winnings on the first race are placed on the second, those of the second on the third, and so on, so that the *punter* finally either wins everything or loses everything. Compare *double*[3].

Act (of Parliament) /ækt (əv ˈpɑːləmənt)/ (law) A law that has been passed by the *House of Commons* and *House of Lords* and given the *royal assent*.

act of God /ˌækt əv ˈɡɒd/ (law) A legal term used for damage caused by a sudden natural force such as a flood, hail storm or landslide, and not by man.

Act of Supremacy /ˌækt əv suːˈpreməsɪ/, **the** (history) The *Act* of 1534 that declared the sovereign to be the secular head of the *Church of England*.

Act of Union /ˌækt əv ˈjuːnɪən/, **the** (history) The *Act* of 1707 that declared the union of *England* and *Wales* and *Scotland* as a single kingdom under the name of *Great Britain*.

Adam (style) /ˈædəm (ˌædəm ˈstaɪl)/ (style) An elegant, neo-classical style of architecture and furniture created by the two Scots brothers Robert and James Adam in the 18th century.

ADC call /ˌeɪ diː ˈsiː kɔːl/ (daily life) A long distance telephone call whose cost is supplied to the caller by the operator after the call. [*a*dvice of *d*uration and *c*harge]

Admiral's Cup /ˌædmərəlz ˈkʌp/, **the** (sport and leisure) The main prize for the biennial international yachting contest of four races (the *Fastnet*, the Britannia Cup and two others). It is presented by the admiral who is the head of the Royal Ocean Racing Club, which established the prize in 1957.

Admiralty /ˈædmərəltɪ/, **the** (1 defence 2 government) 1 The former name (to 1964) of the *Royal Navy* department of the Ministry of Defence. 2 The government building in *Whitehall, London*, where the Admiralty was and where now the headquarters of the *Civil Service* is.

Admiralty Arch /ˌædmərəltɪ ˈɑːtʃ/ (London) A triumphal arch at the east end of The Mall, *London*, built as a memorial to *Queen Victoria* and named after the *Admiralty²*, next to which it stands.

Advent /ˈædvent/ (religion) For Christians, the time of preparation for the celebration of Christ's birth at *Christmas*, lasting from the *Sunday* nearest 30 November (called Advent Sunday) to Christmas. [from the *advent* or coming of Christ]

Advertising Standards Authority /ˌædvətaɪzɪŋ ˈstændədz ɔːˌθɒrətɪ/, **the (ASA, the)** (daily life) The independent (non-governmental) body that monitors professional standards of advertising in the interests of the public and of industry, in particular by means of the British Code of Advertising Practice. This Code aims to ensure that all advertisements are truthful, within the law, and morally decent (their slogan is 'legal, decent, honest and truthful'). Members of the public have the right to complain to the ASA about any specific advertisement, and the Authority may subsequently ask for the offending advertisement to be reworded or withdrawn altogether.

age of consent /ˌeɪdʒ əv kənˈsent/, **the** (law) The minimum age, at present 16, at which a young person may legally have sexual intercourse.

age of discretion /ˌeɪdʒ əv dɪˈskreʃn/, **the** (law) The minimum age, at present 14, at which a young person is judged legally competent to manage his or her own affairs.

Aintree /ˈeɪntriː/ (sport and leisure) A horse-racing course near Liverpool, where the *Grand National* is run annually.

Airedale (terrier) /ˈeədeɪl (ˌeədeɪl ˈterɪə(r))/ (animal world) A large, rough-haired, tan-coloured breed of dog with black back and sides. [originally bred in the valley of the river Aire, Yorkshire]

Al-Anon /ˌæl əˈnɒn/ (charities) A fellowship (founded in 1960) for the families of alcoholics, who meet to share experiences and discuss problems caused by living with an alcoholic. Many such alcoholics are themselves already being aided by *Alcoholics Anonymous*.

Albert Hall /ˌælbət ˈhɔːl/, **the** (London) A large hall in *London*, with seating for 8,000, where the annual *Promenade Concerts* are held, as well as a number of other concerts, parades, meetings, and ceremonial and sporting events. [in full, the Royal Albert Hall, built in 1867–71 and named in honour of Prince Albert, the husband of *Queen Victoria*]

Albert Memorial /ˌælbət məˈmɔːrɪəl/, **the** (London) A large monument opposite the *Albert Hall, London*, and containing a seated bronze figure of Prince Albert, to whom it was built as a national memorial in 1863–76.

Alcoholics Anonymous /ˌælkəˌhɒlɪks əˈnɒnəməs/ **(AA)** (charities) A voluntary organization for people who need help in fighting alcoholism. Compare *Al-Anon*.

Aldeburgh Festival /ˌɔːldbrə ˈfestɪvl/, **the** (arts) An annual music festival at Aldeburgh, Suffolk, where it was started in 1948 by the composer Benjamin *Britten* (1913–76), who lived in Aldeburgh.

alderman /ˈɔːldəmən/ (government) The title of a senior governor of the *City of London* and, before 1974, that of a senior member of a local council, elected by other *councillors*. Aldermen have not been members of the *GLC* since the 1977 elections and they have not been members of London *borough*[2] councils since the 1978 elections.

Aldermaston /ˈɔːldəmɑːstən/ (defence) A village in Berkshire where the Atomic Weapons Research Establishment is, and one of the main places selected by *CND* for anti-nuclear demonstrations, especially the marches to and from *London* in 1958–63.

Alderney (cow) /ˈɔːldənɪ (ˌɔːldənɪ ˈkaʊ)/ (animal world) A breed of light brown dairy cow, originally from Alderney, *Channel Islands*.

Alexandra Palace /ˌælɪgzɑːndrə ˈpælɪs/ (London) A large building on a hill in *Alexandra Park*, north *London*, used mainly for exhibitions and concerts. It formerly housed the main television studios of the *BBC*. The Palace was badly damaged by fire in July 1980 and is now being rebuilt. The outside will be restored to its original Victorian style (see *Victoriana*), while the inside will be used for conferences and concerts.

Alexandra Park /ˌælɪgzɑːndrə ˈpɑːk/ (sport and leisure) A park in north *London* containing *Alexandra Palace* and a well-known race-course. The park is currently being improved and part of it will be used for rare plants and for wild birds and animals.

Alf Garnett /ˌælf ˈgɑːnɪt/ see *Garnett* (media)

All England Club /ˌɔːl ˈɪŋglənd klʌb/, **the** (sport and leisure) A tennis club in *Wimbledon, London*, on whose courts the annual open lawn tennis championships are held. [full title: All England Lawn Tennis and Croquet Club]

Alliance /əˈlaɪəns/, **the** (politics) A short name for the *Liberal-SDP Alliance*.

Alliance Party (of Northern Ireland) /əˈlaɪəns ˌpɑːtɪ (əˌlaɪəns ˌpɑːtɪ əv ˌnɔːðən ˈaɪələnd)/, **the** (politics) The Party was formed in 1970 as a reaction to the *Troubles*. It aims to break down divisions between Protestants and Catholics in *Northern Ireland* and to unite both sections of the community by working for moderate policies.

allotment /ə'lɒtmənt/ (daily life) A small piece of land, often on the outskirts of a town, that is rented by a private individual (usually from a *local authority*) who grows vegetables there. Usually several allotments are grouped together. They were started during the First World War.

allotment

Ally Pally /ˌælɪ 'pælɪ/ (London) A nickname for *Alexandra Palace.*

almshouse /'ɑːmzhaʊs/ (charities) A house provided by the church or a charity organization for poor or elderly people. [from 'alms', donations made to the poor or elderly]

Alsatian /æl'seɪʃn/ (animal world) A large, wolf-like dog kept as a pet or for use as a guide dog or guard dog. [originally from Alsatia, in Germany, now Alsace, France]

Amateur Athletics Association /ˌæmətər æθ 'letɪks əsəʊsɪˌeɪʃn/ **the (AAA, the/three As, the)** (sport and leisure) The national governing body of men's amateur athletics in *England*, founded in 1880. The corresponding organization for women is the Women's AAA, founded in 1922. ['amateur' as opposed to 'professional']

Amnesty International /ˌæmnəstɪ ɪntə'næʃnəl/ (charities) A human rights movement funded by members' fees and gifts of money. It was founded in *Britain* in 1961. It works to release people who have been imprisoned, in any country, for their beliefs, colour, language, ethnic origin or religion, provided that they have not used or advocated violence. Such prisoners are called 'prisoners of conscience'. The movement, which also campaigns against torture and *capital punishment*, has over 100,000 members today in more than 70 countries.

ancient monument /ˌeɪnʃənt 'mɒnjʊmənt/ (history) A monument or other building officially listed as being of historic, architectural or archaeological interest and so protected by *Act (of Parliament)* from being damaged or destroyed.

Andy Capp /ˌændɪ 'kæp/ (media) A character in a strip cartoon by the artist Reg Smythe in the *Daily Mirror*. He represents, in humorously exaggerated form, a typical *working class* man and has what are supposed to be the two main characteristics of the working man, that is, idleness and flippancy. These are usually shown in his treatment of his wife, Florrie, and his reaction to daily life. [from a pun on 'handicap', and with a reference to the flat *cap*[1] which many working men wear, and which Andy Capp himself wears]

Anglesey /'æŋglsɪ/ (geography) A Welsh island in the Irish Sea, close to mainland *Britain* and joined to it by a rail bridge and a road bridge. It is a popular tourist centre and the town of Holyhead on Anglesey is one of the main departure points for sea crossings to *Ireland*.

Anglia TV /ˌæŋglɪə ti: 'vi:/ (media) One of the 15 television companies of the *IBA*, transmitting programmes to *East Anglia*.

Anglican /'æŋglɪkən/ (religion) A member of the *Church of England*.

Anglo-Catholic /ˌæŋgləʊ 'kæθəlɪk/ (religion) An *Anglican* who accepts much of the teaching of the *Roman Catholic church*, without wishing to join it. He usually regards church ritual as important, and believes in the authority of the clergy. See *High Church*.

Anglo-Saxon /ˌæŋgləʊ 'sæksn/ (language) **1** The language of the Anglo-Saxons, the Germanic people who were dominant in *Britain* from the 5th century to the *Norman Conquest* in 1066. The language is also known as Old English. **2** Another term for 'plain' English, especially containing *four-letter words* and other normally taboo words and phrases.

Anne Hathaway's Cottage /ˌæn ˌhæθəweɪz 'kɒtɪdʒ/ (history) The old house near *Stratford-(up)on-Avon* in which *Shakespeare*'s wife, Anne Hathaway (1557-1623), was born. Today the house is a museum and a popular tourist attraction.

annual /'ænjʊəl/ (media) A book or magazine published once a year, usually just before *Christmas* (for the following year). The term often applies to a children's book that has the title of a *comic*, for example 'The *Dandy* Annual 1984'. Such a book contains longer versions of many of the comic's regular features.

another place /əˌnʌðə 'pleɪs/ (government) A parliamentary phrase used in the *House of Commons* to refer to the *House of Lords* and in the House of Lords to refer to the House of Commons.

Antonine Wall /ˌæntənaɪn 'wɔ:l/**, the** (history) A Roman wall in southern *Scotland* running from the river *Forth* in the east to the river *Clyde* in the west. It was built in the reign of the Roman emperor Antoninus Pius (86-161 AD). Compare *Hadrian's Wall*.

Antonine Wall

A-1 /ˌeɪ 'wʌn/ (**1** transport **2** daily life) **1** The classification of a ship in *Lloyd's Register* when it is in first class condition. **2** The expression is also used colloquially to mean 'excellent, first class'.

APEX /'eɪpeks/ (**Association of Professional, Executive, Clerical and Computer Staff, the**) (work) A trade union to which belong a number of *civil servants* and government office workers, with a membership (in 1984) of over 100,000.

Apprentice Boys' Parade /æˌprentɪs ˌbɔɪz pə'reɪd/, **the** (tradition) An annual parade of *Orangemen* in Derry (Londonderry) and other towns in *Northern Ireland*, on 12 August. The parade marks the defeat of the Catholics by the Protestants in the seige of Derry in 1688, in which Protestant apprentice boys took part. In recent years the parade has led to scenes of violence between Catholics and Protestants in Northern Ireland.

approved school /əˈpruːvd skuːl/ (education) A former name for a *community home*.

April Fools' Day /ˌeɪprəl 'fuːlz deɪ/ (tradition) 1 April, when, traditionally, practical jokes are played. The day is also known as All Fools' Day.

APT /ˌeɪ piː 'tiː/, **the (Advanced Passenger Train, the)** (transport) A special high-speed electric train designed to take curves faster than conventional trains, and used experimentally as forerunner to the next design, which might be called the 225 or the Electra.

Archbishop of Canterbury /ˌɑːtʃbɪʃəp əv 'kæntəbrɪ/, **the** (religion) The title of the religious head of the *Church of England*, who is also bishop of *Canterbury*. His official title is *Primate of All England*. Compare *Archbishop of York*.

8

Archbishop of York /ˌɑːtʃbɪʃəp əv ˈjɔːk/, **the** (religion) The title of the deputy religious head of the *Church of England,* who is also bishop of York. His official title is *Primate of England.* Compare *Archbishop of Canterbury.*

Archers /ˈɑːtʃəz/, **the** (media) A popular daily radio programme on *Radio 4* telling of the day-to-day life of an imaginary farming family, which has been broadcast since 1950, thus being the longest-running radio serial. Each episode continues the story from the previous programme.

area of outstanding natural beauty /ˌeərɪə əv aʊtˌstændɪŋ ˌnætʃrəl ˈbjuːtɪ/ (geography) An area of countryside similar to a *national park* but not usually having car-parks, camping areas, information centres and other facilities for the public. Areas of outstanding natural beauty are specially protected, and development in them is strictly controlled. In 1984 there were 35 such areas.

Armada /ɑːˈmɑːdə/, **the** (history) The name of the Spanish fleet sent by Philip II, King of Spain, in 1588 against England but defeated by the English navy. [in full, 'Spanish Armada']

Armistice Day /ˈɑːmɪstɪs ˌdeɪ/ (history) 11 November 1918, the final day of the First World War. See also *Remembrance Sunday.*

Army /ˈɑːmɪ/, **the** (defence) The British Army was originally formed from the regiments that were under the command of the sovereign. At the end of the seventeenth century the British Government took over its control. In both the First and Second World Wars the numbers of men and women serving in the Army rose considerably as a result of conscription, with a maximum of nearly four million in the First World War and nearly three million in the Second. Conscription in the form of *national service* ended in 1957, however. By early 1984 the total number of men and women in the Army was down to almost 161,000, although this figure is twice as large as that of personnel in the *Royal Navy.* As in the two other armed services, men and women can serve in the Army for terms ranging from three to 22 years.

A-road /ˈeɪ rəʊd/ (transport) The official name of a main road, often running between major towns and cities. All A-roads are numbered, and among the most important are the A1 from *London* to *Edinburgh* (mostly following the route of the old *Great North Road*) and the A40 London to South *Wales.* See also *B-road* and compare *motorway.*

Arsenal /ˈɑːsənl/ (sport and leisure) A popular football club with a stadium at Highbury, and nicknamed the Gunners. [formerly based near Woolwich Arsenal, south *London,* a government arsenal closed in 1966]

Arthur /ˈɑːθə(r)/ see *King Arthur* (people)

Arthur Scargill /ˌɑːθə ˈskɑːgɪl/ see *Scargill* (people)

Arts Council (of Great Britain) /ˈɑːts ˌkaʊnsl (ˌɑːts ˌkaʊnsl əv ˌgreɪt ˈbrɪtn)/, **the** (media) A government organization established in 1946 to promote the arts generally in *Britain*, and in particular drama, music and the visual arts.

A-road

Ascension Day /əˈsenʃn deɪ/ (religion) A festival day for Christians, celebrating the ascension of Christ to heaven, and held on the 40th day after *Easter* (always a Thursday). Unlike other major church festivals, it is not a *bank holiday*.

Ascot /ˈæskət/ (sport and leisure) A racecourse near Windsor. Each year the *Royal Ascot* four-day meeting is held here. [named after village here]

ASH /æʃ/ **(Action on Smoking and Health)** (charities) A voluntary organization founded in 1971 to discourage smoking and to find ways for decreasing the damage done to health by smoking. The organization has over 350 members. [name partly chosen to indicate cigarette ash]

Ash Wednesday /æʃ ˈwenzdɪ/ (religion) The first day of *Lent* in the Christian church. [from the practice of sprinkling ashes on the heads of penitents]

Ashmolean (Museum) /æʃˈməʊlɪən (æʃˌməʊlɪən mjuːˈzɪəm)/, **the** (arts) A museum and library of ancient history, fine arts and archaeology at *Oxford University*, founded in 1683 by Elias Ashmole (1617-92).

Aslef /ˈæzlef/ **(Associated Society of Locomotive Engineers and Firemen, the)** (work) An influential trade union for train drivers and other railway staff which is more left-wing than the *NUR*, its traditional rival. In 1984 it had 23,500 members.

assisted area /əˌsɪstɪd ˈeərɪə/ (work) A region of high unemployment where the government encourages industrial development by means of special grants and loans of money. There are two types of assisted area: *development areas* and *intermediate areas.* See also *special development area.*

assisted place /əˌsɪstɪd 'pleɪs/ (education) A place gained at an
independent school by a student whose tuition fees are partly
paid by the government. The scheme is intended to aid
academically gifted children whose parents cannot afford the
full tuition fees.

association football /əˌsəʊsɪeɪʃn 'fʊtbɔːl/ (sport and
leisure) The formal name of football, as distinct from rugby
football. See the *FA* and the *Football League* and compare
rugby league and *rugby union.* [from the FA, who established
the rules of football, and whose title gave the term 'soccer' as
a colloquial word for football]

ASTMS /ˌeɪ es ˌtiː em 'es/ **(Association of Scientific, Technical
and Managerial Staffs, the)** (work) An influential trade
union with 390,000 members. It was created in 1969 by the
amalgamation of two other unions, ASSET (the Association
of Supervisory Staffs, Executives and Technicians) and AScW
(the Association of Scientific Workers). Its members are
employed in a wide range of industrial and commercial jobs,
both in private firms and in the state sector, including the
NHS.

Aston (University) /'æstən (ˌæstən juːnɪ'vɜːsətɪ)/ (education) A
university in Birmingham, founded in 1966. [from the district
of Birmingham where it is]

Aston Villa /ˌæstən 'vɪlə/ (sport and leisure) A popular
Birmingham football club, with a stadium, Villa Park, in the
district of Aston.

Astronomer Royal /əˌstrɒnəmə 'rɔɪəl/, **the** (science and
technology) An honorary title given to an eminent British
astronomer. Until 1972 it was the official title of the director
of the *Royal Greenwich Observatory.* The title 'Astronomer
Royal for Scotland' is still used for the director of the Royal
Observatory at *Edinburgh.*

attendance centre /ə'tendəns ˌsentə(r)/ (law) A centre where
young offenders (under 17) are required to attend for physical
training and instruction in practical subjects instead of going
to prison. Offenders may be ordered to spend up to a total of
24 hours at an attendance centre, usually on Saturdays and
for a maximum of three hours at a time. Compare *borstal,
community home, detention centre, remand home* and *youth
custody centre.*

attorney /ə'tɜːnɪ/ (law) A person, especially a lawyer,
appointed to act for someone in business or legal matters.

Attorney General /əˌtɜːnɪ 'dʒenrəl/, **the** (law) In *England* and
Wales, the senior law officer and chief legal counsel to the
Crown[1].

AUEW /ˌeɪ juː iː 'dʌbljuː/, **the (Amalgamated Union of
Engineering Workers, the)** (work) A large trade union with
members in the engineering industry, and regarded as
usually having a left-wing leadership sympathetic to the aims

of the *Labour Party*. In 1984 it had about 1 million members.

August Bank Holiday /ˌɔːɡəst bæŋk 'hɒlədeɪ/, **the** (daily life) The summer *bank holiday*, held in *England* and *Wales* on the last Monday in August, and in *Scotland* on the first Monday.

Auld Lang Syne /ˌɔːld læŋ 'saɪn/ (tradition) A traditional song sung at the end of a gathering, to remember times past, especially as midnight strikes on *New Year's Eve*. Compare *Burns' Night*. [Scottish, literally 'good times long ago'. The words of the song are from a poem by Robert Burns (1759-96)]

Aunt Sally /ˌɑːnt 'sælɪ/ (tradition) **1** A figure, usually of an old woman's head, that is set up at fairgrounds and *fêtes* as a target for balls or other objects. The aim is to knock off the head or to knock the figure down. **2** A person or thing that is a target for attack or criticism.

Auntie/Aunty /'ɑːntɪ/ (media) An affectionate name for the *BBC*. [seen as a staid old aunt, or keeper of moral values]

Austen, Jane /'ɒstɪn, dʒeɪn/ (people) The novels of Jane Austen (1775–1817) are remarkable for the skilful and sensitive way in which the unremarkable *upper class* lives of the characters are described, either in *country houses* or in the city of Bath which was then very fashionable and elegant. The society of such people, with all their loves and ambitions, was one that Jane Austen knew well, and her novels remain as realistic portraits of the period. The main novels are: 'Pride and Prejudice' (1813), 'Sense and Sensibility' (1811), 'Northanger Abbey' (a satire on the *Gothic Novel*[1]) (1818), 'Mansfield Park' (1814), 'Emma' (1815) and 'Persuasion' (1818). Devotees of Jane Austen and her novels are still sometimes known as 'Janeites'.

Authorized Version /ˌɔːθəraɪzd 'vɜːʃn/, **the (AV, the)** (religion) An English translation of the Bible made in 1611 and 'authorized' by King James VI and I, for which reason it is also known as the *King James Bible*. The Authorized Version is used in many *Anglican* churches, although some churches today favour the use of a more modern translation of the Bible.

autumn double /ˌɔːtəm 'dʌbl/, **the** (sport and leisure) A bet placed simultaneously on two horse races held in the autumn—the Cesarewitch and the Cambridgeshire.

Avebury /'eɪvbrɪ/ (tradition) A village in Wiltshire where one of the largest pre-Celtic temples in Europe is located. The site, which probably dates back to about 2000 BC, includes Silbury Hill, the largest ancient man-made mound in Europe. Despite several attempts to excavate it, the exact purpose of the hill remains uncertain. Over the centuries, many of the standing stones have either been destroyed or removed, and although some remain to form an impressive display, Avebury has never been as popular with tourists and visitors as *Stonehenge*.

avoirdupois /ˌævədə'pɔɪz/ (daily life) A system of weights based on the pound divided into 16 ounces. [from Old French 'aver de peis', 'goods of weight']

Aylesbury (duck) /'eɪlzbrɪ (ˌeɪlzbrɪ 'dʌk)/ (animal world) A breed of white domestic duck, regarded as of good quality for eating. [originating from Aylesbury, Buckinghamshire]

Ayrshire (cow) /'eəʃə(r) (ˌeəʃə 'kaʊ)/ (animal world) A breed of brown and white dairy cow. [originally from Ayrshire, *Scotland*]

BA /ˌbiː ˈeɪ/ **(Bachelor of Arts)** (education) A degree obtained by the student at a university or *polytechnic* on successfully completing a course of studies, usually in a non-science subject. However, at *Oxford²* and *Cambridge²*, as well as at some of the newer universities, the BA is a *first degree* in either non-science or science subjects.

Bach Choir /ˌbɑːk ˈkwaɪə(r)/, **the** (arts) A well-known London *choir* that performs not only the works of J.S. Bach but those of other important composers. Bach Choirs also exist in other towns and cities.

backbencher /ˌbæk ˈbentʃə(r)/ (government) An *MP* who does not hold any special office and who, therefore, in the *House of Commons* sits on the back benches (as distinct from the *front benches*, on which sit *ministers²* and members of the *Shadow Cabinet*).

Backs /bæks/, **the** (education) The attractive gardens and lawns in *Cambridge¹*, between several *colleges¹* and the river Cam. Each garden belongs to a particular college, and is at the back of it.

bacon and eggs /ˌbeɪkən ən ˈegz/ (food and drink) A popular main dish of a traditional *English breakfast*: fried rashers (slices) of bacon and one or more fried eggs.

Badminton (Horse Trials) /ˈbædmɪntən (ˌbædmɪntən ˈhɔːs traɪəlz)/, **the** (sport and leisure) The most important *three-day event* in *Britain*, held annually in the grounds of Badminton House, Avon. The event is usually attended by members of the *royal family*.

bailiff /ˈbeɪlɪf/ (law) An officer employed to serve *writ*s and *summons*es, make arrests, collect fines, and ensure that a *court³* sentence is carried out.

Baker Street /ˈbeɪkə striːt/ (London) A central street in *London*. It was at number 221B Baker Street that the famous fictional detective *Sherlock Holmes* lived.

Bakewell tart /ˌbeɪkwel ˈtɑːt/ (food and drink) An open tart made of pastry lined with a layer of jam and filled with almond-flavoured sponge cake. [originally made in Bakewell, Derbyshire]

ball boy/girl /ˈbɔːl bɔɪ/gɜːl/ (sport and leisure) A boy or girl who retrieves the balls on tennis courts, especially at *Wimbledon* and other important tennis matches.

Ballet Rambert /ˌbæleɪ ˈrɑːmbeə(r)/, **the** (arts) A leading ballet company, which specializes in performing modern ballets, and often tours abroad. It was founded in *London* in 1930 by the ballet dancer and teacher Marie Rambert (1888–1982).

ballot paper /ˈbælət ˌpeɪpə(r)/ (government) The special slip of paper on which an elector records his vote in a political election such as a *by-election* or a *general election*. It has the names of the candidates and their parties printed on it, and the voter makes his choice by marking a letter 'X' against the name of the candidate he supports. He does this in a *polling booth* where no-one else can see which candidate he has voted for.

1	**BROWN** JOHN EDWARD Brown, 2 The Cottages, Barlington, Grayshire Labour	
2	**BROWN** THOMAS WILLIAM Brown, 15 Barchester Road, Barlington, Grayshire Liberal	
3	**JONES** William David Jones, The Grange, Barlington, Grayshire Conservative	

ballot paper

Balmoral /bælˈmɒrəl/ (royal family) A castle in northeast *Scotland* that has been a private home of the *royal family* since 1852.

Baltic Exchange /ˈbɔːltɪk (ˌbɔːltɪk ɪksˈtʃeɪndʒ)/, **the** (finance) An important market in *London* for the chartering of cargo vessels of all nationalities. It also deals with marine insurance. [in full, the Baltic Mercantile and Shipping Exchange, named after the coffee-house where merchants involved in the Baltic trade met in the 18th century]

Bampton fair /ˌbæmptən ˈfeə(r)/ (tradition) An annual fair at Bampton, Devon, famous for its sale of *Exmoor ponies*.

Banbury cake /ˈbænbrɪ keɪk/ (food and drink) A cake containing currants, raisins, candied peel and sugar, and with a criss-cross pattern on top. [originally made at Banbury, Oxfordshire]

bangers and mash /ˌbæŋəz ən ˈmæʃ/ (food and drink) A colloquial term for sausages and mashed potatoes.

bank holiday /ˌbæŋk ˈhɒlədeɪ/ (daily life) An official public holiday (on a day other than Saturday and Sunday) when all banks and post offices are closed, as well as most factories, offices and shops. At present (1985) the following days are bank holidays in *England* and *Wales*: *New Year's Day* (or the first working day after it), *Good Friday*, *Easter Monday*, the first Monday in May (*May Day* bank holiday), the last Monday in May (spring bank holiday), the last Monday in August (summer bank holiday, known as the *August Bank Holiday*), *Christmas Day* (or the Monday after it, if it falls on a Saturday or Sunday) and *Boxing Day* (or the next working day following Christmas Day). There are some other bank holidays in *Scotland* and *Northern Ireland*.

Bank of England /ˌbæŋk əv ˈɪŋɡlənd/, **the** (finance) The central bank of *England* and *Wales*, in *London*, founded in 1694 and nationalized in 1946. It issues bank notes, advises the government on financial matters, and determines the *bank rate*.

Bank of Scotland /ˌbæŋk əv ˈskɒtlənd/, **the** (finance) The second largest of the three main Scottish banks (after the *Royal Bank of Scotland* and before the *Clydesdale Bank*). It was founded in 1695. Like the other two Scottish banks (but unlike English banks, except for the *Bank of England*), it issues its own banknotes (for values from £5 to £100). These notes are not legal tender. However, in *Scotland* and almost always in *England* they are given the same status as notes issued by the Bank of England.

bank rate /ˈbæŋk reɪt/ (finance) The rate of interest at which the *Bank of England* lends money to other financial institutions. Regular public announcements of the current rate were stopped in 1981.

bannock /ˈbænək/ (food and drink) A round, flat cake, made from wheat or barley and sometimes filled with currants. It is specially popular in *Scotland* and the north of *England*.

Banqueting House /ˈbæŋkwɪtɪŋ haʊs/, **the** (London) One of the most famous buildings in *Whitehall*[1], *London*, and the only surviving part (built 1622) of Whitehall Palace, which was mostly destroyed by fire in 1698. Today it is used for official receptions.

BAOR /ˌbiː eɪ əʊ ˈɑː(r)/ **(British Army of the Rhine, the)** (defence) A force of about 55,000 British army servicemen and officers stationed in West Germany.

bap /bæp/ (food and drink) A kind of soft, round, flat bread roll.

Baptists /ˈbæptɪsts/ (religion) A large Protestant (but non-*Anglican*) church that has approximately 168,000 members. Those members are almost all grouped in associations of churches, most of which belong to the Baptist Union of Great

Britain and Ireland (formed 1813). There is a particularly strong Baptist following in *Wales*. Baptists reject infant baptism, as practised in most other Christian churches, on the grounds that there is no evidence of it in the Bible. Only adult members of the church are baptised. Each church member being baptised is completely immersed in the water during the ceremony.

bar /bɑː(r)/ (**1** food and drink **2, 3** law) **1** A counter or room for the sale and consumption of alcoholic drinks (*public bar*, *saloon bar*, *lounge bar*) in a *pub*, or in general in a hotel, restaurant, or other public place such as a theatre or concert hall. **2** The area in a law *court*³ separating the part reserved for the judge or *magistrate* and *QC* from the part reserved for junior *barristers, solicitors* and the general public. **3** The place in a law court where the accused person ('prisoner at the bar') stands during his or her trial.

bar billiards /bɑː ˈbɪliədz/ (sport and leisure) A version of billiards popular in *pubs*, in which the balls are hit into holes on the surface of the billiard table.

bar snacks /ˈbɑː snæks/ (food and drink) A light meal in one of the *bars*¹ of a *pub*, such as a *ploughman's lunch* or a snack of sandwiches or meat pies.

Barbarians /bɑːˈbeəriənz/, **the** (sport and leisure) The name of the *rugby football* club whose members are the best players of *Britain*, France and the *Commonwealth*¹.

Barbican (Centre) /ˈbɑːbɪkən (ˌsentə(r))/, **the** (arts) A large cultural centre in *London* opened in 1982. It contains a conference hall, a concert hall, three cinemas, a theatre, an art gallery, a public library and two exhibition halls, as well as *bars* and restaurants. The theatre is the London home of the *Royal Shakespeare Company*.

Barchester Chronicles /ˌbɑːtʃɪstə ˈkrɒnɪklz/, **the** (arts) The collective title of six novels by Anthony Trollope (1815–92), set in the fictional cathedral city of Barchester (believed to be based on either Salisbury or Wells) and portraying the intrigues and struggle for power of the local *Anglican* clergy.

Barclaycard /ˈbɑːklɪkɑːd/ (finance) A credit card issued by *Barclays (Bank)* and certain other financial institutions. Each institution issues such cards independently of the others but within the international *VISA* system.

Barclays (Bank) /bɑːklɪz (ˌbɑːklɪz ˈbæŋk)/ (finance) One of the four main English banks, founded in 1896 and with branches in most towns and cities.

bard /bɑːd/ (arts) The title of the poet who wins a competition at an *eisteddfod*, especially in *Wales*. (A bard was originally a wandering musician who sang about the deeds of his tribe.)

Bard of Avon /ˌbɑːd əv ˈeɪvn/, **the** (arts) A nickname for William *Shakespeare* (1564–1616), the great poet (*bard*) and dramatist who was born, and is buried, at *Stratford-(up)on-Avon*.

bargain basement /'bɑːgɪn ˌbeɪsmənt/ (commerce) **1** In some large shops and stores, a basement (floor below street level) where goods are sold at reduced prices. **2** In some local papers, a section where second-hand goods for sale can be advertised at low rates, or even free of charge.

Barnardo's /bə'nɑːdəʊz/ see **Dr Barnardo's (Homes)** (charities)

barrister /'bærɪstə(r)/ (law) In *England*, a lawyer who has been 'called to the bar' (see *bar²*), or admitted to the *Inns of Court*. He can advise on legal problems submitted through a *solicitor*, and present a case in the higher *courts³*.

Bart's /bɑːts/ (medicine) A colloquial abbreviation for *St Bartholomew's Hospital*.

base lending rate /ˌbeɪs 'lendɪŋ reɪt/ (finance) The rate (expressed as a percentage of interest) at which banks will lend money. The rate may differ between one bank and another.

Basic English /ˌbeɪsɪk 'ɪŋglɪʃ/ (language) A simplified form of English intended as an international language. It contains a vocabulary of 850 basic words and was invented by I.A.Richards (1893–1979). The psychologist Charles Ogden (1889–1957) was also involved. [pun on 'basic' and initials of 'British American Scientific International Commercial']

Bateman cartoon /ˌbeɪtmən kɑː'tuːn/ (arts) A cartoon (comic drawing) by H M Bateman (1887–1974), portraying a man in an embarrassing situation, especially one who has unknowingly broken some code of social conduct. The cartoons usually have a caption beginning, 'The Man Who. . . . . .', or something similar, for example, 'The Guest who Called 'Pâté de Foie Gras' Potted Meat'.

Bath and West /ˌbɑːθ ən 'west/, **the** (tradition) One of the most important annual agricultural shows, held in Bath, Avon, or some other town in the west of *England*.

Bath bun /ˌbɑːθ 'bʌn/ (food and drink) A type of sweet bun containing spices and dried fruit. [originally made in Bath, Avon]

Bath Festival /ˌbɑːθ 'festɪvl/, **the** (arts) An annual music festival held in Bath, Avon, and running at the same time as various theatre and ballet performances, exhibitions, lectures, etc.

Bath Oliver /ˌbɑːθ 'ɒlɪvə(r)/ (food and drink) A type of unsweetened dry biscuit, whose recipe was originally invented in the 17th century by William Oliver, a doctor, of Bath, Avon.

Battersea Dogs' Home /ˌbætəsɪ 'dɒgz həʊm/, **the** (animal world) A *London* centre for lost and unwanted dogs and cats. [situated in Battersea]

Battle of Britain /ˌbætl əv 'brɪtn/, **the** (history) The battle between British and German aircraft over *London* and the south of *England* in the early years of the Second World War, in particular 1940. The Battle was to have been the start of the

German invasion of *Britain*.

Battle of Britain Day /ˌbætl əv ˈbrɪtn deɪ/ (history) 15 September, when a fly-past of aircraft is held over *London* to mark the anniversary of the climax of the *Battle of Britain* in 1940. On the following Sunday a special commemorative service is held in *Westminster Abbey*.

BBC /ˌbiː biː ˈsiː/, **the (British Broadcasting Corporation, the)** (media) One of the two main radio and television broadcasting companies in *Britain*, under government control since 1927, but free to manage its own policy and decide the content of its programmes. Within Britain, it broadcasts radio programmes on *Radio 1, Radio 2, Radio 3, Radio 4* and *local radio*, and television programmes on *BBC 1* and *BBC 2*. Outside Britain, it broadcasts worldwide on the *BBC World Service*. See also *Broadcasting House, Bush House, BBC Television Centre*, and compare *IBA*.

BBC English /ˌbiː biː siː ˈɪŋglɪʃ/ (language) Traditionally correct English, especially as formerly spoken by *BBC* announcers and news readers.

BBC 1 /ˌbiː biː siː ˈwʌn/ (media) The main television channel of the *BBC*, transmitting mostly programmes of general interest such as light entertainment, news, sport, current affairs and children's programmes.

BBC Television Centre /ˌbiː biː siː ˈtelɪvɪʒn ˌsentə(r)/, **the** (media) The main television studios of the *BBC* in west *London*.

BBC 2 /ˌbiː biː siː ˈtuː/ (media) The second television channel of the *BBC*, transmitting mainly programmes that are more specialized than those of *BBC 1*, such as documentaries, travel programmes, serious plays, concert performances, programmes on leisure interests and international (foreign language) films.

BBC World Service /ˌbiː biː siː ˌwɜːld ˈsɜːvɪs/, **the** (media) A 24-hour service of English radio programmes broadcast to overseas countries by the *BBC*. See also *Bush House*.

beagle /ˈbiːgl/ (animal world) A small breed of hound used for hunting hares, and with a short, smooth black and white or brown and white coat. Hunting hares with such hounds is known as 'beagling'.

Beano /ˈbiːnəʊ/, **the** (media) A popular weekly *comic* for children, founded in 1938. ['beano', a colloquial term for 'good time', 'party']

bear /beə(r)/ (finance) On the *Stock Exchange*, a term for a speculator who sells his shares hoping that the price will fall and that he can then make a profit by buying them back. Compare *bull*. [probably from the proverb, 'sell the bear's skin before you have caught the bear']

beating the bounds /ˌbiːtɪŋ ðə ˈbaʊndz/ (tradition) An old custom, still kept in some parts of *Britain*, of marking the boundaries of a parish by marching round them and beating the ground, or certain boundary marks, with rods. The custom usually takes place annually on either *Ascension Day* or before *Easter*. In former times, small boys were beaten at boundary marks so that they would remember the boundaries of their parish.

Beatles /'biːtlz/**, the** (people) One of *Britain*'s most influential pop groups, first performing in 1959 in Liverpool. The group included Paul McCartney (1942–), John Lennon (1940–80), George Harrison (1943–) and Ringo Starr—real name Richard Starkey—(1940–). At first, the group performed music that was influenced by American rock 'n' roll and rhythm-and-blues. Lennon and McCartney's songs, however, became increasingly sophisticated and experimental, and their imaginative lyrics and memorable melodies soon contributed to the distinctive *Mersey sound*. Their records were consistently top of the pop music charts in the mid-1960s, their first great success being 'Please Please Me' in 1962. They also made several successful films. In the late 1960s the group studied Indian mysticism and used hallucinatory drugs, and both activities influenced their music. The Beatles broke up in 1971. Paul McCartney then formed the successful group 'Wings' while John Lennon wrote and recorded music in America with his second wife Yoko Ono. Lennon was assassinated in New York in 1980.

Beaulieu /'bjuːlɪ/ (transport) A village in Hampshire famous for the National Motor Museum, opened by Lord Montague in 1952 in the grounds of his house here.

Becher's Brook /ˌbiːtʃəz 'brʊk/ (sport and leisure) A difficult jump in the course of the *Grand National*. [named after Captain Becher, who fell here with his horse in the first Grand National in 1839]

bed and breakfast /ˌbed ən 'brekfəst/ (daily life) A bed for the night and breakfast the following morning in a hotel, boarding house or private house, charged to a guest as a single unit. The term is often used colloquially to refer to private houses which provide such a service.

bedsit(ter) /bed'sɪt(ə(r))/ (daily life) A combined sitting-room and bedroom, often with cooking and washing facilities, and usually rented out in a private house to a single tenant.

Beeb /biːb/**, the** (media) A familiar nickname for the *BBC*. [from the pronunciation of BBC]

Beefeater /'biːfiːtə(r)/ (tradition) The nickname of a *Yeoman Warder* at the *Tower of London*. [in the sense 'one who eats beef', 'one who is well fed']

beer garden /'bɪə gɑːdn/ (daily life) The garden of a *pub* in which customers can sit in fine weather to eat the food and drink bought inside the pub. Beer gardens are popular with families in the summer months since young children, who are not allowed inside a pub, can be with their parents.

Belfast /'belfɑːst/ (geography) The capital of *Northern Ireland*, and in normal times the seat of the government of Northern Ireland. The city, which has a population of nearly 300,000, is an important industrial centre (in particular ship-building and the manufacture of aircraft), but at the same time has relatively high unemployment. Most of its buildings are comparatively modern. Since the 1960s it has been almost continuously one of the key points in the *Troubles*.

Belgravia /bel'greɪvɪə/ (London) A fashionable residential district of *London* centring on Belgrave Square, near *Hyde Park*.

Belisha beacon /bəˌliːʃə 'biːkən/ (transport) A road sign in the form of a flashing light in an orange globe on a striped pole, marking a pedestrian crossing. See *zebra crossing* and *pelican crossing*. [named after Leslie Hore-Belisha, minister of transport in the 1930s, when such signs were introduced]

Belisha beacon

bell ringing /'bel rɪŋɪŋ/ see *change ringing* (tradition)

BEM /ˌbiː iː 'em/, **the (British Empire Medal, the)** (life and society) A medal awarded to both military personnel and civilians 'for meritorious service'.

Ben Nevis /ˌben 'nevɪs/ (geography) The highest mountain in *Britain*, in western *Scotland*. Its height is 1,343 metres.

benchmark /'bentʃmɑːk/ (geography) A mark in the form of a broad arrow below a horizontal line, engraved on a wall, pillar, etc to indicate a particular height above sea level at that point and so serve as a reference mark in surveying.

Benjamin Britten /ˌbendʒəmɪn 'brɪtn/ see *Britten* (people)

Benn, Tony /ben, 'təʊnɪ/ (people) Tony Benn (born 1925) became a Labour MP (see *Labour Party*) in 1950. However, he was the son of a viscount, and when his father died in 1960 he had to relinquish his *seat* in the *House of Commons* since he had legally inherited his father's title. He refused to accept it, and started a campaign to introduce a law that would enable those inheriting titles to disclaim them, if they wished. His campaign resulted in the passing of the Peerage Act of 1963, whereupon Tony Benn disclaimed his title (he would have been The *Right Honourable* Anthony Wedgwood Benn, 2nd Viscount Stansgate) and was re-elected as an *MP*. He has been fiercely critical of the British class system and has earned the reputation of being one of the most influential of left-wing thinkers.

Bennism /'benɪzəm/ (politics) A colloquial term in politics for a group of policies that include state ownership (the state becoming the owner of private industry), as put forward by Tony *Benn*, *Labour Party* politician and *Secretary of State* for Industry in 1974.

Bentley /'bentlɪ/ (transport) A luxury car made by the *Rolls-Royce* Company.

Bernard Levin /ˌbɜːnəd 'levɪn/ see *Levin* (people)

best man /ˌbest 'mæn/ (tradition) The chief attendant on the bridegroom at a wedding. Traditionally, he presents the ring at the moment when the bride is ready to put it on, and after the wedding makes the leading speech at the *wedding breakfast* or reception.

betting shop /'betɪŋ ʃɒp/ (sport and leisure) The licensed premises of a *bookmaker* in a town. Such premises take nearly 90% of all money staked on horse and *greyhound racing*.

B'ham /'bɜːmɪŋəm/ (geography) A conventional abbreviation, for example on road signs and lanes, for Birmingham.

Big Ben /ˌbɪg 'ben/ (London) The clock in the clock tower of the *Houses of Parliament*, *London*, famous for its accurate time-keeping and for its use as a broadcast time signal by the *BBC*. The name properly refers to the bell of the clock, so nicknamed after Benjamin Hall, Chief Commissioner of Works when it was cast in 1856.

big four /ˌbɪg 'fɔː(r)/, **the** (finance) A collective nickname for the four main English banks: *Barclays Bank*, *Lloyds Bank*, the *Midland Bank* and the *National Westminster Bank*.

bill /bɪl/ (government) The term for the draft of an *Act of Parliament*, which when under discussion in the *Houses of Parliament* passes through five stages: *first reading*, *second reading*, committee stage, report stage and *third reading*.

Billy Bunter /ˌbɪlɪ 'bʌntə(r)/ (education) A famous fat and greedy boy in the stories about *Greyfriars*.

bingo /'bɪŋgəʊ/ (sport and leisure) A popular gambling game. It is normally played in halls and converted cinemas. Players buy cards printed with rows of numbers and cross off the numbers as they are called out at random. The winner is the first player to cross out all the numbers on his or her card. In recent years it has also been possible to play bingo by filling in similar cards published in *popular papers*. [said to represent a cry of joy on winning or achieving something]

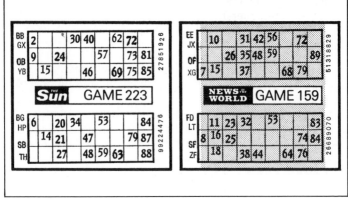

bingo

Birkbeck (College) /'bɜːkbek (ˌbɜːkbek 'kɒlɪdʒ)/ (education) A *college[1]*, of *London University*, founded in 1823 by George Birkbeck as an institute of mechanics.

Birmingham Post /ˌbɜːmɪŋəm 'pəʊst/, **the** (media) A daily newspaper published in Birmingham and inclined to the *Conservative Party* viewpoint in its politics. Its circulation in 1980 was about 40,000.

Biro /'baɪərəʊ/ (daily life) The trade name of a popular make of ball-point pen, although the name is also used for any such pen. [from the name of its Hungarian inventor, Biró]

Birthday Honours /ˌbɜːθdeɪ 'ɒnəz/, **the** (life and society) The announcement of honorary titles, orders and medals awarded annually on the sovereign's *Official Birthday*. Compare *New Year Honours*.

Bisley /'bɪzlɪ/ (sport and leisure) A shooting range near Woking, Surrey, where international and other important shooting contests are held. [from the name of the village nearby]

bitter /'bɪtə(r)/ (food and drink) A type of draught beer with a high hop content and a rather bitter taste. Compare *light ale*.

BL /ˌbiː 'el/ (transport) One of the four main motor manufacturing companies in *Britain*, formerly the British Leyland Motor Corporation (nationalized in 1975).

black /blæk/, **the** (finance) A colloquial term for a bank account in credit, said to be 'in the black'. [as opposed to a debit account 'in the *red*'. Credit entries were originally written in black ink and debit entries were written in red ink]

Black Country /'blæk ˌkʌntrɪ/, **the** (geography) The industrialized region of the West *Midlands*, where there are many collieries and steelworks. [from the black smoke and blackened buildings here]

Black Maria /ˌblæk mə'raɪə/ (law) A police van for taking prisoners to and from prison. [from the original colour of the vans: Black Maria was said to be the name of a strong black woman in Boston, USA, who helped the police in the handling of prisoners]

Black Prince /ˌblæk ˈprɪns/, **the** (history) The nickname of Edward, Prince of Wales (1330–76), son of King Edward III. [either from the colour of his armour or for his cruelty]

black pudding /ˌblæk ˈpʊdɪŋ/ (food and drink) A kind of black sausage made mainly from minced pork fat and pig's blood.

Black Rod /ˌblæk ˈrɒd/ (government) In the *House of Lords*, an officer whose main duty is calling the members of the *House of Commons* to attend the annual *Speech from the Throne* at the opening of parliament. [from the black rod topped by a gold lion that he carries during this ceremony]

black tie /ˌblæk ˈtaɪ/ (clothing) **1** A black bow tie worn with a *dinner jacket*. **2** A conventional indication on an official invitation that *evening dress* must be worn. Compare *white tie*.

Black Watch /ˌblæk ˈwɒtʃ/, **the** (defence) The nickname of the *Royal Highland Regiment* in the British *Army*. [from the dark colour of the *tartan* of the men's *kilts*]

blacking /ˈblækɪŋ/ (work) The boycott of specific goods, work etc by a trade union in a firm where there are *blacklegs*.

blackleg /ˈblækleg/ (work) A strike-breaker or person who works in place of another striker when ordered not to by his trade union.

Blackpool /ˈblækpuːl/ (geography) A popular seaside resort in Lancashire, famous for its Tower, its trams, its illuminated seafront and its facilities as a conference centre.

Blackwell's /ˈblækwelz/ (commerce) A famous bookshop in *Oxford*.

blazer /ˈbleɪzə(r)/ (clothing) A distinctive jacket, usually with a badge on the breast pocket, and often having gold or silver buttons, worn by a pupil as part of a school uniform, by a member of a sports team, or by a member, or former member, of an association or organization of some kind.

Blenheim /ˈblenɪm/ **(Battle of Blenheim, the)** (history) The battle of 1704 in which the Anglo-Austrian forces won a victory over the French and Bavarian troops in the War of the Spanish Succession. [from the name of the village, now Blindheim, West Germany, where it was fought]

Blenheim Orange /ˌblenɪm ˈɒrɪndʒ/ (food and drink) A type of winter eating apple, with large, round, golden fruit. [first grown in the gardens of *Blenheim Palace*]

Blenheim Palace /ˌblenɪm ˈpælɪs/ (history) A large country house and estate near *Oxford¹*, built for the Duke of Marlborough, leader of the English forces in the Battle of *Blenheim*, in memory of his victory in this battle.

Blighty /ˈblaɪtɪ/ (tradition) A former nickname for *England*, common among soldiers returning from service overseas. [from Anglo-Indian form of Hindi 'bilayati', 'foreign']

Blitz /blɪts/, **the** (history) The bombing of *Britain*, and especially *London*, by the German air force in the Second World War, in particular 1940–1. [from German 'Blitzkrieg', 'lightning war']

block vote /ˌblɒk 'vəʊt/ (work) A method of voting in which a single delegate's vote represents not one vote but the total number of votes cast by the section he represents. Such a method is commonly used by the *TUC*.

blood sports /'blʌd spɔːts/ (sport and leisure) The hunting of wild animals such as foxes, hares and otters with the aim of killing them. Such hunting has been increasingly criticized and actively opposed by supporters of the *League Against Cruel Sports*. ['blood' from the blood that is shed]

Bloody Mary /ˌblʌdɪ 'meərɪ/ (**1** history **2** food and drink) **1** A nickname of Queen Mary Tudor (1516–58), given her by the Protestants whom she persecuted cruelly. **2** A type of cocktail, made from vodka and tomato juice. [from its red colouring]

Bloody Tower /ˌblʌdɪ 'taʊə(r)/, **the** (history) A tower in the *Tower of London* built in the 14th century and supposedly where the *Princes in the Tower* were murdered.

Bloomsbury Group /'bluːmzbrɪ ˌgruːp/, **the** (arts) A group of writers, artists and intellectuals living and working in the early 20th century in the *London* district of Bloomsbury, near the *British Museum*. Among them were the writers E M Forster (1879–1970), Virginia Woolf (1882–1941) and Lytton Strachey (1880–1932), the philosopher and mathematician Bertrand Russell (1872–1970) and the economist John Maynard Keynes (1883–1946). The Group were critical of many aspects of contemporary society, notably morality, religion and aesthetics.

blue /bluː/ (**1** politics **2, 3** sport and leisure) **1** A member of the *Conservative Party*, whose campaigning colour is blue. **2** A member of a sports team playing for *Oxford University* (and wearing dark blue) or *Cambridge University* (wearing light blue). **3** An award at either Oxford University or Cambridge University to such a member.

blue chip /ˌbluː 'tʃɪp/ (finance) On the *Stock Exchange*, a share regarded as reliable for providing a good *dividend* and for retaining a high value. [from gambling jargon: in poker a blue 'chip' (counter) has a high value]

Blue Ensign /ˌbluː 'ensən/ (defence) A flag flown by ships chartered by the government (and formerly by ships under the command of naval reserve officers). The flag is blue, with a *Union Jack* in the upper left quarter.

Blue Peter /ˌbluː 'piːtə(r)/ (media) An informative and entertaining television programme for children, broadcast twice weekly on *BBC 1*. [from the 'blue peter', the signal flag displayed by a ship about to sail]

Bluebell Line /ˈbluːbel ˌlaɪn/, **the** (transport) A private railway line in Sussex, operating with old-style steam engines and coaches. The track runs for five miles from Sheffield Park to Horsted Keynes, and follows a picturesque route along a track bordered by bluebells in spring.

Bluebird /ˈbluːbɜːd/ (sport and leisure) The name of a series of racing cars and speed boats in which the racing drivers (father and son) Malcolm and Donald Campbell set several world speed records over the period 1935–67.

blue-collar worker /ˌbluː ˈkɒla ˌwɜːkə(r)/ (work) A nickname for an industrial worker, who often wears blue overalls. [as distinct from a *white-collar worker*]

Blues and Royals /ˌbluːz ən ˈrɔɪəlz/, **the** (defence) A British army regiment formed in 1969 when the *Royal Horse Guards*, nicknamed the Blues from the colour of their uniform, joined with the Royal Dragoons, nicknamed the *Royals*.

bluestocking /ˈbluːstɒkɪŋ/ (life and society) A (usually disparaging) name for a scholarly woman. [from the blue stockings originally worn by male members of an 18th century literary society]

BNOC /ˈbiːnɒk/ **(British National Oil Corporation, the)** (science and technology) The state industry set up in 1975 to exploit oil in the North Sea and to act as an oil trading company. In 1982 its oil-producing business was transferred to *Britoil*, although BNOC itself remains the largest oil trader in Britain. In 1985, the government announced that it would abolish BNOC.

Boat Race /ˈbəʊt reɪs/, **the** (sport and leisure) The traditional annual rowing race between teams (eight rowers and a cox) from *Oxford University* and *Cambridge University*, held on a section of the river Thames in London in March or April. The length of the course is 7.2km. [in full, University Boat Race]

Boat Show /ˈbəʊt ʃəʊ/, **the** (sport and leisure) An annual international exhibition of yachts and boats, held in *London* every January at *Earls Court*.

boater /ˈbəʊtə(r)/ (clothing) A stiff straw hat with a low, flat crown, straight brim, and broad ribbon round it, in fashion at cricket matches, boating parties and picnics in the 1920s. Today it still forms part of the uniform of some *public schools*[1] (notably *Harrow*) and *college*[1] sports clubs.

bob /bɒb/ (daily life) A nickname for a *shilling*, still occasionally used for the 5p piece which superseded it in 1971, and also in colloquial expressions such as 'a couple of bob', or 'a bob or two'.

bobby /ˈbɒbɪ/ (law) A common nickname for a policeman, especially one regarded as friendly and helpful, for example when controlling traffic or giving directions to a passer-by. The word often occurs in such phrases as 'the British bobby' or 'the bobby on his beat' (one making a regular patrol of a district on foot or by bicycle). [from the name *Bobby*, a form of Robert, referring to Sir Robert Peel, the *Home Secretary* who founded the *Metropolitan Police Force* in 1828]

bobby

Bodleian (Library) /ˈbɒdlɪən (ˌbɒdlɪən ˈlaɪbrərɪ)/, **the** (arts) The main library of *Oxford University*, with about 3.5 million printed volumes and many thousands of manuscripts. It is a *copyright library*. [from Thomas Bodley, who refounded the old library with new furnishings and books in 1598]

Boer War /ˌbɔː ˈwɔː(r)/, **the** (history) The Anglo-Boer War of 1899–1902, in which *Britain* fought against the South African Boer republics of Transvaal and Orange Free State and gained control of them.

Bond Street /ˈbɒnd striːt/ (London) One of the main shopping streets of *London*, famous for its fashion stores and in particular its jewellers' shops and private picture galleries. [named after Sir Thomas Bond, who built it in the 17th century]

Bonnie Prince Charlie /ˌbɒnɪ prɪns ˈtʃɑːlɪ/ (history) One of the nicknames of the Scottish prince Charles Edward Stuart (1720–88), the son of James Edward Stuart. See also *Young Pretender, Culloden*. [from Scottish 'bonnie' meaning 'handsome']

Book of Common Prayer /ˌbʊk əv ˌkɒmən ˈpreə(r)/, **the** (religion) The official prayer and service book of the *Church of England*, first published in 1549 and later in a new version in 1662. Many churches today use a modernized and simplified version of it, the Alternative Service Book.

book token /ˈbʊk ˌtəʊkən/ (commerce) A voucher, usually in the form of a greetings card, which can be exchanged at a bookshop for a book or books at the stated value of the card. Book tokens are frequently given as presents or prizes, especially when the giver wishes to leave the choice of gift or prize to the receiver. They were first introduced in the 1930s. Compare *gift token*.

Booker prize /ˌbʊkə ˈpraɪz/, **the** (arts) An annual prize sponsored by Booker McConnell Ltd. and awarded for the best novel written in English and published for the first time in *Britain* by a British publisher. Its 1984 value was £15,000.

bookie /ˈbʊkɪ/ (sport and leisure) A colloquial term for a *bookmaker*.

bookmaker /ˈbʊkmeɪkə(r)/ (sport and leisure) A man whose business is to accept bets, especially on horse and dog races, and to pay out the winnings. See *betting shop*. [literally, 'one who makes a betting book']

Boots /buːts/ (commerce) A chain store chemist's shop, managed by The Boots Company. Most of the stores also sell other goods, especially household items, photographic equipment, records, tapes and video cassettes, home computers and garden equipment. [founded by Jesse Boot (1850–1931)]

Border Television /ˌbɔːdə ˈtelɪvɪʒn/ (media) One of the 15 television companies of the *IBA*, transmitting programmes to areas of northern *England*, southern *Scotland* and the *Isle of Man*. See *Borders*.

Borders /ˈbɔːdəz/, **the** (geography) The district either side of the border between *England* and *Scotland*. Compare *Border Television*.

borough /ˈbʌrə/ (government) **1** A town represented in the *House of Commons* by one or more *MPs*. **2** One of the 32 administrative districts of *London*.

borough council /ˌbʌrə ˈkaʊnsl/ (government) A *local authority* within a *borough*. Like a *district council*, it deals mainly with local services, for example, environmental health, housing, decisions on *planning permission* and rubbish collection.

borstal /ˈbɔːstəl/ (law) The former name of a *youth custody centre*. Compare *attendance centre, community home, detention centre* and *remand home*. [from Borstal, now a suburb of

Rochester, Kent, where the first such establishment opened in 1902]

Boston Stump /ˌbɒstən 'stʌmp/, **the** (geography) The colloquial name of the main church in Boston, Lincolnshire, whose tall, square tower, near the North Sea coast, serves as a landmark for ships.

bottle party /'bɒtl ˌpɑːtɪ/ (life and society) An evening party to which each guest brings a bottle of wine or some other type of drink.

Bournemouth /'bɔːnməθ/ (geography) A large and fashionable seaside town and resort in Dorset, well-known also as a conference centre.

Bow Bells /ˌbəʊ 'belz/ (London) The bells of the *London* church *St Mary-le-Bow*. According to tradition, a true Londoner or *cockney*[2] is a person who was born within the sound of these bells.

Bow Group /'bəʊ gruːp/, **the** (politics) An influential society of younger members of the *Conservative Party*, whose first meeting in 1951 was held in the Bow and Bromley Club, southeast *London*.

Bow Street /'bəʊ striːt/ (law) The chief police criminal court in *London*, in the street of this name.

bowl /bəʊl/ (sport and leisure) A large, heavy, wooden ball containing a metal bias used in the game of *bowls*.

bowler /'bəʊlə(r)/ (clothing) A type of man's hat, usually black, and rigid with a round crown, traditionally worn by businessmen in the *City (of London)*. [in full, 'bowler hat', named after John Bowler, a 19th century *London* hatter]

bowling /'bəʊlɪŋ/ (sport and leisure) **1** An alternative name for *bowls*. **2** The sport of tenpin bowling.

bowls /bəʊlz/ (sport and leisure) A game in which a heavy wooden ball (*bowl*) is rolled over a smooth lawn (bowling green) in such a way that it stops as close as possible to a small white ball (jack). The game has from two to eight players, each bowling two or more bowls.

box junction /'bɒks ˌdʒʌŋkʃn/ (transport) A special marking on the road at a crossroad or junction, consisting of a yellow square ('box') marked with criss-cross lines. In order to control traffic flow at the junction, no vehicle should drive onto the box while another vehicle is still on it.

box junction

bowls

Boxing Day /ˈbɒksɪŋ deɪ/ (tradition) The day (26 December)
following *Christmas Day*, and celebrated as a *bank holiday*. It
was formerly the custom to give 'Christmas boxes', or gifts of
money, to servants and tradesmen on this day. Today many
people still give an annual Christmas gift to regular callers
such as dustmen and *paperboys*.

boy scout /ˌbɔɪ ˈskaʊt/ (sport and leisure) A term still used for
a *scout*[1].

Boyne /bɔɪn/, **the (Battle of the Boyne, the)** (history) A battle
in 1690 on the river Boyne, *Ireland*. The Roman Catholics in
Ireland rose in favour of the former King James II (reigned
1685–89), but their rebellion was crushed by his successor,
the Protestant King William III (reigned 1689–1702). See also
Orangemen.

BP /ˌbiː ˈpiː/ **(British Petroleum)** (science and technology) One
of the two leading oil companies in *Britain*, in which the
government holds 32% of the shares.

BR /ˌbiː ˈɑː(r)/ **(British Rail(ways))** (transport) The state
company that controls *Britain*'s railways, divided into five
administrative regions: London Midland Region, Western
Region, Southern Region, Eastern Region and Scottish
Region.

Bradshaw /ˈbrædʃɔː/ (transport) A railway timetable
published from 1839 to 1961 and covering the whole of
Britain. [from the name of the original publisher, George
Bradshaw]

Braemar Gathering /ˌbreɪmɑː ˈɡæðrɪŋ/, **the** (sport and leisure) The annual *Highland gathering* held at Braemar, *Scotland*, in September and traditionally attended by members of the *royal family*. The activities include *tossing the caber*, wrestling and Scottish country (ie, folk) dancing.

Brain of Britain /ˌbreɪn əv ˈbrɪtn/ (media) A weekly general knowledge quiz programme on *Radio 4*, in which contestants answer questions in front of a studio audience. The winner at the end of the series is declared 'Brain of Britain' for that year.

Bramley's (Seedling) /ˈbræmlɪz (ˌbræmlɪz ˈsiːdlɪŋ)/ (food and drink) A type of winter cooking apple with large, juicy, greenish-yellow fruit. [said to have been first grown in the 19th century by Matthew Bramley, an English butcher]

Brand's Hatch /ˌbrændz ˈhætʃ/ (sport and leisure) The name of a motor-racing track in Kent, near the village of that name. The *British Grand Prix[1]* is held here every second year.

brass band /ˌbrɑːs ˈbænd/ (arts) A band or orchestra of players of brass musical instruments, often together with other wind instruments and almost always with drums. Brass bands are found throughout *Britain*, but are particularly popular in the north of *England*. Their players come from a wide range of commercial and voluntary organizations, although some of the best have players from factories (so called 'works bands'), coal mines and religious or charitable organizations such as the *Salvation Army*. There are also good bands with young players, especially in schools.

bread and butter pudding /ˌbred ən ˌbʌtə ˈpʊdɪŋ/ (food and drink) A hot sweet dish consisting of slices of bread baked in egg *custard* with raisins and sugar.

breakfast TV /ˌbrekfəst tiː ˈviː/ (media) A colloquial name for early morning television, designed to be watched while people are having breakfast and getting ready to go to work. The two main breakfast television programmes are 'Breakfast Time', broadcast by *BBC 1*, from Monday to Friday and 'Good Morning Britain', broadcast by *TV-am* seven days a week. Both programmes include news bulletins, weather reports, sports features and interviews with people in public life.

Brecon Beacons /ˌbrekən ˈbiːkənz/, **the** (geography) The name of two high hills in Powys (formerly in Breconshire), South *Wales*, on which signal fires were lit in medieval times. They are now part of a *national park*.

Brewer /ˈbruːə(r)/ (language) The short title of 'Brewer's Dictionary of Phrase and Fable', a reference book explaining the origins of words and phrases from mythology, history, religion, art and related themes, and originally compiled in 1870 by a clergyman, Ebenezer Brewer.

Bridge of Sighs /ˌbrɪdʒ əv ˈsaɪz/, **the** (style) A picturesque covered bridge over the river Cam at *Cambridge[1]* belonging to St John's *College[1]*. A bridge like this and with the same name links two of the buildings of Hertford College[1], Oxford. [from its appearance, similar to the Bridge of Sighs in Venice]

bridleway /ˈbraɪdlweɪ/ (geography) A public track or path along which a horse may be ridden or led.

Brighton /ˈbraɪtn/ (geography) A fashionable seaside resort in East Sussex, famous for its architecture (especially the *Royal Pavilion*), its long, broad seafront, and its large conference centre, where many important political and scientific meetings are held. See also *Veteran Car Run*.

bring-and-buy (sale) /ˌbrɪŋ ən ˈbaɪ (seɪl)/ (daily life) A sale, often held as part of a *coffee morning*, in which people bring goods they wish to sell, and buy the goods brought by others. It is usually held to raise money for a charity.

Bristol Cream /ˌbrɪstl ˈkriːm/ (food and drink) The brand name of a type of superior full-bodied, medium sweet sherry. [named in the 19th century by comparison with *Bristol Milk*]

Bristol Milk /ˌbrɪstl ˈmɪlk/ (food and drink) The brand name of a type of superior fine, medium dry sherry. [originally a nickname for sherry, as this was imported to *England* from Spain via the port of Bristol]

Brit /brɪt/ (geography) A colloquial term, sometimes used critically, for a British person.

Britain /ˈbrɪtn/ (geography) A frequently-used name for *Great Britain*. See also *United Kingdom* and *British Isles* and maps on p 380.

Britannia /brɪˈtænjə/ (1 history 2 tradition 3 royal family) **1** The Roman name for the southern part of *Great Britain*. **2** A personification of *Great Britain* on coins, etc in the form of a seated woman holding a trident in one hand and wearing a helmet. **3** The name of the *Royal Yacht*.

Britannia Royal Naval College /brɪˌtænjə ˌrɔɪəl ˈneɪvl ˌkɒlɪdʒ/, **the** (education) A *college*[2] for officer cadets of the *Royal Navy*, at Dartmouth, Devon.

British Academy /ˌbrɪtɪʃ əˈkædəmɪ/, **the** (arts) A learned society founded in 1901 for the purpose of promoting historical, philosophical and philological studies, and which fulfils almost the same role for the humanities as the *Royal Society* does for the natural sciences.

British Aerospace /ˌbrɪtɪʃ ˈeərəʊspeɪs/ **(BA)** (science and technology) The largest British company to design and produce military and civil aircraft, guided missiles and space systems, and provide defence support services. It was formed as a nationalized corporation in 1978 from various aircraft manufacturing companies, but in 1981 became a public limited company (see *PLC*). The British government sold its remaining 48% share in the company in 1985.

British Airways /ˌbrɪtɪʃ ˈeəweɪz/ (transport) The largest airline in *Britain*, set up in 1974 as a state company formed from British European Airways (BEA) and the British Overseas Airways Corporation (BOAC). The British Government intends to privatize British Airways in 1986.

British Association /ˌbrɪtɪʃ əsəʊsɪˈeɪʃn/, **the** (science and technology) An organization founded in 1831 to promote general interest in science in all its branches by means of lectures, exhibitions and the publication of pamphlets. [full name: the British Association for the Advancement of Science]

British Board of Film Censors /ˌbrɪtɪʃ ˌbɔːd əv ˈfɪlm ˌsensəz/, **the** (arts) A body set up in 1912 to grant an appropriate certificate to cinema films. The Board currently places films in one of four main categories: *U certificate*, *PG*, *15* and *18*. Occasionally it will refuse to place a film in any category, if the film is considered too violent or too indecent.

British Broadcasting Corporation /ˌbrɪtɪʃ ˈbrɔːdkɑːstɪŋ ˌkɔːpəˌreɪʃn/ see *BBC* (media)

British Caledonian (Airways) /ˌbrɪtɪʃ kælɪˈdəʊnɪən (ˌbrɪtɪʃ kælɪˌdəʊnɪən ˈeəweɪz)/ **(BCal)** (transport) The largest independent (private) airline in *Britain*, formed in 1970 from British United Airways and Caledonian Airways.

British Council /ˌbrɪtɪʃ ˈkaʊnsl/, **the** (education) A government organization founded in 1934 to promote a wider knowledge of *Britain* and the English language abroad and to develop closer cultural ties with other countries.

British Empire /ˌbrɪtɪʃ ˈempaɪə(r)/, **the** (history) A term formerly used for *Great Britain* and its overseas dominions and colonial possessions, today replaced by the *Commonwealth[1]*. The British Empire was at its greatest in about 1920, when it included approximately 25% of the world's population and more than a quarter of the world's land territory.

British Film Institute /ˌbrɪtɪʃ ˈfɪlm ˌɪnstɪtjuːt/, **the** (arts) An organization founded in 1933 to encourage film making. It administers the *National Film Theatre* and has a large library of scripts and books on film and television. It is financed mainly by the government.

British Gas Corporation /ˌbrɪtɪʃ ˈɡæs kɔːpəˌreɪʃn/, **the** (science and technology) A state organization set up in 1973 (replacing the former Gas Council) to control the manufacture and distribution of gas throughout *Britain*.

British Grand Prix /ˌbrɪtɪʃ ˌɡrɒn ˈpriː/, **the** (sport and leisure) **1** An important motor racing championship held in alternate years at *Brands Hatch* and *Silverstone*. **2** An important motorcycle racing championship held annually at Silverstone.

British Isles /ˌbrɪtɪʃ ˈaɪlz/, **the** (geography) A frequently-used name for *England, Scotland, Wales* and the whole of *Ireland*. Compare *Great Britain* and the *United Kingdom*. See p 380.

British Legion /ˌbrɪtɪʃ ˈliːdʒən/ see *Royal British Legion* (charities)

British Leyland /ˌbrɪtɪʃ ˈleɪlənd/ see *BL* (transport)

British Library /ˌbrɪtɪʃ ˈlaɪbrərɪ/, **the (BL, the)** (arts) The largest public library in *Britain*, and a *copyright library*. It has three divisions: the Reference Division, including the former *British Museum* Library, *London* and the Newspaper Library in north London; the Lending Division, at Boston Spa, West Yorkshire; the Bibliographic Services Division in London.

British Lions /ˌbrɪtɪʃ ˈlaɪənz/, **the** (sport and leisure) A party of *rugby football* players chosen from the best professional players in the *United Kingdom*. They play as a team on tours overseas.

British Museum /ˌbrɪtɪʃ mjuːˈzɪəm/, **the (BM, the)** (arts) A famous museum in *London* founded in 1753 and containing one of the world's richest collections of antiquities. It also holds the main collection and the reading room of the Reference Division of the *British Library*. The Museum regularly organizes exhibitions in special halls.

British Nuclear Fuels (Plc) /ˌbrɪtɪʃ ˌnjuːklɪə ˈfjuːəlz (ˌpiː el ˈsiː)/ (science and technology) One of the world's largest nuclear fuel businesses which is owned by the British govenment. It produces nuclear fuel and reprocesses nuclear waste. The company runs the *Sellafield* (formerly *Windscale*) plant where nuclear waste is reprocessed. British Nuclear Fuels has been criticized for poor safety standards at Sellafield and for its methods of disposing of nuclear waste. It is one of the government-owned companies that Mrs *Thatcher*'s Conservative administration (see *Conservative Party*) would like to privatize.

British Open (Championship) /ˌbrɪtɪʃ ˈəʊpən (ˌbrɪtɪʃ ˌəʊpən ˈtʃæmpɪənʃɪp)/, **the** (sport and leisure) The most important annual golf tournament in *Britain*, open to professional and amateur players, and held since 1860 at different courses in the *British Isles*.

British Shipbuilders /ˌbrɪtɪʃ ˈʃɪpbɪldəz/ (transport) A state corporation established in 1977 to manage all publicly owned shipyards in *Britain*.

British Technology Group /ˌbrɪtɪʃ tekˈnɒlədʒɪ gruːp/, **the (BTG, the)** (science and technology) An organization formed in 1981 by combining the National Research Development Corporation and the *NEB*. It promotes the development of technology, especially in *assisted areas*, supports the growth of small firms and provides finance for technological innovation and progress by itself investing in industrial companies.

British Telecom /ˌbrɪtɪʃ ˈtelɪkɒm/ (commerce) The state company (formally known as British Telecommunications) set up in 1981 to operate telecommunications (in particular *Britain*'s telephone network) and data processing services. It was formerly part of the *Post Office* and in 1984 became a public limited company (see *PLC*).

Britoil /ˈbrɪtɔɪl/ (commerce) A private company formed in 1982 to manage the oil-producing business of the *BNOC*, a state body.

Briton /'brɪtn/ (**1** geography **2** history) **1** A native or inhabitant of *Britain*, or a citizen of the *United Kingdom*. **2** An early Celtic inhabitant of southern Britain before the 5th century, also sometimes called an Ancient Briton.

Britten, Benjamin /'brɪtn, 'bendʒəmɪn/ (people) Benjamin Britten (1913–76), a noted composer, pianist and conductor, wrote works that range widely from arrangements of simple folk songs for voice and piano to such large, dramatic executions as the children's opera 'Noyes Fludde' (1958) and the sombre, serious 'War Requiem' (1962). He was noted for his skill as an opera writer and for his use of children's voices in both religious and secular works. His output also extended to music for radio and films. His greatest achievement, however, was as an opera writer. Benjamin Britten was awarded the *Companion of Honour* in 1953, the *Order of Merit* in 1965, and was made a *life peer* in 1976. See also *Aldeburgh Festival*.

B-road /'biː rəʊd/ (transport) A secondary or minor road (compare *A-road*), often running cross country to connect two A-roads.

B-road

Broadcasting House /ˌbrɔːdkɑːstɪŋ 'haʊs/ (media) The main building and central office of the *BBC* in *London*, where a number of radio and television studios are. Compare *Bush House*.

Broadmoor /'brɔːdmɔː(r)/ (law) An institution (officially Broadmoor Hospital) in Berkshire where patients suffering from mental illness are treated and, in particular, where there is a residential centre for people who have been convicted of a criminal offence but who cannot be sent to an ordinary prison as they are seriously mentally disturbed. [opened in 1873 as Broadmoor Asylum]

Broads /brɔːdz/, **the** (geography) A group of shallow
navigable lakes, interconnected by rivers, in *East Anglia*
(Norfolk and Suffolk). They are popular as a tourist centre
and for their many bird sanctuaries.

brogues /brəʊgz/ (clothing) A type of stout walking shoe,
often with ornamental decorations in the form of small holes.
[The holes were originally punched through the leather to let
water drain out when the wearer was walking over wet
ground]

brogues

broker /ˈbrəʊkə(r) (1 commerce 2 finance) 1 An agent who
buys or sells goods on someone's behalf in return for
payment. 2 A short word for a *stockbroker*.

brother /ˈbrʌðə(r)/ (life and society) A form of address in
some religious organizations and in trade unions, used to
show a friendly relationship between members of the group.

Brownie (Guide) /ˈbraʊnɪ (ˌbraʊnɪ ˈgaɪd)/ (sport and leisure) A
girl aged 7 to 10 who is a member of the Brownie Guides, the
junior branch of the *Girl Guides Association*. [from the colour
of their uniform]

Brown's Hotel /ˌbraʊnz həʊˈtel/ (London) A superior *London*
hotel in the district of *Mayfair*.

Brum /brʌm/ (geography) A colloquial nickname for
Birmingham. Compare *Brummie*.

Brummie /ˈbrʌmɪ/ (geography) A colloquial name for a native
or inhabitant of Birmingham. Compare *Brum*.

BSc /ˌbiː es ˈsiː/ **(Bachelor of Science)** (education) A degree
obtained by the student of a university or *polytechnic* on
successfully completing a course of studies in one of the
sciences.

BSC /ˌbiː es 'siː/, **the (British Steel Corporation, the)**
(work) The state industry established in 1967 to manufacture
steel at a number of plants in *Britain*.

BSI /ˌbiː es 'aɪ/, **the (British Standards Institution, the)** (science
and technology) An association formed in 1901 to establish
and maintain standards relating to the dimensions,
performance and safety criteria, and testing methods, of a
wide range of products and processes.

BST /ˌbiː es 'tiː/ **(British Summer Time)** (daily life) A period in
the summer, usually from March to October, when clocks are
advanced one hour ahead of *GMT* in order to gain maximum
use of daylight hours.

BTA /ˌbiː tiː 'eɪ/, **the (British Tourist Authority, the)**
(commerce) The state industry established in 1969 for the
promotion overseas of tourism in *Great Britain* and for
tourism generally in *Britain*, the latter through three national
tourist boards (English, Scottish and Welsh).

bubble and squeak /ˌbʌbl ən 'skwiːk/ (food and drink) A dish
made from cold cabbage and potatoes left over after a meal.
The cold, already cooked, ingredients are heated together and
served.

Buck House /ˌbʌk 'haʊs/ (royal family) A colloquial name
sometimes used for *Buckingham Palace*.

bucket shop /'bʌkɪt ʃɒp/ (transport) A shop or agency that
sells airline tickets unofficially at reduced prices. [said to be
from an old *Stock Exchange* expression with reference to
stockbrokers who disposed of worthless share certificates 'by
the bucketload']

Buckingham Palace /ˌbʌkɪŋəm 'pælɪs/ (royal family) The
official *London* residence of the sovereign. The daily
ceremony of the *Changing of the Guard* takes place in its
courtyard. The palace was built in 1703 by the Duke of
Buckingham.

Buck's fizz /ˌbʌks 'fɪz/ (food and drink) An alcoholic drink of
champagne and orange juice. [apparently from the slang
words 'buck', meaning 'dandy', and 'fizz', meaning
'champagne']

budgerigar /'bʌdʒəriːgaː(r)/ (animal world) A small green
Australian parrot popular in many homes as a cage bird. It
can be trained to talk.

Budget /'bʌdʒɪt/, **the** (government) The annual proposals
made by parliament for taxes, government spending and
related financial matters for the coming *financial year*. It is
presented by the *Chancellor of the Exchequer* in the *House of
Commons* in a special speech made in March or April.
Compare *mini-budget*. [from an old word meaning 'wallet' or
'pouch', related to modern English 'bag']

budget leak /'bʌdʒɪt liːk/ (government) A 'leak of
information', when the *Chancellor of the Exchequer* or some
other *minister*[2] makes known (deliberately or by mistake)

details from a coming *budget*. If this is done deliberately, the purpose is usually to test public reaction or to see what the effect on the *Stock Exchange* will be.

budgie /'bʌdʒɪ/ (animal world) A colloquial term for a *budgerigar*.

building society /'bɪldɪŋ səˌsaɪətɪ/ (finance) A banking organization financed by deposits from members of the public on which interest is paid and from which loans called *mortgages* are made to people who wish to build or buy a house. In recent years building societies have been increasingly competing with banks to offer investors such facilities as cheque books, credit cards and *standing orders*.

bull /bʊl/ (finance) On the *Stock Exchange*, a term for a speculator who buys shares hoping that their value will rise so that he can make a profit when he sells them. [perhaps by association with *bear*, the opposite term]

Bull Ring /'bʊl rɪŋ/, **the** (commerce) A large shopping centre in Birmingham, built in the 1960s on the site of a covered market where bulls were once sold.

bull terrier /ˌbʊl 'terɪə(r)/ (animal world) A stocky breed of working dog that is a cross between a *bulldog* and a terrier. It has a short smooth coat and is usually white in colour.

bulldog /'bʊldɒg/ (animal world) A sturdy breed of dog with a broad head, the lower jaw projecting beyond the upper, and a short, smooth coat on a muscular body. The aggressive appearance of the dog and the association of its name with that of *John Bull* have caused it to be used as a personification of *Britain*, especially in a military context. [named from its former use in the sport of bull-baiting—exciting bulls with dogs]

bullseye /'bʊlzaɪ/ (food and drink) A round, hard, peppermint-flavoured boiled sweet, usually striped black and white. [from its supposed likeness to a bull's eye]

Bunty /'bʌntɪ/ (media) A weekly *comic* for young girls, founded in 1958. [girl's name]

BUPA /'buːpə/ (medicine) An insurance association providing financial cover for private medical treatment for regular subscribers. [in full British United Provident Association]

Burberry /'bɜːbərɪ/ (clothing) The trade name of a make of light, good quality raincoat.

burgh /'bʌrə/ (government) A Scottish town that has approximately the same status as an English *borough*[2].

Burke('s Peerage) /bɜːk(s 'pɪərɪdʒ)/ (life and society) An annual reference work that lists biographical details of members of the *peerage* and other titled people. Compare *Debrett*. [from John Burke, who first published 'Burke's Peerage, Baronetage and Knightage' in 1826]

Burlington House /ˌbɜːlɪŋtən 'haʊs/ (London) A large building in *Piccadilly*, *London*, in which are the *Royal Academy* and

other learned societies (including the *Royal Society* to 1967).
In it is held the annual summer exhibition of contemporary
works by the Royal Academy. [originally built for Richard
Boyle, Earl of Burlington, in the 17th century]

Burnham scale /ˈbɜːnəm skeɪl/**, the** (education) The standard
salary scale for most teachers in British schools and *colleges²*.
[first established in 1924 by a committee chaired by Lord
Burnham]

Burns' Night /ˈbɜːnz naɪt/ (tradition) A celebration held every
year on 25 January, the anniversary of the birth of Robert
Burns (1759–96), *Scotland*'s great 'national' poet. The
celebration usually takes the form of a supper at which
traditional Scottish dishes are eaten (including *haggis* and
mashed potatoes and turnips, known as 'bashed tatties and
neeps') and during which a Scottish piper plays, wearing
traditional Highland dress. Some of Burns' most popular
poems are recited and there may be Scottish dancing after the
meal is finished. Burns' Night celebrations are held not only
in Scotland and in many places in *England*, but also amongst
British people living in other countries, with several British
embassies regarding Burns' Night as one of the social events
of the year. See also *Auld Lang Syne*.

Burrell Art Collection /ˌbʌrəl ˈɑːt kəˌlekʃn/**, the** (arts) An
important collection of paintings, tapestries, porcelain, and
bronzes given in 1944 to the city of *Glasgow* by Sir William
Burrell (1861–1958). In 1983, the collection was put on show in
a special gallery in Glasgow now called the Burrell Gallery.

bursar /ˈbɜːsə(r)/ (finance) An official in charge of the finances
of a school, *college¹,²* or other establishment.

busby /ˈbʌzbɪ/ (clothing) A special type of tall fur hat or
helmet, with a bag hanging from the top to the right side,
worn as part of their ceremonial uniform by certain
regiments of the British army.

Bush House /ˌbʊʃ ˈhaʊs/ (media) A large building in central
London containing the headquarters and studios of the
External Services of the *BBC*, which broadcast radio
programmes in different languages to overseas countries.
[named after its designer in 1931, the American business
executive Irving T. Bush]

busker /ˈbʌskə(r)/ (tradition) A performer who makes money
by singing, playing, acting, etc. in public places, for example,
in front of theatre queues or in *Underground* railway stations.

but and ben /ˌbʌt ən ˈben/ (style) In *Scotland*, a small cottage
with two rooms, 'but' being the outer room and 'ben' the
inner.

Butlin's /ˈbʌtlɪnz/ (sport and leisure) A name for self-
contained holiday camps, run by a company with the same
name. The camps are often by the sea and are designed so
that the holidaymaker has a wide range of amenities and
entertainments, and need not leave the camp. The first such

camp was opened at Skegness, Lincolnshire, in 1936 by Billy Butlin.

busker

butterscotch /ˈbʌtəskɒtʃ/ (food and drink) A kind of hard, brittle toffee made chiefly from butter and burnt sugar. [said to have been originally made in *Scotland*]

butty /ˈbʌtɪ/ (food and drink) In the north of *England*, a colloquial word for a sandwich, for example, a jam butty. [from 'buttered bread']

by-election /ˈbaɪ ɪlekʃn/ (politics) An election held in a single *constituency* between one *general election* and the next. It may be held because an *MP* has retired or died, or because he has been transferred to the *House of Lords*.

by-law /ˈbaɪ ˌlɔː/ (law) A law passed by a *local authority* such as a *town council*.

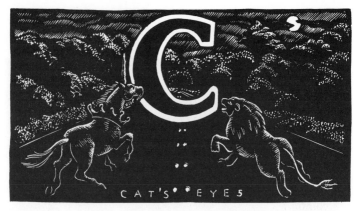

CAT'S EYE 5

CAA /ˌsiː eɪ ˈeɪ/, **the (Civil Aviation Authority, the)**
(transport) A semi-government organization that supervises
the operation of British airline companies and provides air
navigation facilities.

CAB /ˌsiː eɪ ˈbiː/, **the (Citizens Advice Bureau, the)** (daily
life) A voluntary organization found in most towns and
cities. It gives advice to people who are uncertain about their
rights or who seek special state or voluntary aid but do not
know where to find it.

Cabinet /ˈkæbɪnɪt/, **the** (government) The executive group of
ministers[2,4], usually about 20 in number, who are chosen by
the *Prime Minister* to determine government policies, exercise
supreme control of government and co-ordinate government
departments. The Cabinet usually meets once or twice a week
in private at *No 10*, *Downing Street*, while parliament is
sitting. Its members may be departmental or non-
departmental ministers.

Caernarfon /kəˈnɑːvn/ (geography) A town and tourist resort
in North *Wales*, famous for its 13th-century castle where the
ceremony of the investiture of the *Prince of Wales* is held.

Caerphilly /keəˈfɪlɪ/ (food and drink) A type of white, mild-
flavoured cheese originally made in Caerphilly, South *Wales*.

cairn (terrier) /keən (ˈterɪə(r))/ (animal world) A small breed
of rough-haired terrier, once used for hunting foxes and other
animals in hilly country, and originating from *Scotland*,
where it worked among cairns, ie, mounds of stones built as
landmarks on mountain tracks.

Cairngorms /ˈkeəngɔːmz/, **the** (geography) A group of
mountains in north central *Scotland*, in the larger *Grampians*.
They have become popular in recent years as a winter sports
centre, with good facilities for skiing and are a year-round
centre for climbing and walking.

Caledonia /ˌkælɪˈdəʊnɪə/ (geography) A poetic name for
Scotland, also found in adjective form (Caledonian) in the
name of commercial companies (eg, *British Caledonian*) and
other Scottish organizations. See also *Caledonian Canal*.
[originally the Roman name for northern *Britain*]

Caledonian Canal /ˌkælɪdəʊnɪən kəˈnæl/, **the** (geography) A canal in northern *Scotland*, running across the country through a series of lochs (lakes) (including *Loch Ness*) from the North Sea at its northeast end to the Atlantic at the southwest end.

Caledonian Market /ˌkælɪdəʊnɪən ˈmɑːkɪt/, **the** (London) A market held on Friday mornings by antique dealers in Bermondsey Street, in the *East End* of *London*. [properly, the New Caledonian Market, as it was originally on the Caledonian Road in North London]

Cambria /ˈkæmbrɪə/ (geography) A poetic name for *Wales*, found in adjective form (Cambrian) in the names of commercial organizations and in some specialist uses. [originally the medieval Latin name for Wales]

Cambridge /ˈkeɪmbrɪdʒ/ (**1** geography **2** education) **1** The chief city and administrative centre of Cambridgeshire, famous for its university, and a major tourist centre. **2** A short name for *Cambridge University*. Compare *Oxford*[2].

Cambridge blue /ˌkeɪmbrɪdʒ ˈbluː/ (**1** daily life **2** sport and leisure) **1** A light blue colour. Compare *Oxford blue*[1]. **2** A *blue*[3] at *Cambridge University*.

Cambridge University /ˌkeɪmbrɪdʒ juːnɪˈvɜːsətɪ/ (education) One of the two oldest and most famous British universities, the other being *Oxford University*. It was founded in the 13th century. There are at present 28 *colleges*[1], of which only one is for men students only and two for women only. The remaining 25 take both men and women. Among the best known colleges are: King's College, founded in 1441, famed for its fine *chapel*[2] in the *perpendicular style* and for the *choir* that sings here; Trinity College, founded in 1546, with its large *court*[2] and excellent library; Magdalene College, founded in 1542, with a famous library containing the original diaries of Samuel Pepys (1633–1703); and St John's College, founded in 1511, with its well-known *Bridge of Sighs*. There are at present over 9,000 students in residence, of whom a third are women. Cambridge University has made the city of *Cambridge*[1] an internationally famous tourist centre. See also *Backs, Fitzwilliam Museum, Mays*.

CAMRA /ˈkæmrə/ (**Campaign for Real Ale, the**) (daily life) A voluntary organization (also a *limited company*) formed in 1971 with the aim of conserving and promoting the brewing and drinking of *real ale* (*draught beer*), as distinct from canned and bottled beer. The organization also promotes the traditional *pub* that sells such beer.

Canterbury /ˈkæntəbrɪ/ (geography) A historic walled city in Kent, famous for its cathedral, built in the 11th–15th centuries, which became a place of pilgrimage in medieval times after the murder of Thomas à Becket, *Archbishop of Canterbury*.

Canterbury bell /ˌkæntəbrɪ ˈbel/ (tradition) A plant with blue, violet or white bell-shaped flowers, and said to be so named since the flowers look like (or, remind one of) the bells on the horses of pilgrims riding to *Canterbury*, or else the metal badges, called St Thomas's Bells, sold to these pilgrims.

cap /kæp/ (**1** clothing **2, 5** education **3, 4, 6, 7** sport and leisure) **1** The traditional headwear of the *working class* man, especially a flat cloth cap (see *Andy Capp*). **2** Part of the uniform of some boys' *public schools*[1] and *preparatory schools*. **3** Part of the uniform of the member of a sports team, especially one representing his *county*, university, school, etc. **4** A player awarded a *cap*[3] as a team member. **5** A *mortarboard* worn with a gown by a university student or *graduate*, especially in the phrase 'cap and *gown*[1]'. **6** A contribution of money to a *hunt* by a follower who is not a member of that hunt, to allow him or her to join in hunting for a day, and traditionally collected in a huntsman's cap before the start of the day's hunting. **7** A collection of money for charity taken by a *hunt* before the start of the day's hunting, traditionally made in a huntsman's cap.

capital gains tax /ˌkæpɪtl 'ɡeɪnz tæks/ (finance) A special tax (at present charged at a rate of 30%) on profit made from the sale of goods, property or assets. The tax does not apply to the sale of a person's private house or car. A similar tax charged to companies is *corporation tax*.

capital punishment /ˌkæpɪtl 'pʌnɪʃmənt/ (law) The execution of a criminal by hanging. This was abolished in Britain in 1965, but can still, at least in theory, be the punishment awarded for treason. Capital punishment (also known as the 'death penalty') has been replaced by life imprisonment, which usually means imprisonment for a minimum of 20 years.

Capital Radio /ˌkæpɪtl 'reɪdɪəʊ/ (media) A *London local radio* station opened in 1973 by the *IBA* and mainly transmitting popular music and entertainment and information programmes round the clock, together with advertisements.

capital transfer tax /ˌkæpɪtl 'trænsfɜː tæks/ (finance) A special tax charged on transfers of personal wealth, such as a large gift of money, or money left in a will. At present (1984) no tax is charged on transfers of under £64,000.

Cardiff /'kɑːdɪf/ (geography) The capital city of *Wales*, in the southeast, and an important industrial centre and port.

Cardiff City /ˌkɑːdɪf 'sɪti/ (sport and leisure) A popular Welsh football club with a stadium at *Ninian Park, Cardiff*.

Carnaby Street /'kɑːnəbɪ striːt/ (London) A small street in central *London* famous in the 1960s for its fashion shops.

carol service /'kærəl ˌsɜːvɪs/ (religion) A special religious service held in the weeks before *Christmas* either in a church or in a public place such as a town square, and consisting chiefly of carols (Christmas hymns) and readings from the Bible.

Carroll, Lewis /ˈkærəl ˈluːɪs/ (people) Although by profession a mathematician at *Oxford University*, Lewis Carroll (1832–98, real name Charles Lutwidge Dodgson), is known internationally as the popular author of 'Alice in Wonderland' (1865) and 'Through the Looking-Glass' (1871). These two books are very popular not only with children but with adults. Both books tell stories of exciting and original adventures and have humorous characters. In the original editions, the imaginative illustrations by John Tenniel added to the attractiveness of the text. In many ways, the books show that Carroll was a typical British eccentric or 'dual personality'—outwardly a matter-of-fact lecturer in mathematics, but inwardly an inspired and original storyteller and writer.

Cashpoint /ˈkæʃpɔɪnt/ (finance) The trade name of the automatic cash dispensers in branches of *Lloyds Bank*.

cathedral school /kəˈθiːdrəl skuːl/ (education) A school in a cathedral city, usually a *preparatory school* or, occasionally, a *public school[1]*, some of whose pupils sing in the cathedral choir. Compare *choir school*.

cat's-eyes /ˈkæts aɪz/ (transport) Glass reflectors set into rubber pads down the centre of a road to indicate traffic lanes at night. [from their resemblance to the eyes of a cat, which glow in the dark when facing a light]

cavalry twill /ˌkævlrɪ ˈtwɪl/ (clothing) A strong wool fabric used for trousers and woven with a 'twill' or ribbed effect. [originally worn by soldiers on horseback]

CB (radio) /ˌsiː ˈbiː (ˌsiː biː ˈreɪdɪəʊ)/ **(Citizens Band radio)** (sport and leisure) A local radio communication system operated by private citizens, chiefly from travelling motor vehicles. It became popular in *Britain* from the early 1980s and uses a complex and semi-secret jargon, with each operator having his own call-sign.

CBer /ˌsiːˈbiːə(r)/ (sport and leisure) An operator of *CB radio*.

CBI /ˌsiː biː ˈaɪ/, **the (Confederation of British Industry, the)** (work) An organization set up in 1965 to represent the employers of British industrial companies (in 1984, approximately 300,000) with the aim of ensuring that both the government and the public understand the needs and objectives of businessmen.

Ceefax /ˈsiːfæks/ (media) A teletext service provided by the *BBC*. Compare *Oracle*. [a stylized spelling of 'see facts']

CEGB /ˌsiː iː dʒiː ˈbiː/, **the (Central Electricity Generating Board, the)** (science and technology) The state organization that supplies electricity throughout *England* and *Wales*, with the distribution network administered by 12 regional boards. Two separate boards in *Scotland* and a publicly-owned board in *Northern Ireland* supply electricity in those countries.

ceilidh /ˈkeɪlɪ/ (tradition) In *Scotland* and *Ireland*, an informal gathering with folk music, singing, dancing and story telling.

[*Gaelic* word, meaning 'visit']

Celtic /'seltɪk/ (sport and leisure) A popular Scottish football club with its stadium at Parkhead in *Glasgow*. It draws support especially from the local Roman Catholic community and its traditional rivals are *Rangers*.

Celtic fringe /ˌkeltɪk 'frɪndʒ/, **the** (geography) A name for those parts of the *United Kingdom* whose population is of Celtic origin—*Wales*, *Cornwall*, *Scotland* and *Northern Ireland*, such parts being on the 'fringe' or borders of *England*.

Cenotaph /'senətɑːf/, **the** (London) A war memorial in *Whitehall, London*, built after the First World War in memory of the dead. On *Remembrance Sunday* every year there is a short memorial service here, with the laying of wreaths, to commemorate those who died in both world wars. The ceremony is attended by the sovereign, the *Prime Minister* and other leading figures of state. See also *two-minute silence*.

Central Criminal Court /ˌsentrəl 'krɪmɪnl kɔːt/, **the** (law) The official name of the leading criminal court in *Britain*, at the *Old Bailey, London*.

Central TV /ˌsentrəl ti: 'vi:/ (media) One of the 15 television companies of the *IBA*, transmitting programmes to central *England*, in particular the *Midlands*.

Centre Point /ˌsentə 'pɔɪnt/ (London) A 33-storey office building in central *London*. When originally built, in 1965, it was deliberately kept empty for several years by the owner, which greatly angered many people.

Ceremony of the Keys /ˌserɪmənɪ əv ðə 'ki:z/, **the** (tradition) A ceremony held every night at 9.30 at the *Tower of London*. The Chief Warder closes the gates and after exchanging passwords with a sentry hands him the keys of the Tower for safe-keeping with the Resident Governor.

Cerne Giant /ˌsɜːn 'dʒaɪənt/, **the** (geography) A huge figure of a man holding a club, carved out of the chalk hillside near the village of Cerne Abbas, Dorset. The figure, 55m in length, dates back to at least the 2nd century AD and may represent Hercules.

CFE /ˌsi: ef 'i:/ **(college of further education)** (education) An educational establishment, other than a *polytechnic* or university, where people can go after they leave school for additional full-time or part-time education. See *further education* and compare *higher education*.

chamber of commerce /ˌtʃeɪmbər əv 'kɒmɜːs/ (commerce) An association of local businessmen, shop owners and industrialists in a town, formed to promote, regulate and protect their interests.

Chamber of Horrors /ˌtʃeɪmbər əv 'hɒrəz/, **the** (London) At *Madame Tussaud's* waxworks museum, *London*, a special exhibition room containing models of famous criminals, murder scenes etc.

chambers /'tʃeɪmbəz/ (law) 1 The room of a *barrister* where

clients are interviewed. In *London*, such rooms are mostly in
the *Inns of Court*. **2** A judge's room in which cases are heard
'in camera' and in which he also hears minor cases.

Cerne Giant

chancellor /'tʃɑːnsələ(r)/ (education) The title of the nominal
head of a university. He is appointed for life and attends the
university only on formal occasions once or twice a year.
Compare *vice-chancellor*.

Chancellor of the Duchy of Lancaster /ˌtʃɑːnsələr əv ðə ˌdʌtʃɪ əv
'læŋkəstə(r)/, **the** (government) The title of a *minister*[4] in the
Cabinet who is nominally responsible for crown lands in the
county of Lancashire (the 'Duchy of Lancaster'), but who
actually has few or no departmental duties and so is able to
carry out any special responsibilities the *Prime Minister* may
require.

Chancellor of the Exchequer /ˌtʃɑːnsələr əv ðɪ ɪksˈtʃekə(r)/,
the (government) The title of the British finance minister.
He is a member of the *Cabinet* and responsible for the annual
Budget, which makes him one of the most important
ministers[2] in the government.

Chancery /'tʃɑːnsərɪ/ (**1** law **2** government) **1** A division in the
High Court of Justice that examines civilian cases (in full,
Chancery Division). **2** A section in a British embassy or
legation that deals with political matters, the head of such a
section usually being called a counsellor.

change ringing /'tʃeɪndʒ ˌrɪŋɪŋ/ (tradition) The special method
of ringing church bells in *England*, especially those of an
Anglican church. Members of a team of ringers (usually six,
but depending on the number of bells) stand some way
below the bells and pull on the end of a long rope attached to

the bells (one rope to each bell) in such a way that the bell swings, causing the clapper inside the bell to strike the side of the bell. Each bell is rung according to a mathematical sequence, instead of being rung to give the notes of a melody.

change ringing

Changing of the Guard /ˌtʃeɪndʒɪŋ əv ðə ˈgɑːd/, **the** (London) The formal ceremony of changing the royal guard in *London*, held every morning in the forecourt of *Buckingham Palace* and also in front of the main building of the *Royal Horse Guards* in *Whitehall*[1]. The sight is a popular tourist attraction.

Channel Four /ˌtʃænl ˈfɔː(r)/ (media) A television channel of the *IBA* that first operated in 1982. It broadcasts a more selective and specialized range of programmes than the popular main *ITV* channel, including documentaries, detailed news reports, films and the more 'permissive' type of play and comedy. One of its responsibilities is to show some programmes that are of interest to minority groups. See also *S4C*. ['Four' as the fourth channel after *BBC 1*, *BBC 2* and *ITV*; the name was in use before the channel was allocated to the IBA]

Channel Islands /ˈtʃænl ˌaɪləndz/, **the** (geography) A group of islands off the northwest coast of France that since the *Norman Conquest* have belonged to *Britain*. Like the *Isle of Man*, they are not officially part of the *United Kingdom* and are a self-governing crown dependency with their own parliaments (called the 'States' in the three main islands of Jersey, Guernsey and Alderney, and the 'Court of Chief Pleas' in the smaller island of Sark). They also have their own systems of local administration and their own courts. They are popular with British tourists, because of their mild, sunny climate and their favourable tax rates. The official languages of the islands are French and English, although English has virtually supplanted French. A local Norman-French dialect is still spoken, however, in some of the rural districts.

Channel Tunnel /ˌtʃænl ˈtʌnl/, **the** (transport) The proposed tunnel under the English Channel that would link *England* and France. The idea for such a tunnel was first suggested in the early 19th century. In 1964 the British and French governments announced that a tunnel would be built. Work began in both countries but was halted in 1975 because of the very high cost. The project was discussed in 1978 by *BR* and the French national railway company (SNCF). Once again, however, the problems were too great and the project was temporarily abandoned. At last, in 1985, Britain and France finally agreed on a way of building the tunnel. The colloquial name for the planned Channel Tunnel is the *Chunnel*.

chapel /ˈtʃæpl/ (**1, 2, 3, 4,** religion **5, 6** work) **1** A separate place of worship, with an altar, in a cathedral or *church*. **2** A private church or place of worship in a *college[1]*, school, hospital, military barracks, prison etc. **3** A *Nonconformist* (non-*Anglican*) church or place of worship, sometimes used as a term of criticism by contrast with the *Church of England*. **4** A *chapel royal*. **5** A division of a trade union, usually in a newspaper press or a publishing house. **6** A meeting of the members of a chapel[5].

chapel of rest /ˌtʃæpl əv ˈrest/ (daily life) A euphemistic expression for an undertaker's mortuary. It usually does not have any specific Christian or even religious furnishings in the normal sense of 'chapel', except in the most general way.

chapel royal /ˌtʃæpl ˈrɔɪəl/ (religion) A *chapel[2]* or church belonging to a royal palace or residence, such as the one at *Windsor Castle*.

Charing Cross /ˌtʃærɪŋ ˈkrɒs/ (**1, 4** London **2, 3** transport) **1** A crossroads in *London* between *Trafalgar Square* and *Whitehall[1]* regarded as the centre of London when distances are measured in miles from London. **2** A main line railway station here that is a terminus of the Southern Region of *BR*. **3** An underground railway station just north of here, previously called *Trafalgar Square*. (The station now called *Embankment*, south of the main line terminus, was previously called Charing Cross.) **4** A good hotel on the *Strand*, near the main line station (in full, Charing Cross Hotel). [Named after a cross, set up here in the 14th century by King Edward I, to mark the funeral procession of his queen, Eleanor. The cross was set up at a location already known as 'charing', meaning 'place at the bend' in Old English]

Charing Cross Hospital /ˌtʃærɪŋ krɒs ˈhɒspɪtl/ (medicine) A large *London* hospital founded in 1818 near *Charing Cross[1]* but in 1971 transferred to the district of Fulham, West *London*.

Charity Commission /ˈtʃærətɪ kəˌmɪʃn/, **the** (charities) A government body that keeps a record of all charities and controls charitable trusts.

Charles Dickens /ˌtʃɑːlz ˈdɪkɪnz/ see *Dickens* (people)

chartered accountant /ˌtʃɑːtəd əˈkaʊntənt/ (finance) An accountant who has passed the examinations of the Institute of Chartered Accountants and so is professionally qualified.

Charterhouse (School) /ˈtʃɑːtəhaʊs (ˌtʃɑːtəhaʊs ˈskuːl)/ (education) A leading *public school[1]* founded in 1611 on the site of a former 'charterhouse' (Carthusian monastery) in *London*, but in 1872 transferred to Surrey. It has approximately 700 students.

Chartwell /ˈtʃɑːtwel/ (history) A *country house* (in full Chartwell Manor) in Kent that for many years was the home of Winston *Churchill* (1874–1965) and which is now open to the public as a museum.

Cheddar (cheese) /ˈtʃedə(r) (ˌtʃedə ˈtʃiːz)/ (food and drink) One of several types of smooth, firm, yellow cheese, originally made in the village of Cheddar, Somerset.

Chelsea /ˈtʃelsɪ/ (**1** London **2** sport) **1** A fashionable district in west *London*, famous as an artists' quarter. **2** A London football club with a stadium in Fulham, west of Chelsea[1].

Chelsea bun /ˌtʃelsɪ ˈbʌn/ (food and drink) A type of rolled currant bun sprinkled with sugar. [originally made in *Chelsea[1]*]

Chelsea Flower Show /ˌtʃelsɪ ˈflaʊə ʃəʊ/, **the** (London) The most important flower show in *Britain*, held in May every year in the grounds of *Chelsea Hospital*.

Chelsea Hospital /ˌtʃelsɪ ˈhɒspɪtl/ (London) A home for over 400 old or invalid soldiers (*Chelsea Pensioners*) in *Chelsea[1]*, founded in 1682. [full title, Chelsea Royal Hospital]

Chelsea Pensioners /ˌtʃelsɪ ˈpenʃənəz/ (tradition) The inhabitants of *Chelsea Hospital*, famous for their traditional, knee-length coats, scarlet in summer and navy blue in winter.

Cheltenham /ˈtʃeltnəm/ (geography) A fashionable town and former health resort in Gloucestershire, famous for its *public schools[1]*, mineral springs and race course. See *Cheltenham Gold Cup*.

Cheltenham Festival /ˌtʃeltnəm ˈfestɪvl/, **the** (arts) An annual music festival in *Cheltenham*, Gloucestershire, where mainly modern British music is performed.

Cheltenham Gold Cup /ˌtʃeltnəm ɡəʊld ˈkʌp/, **the** (sport and leisure) An annual horse race at *Cheltenham*, for which the prize is a gold cup.

Chequers /ˈtʃekəz/ (government) The *country house* in Buckinghamshire that is the official country residence of the *Prime Minister*. Compare *Downing Street, No 10*. [full name Chequers Court]

Cheshire (cheese) /ˈtʃeʃə(r) (ˌtʃeʃə ˈtʃiːz)/ (food and drink) One of several types of cheese, of various colours, flavours and textures, the most common being white, mild and crumbly, and originally produced in Cheshire.

Chelsea Pensioners

Cheshire Cat /ˌtʃeʃə ˈkæt/, **the** (tradition) An animal character in Lewis *Carroll*'s 'Alice in Wonderland' (who 'vanished quite slowly . . . ending with the grin'). Carroll was using the animal to illustrate the already existing idiom, 'to grin like a Cheshire cat', although many people today think that Carroll's character was the origin of the expression. If the true origin of the idiom is not known, it may refer to the fact that a round *Cheshire cheese* looks like a cat's face.

Cheshire Homes /ˌtʃeʃə ˈhəʊmz/ (charities) Special homes for the permanently disabled and incurably ill, run by the Cheshire Foundation Homes for the Sick, a charity set up in 1948 by Leonard Cheshire (1917–), a retired *RAF* officer.

Cheviot (sheep) /ˈtʃeviət (ˌtʃeviət ˈʃiːp)/ (animal world) A breed of hill sheep famous for their wool, and reared in the south of *Scotland* and in the English county of Northumberland, through which run the Cheviot Hills.

Chichester Festival /ˌtʃɪtʃɪstə ˈfestɪvl/, **the** (arts) An annual drama festival in Chichester, West Sussex, held since 1962.

Chief Constable /ˌtʃiːf ˈkʌnstəbl/ (law) The rank of a senior police officer who is in command of an administrative area, usually corresponding to that of an English *county* or a Scottish region. He is responsible for the direction and control of the police forces in his area, and for the appointment, promotion and discipline of all police officers below assistant chief constable. He is also responsible for all *traffic wardens* in his area.

Chief Scout /ˌtʃiːf ˈskaʊt/, **the** (sport and leisure) The official title of the head of the *Scout Association*.

Chief Whip /ˌtʃiːf 'wɪp/, **the** (politics) In the *House of Commons*, a leading member of a political party who is appointed to keep party discipline, encourage active support for the party and its policies, and make sure party members attend meetings and vote. See *whip¹, three-line whip*.

chieftain /'tʃiːftən/ (life and society) In *Scotland*, the title of the leader or hereditary head of a *clan*.

child care /'tʃaɪld keə(r)/ (life and society) Care provided by a *local authority* in a home for abandoned or disturbed children.

Chiltern Hundreds /ˌtʃɪltən 'hʌndrədz/, **the** (government) A historic administrative division (see *hundred*) of Buckinghamshire, used when an *MP* retires. He 'applies for the Chiltern Hundreds' and thus gives up his seat, since the (purely nominal) position of managing the Chiltern Hundreds is incompatible with his post as an MP in the *House of Commons*.

Chilterns /'tʃɪltənz/, **the** (geography) A range of chalk hills between *London* and *Oxford¹*, famous for their beautiful scenery and old houses, including *Chequers*. The hills have been designated an *area of outstanding natural beauty*.

Chippendale /'tʃɪpəndeɪl/ (style) A style of 18th-century furniture characterized by flowing lines, carved work, and a combination of strength and elegance. Compare *Hepplewhite, Sheraton*. [from the cabinet-maker and furniture designer Thomas Chippendale (?1718–79)]

chippy /'tʃɪpɪ/ (**1** food and drink **2** work) **1** A colloquial name for a shop selling *fish and chips*. **2** A colloquial name for a carpenter.

choir /'kwaɪə(r)/ (arts) A group of singers formed to perform choral works, whether accompanied or unaccompanied. There is strong British tradition of choral singing, both by choirs in churches and by local 'choral societies'. Some choirs in cathedrals or *Oxford²* and *Cambridge² colleges¹* are internationally famous. Choral singing is particularly associated with *Wales*, where *chapel³* and miners' choirs are well known for their enthusiastic and fine singing.

choir school /'kwaɪə skuːl/ (education) A *preparatory school* or *public school¹* attached to a church, cathedral or *chapel²* (especially that of a *college¹* at *Oxford University* or *Cambridge University*), in which certain pupils, apart from receiving a normal school education, are trained to sing in the choir of the church, cathedral or chapel. Compare *cathedral school*.

Christian Aid /ˌkrɪstʃən 'eɪd/ (charities) A well-known charity organization raising funds for practical aid and relief operations in developing countries.

Christie's /'krɪstɪz/ (commerce) A well-known firm of *London* auctioneers, famous for its fine art sale-room. Compare *Sotheby's*. [founded in 1766 by James Christie]

Christmas /'krɪsməs/ (religion) The second greatest religious festival (after *Easter*) in the Christian year. It is the most popular family holiday season after the summer, and centres on *Christmas Day*. At this time presents and Christmas greetings cards are exchanged, a *Christmas tree* (traditionally a fir tree) is decorated, parties are held, and *pantomimes* and *carol services* take place. The Christmas season traditionally begins on *Christmas Eve* and continues until *Twelfth Night*. See also *Advent*, *Christmas dinner* and *Boxing Day*.

Christmas Day /ˌkrɪsməs 'deɪ/ (tradition) 25 December, the central day of the *Christmas* season, and a traditional family reunion day. On this day, many people attend a church service, open their presents, eat a *Christmas dinner* and watch the sovereign's annual Christmas broadcast on television (or listen to it on the radio). The day is regarded as a special one for children, who receive much attention from their families and friends.

Christmas dinner /ˌkrɪsməs 'dɪnə(r)/ (food and drink) A traditional midday meal eaten on *Christmas Day*, and usually including roast turkey and *Christmas pudding* with *mince pies*, and accompanied by wine. Often *crackers* are pulled and the paper hats they contain are worn throughout the meal.

Christmas Eve /ˌkrɪsməs 'iːv/ (tradition) 24 December, the day before *Christmas Day*, when all preparations for *Christmas* are complete and when almost everyone starts a holiday of several days (in recent times, often until the next working day after *New Year's Day*). It is a traditional time for parties, especially the annual *office party*, and many work places, including shops and banks, close earlier than usual. In the late evening, many people go to a church service (in the *Church of England* and the *Roman Catholic Church* often called a 'midnight mass'), and children, on going to bed, traditionally hang up an old sock ('stocking') at the head of their bed for *Santa Claus* to fill with presents during the night. (This role is actually played by the child's parents.)

Christmas pudding /ˌkrɪsməs 'pʊdɪŋ/ (food and drink) A rich steamed pudding containing dried fruit, spices and often brandy, served as part of a *Christmas dinner* and traditionally decorated with a small piece of *holly* 'planted' in the top. Compare *plum pudding*.

Christmas tree /'krɪsməs triː/ (tradition) A fir tree that is decorated with small, brightly-coloured lights and small coloured glass ornaments. Decorating the tree is part of the *Christmas* festivities.

Christ's Hospital /ˌkraɪsts 'hɒspɪtl/ (education) A *public school*[1] for boys in Horsham, East Sussex, also known as the *Bluecoat School*. It was founded in London in 1552 as a religious home or 'hospital' for foundlings but soon became a school and moved to Sussex in 1902. Unlike most public schools[1], its fees

depend on the income of the parents, and are graded
accordingly.

Christmas tree

Chubb (lock) /'tʃʌb (lɒk)/ (daily life) The trade name of a type
of patent lock that contains a special device to prevent it from
being picked. [from the name of its inventor, Charles Chubb
(1773–1845), a *London* locksmith]

Chunnel /'tʃʌnl/, **the** (transport) A colloquial term for the
proposed *Channel Tunnel* linking *England* and France under
the English Channel. [a blend of *Ch*annel and *t*unnel]

church /tʃɜːtʃ/ (religion) A term sometimes used to apply to
the *Church of England*, or other established church, by
contrast with *chapel*³.

Church Army /ˌtʃɜːtʃ 'ɑːmɪ/, **the** (charities) An evangelistic
organization within the *Church of England*, founded in 1882
with the aim of aiding all who are disadvantaged, such as the
poor, the homeless and the elderly, by offering them homes,
hostels and practical assistance on Christian lines.

Church Commissioners /ˌtʃɜːtʃ kə'mɪʃənəz/, **the** (religion) An
organization appointed by the government to manage the
finances of the *Church of England*.

Church House /ˌtʃɜːtʃ 'haʊs/ (religion) The headquarters in
London of the *General Synod* of the *Church of England*.

Church of England /ˌtʃɜːtʃ əv 'ɪŋglənd/, **the** (religion) The
official (established) church of the *United Kingdom*, created in
the 16th century as a protestant church by the *Act of
Supremacy*. Its secular head is the sovereign, and its religious

head, the *Archbishop of Canterbury*. Its senior clergy—
archbishops, bishops and *deans*[3]—are appointed by the
sovereign on the recommendation of the *Prime Minister*. It is
one of the main forces of the *Establishment* in *Britain*. See also
High Church, Low Church, Anglo-Catholic, General Synod.

Church of Scotland /ˌtʃɜːtʃ əv ˈskɒtlənd/, **the** (religion) The
official title of the national Presbyterian church in *Scotland*.
Unlike the *Church of England*, it is completely free to control
its own spiritual matters, and all its *ministers*[1] have equal
status. Each church is locally governed by a 'Kirk Session',
consisting of the minister and elected senior members
('elders') of the Church. The total adult membership of the
Church of Scotland is currently over 900,000, but falling, as in
many churches (1970—1.2 million).

church school /ˈtʃɜːtʃ skuːl/ (education) A *state school*
subsidized by the *Church of England* and under its authority.
See *voluntary school*.

Churchill, Winston /ˈtʃɜːtʃɪl, ˈwɪnstən/ (people) Winston
Churchill (1874–1965) became a major political figure during
the Second World War. In 1940 he became both *Prime Minister*
(of a *coalition* government) and Minister of Defence. He
inspired the confidence of the British people in their struggle
for victory and his radio speeches did much to boost the
nation's morale at a time of crisis and deprivation. Churchill
was a gifted orator and many of his speeches contained
memorable phrases, for example, 'This was their finest hour',
and, of fighter pilots in the *Battle of Britain*, 'Never in the field
of human conflict was so much owed by so many to so few'.
Churchill became a popular symbol of Britain's fighting
optimism. Churchill's other talents and achievements—his
historical writings, his paintings and his subsequent career
as Prime Minister (of the *Conservative Party*) after the war, to
say nothing of his international role as statesman—are today
mostly overshadowed by his unique contribution as one of
Britain's finest wartime leaders. The adjective 'Churchillian'
survives (meaning 'grand', 'great') as a modern legacy of his
standing and popularity.

churchwarden /ˌtʃɜːtʃ ˈwɔːdn/ (religion) An elected
representative of a parish (not a priest) in the *Church of
England*. He helps with the day-to-day running of a church,
such as showing people to seats, taking the collection and
managing church money and other business.

CID /ˌsiː aɪ ˈdiː/, **the (Criminal Investigation Department, the)**
(law) A regional crime and detection department of the
British police force, with the best known being that of the
Metropolitan Police Force in *London*. This operates at *New
Scotland Yard* and is divided into a number of branches,
including the *Special Branch*, the Criminal Record Office and
the *Flying Squad*.

Cinque Ports /ˈsɪŋk pɔːts/ (geography) The collective historic title of the five coastal towns (some now no longer on the coast) of Hastings, Dover, Sandwich, Romney and Hythe (and, later, Winchelsea and Rye), all in southeast *England* (Sussex and Kent), which formerly had special privileges as ports. [from old French, meaning 'five ports']

citizen's arrest /ˌsɪtɪznz əˈrest/ (law) The right of a British citizen to arrest any person he suspects of committing an arrestable offence, or of having committed such an offence. An arrestable offence is one which has a fixed penalty by law, (eg, a number of years' imprisonment), such as murder, theft, rape or unlawful wounding. Most arrests, however, are made by police officers.

city /ˈsɪtɪ/ (geography) The title of many large towns in *Britain*, traditionally ones with a cathedral, but also of a smaller town awarded the title as an honour.

City (of London) /ˈsɪtɪ (ˌsɪtɪ əv ˈlʌndən)/, **the** (London) A self-governing administrative region, with its own police force, in the east of *London*, and the historic centre of London as a whole. It is one of the chief financial and commercial centres of the western world, and its territory of just over one square mile contains several banks, including the *Bank of England*, the *Stock Exchange* and the offices of many financial companies.

civic centre /ˌsɪvɪk ˈsentə(r)/ (government) The public administrative buildings of a town, where the *town council* offices are, as well as other local government offices and, often, recreational facilities.

Civic Trust /ˌsɪvɪk ˈtrʌst/, **the** (charities) A non-government organization that contributes towards the preservation and maintenance of ancient monuments, historic buildings and picturesque areas of the country, and undertakes protection and improvement of the aesthetic environment.

Civil List /ˌsɪvl ˈlɪst/, **the** (royal family) An annual allowance, approved by parliament, made to the sovereign and members of the *royal family* for the expense involved in carrying out their public duties.

civil servant /ˌsɪvl ˈsɜːvənt/ (government) A person employed as a member of the *Civil Service*, that is, a civilian employed by the government. As such he has no right to be actively engaged in politics or to become an *MP*. His position is not affected by a change of government. ['civil' as not military, 'servant' as serving both the government and the public]

Civil Service /ˌsɪvl ˈsɜːvɪs/, **the** (government) The state organization, composed of several ministries or departments, that is responsible for carrying out the work of the government at all levels. See also *civil servant*.

clan /klæn/ (life and society) In *Scotland* and (mainly historically) *Ireland*, the collective term for members of a family having a common ancestor and, usually, bearing the same surname and acknowledging the same leader. See *chieftain*.

Clansman /'klænzmən/, **the** (transport) The name of a daily express train that runs between *London* and Inverness, *Scotland*. [literally, 'member of a *clan*']

Clapham Junction /ˌklæpəm 'dʒʌŋkʃn/ (transport) An important railway junction in south *London*, one of the largest and busiest in *Britain*.

clearing bank /'klɪərɪŋ bæŋk/ (finance) A bank that is a member of the central clearing house in *London* that arranges the transfer of credits and cheques between banks, the clearing house itself settling the amounts due to and from each bank through that bank's account with it. In *England* and *Wales* the chief clearing banks are *Barclays*, *Lloyds*, the *Midland* and the *National Westminster*; in *Scotland* they are the *Bank of Scotland*, the *Clydesdale Bank* and the *Royal Bank of Scotland*. An alternative name for a clearing bank is a 'deposit bank'.

clearway /'klɪəweɪ/ (transport) A stretch of road that is of *A-road* status but is not a *motorway*, on which traffic may stop only in an emergency.

Cleopatra's Needle /ˌklɪəpætrəz 'niːdl/ (London) An obelisk of pink granite placed on the (*Thames*) *Embankment*, *London* in 1878. It is one of two such obelisks originally standing at Heliopolis, Egypt, in about 1500 BC. The other was placed in Central Park, New York, USA, in 1880.

clerihew /'klerɪhjuː/ (language) A humorous verse in four lines serving as a 'mini-biography' of some famous person, for example:
> George the Third
> Ought never to have occurred.
> One can only wonder
> At so grotesque a blunder.

[named after their inventor, Edmund Clerihew Bentley (1875–1956), whose first such verse appeared in 1905]

Clerk of the House (of Commons) /ˌklɑːk əv ðə 'haʊs (ˌklɑːk əv ðə ˌhaʊs əv 'kɒmənz)/, **the** (government) A senior official of the *House of Commons*. He is the principal adviser to the *Speaker* on matters of procedure and he attends all sittings of the *House*[1].

clerk of works /ˌklɑːk əv 'wɜːks/ (work) A person who supervises building work in progress or who is responsible for the maintenance of existing buildings.

Clifton (College) /'klɪftən (ˌklɪftən 'kɒlɪdʒ)/ (education) A *public school*[1] for boys in Bristol, founded in 1862 and having 470 students. [named for its location on Clifton Down]

Clifton Suspension Bridge /ˌklɪftən sə'spenʃn brɪdʒ/, **the** (transport) A road and pedestrian bridge high over the river Avon in Bristol, Avon, and notorious for the suicides committed by people jumping from it.

Clive Sinclair /ˌklaɪv 'sɪŋkleə(r)/ see *Sinclair* (people)

clock golf /ˌklɒk ˈɡɒlf/ (sport and leisure) A type of *putting* played on a lawn on which a course is laid out in the form of a clock face, with 12 numbers. Players start at figure 1 and move round the clock face in turn, driving their ball into a hole at the centre of the 'clock'.

close /kləʊs/ (**1** style **2** religion) **1** A courtyard enclosed by buildings, or the entry to such a courtyard. **2** The land surrounding a cathedral, usually with houses facing inwards on roads that form the four sides of a square, with lawns extending between the roads and the cathedral.

closed shop /ˌkləʊzd ˈʃɒp/ (work) An arrangement whereby the whole of the work force of a factory or other establishment is obliged to join one of the trade unions recognized in that establishment. Compare *open shop*.

closing price /ˈkləʊzɪŋ praɪs/, **the** (finance) The price of stocks and shares recorded at the end of the working day (3.30) at the *London Stock Exchange*.

cloth cap /ˌklɒθ ˈkæp/ (clothing) A flat *cap¹* made of cloth that has become the symbol of the *working-class* man. Compare *Andy Capp*.

clotted cream /ˌklɒtɪd ˈkriːm/ (food and drink) A thick, rich cream made with scalded milk, produced chiefly in Devon and *Cornwall*, and regarded as especially tasty. It is usually eaten with fruit, or added to jam on bread or in cakes. [so called as the cream is not liquid but has *clotted* or thickened to a soft but firm consistency]

club /klʌb/ (life and society) An association of people, linked by a common interest, such as sport, who have their own premises for meetings and relaxation. Many clubs have a restricted membership (some *London* clubs still do not admit women) and charge a high entrance fee and annual subscription.

Clubland /ˈklʌblænd/ (London) A nickname for the area of *London* near *St James's Park*, where there are many *clubs*.

Clyde /klaɪd/, **the** (geography) The most important river of southwest *Scotland*, long famous for the industries that have developed on its banks and at its estuary, especially where it flows through *Glasgow*. Its length is about 106 miles (170 km).

Clydesdale (horse) /ˈklaɪdzdeɪl (ˌklaɪdzdeɪl ˈhɔːs)/ (animal world) A heavy breed of powerful cart-horse, usually reddish-brown in colour. [originally from the valley of the river *Clyde*, *Scotland*]

Clydesdale Bank /ˌklaɪdzdeɪl ˈbæŋk/, **the** (finance) The third largest of the major Scottish banks (after the *Royal Bank of Scotland* and the *Bank of Scotland*). It was founded in 1838 and has its head office in *Glasgow*. Unlike English banks, but like the other two main Scottish banks, it issues its own banknotes (for values of £5 to £100). Such notes are not legal tender, but in Scotland have a status equal to a note issued by the *Bank of England*.[called this because Glasgow is in

Clydesdale, a general name for the region that lies in the broad valley of the river Clyde]

CND /ˌsi: en ˈdi:/, **the (Campaign for Nuclear Disarmament, the)** (defence) A movement started by the philosopher Bertrand Russell (1872–1970) in 1958 to work for the abolition of nuclear weapons. It has a growing membership (1983) of over 60,000 and the active support of nearly 500,000 people in *Britain*.

coalition /ˌkəʊəˈlɪʃn/ (politics) A government formed from the alliance of normally opposed political parties, especially at a time of crisis, as during war. There have been coalition governments in *Britain* in the periods 1915–16, 1916–22, 1931–5 and 1940–5.

Coalport /ˈkəʊlpɔːt/ (style) A type of fine porcelain made at the potteries in the village of this name in Shropshire since the end of the 18th century.

cock-a-leekie /ˌkɒkəˈliːkɪ/ (food and drink) A type of soup popular in *Scotland*, made from chicken boiled with leeks. [from *cock*, 'chicken', and *leek*]

cocker (spaniel) /ˈkɒkə(r) (ˌkɒkə ˈspænjəl)/ (animal world) A breed of working spaniel with a short, silky, black, reddish or golden coloured coat and long ears. [from its use in hunting woodcock]

cockney /ˈkɒknɪ/ (London) **1** The standard *London* dialect, with characteristic pronunciation and the use of *rhyming slang*. **2** A native Londoner, who speaks such a dialect, traditionally a person born within hearing of *Bow Bells*.

cod war /ˌkɒd ˈwɔː(r)/ (politics) A dispute between *Britain* and Iceland concerning Iceland's extension of her fishing limits and involving the deliberate collisions of British and Icelandic fishing boats at sea. Such disputes occurred in 1958, 1972–3 and 1975–6.

coffee morning /ˈkɒfɪ ˌmɔːnɪŋ/ (daily life) A sale of second-hand or new clothes or other goods held in a public hall, *club* or private home. Coffee is served during the sale, which is usually in aid of a particular charity and run by housewives. Compare *bring-and-buy (sale)*, *sale of work*.

coffee-table book /ˈkɒfɪ ˌteɪbl bʊk/ (arts) A large size illustrated book printed on good quality paper and designed to be glanced at rather than read. [from its display on a coffee-table—a low table on which coffee is served in a sitting-room]

COHSE /ˈkəʊzɪ/ **Confederation of Health Service Employees, the)** (work) A trade union to which many nurses and hospital workers belong, having in 1984 over 222,000 members.

COI /ˌsi: əʊ ˈaɪ/, **the (Central Office of Information, the)** (government) A state organization responsible for the preparation and dissemination of government information, both at home and abroad. It publishes booklets and brochures, organizes exhibitions and film shows, and arranges the distribution of British publications, television films, etc overseas.

Coldstream Guards /ˌkəʊldstriːm 'gɑːdz/, **the** (defence) The second oldest regiment in the British army (after the *Royal Scots*), raised in 1650 and forming part of the *Guards Division*. See *Army*. [originating in the village of Coldstream, *Scotland*]

Coliseum (Theatre) /ˌkɒliˈsɪəm (ˌkɒlɪsɪəm 'θɪətə(r))/, **the** (arts) A large *London* theatre that is the home of the *English National Opera*.

collective bargaining /kəˌlektɪv 'bɑːgɪnɪŋ/ (work) A term used for joint negotiation and discussion between employers and trade unions in order to agree wages and conditions of employment, especially when employers and employees are in dispute. When collective bargaining fails to resolve a dispute, matters are usually referred to *ACAS*.

college /'kɒlɪdʒ/ (education) **1** An independent institution of higher education within a university, typically one at *Oxford University* or *Cambridge University*. **2** A specialized professional institution of secondary or higher education, such as a college of music or a *college of education*. **3** The official title of certain *public schools[1]*, such as *Eton College*. **4** The building or buildings of any of these.

College of Arms /ˌkɒlɪdʒ əv 'ɑːmz/, **the** (life and society) An organization established in the 15th century that grants armorial bearings and is responsible for all matters relating to the coats of arms and pedigrees of English, Irish and *Commonwealth[1]* families. Its head is the *Earl Marshal*. It is also known as the College of Heralds.

college of education /ˌkɒlɪdʒ əv edʒʊ'keɪʃn/ (education) A *college[2]* where teachers are trained.

collie /'kɒlɪ/ (animal world) A breed of Scottish sheepdog with a long or short silky coat, usually reddish or black in colour and with a long narrow head. [said to be so called as its coat was as black as coal]

colours /'kʌləz/ (sport and leisure) A distinguishing badge or item of clothing, such as a tie, awarded to a player who has become a member of a particular sports team, especially at a school or *college[1]*. Compare *blue[2,3]*, *cap[3,4]*.

comic /'kɒmɪk/ (media) A weekly magazine for children containing mostly humorous or entertaining stories in the form of a series of pictures. There are also so called 'adult' comics containing picture stories on subjects such as adventure, war and romance.

coming of age /ˌkʌmɪŋ əv 'eɪdʒ/ (law) The 18th birthday of a young person, when he or she legally becomes an adult. At 18, a person gains several additional rights, including the ability to vote at a political election, to serve on a *jury* (if asked to), to see a film rated '*18*', drink alcohol in a *pub* (or buy it from an *off-licence*) and marry without the consent of his or her parents (although in *Scotland* a person has always been able to, and can still, marry at 16 without the consent of his or her parents).

Commandos /kə'mɑːndəʊz/, **the** (defence) A branch of the *Royal Marines* specially trained to carry out landings on enemy coasts and to prepare the way for landings by sea, air or land forces. [originating as an Afrikaans word for troops used in the *Boer War*]

commercial radio /kə,mɜːʃl 'reɪdɪəʊ/ (media) A term sometimes used for broadcasts made by *local radio* stations operated by the *IBA*, since these are financed by commercial advertising.

commercial subjects /kə'mɜːʃl ,sʌbdʒɪkts/ (education) Subjects taught at some schools and *colleges²* to prepare students for employment in a business office. Among such subjects (today more often known as business studies) are shorthand, typing and book-keeping.

commercial television /kə,mɜːʃl 'telɪvɪʒn/ (media) A term sometimes used for the 15 television companies operated by the *IBA*. Compare *commercial radio*.

Commission for Racial Equality /kə,mɪʃn fə ,reɪʃl ɪ'kwɒlətɪ/, **the (CRE, the)** (life and society) An official body established by the Race Relations Act of 1976 in order to eliminate racial discrimination and to promote equality of opportunity and good relations between people of different racial groups.

Common Entrance /,kɒmən 'entrəns/ (education) In *preparatory schools*, a school-leaving examination taken to gain entrance to a *public school¹* (usually by boys at age 13, girls at age 10). [from the examination being used by all schools in common to gain entrance]

common law /,kɒmən 'lɔː/ (law) The traditional unwritten law of *England*, based on judges' decisions and custom rather than on written laws passed by *Parliament*.

common law husband/wife /,kɒmən lɔː 'hʌzbənd/'waɪf/ (law) A husband or wife recognized by *common law* only, that is, one who is not married but who has lived for some time with his or her partner.

Common Market /,kɒmən 'mɑːkɪt/, **the** (government) The popular name of the *EEC* (European Economic Community), which *Britain* joined at the beginning of 1973. Many people felt uneasy about the conditions of Britain's membership, although a referendum held by the *Labour Party* in 1975 showed that two to one of the population were in favour of Britain remaining in the Common Market. As a result of negotiations carried out between Britain and her EEC partners in the early 1980s, some important difficulties were partly resolved, although there is still considerable support at a popular level for Britain to leave the EEC.

commoner /'kɒmənə(r)/ (**1** education **2** life and society) **1** A student at a university, especially at *Oxford* and *Cambridge*, who is not receiving a *scholarship*. **2** A person who is not a *peer*.

Commons /'kɒmənz/, **the** (government) A short name for the *House of Commons*.

Commonwealth /'kɒmənwelθ/, **the** (**1** politics **2** history) **1** An association of countries (in 1984, 49 in number) that have been, or in some cases still are, ruled by *Britain*. All such countries recognize the reigning British sovereign as the head of the Commonwealth. [full title, Commonwealth of Nations] **2** The title of the republic that existed in Britain from 1649 to 1660, in particular the period 1649–53.

Communist Party (of Great Britain) /'kɒmjʊnɪst ˌpɑːtɪ (ˌkɒmjʊnɪst ˌpɑːtɪ əv ˌɡreɪt 'brɪtn)/, **the (CPGB, the)** (politics) The British Communist Party was founded in 1920. Its present aims are to achieve unity among left-wing 'progressive' forces against the threat of world war and to combat the power of the commercial monopolies. As a parliamentary party it has had little success, and its membership has declined from about 29,000 in 1971 to under 16,000 in 1983. Its views and policies are expressed in the daily newspaper *Morning Star*, as well as in a small number of specifically political journals such as 'Marxism Today' and 'Comment'.

community centre /kə'mjuːnətɪ ˌsentə(r)/ (daily life) A building used by members of a community, such as a town or village, for social gatherings, sports meetings and so on.

community council /kəˌmjuːnətɪ 'kaʊnsl/ (government) A *local authority* in *Wales* that has replaced the former *parish council*, county borough council, *borough* council or urban district council. There are also community councils in *Scotland*, but these are merely local advisory bodies and do not have the status of a local authority.

community home /kə'mjuːnətɪ ˌhəʊm/ (law) A state residential home for young offenders under the age of 17. Compare *borstal, attendance centre, detention centre, youth custody centre, remand home*.

Companion of Honour /kəmˌpænjən əv 'ɒnə(r)/, **the (CH, the)** (life and society) An order instituted in 1917 as an award to someone who has performed a special service of national importance. It is similar to the *Order of Merit*.

comprehensive school /ˌkɒmprɪ'hensɪv skuːl/ (education) A large state *secondary school* for children of all abilities from a single district, providing a wide ('comprehensive') range of education. About 90% of all secondary school students attend a comprehensive school. Compare *grammar school, secondary modern school*.

Concorde /'kɒŋkɔːd/ (transport) The name of the first commercial supersonic airliner, of joint British and French design and construction, first flown in 1969 and entering into passenger service in 1976.

Concorde

Conference (pear) /'kɒnfərəns (ˌkɒfərəns 'peə(r))/ (food and drink) A popular type of autumn pear with a good flavour and a long, tapering, brownish-coloured fruit.

Congress House /ˌkɒŋgres 'haʊs/ (work) The headquarters of the *TUC*, in central *London*.

conkers /'kɒŋkəz/ (sport and leisure) A game popular among children in the autumn. One player threads a shelled horse chestnut ('conker') onto a string and with this strikes the conker of another player, with the aim of breaking it.

conkers

Conqueror /'kɒŋkərə(r)/, **the** (history) The nickname of King William I, Duke of Normandy (1028–87), who in 1066 led the Normans to victory in *Britain*. See *Norman Conquest*.

Conquest /'kɒŋkwest/**, the** (history) A short name for the *Norman Conquest*.

conservation area /kɒnsə'veɪʃn ˌeərɪə/ (geography) An area of particular architectural or historic interest, usually in a town or city, where building and development is carefully controlled by the *local authority*. There are over 5,000 conservation areas in *Britain*.

Conservative Party /kən'sɜːvətɪv ˌpɑːtɪ/**, the** (politics) One of the two largest political parties of *Britain* (together with the *Labour Party*) and the major right-wing party. It developed in its present form in the 1830s, and supports free enterprise, encourages property owning and has been responsible for many important social reforms. It finds its support mainly in *middle* and *upper class* or *Establishment* circles, traditionally in rural areas. Compare *Liberal Party* and *SDP*. ['conservative' implying that it aims to maintain and preserve existing constitutions, and conserve what is good]

constable /'kʌnstəbl/ (**1** law **2** life and society) **1** A police officer (in full, police constable (PC) or woman police constable (WPC)) of the lowest rank. See *Chief Constable*. **2** The title of the commandant or governor of a royal castle or fortress, such as the *Tower of London* or *Windsor Castle*. This title is always written with a capital C, ie, Constable.

Constable country /'kʌnstəbl ˌkʌntrɪ/ (geography) A tourist name for the picturesque rural districts of Suffolk and Essex, especially along the river Stour, where the landscape painter John Constable (1776–1837) lived and worked.

constituency /kən'stɪtjʊənsɪ/ (government) A political administrative district whose voters elect a single *MP* to represent them in the *House of Commons*.

constitutional monarchy /ˌkɒnstɪtjuːʃənl 'mɒnəkɪ/ (government) The official status in *Britain* of the monarchy, meaning that the power of the monarch is limited by the country's constitution. The legal authority (the passing of acts) is given to *Parliament*, and executive authority (the carrying out of laws) to the government.

Consumers Association /kən'sjuːməz əsəʊsɪˌeɪʃn/**, the (CA, the)** (commerce) A non-governmental organization that works to promote the interests of consumers and everyday shoppers by monitoring and testing the quality and cost of goods and services. It publishes its findings in the magazine *Which?*

continental breakfast /ˌkɒntɪnentl 'brekfəst/ (food and drink) A light breakfast without a cooked dish, and usually consisting of fruit juice or cereal, rolls or *toast* and *marmalade* and coffee. Such a breakfast has become increasingly popular in *Britain* in recent years. Compare *English breakfast*.[regarded as typical of the 'continent' or mainland Europe]

Co-op /'kəʊ ɒp/**, the** (commerce) One of a number of multiple stores run by the *Co-operative Wholesale Society*.

Co-operative Movement /kəʊˈɒpərətɪv ˌmuːvmənt/, **the**
(commerce) The Co-operative Movement began in the 19th
century to help poorly-paid factory workers in early
industrialized *Britain*. Individual workers contributed small
amounts of money so that, as a group, they could afford to
produce and sell goods to earn more money than they would
earn in factories. The groups also bought important items of
food and household goods more cheaply than any one person
could. This part of the movement's activities became the *Co-
operative Wholesale Society*. The Co-operative Movement also
worked to improve housing, education and employment
conditions. Today, the Movement has about 9.5 million
members in retail, wholesale and manufacturing sectors, and
over 400,000 in the agricultural sector.

Co-operative Wholesale Society /kəʊˌɒpərətɪv ˈhəʊlseɪl
səˌsaɪətɪ/, **the (CWS, the)** (commerce) The national trading
and manufacturing organization of the *Co-operative
Movement* in *England* and *Wales*, established in 1863, with its
products, mainly consumer goods, sold through *Co-ops*. The
Scottish Co-operative Wholesale Society (SCWS), set up in
1868, amalgamated with the CWS in 1973 to form a single co-
operative wholesale and productive organization for the
United Kingdom. Customers of the CWS are encouraged to
become shareholders in the company and to attend local
company policy meetings. The CWS also operates its own
bank, the Co-operative Bank.

copper /ˈkɒpə(r)/ **(1** daily life **2** law) **1** A low-value coin (1p,
2p) which is made of bronze and is copper-coloured. **2** A
colloquial term for a policeman. [from colloquial 'to cop',
meaning 'to catch']

copyright library /ˈkɒpɪraɪt ˌlaɪbrərɪ/ (arts) One of six libraries
in the *British Isles* entitled to receive a free copy of every book
published in the *United Kingdom*. They are: the *British Library*,
Bodleian Library, Cambridge University Library, the Scottish
National Library, the National Library of Wales and the
library of Trinity College, Dublin.

corgi /ˈkɔːgɪ/ (animal world) A breed of small dog with a
smooth coat and usually reddish-brown in colour. Corgis are
popular with the *royal family*. [from Welsh meaning 'dwarf
dog']

corn exchange /ˈkɔːn ɪksˌtʃeɪndʒ/ (tradition) A building where
corn was, or still is, bought and sold. In many towns the corn
exchange serves as a public hall for concerts, exhibitions etc.

corner shop /ˈkɔːnə ʃɒp/ (commerce) A small, often privately
owned, general shop frequently on or near a street corner in
the residential district of a town or city. See also *Sunday*.

Cornish pasty /ˌkɔːnɪʃ ˈpæstɪ/ (food and drink) A pastry case
filled with meat and vegetables and usually eaten hot. The
pasty was a traditional product in *Cornwall*, where it often
served as a complete midday meal for fishermen, miners,

farmers and schoolchildren.

Cornish Riviera /ˌkɔːnɪʃ rɪ'vɪərə/, **the** (transport) A daily express train running between *London* and Penzance, *Cornwall*. [from the Cornish Riviera, the southern coast of Cornwall with its many resorts]

Cornwall /'kɔːnwəl/ (geography) The county at the western end of the southwestern peninsula of *England*. It is an historically distinct part of *Britain*, with its own Celtic language (Cornish, once extinct, but now revived by experts). It is a popular tourist centre and has a picturesque indented coastline.

Coronation /ˌkɒrə'neɪʃn/, **the** (history) The religious ceremony in *Westminster Abbey* when the crown is placed on the head of a new sovereign. The year when this occurs is regarded as an historical milestone. The present sovereign, *Queen Elizabeth* II, had her Coronation ceremony in 1953.

Coronation

Coronation Chair /ˌkɒrəneɪʃn 'tʃeə(r)/, **the** (history) The special throne in *Westminster Abbey* on which the sovereign sits during the *Coronation* ceremony. In an open box under the seat of the throne is the *Stone of Scone*.

Coronation Street /kɒrə'neɪʃn striːt/ (media) A popular twice-weekly television series on *ITV* about the everyday life of several families who live in the same street in a town in the north of *England*, with much of the action centring on a *pub*. The programme was first broadcast in 1960. See also *Crossroads*. [named after a typical residential street, itself built (or named) shortly after the *Coronation* of a British sovereign, such as Victoria (1837), George V (1910), or George VI (1936)]

coroner /ˈkɒrənə(r)/ (law) A local government officer responsible for investigating sudden or violent deaths, especially in suspicious circumstances. Compare *procurator fiscal*.

corporal punishment /ˌkɔːpərəl ˈpʌnɪʃmənt/ (life and society) The punishment of criminals or offending schoolchildren by physically striking them, either with the cane or with a leather belt. Until recently, law breakers in the *Isle of Man* could be sentenced to be beaten ('birching'), but this practice, though still legally enforceable, is now rarely observed. Although corporal punishment has been abolished in many schools, *Britain* remains one of the few countries where it is lawful for an adult to strike a child. There is widespread and increasing opposition to corporal punishment.

corporation tax /ˌkɔːpəˈreɪʃn tæks/ (finance) A tax paid by a company on its profits. For several years it was 52%, but for the financial year 1985/86 it was 40% for large companies and 30% for small. (By 1987 the full rate will be down to 35%.) Compare *capital gains tax*.

correspondence college /ˌkɒrɪˈspɒndəns ˌkɒlɪdʒ/ (education) A *college²* that prepares students for examination by means of correspondence, the student working at home and sending his work to the college by post for assessment and return.

correspondence course /ˌkɒrɪˈspɒndəns kɔːs/ (education) An educational course, usually for an official examination, in which a student studies by means of correspondence (by post) with a particular tutor or lecturer, either at a standard educational establishment or at a special *correspondence college*. Especially well-known are the correspondence courses run by *London University* and the *Open University*, with both leading to a *first degree*.

Cosmopolitan /ˌkɒzməˈpɒlɪtən/ (media) A monthly quality magazine for younger women, first published in 1972, and having a circulation (1982) of over 440,000.

cottage /ˈkɒtɪdʒ/ (style) A small house, usually in the country and often old and picturesque, and having an attractive garden. Some people, especially those living in towns and cities, rent a cottage as a holiday home in the summer or to live in at weekends.

cottage hospital /ˌkɒtɪdʒ ˈhɒspɪtl/ (medicine) A small hospital in a town or rural district, often laid out as several individual buildings resembling *cottages*.

cottage loaf /ˌkɒtɪdʒ ˈləʊf/ (food and drink) A type of loaf baked in the form of a round bread base with a smaller piece on top. [once traditionally made in *cottages*]

cottage pie /ˌkɒtɪdʒ ˈpaɪ/ (food and drink) Another name for *shepherd's pie*.

council estate /ˈkaʊnsl ɪˌsteɪt/ (daily life) A residential, usually modern, district of a town or city consisting of *council houses*.

cottage loaf

council house /ˈkaʊnsl haʊs/ (daily life) A house provided by a *local authority* council such as a *town council*, usually at a low (subsidized) rent. Such houses are mainly occupied by *working-class* people who cannot afford to buy a house. Since 1980 it has become possible for council house tenants to buy their houses at favourable rates after they have lived in them for at least two years.

councillor /ˈkaʊnsələ(r)/ (government) A member elected to serve, without pay, under the chairman of a *local authority* council such as a *town council* or *county council*.

Country Code /ˌkʌntrɪ ˈkəʊd/, **the** (life and society) A code of conduct issued by the *Countryside Commission* for visitors to the countryside, recommending a considerate attitude to the property of country people such as farmers, and respect for the natural environment, for example, shut farm gates, don't let your dogs chase farm animals, etc.

country house /ˌkʌntrɪ ˈhaʊs/ (style) A large, often historic and privately owned, house in the country. Some such houses, together with their estates or gardens, are open to the public for an admission fee. See also *stately home*.

Country Life /ˌkʌntrɪ ˈlaɪf/ (media) An illustrated weekly magazine founded in 1897 and chiefly concerned with such aspects of rural life as social and local history, architecture and the fine arts, natural history, gardening and sport.

Countryside Commission /ˈkʌntrɪsaɪd kəˌmɪʃn/, **the** (geography) An independent (non-governmental) organization set up in 1968 to promote the conservation and improvement of the countryside and to provide facilities for enjoyment and recreation. The Commission is responsible for *national parks, areas of outstanding natural beauty, heritage coasts*, and footpaths and *bridleways*. See also *Country Code*.

county /'kaʊntɪ/ (geography) One of the 53 geographical units into which, with the exception of seven major conurbations (*London* and the six *metropolitan counties*), *England* and *Wales* have been divided for the purposes of local government since 1974.

county council /ˌkaʊntɪ 'kaʊnsl/ (government) The *local authority* of a *county*, consisting o.h)h&%–:h'.hcouncillors presided over by a chairman.

county cricket /ˌkaʊntɪ 'krɪkɪt/ (sport and leisure) *Cricket* matches played between teams of different *counties*, ie, those that existed before the reorganization of local government boundaries in 1974. There are 17 county teams who play matches over a three-day period, as well as one-day matches. All such games are financially sponsored by a commercial firm.

County Hall /ˌkaʊntɪ 'hɔːl/ (government) 1 The headquarters of the *GLC* on the banks of the *Thames* in *London*. [so named from the previous title of the Council to 1965—the London County Council (LCC)] **2 (county hall)** The headquarters of some *county councils*, located in a *county town*.

county school /ˌkaʊntɪ 'skuːl/ (education) A state school provided and maintained in a *county* by the *LEA*. Compare *voluntary school*.

county town /ˌkaʊntɪ 'taʊn/ (geography) The town in a *county* where the headquarters of the *county council* are, the town being regarded as the county 'capital' for purposes of local government and administration.

court /kɔːt/ (**1** daily life **2** style **3** law) **1** In street names, a block of flats, such as 'Hastings Court'. **2** An inner courtyard of a *college¹*, especially one at *Cambridge University*. Compare *quadrangle*. **3** A place where law cases are held, such as the *Central Criminal Court*.

court circular /ˌkɔːt 'sɜːkjʊlə(r)/ (royal family) A daily report of the activities and engagements of the sovereign and members of the *royal family*, as published in a newspaper.

Courtauld Institute (Galleries) /'kɔːtəʊld ˌɪnstɪtjuːt (ˌkɔːtəʊld ˌɪnstɪtjuːt 'gælərɪz)/, **the** (arts) An art gallery in *London* open to the public and famous for its collections of Italian paintings, English and Dutch portraits, and impressionist and post-impressionist works. It grew from the paintings left by the industrialist Samuel Courtauld (1876–1947).

Covent Garden /ˌkɒvənt 'gɑːdn/ (**1** London **2** arts) **1** *London*'s wholesale fruit, flower and vegetable market, formerly in central London but in 1975 moved to new buildings (New Covent Garden Market) south of the *Thames*. In 1980 the restored buildings of the old market were opened as a complex of shops, cafés and promenades, with the former flower market housing the museum of *London Transport*. [formerly 'convent garden', as the market was on the site of the garden of a convent attached to *Westminster Abbey*] **2** The name used for the *Royal Opera House*, which is near the former site of the Covent Garden market in central London.

Cowes (Week) /'kaʊz (wiːk)/ (sport and leisure) An annual sailing and yachting regatta at Cowes, *Isle of Wight*, regarded as one of the most important sporting and social events of the year. Among the many races one of the best known is the Britannia Cup.

Cox's (Orange Pippin) /'kɒksɪz (ˌkɒksɪz ˌɒrɪndʒ 'pɪpɪn)/ **(Coxes, Cox)** (food and drink) **1** A popular variety of eating apple with a sweet, somewhat spicy taste and a greenish-yellow fruit tinged with red. [first propagated in the 19th century by R Cox] **2** A name used for a number of similar varieties of apple.

cracker /'krækə(r)/ (tradition) A *Christmas* decoration placed either on a *Christmas tree* or on a dining table for the *Christmas dinner* or other meal of the season. It consists of a cardboard tube covered with coloured paper. This traditionally contains an explosive strip and a small present (and often a printed joke), as well as a tightly folded paper hat. When pulled apart by two people, one holding each end, the strip explodes ('cracks') and the contents of the cracker are kept by the person holding the half that contains them. Crackers are usually pulled at the start of a meal or party, and the paper hats worn throughout the celebration.

crammer /'kræmə(r)/ (education) A colloquial, rather critical term for a private school or institution that prepares students for an examination, especially one that a student has already taken but failed. A more formal and respectable name for such an establishment is a 'tutorial college'. [from the colloquial verb 'to cram', meaning to 'fill forcibly (with knowledge)']

Cranwell /'krænwel/ (education) A *college*[2] for officer cadets of the *RAF*, near the village of Cranwell, Lincolnshire. Compare *Dartmouth*, *Sandhurst*.

cream cracker /ˌkriːm 'krækə(r)/ (food and drink) A type of crisp, flaky, unsweetened biscuit, usually eaten with butter and cheese. [from 'cracker', meaning 'biscuit', and the 'cream' or dairy products eaten with it]

credit union /'kredɪt ˌjuːnɪən/ (finance) A type of small savings and loan club in which the members agree to pool part of their savings so as to obtain credit at low cost. Members normally have a common bond, such as working in the same factory.

cricket /'krɪkɪt/ (sport and leisure) A very popular summer sport which is played between two teams, each of eleven people. They play on a mown grass field at the centre of which is the 'pitch' (playing area). The aim is for one team (the batsmen) to score a large number of runs by hitting the ball 'bowled' (thrown) to them by the other team (the fielders). The fielders try to send the batsmen out of the game as quickly as possible, for example by catching a ball hit by a batsman before it touches the ground. Cricket is usually played by men and boys though there are teams of women and girls as well. Players traditionally wear white clothes.

cricket

Crockford /'krɒkfəd/ (religion) The short title of 'Crockford's Clerical Dictionary', the standard annual register of clergy in the *Church of England*. The Directory appeared for the last time in 1983, having been first published in 1857 by John Crockford.

crofter /'krɒftə(r)/ (life and society) In *Scotland*, the owner or tenant of a small farm, whose land is known as a 'croft'.

crossbencher /'krɒsbentʃə(r)/ (government) In the *Houses of Parliament*, an independent or neutral member, who belongs neither to the government nor to the *Opposition*, and who sits on the 'crossbenches' which are at one end of the chamber at right angles to the main benches of the government and the Opposition (which face each other). Compare *backbencher*, *frontbencher*.

Crossroads /'krɒsrəʊdz/ (media) A popular television series on *ITV* about the lives and intrigues of the staff and guests in a motel in the *Midlands*. The programme, which is broadcast three times a week, has been running since 1964. Compare *Coronation Street*.

Crown /kraʊn/, **the** (government) **1** A term used to refer to the realm or authority of the sovereign. **2** A term used to refer to the government, with the sovereign being the head of state.

Crown Agent /ˌkraʊn 'eɪdʒənt/ (government) 'Crown Agent' is the title of one of seven individuals appointed by the Minister for Overseas Development to provide financial, commercial and professional services for a number of overseas governments and international organizations. Although appointed by a government minister, the Office of Crown Agents is not itself a department of the British government. Crown Agents currently act for about 100 governments and over 300 public authorities and have about 2,000 staff in *Britain* and 60 overseas. They do not act for private individuals or companies.

crown court /ˌkraʊn 'kɔːt/ (law) A criminal court that deals with the more serious cases and holds sessions in towns throughout *England* and *Wales*. It is presided over either by a judge from the *High Court of Justice* or a local full-time judge.

Crown Derby /ˌkraʊn 'dɑːbɪ/ (style) A type of fine porcelain manufactured in Derby in the 18th and 19th centuries, marked with a crown over the letter 'D' (for 'Derby').

Crown Jewels /ˌkraʊn 'dʒuːəlz/, **the** (tradition) The jewellery that is used by the sovereign on state occasions. When not in use, it is displayed to the public in the *Tower of London*.

Cruft's /krʌfts/ (animal world) The most important annual dog show in *Britain*, held every February at *Earl's Court* in *London*. [in full, Cruft's Dog Show, and first held by Charles Cruft in 1886]

crumpet /'krʌmpɪt/ (food and drink) A round, light, soft cake full of small holes on the upper side and traditionally toasted, buttered and eaten at teatime, especially in winter. Compare *muffin*.

Crystal Palace /ˌkrɪstl 'pælɪs/ (1 London 2 sport and leisure) **1** The name (originally a nickname) of a huge glass and iron exhibition hall built in *Hyde Park, London,* for the *Great Exhibition* of 1851, and later moved to south London, where it was destroyed by fire in 1936. **2** A London football club with a stadium in south London (originally near the Crystal Palace, but later moved).

CSE /ˌsiː es 'iː/, **the (Certificate of Secondary Education, the)** (education) **1** A school-leaving examination taken in many *comprehensive schools* either with or instead of the *GCE 'O' level*. **2** A certificate showing that a student has successfully passed this examination in one or more subjects, with a grade 1 (the highest) the equivalent of at least a grade 'C' (the third highest) at 'O' level. See also *GCSE*.

cub (scout) /ˌkʌb ('skaʊt)/ (sport and leisure) A boy aged 8 to 10 who is a member of the Cub Scouts, the junior branch of the *Scout Association*.

Culloden /kə'lɒdn/ **(Battle of Culloden, the)** (history) The battle of 1746 in which the Scottish prince Charles Edward Stuart (*Bonnie Prince Charlie* or the *Young Pretender*) and his followers were finally defeated by English troops in the *Forty-Five*. [from Culloden Moor, near Inverness, *Scotland*, where it was fought]

Cunard /kjuː'nɑːd/ (transport) A large shipping company (in full Cunard Steamship Company) that operates the passenger liner *QE2* and previously operated the 'Queen Mary' (sold in 1967) and the 'Queen Elizabeth' (sold in 1968). Today the company operates passenger ships on regular transatlantic crossings and on cruises in the Caribbean and Mediterranean. [founded in 1839 by a Canadian shipowner, Samuel Cunard (1787–1865)]

Cup /kʌp/, **the** (sport and leisure) **1** A short colloquial title for the *FA Cup*. **2** A short colloquial title for the *Cup Final*.

Cup Final /ˌkʌp 'faɪnl/, **the** (sport and leisure) The final match of the *FA Cup* contest, played at *Wembley* in *London*.

cup tie /'kʌp taɪ/ (sport and leisure) An elimination match between two teams in a competition for a cup, especially one in the *FA Cup*.

cuppa /'kʌpə/ (food and drink) A colloquial term for a cup of *tea*[1].

curate /'kjʊərət/ (religion) **1** In the *Church of England*, a clergyman appointed to assist a parish priest such as a *vicar* or *rector*. **2** In the Church of England, a clergyman who has the charge of a parish (in full, 'curate-in-charge') when there is no parish priest.

curling /'kɜːlɪŋ/ (sport and leisure) A game played on ice, mainly in *Scotland*, in which heavy stones with handles are thrown so as to slide across the ice towards a target.

curling

custard /'kʌstəd/ (food and drink) A sweet yellow sauce made of milk and sugar thickened with cornflour and served hot or cold with puddings, pies, fruit and similar sweet dishes. Custard was originally made in the home from a mixture of milk, eggs and sugar, all beaten together and then baked. Today it is available commercially in powder form and simply needs to be boiled with milk (less often, water).

Customs and Excise /ˌkʌstəmz ən 'eksaɪz/, **the** (government)
The Department of Customs and Excise is the government
department responsible for collecting and accounting for
money from Customs (duty paid on imports and exports) and
Excise (tax paid on goods, such as alcoholic drinks and
tobacco, produced for the home market). This money
includes *VAT*. They are also responsible for controlling
certain imports and exports and for compiling overseas trade
statistics.

Cutty Sark /ˌkʌtɪ 'sɑːk/, **the** (history) The name of a famous
tea-clipper built in 1869 and now anchored on the *Thames* at
Greenwich where it is open to the public. [named after a witch
in Robert Burns' poem 'Tam o'Shanter', who wore a 'cutty
sark' or 'short shirt']

daffodil /'dæfədɪl/ (tradition) A yellow flower that is a symbol of *Wales*. Many Welsh people wear it pinned to their coats on *St David's Day*. See also *leek, thistle* and *rose*.

Daily Express /ˌdeɪlɪ ɪk'spres/, **the** (media) A daily *popular paper* with a circulation in 1985 of about 1.9 million (1970, 3.6 million). It is conservative in outlook, but does not always reflect the views of the *Conservative Party*. It was founded in 1900.

Daily Mail /ˌdeɪlɪ 'meɪl/, **the** (media) A daily *popular paper* with a circulation in 1985 of about 1.8 million (1970, 1.9 million). It is politically right of centre, but has no definite party ties and is widely read by a range of social groups. It is probably the most intellectual of the popular papers and was founded in 1896.

Daily Mirror /ˌdeɪlɪ 'mɪrə(r)/ see *Mirror* (media)

Daily Star /ˌdeɪlɪ 'stɑː(r)/, **the** (media) A daily *popular paper* first published in 1978 and having a circulation in 1985 of 1.5 million (1978, 0.9 million). It is like the *Sun* in format and content but has a more aggressively 'popular' approach, aimed in particular at young and female readers.

Daily Telegraph /ˌdeɪlɪ 'telɪgrɑːf/, **the** (media) A daily *quality paper* with a circulation in 1985 of 1.2 million (1970, 1.4 million), the largest of the quality papers. It is politically right of centre and usually reflects the views of the *Conservative Party*. It has gained a reputation for the detail of its reporting and its regular, brightly written features. It was founded in 1855.

Daimler /'deɪmlə(r)/ (transport) An expensive make of car built by *BL*. [named after the original engine designer, the German engineer Gottfried Daimler (1834–1900)]

dalesman /'deɪlzmən/ (geography) **1** An inhabitant of the valleys (dales) of Yorkshire, in particular a farmer there. **2** An inhabitant of the valleys of the *Lake District*.

Daley Thompson /ˌdeɪlɪ 'tɒmpsn/, see *Thompson* (people)

dame /deɪm/ (tradition) One of the main characters in a *pantomime*—the mother, or an elderly female relative, of the *principal boy*. The part is traditionally played by a male actor.

Dame /deɪm/ (life and society) The title of a woman who has been awarded the *OBE* or one of a number of certain other awards.

Dandy /'dændɪ/**, the** (media) A popular weekly *comic* for young children, first published in 1937.

Darby and Joan club /ˌdɑːbɪ ən 'dʒəʊn klʌb/ (charities) A social club for elderly people, usually run on a voluntary basis by charity workers who organize parties, concerts and outings. [from the name of a loving elderly couple in a ballad by Henry Woodfall (died 1769)]

Dartington Hall /ˌdɑːtɪŋtən 'hɔːl/ (education) An unorthodox *independent secondary school* in Devon for co-educational students where much importance is attached to self-expression and to the encouragement of excellence in art, craft and music. The school was founded in 1926 with the aim of being a direct contrast to the traditional English *public school[1]*.

Dartmoor /'dɑːtmɔː(r)/ (1 geography 2 law) **1** A bleak region of moors and hills in Devon, through which flows the river Dart. **2** The short name of Dartmoor Prison for men, located at Princetown in the middle of the moors here.

Dartmoor pony /ˌdɑːtmɔː 'pəʊnɪ/ (animal world) A breed of small pony popular as a riding pony for children and originally bred on *Dartmoor[1]*.

Dartmouth /'dɑːtməθ/ (education) The short name of the *Britannia Royal Naval College*, at Dartmouth, Devon. Compare *Sandhurst, Cranwell*.

darts /dɑːts/ (sport and leisure) An indoor game popular in *pubs* and *working men's clubs*. Short, weighted steel darts with a feathered base are thrown at a circular cork board (dartboard) marked out in numbered sections. The aim is to score a particular number of points, usually 301 or 501.

darts

Datapost /'deɪtəpəʊst/ (commerce) A special overnight delivery service provided by the *Post Office* for urgent packages. [from 'data' and 'post']

Datel /'deɪtel/ (commerce) A service provided by the *Post Office* to give high-speed transmission of computer information, as an extension of the telex system. [from '*da*ta' and '*te*lex']

David Owen /ˌdeɪvɪd 'aʊɪn/ see *Owen* (people)

David Steel /ˌdeɪvɪd 'stiːl/ see *Steel* (people)

day release /ˌdeɪ rɪ'liːs/ (education) The release of apprentices from their place of work one day a week, without loss of pay, so that they can attend a *technical college* and thus improve their qualifications.

day-boy /'deɪbɔɪ/ (education) A boy who attends a boarding school daily, but who lives at home.

day-girl /'deɪgɜːl/ (education) A girl who attends a boarding school daily, but who lives at home.

D-day /'diː deɪ/ (history) **1** 6 June 1944, the day in the Second World War when Anglo-American troops landed in Normandy to fight German forces occupying mainland Europe. **2** 15 February 1971, the day when decimal currency was officially introduced in *Britain*. ['D' for 'decimal']

deacon /'diːkən/ (religion) The lowest ordained minister in the *Church of England*, with a minimum age of 23.

dean /diːn/ (**1, 2** education **3** religion) **1** The administrative head of a college[1] or faculty in a university. **2** The *fellow*[1] of a *college*[1] at *Oxford University* or *Cambridge University* who is responsible for student discipline. **3** A senior clergyman in the *Church of England*.

death penalty /'deθ ˌpenəltɪ/ see *capital punishment* (law)

Debrett /də'bret/ (life and society) The short title of an annual register of the British aristocracy, in full 'Debrett's Peerage, Baronetage, Knightage and Companionage'. Compare *Burke('s Peerage)*. [first issued in 1802 by John Field Debrett]

Decorated (style) /'dekəreɪtɪd (staɪl)/ (style) A *Gothic (style)* of architecture of the first half of the 14th century, characterized by pointed arches, geometrical tracery in windows, curved wooden roofs and many ornamental decorations in external stonework.

decree absolute /dɪˌkriː 'æbsəluːt/ (law) The final decree in a divorce after which both the man and the woman who used to be married to each other are free to marry someone else. Compare *decree nisi*.

decree nisi /dɪˌkriː 'naɪsaɪ/ (law) A judgement made by a court of law that a divorce will be effective at some specified time in the future (usually six weeks) unless someone shows a good reason why the divorce should not happen. Compare *decree absolute*. ['nisi' from the Latin word meaning 'unless', i.e. 'unless cause is shown to the contrary']

deerstalker (hat) /'dɪəstɔːkə(r) (hæt)/ (clothing) A woollen hat with a peak at the front and the back, and with ear flaps usually tied together on top. Such a hat was traditionally worn by *Sherlock Holmes*. [so called from their use by hunters, stalking deer on foot]

deerstalker (hat)

department /dɪˈpɑːtmənt/ (government) A major branch of the government. Many departments are *ministries*[2] (for example, the Department of Education and Science) and have a *minister*[2] at their head.

Depression /dɪˈpreʃn/, **the** (history) The economic slump that occurred in Britain in 1929 and at times throughout the 1930s.

Deputy Lieutenant /ˌdepjʊtɪ lefˈtenənt/ (government) The deputy of a *Lord-Lieutenant* of a *county*.

Derby /ˈdɑːbɪ/, **the** (sport and leisure) A popular annual horse race for three-year-olds held on the course at *Epsom* Downs. [named after the Earl of Derby who first organized such a race in 1780]

derv /dɜːv/ (transport) A name for diesel oil when used as fuel for road transport. [from the initials *d*iesel *e*ngine *r*oad *v*ehicle]

Derwentwater /ˈdɜːwentˌwɔːtə(r)/ (geography) One of the most beautiful lakes in *England*, in the *Lake District*, where it is surrounded by steep rocks, green hills, and mountain peaks. There are a number of small islands in the lake.

Desert Island Discs /ˌdezət ˌaɪlənd ˈdɪsks/ (media) A weekly programme on *Radio 4* in which a well-known personality was interviewed by Roy Plomley to choose six records (discs), one book, and one luxury which he would like to have with him if he was alone on a desert island. The records were played during the interview. The programme was first broadcast in 1942. Roy Plomley died in 1985.

detached house /dɪˌtætʃt ˈhaʊs/ (style) A house standing on its own land and not attached to another building. Such houses are generally more expensive to buy than *semi-detached* or *terraced houses.*

detached house

detention centre /dɪ'tenʃn ˌsentə(r)/ (law) A centre where young male criminal offenders are kept for a period ranging from three weeks to four months and are given a strict programme of work to do. Boys aged 14 to 16 are sent to a junior detention centre, while offenders aged 17 to 20 (16 to 21 in *Scotland*) go to a senior detention centre.

development area /dɪ'veləpmənt ˌeərɪə/ (work) An *assisted area* in which the government offers incentives to encourage industrial development. Compare *intermediate area* and see also *special development area.*

Devizes-Westminster race /dɪˌvaɪzɪz 'westmɪnstə ˌreɪs/, **the** (sport and leisure) An annual canoe race held at *Easter* along the Kennet and Avon Canal and river *Thames* from Devizes, Wiltshire, to *London*. The length of the course is approximately 200 km.

devolution /ˌdiːvə'luːʃn/ (government) The transference of certain powers from central government in *London* to *Scotland*, *Wales* and *Northern Ireland*. Devolution began in *Britain* in 1920 when Northern Ireland gained powers in most areas except foreign affairs and defence. This was suspended in 1972 after outbreaks of violence between the Protestant majority in Northern Ireland and the Roman Catholic minority, and *direct rule* from *Westminster*[2] was imposed instead. Devolution has also been discussed for Scotland and Wales, but has not yet been introduced. This is because when referenda were held in Wales and Scotland in 1979, most people in Wales did not want devolution of government powers to a regional assembly. In Scotland there was a small majority in favour of a Scottish assembly but so few people voted (only 33% of the voters) that the idea of devolution was abandoned.

Devonshire cream /ˌdevənʃə ˈkriːm/ (food and drink) Another name for *clotted cream*.

dewpond /ˈdjuːpɒnd/ (geography) A small pond, usually man-made, occasionally natural, found in the chalk hills of southern *England*, and never drying up, even in a drought. Many such ponds are very old and it was originally thought that dew, or natural condensation kept the ponds wet.

Diamond Sculls /ˌdaɪəmənd ˈskʌlz/, **the** (sport and leisure) The annual rowing race for sculls (single oarsmen) at the *Henley Regatta*. The race is open to amateurs and is regarded as the most important international sculling contest.

Dickens, Charles /ˈdɪkɪnz, tʃɑːlz/ (people) Charles Dickens (1812-70) is popularly regarded as one of the greatest English novelists. He mocked and denounced the social evils of *Victorian England* as well as showing humour and pathos. His sentimentality and caricature are still widely appreciated, and many of his characters, with their unusual names, have entered popular folklore. Among them are the miser Scrooge, the orphan Oliver Twist (who 'asked for more'), the drunken midwife Sarah Gamp, who always carried an old umbrella (so that 'gamp' is now a colloquial word in English for an umbrella), and the pathetic cripple boy Tiny Tim in 'A Christmas Carol' (1843). This last story, with its evocation of a Victorian *Christmas*, is probably still the most popular and best known work that Dickens produced.

Charles Dickens

Dictaphone /'dɪktəfəʊn/ (commerce) The trade name of a machine that records speech to be transcribed, for example, the text of a business letter. The name is sometimes used (incorrectly) for any such make of machine. [from 'dictate' and '-phone' as in 'gramophone', 'telephone']

Dinky Toy /'dɪŋkɪ tɔɪ/ (daily life) The trade name of a small toy vehicle, made of steel, formerly manufactured by the firm of 'Meccano'. Often used (incorrectly) of any metal toy vehicle.

dinner /'dɪnə(r)/ (food and drink) The main meal of the day, taken either in the evening or (traditionally, by working people and children) at midday. Compare *lunch*.

dinner dance /'dɪnə dɑːns/ (sport and leisure) An evening *dinner* followed by a dance.

dinner jacket /'dɪnə ˌdʒækɪt/ (clothing) A man's black jacket with silk lapels, worn, together with black trousers, a white or coloured shirt and a black bow tie, on formal or semi-formal occasions, such as a special *dinner*. See also *black tie*.

dinner lady /'dɪnə ˌleɪdɪ/ (education) The colloquial term for a woman who serves *dinners* at midday in a school.

Diplomatic Service /ˌdɪplə'mætɪk ˌsɜːvɪs/, **the** (government) A department of the *Civil Service* that provides staff for the *Foreign and Commonwealth Office* and for diplomatic and consular posts overseas.

direct debit /ˌdaɪrekt 'debɪt/ (finance) An order from a customer to a named organization that allows that organization to request regular payments (usually monthly or annually) from the customer's bank account. The organization is also allowed to increase the amount of the payments as necessary, although the customer can always stop payments if he wishes. This is a convenient way to pay regular bills and subscriptions. Compare *standing order*.

direct grant school /ˌdaɪrekt 'grɑːnt skuːl/ (education) A *grammar school* financially assisted by a grant from the Department of Education and Science (see *department*). Such schools began to be phased out from 1976, and are now nearly all *independent schools*.

direct rule /ˌdaɪrekt 'ruːl/ (government) The direct control of law and order in *Northern Ireland* by the British government, instead of locally by the Northern Ireland government, from 1972. See also *Northern Ireland Assembly*.

disc parking /'dɪsk ˌpɑːkɪŋ/ (transport) A system whereby cars may be parked in a public car park or on town streets only if they display a special disc indicating their time of arrival or intended time of departure.

Discline /'dɪsklaɪn/ (commerce) A telephone service provided by *British Telecom*, on which a caller can listen to a taped recording of current pop music records.

Discovery /dɪ'skʌvərɪ/, **the** (history) The ship on which Captain Robert Scott made his expeditions to the Antarctic in

1901-4. It is now a museum open to the public on the river *Thames* at *London*.

Disprin /'dɪsprɪn/ (medicine) The trade name of a soluble aspirin-type medicine.

district council /ˌdɪstrɪkt 'kaʊnsl/ (government) A local authority within a *county council*, dealing mainly with local services rather than national ones, for example, environmental health, housing, decisions on *planning permission* and rubbish collection.

district nurse /ˌdɪstrɪkt 'nɜːs/ (medicine) A trained medical nurse who gives care and treatment to people in their homes or elsewhere outside hospital, and who covers a particular district in the town or the country. Compare *district visitor* and *health visitor*.

district visitor /ˌdɪstrɪkt 'vɪzɪtə(r)/ (religion) A member of the *Church of England* who volunteers to visit the sick and needy in a parish.

dividend /'dɪvɪdend/ (finance) A payment made regularly from the profits of a company to its shareholders, usually twice a year.

division /dɪ'vɪʒn/ (**1** government **2** sport and leisure) **1** A formal vote in the *House of Commons*, when *MP*s divide into two groups, for the motion ('aye') or against it ('no'), and go to one of two special corridors (division lobbies) to cast their vote. **2** One of four groups into which professional football clubs are placed in the *Football League*.

divvy/divi /'dɪvɪ/ (finance) A colloquial term for a *dividend*.

DIY /ˌdiː aɪ 'waɪ/ (**do-it-yourself**) (daily life) The popular British hobby of making improvements and additions to one's house without the help of professional or skilled workers such as painters, builders and carpenters. The pastime is not only specially satisfying to the home-owner but is cheaper than engaging professional craftsman to do the work. Many special 'DIY shops' sell equipment and materials for DIY work.

D-notice /'diː ˌnəʊtɪs/ (defence) An instruction circulated to the news media by the government advising against the publication of information on a topic regarded as harmful to the defence interests of the country. ['D' for 'defence']

Doctor Who /ˌdɒktə 'huː/ (media) A television science-fiction series for children broadcast by the *BBC* since 1963. The central character (Doctor Who of the title) has a 'time machine' (the 'Tardis') in which, with one or more companions, he travels backwards or forwards in time to combat a variety of evil forces and characters.

Dodgem /'dɒdʒəm/ (sport and leisure) The trade name of a type of bumper car—a low-powered electrically operated vehicle driven and bumped into similar cars on a special rink at a fairground. [from 'dodge 'em' ('dodge them'), the aim being to bump while dodging the other cars]

dog-collar /ˈdɒɡˌkɒlə(r)/ (clothing) A colloquial term for a priest's stiff white collar (officially, 'clerical collar').

dogs /dɒɡz/, **the** (sport and leisure) A colloquial term for *greyhound racing*. On a special circular track a mechanical hare is chased by greyhounds, on which bets are placed as in horse racing.

dog's nose /ˈdɒɡz nəʊz/ (food and drink) A colloquial name for a mixture of *gin* and beer, popular in the north of *England* as an alcoholic drink.

Domesday Book /ˈduːmzdeɪ bʊk/, **the** (history) The records of a survey of the land of *England* made by order of William the *Conqueror* (William I of Normandy) in 1086, and used for tax purposes and as a general reference book of the population, its property, stock, etc. Some of the remoter areas of northern England were not included in the survey. [probably so named as the records were the final ('day of judgement' or 'doomsday') authority for disputes over property]

don /dɒn/ (education) A member of the teaching staff of a university or *college¹*, especially at *Oxford University* or *Cambridge University*.

donkey derby /ˈdɒŋkɪ ˌdaːbɪ/ (sport and leisure) A race in which people, especially children, ride donkeys, usually at a *fête*.

donkey jacket /ˈdɒŋkɪ ˌdʒækɪt/ (clothing) A short, thick, outdoor jacket, often dark blue in colour, worn either by workmen in bad weather or as a fashionable garment.

Dons /dɒnz/, **the** (sport and leisure) The nickname of Aberdeen football club in *Scotland*, founded in 1903. [from 'Aber*do*nian'; see *Aberdonian*]

doorstep /ˈdɔːstep/ (food and drink) A colloquial word for a thick slice of bread.

door-to-door salesman /ˌdɔː tə dɔː ˈseɪlzmən/ (commerce) A salesman who drives or walks from one house to the next to sell his goods.

Dorchester /ˈdɔːtʃɪstə(r)/, **the** (London) A luxury hotel in *Park Lane, London*.

Dorking /ˈdɔːkɪŋ/ (animal world) A large breed of chicken with silver-grey feathers and short legs. [originally bred at Dorking, Surrey]

double /ˈdʌbl/ (1 food and drink 2 ,3 sport and leisure) 1 A double measure of spirits as an alcoholic drink, especially one measured in a *bar¹*. 2 In *darts*, a hit inside the narrow double ring that runs round the outer edge of a dartboard, thus scoring double the number of points in the particular section. 3 In gambling, a bet placed on two horses in different races, the winnings (and stake) from the first bet being placed as the second. See also *autumn double*, *accumulator*.

double decker /ˌdʌbl ˈdekə(r)/ (transport) A bus with two passenger decks, especially a red bus of this type in *London*.

At many seaside resorts, double deckers with an open top deck are used in the summer season for tourists who are sight-seeing.

double feature /ˌdʌbl ˈfiːtʃə(r)/ (arts) A cinema programme that includes two major films.

double Gloucester (cheese) /ˌdʌbl ˈglɒstə(r) (ˌdʌbl ˌglɒstə ˈtʃiːz)/ (food and drink) A kind of smooth, mellow, orange-red cheese, originally made in the Vale of Gloucester. ['double' by contrast with the former 'single Gloucester' cheese, which was thinner and milder and made with less creamy milk]

Doulton (pottery) /ˈdəʊltən (ˌdəʊltən ˈpɒtəri)/ (style) A type of stoneware, typically brown and salt-glazed, originally made by Henry Doulton in *London*. The name 'Royal Doulton' is the mark of this and other china products.

Downing Street /ˈdaʊnɪŋ striːt/ (government) **1** A short street in central *London*, off *Whitehall[1]*, where the official homes of the *Prime Minister* (*Number Ten*) and of the *Chancellor of the Exchequer* (Number 11) are. **2** A term used for the British government.

Downs /daʊnz/, **the** (geography) The name of a number of chains of low chalk hills in the south of *England*, in particular the South Downs in Sussex.

DPP /ˌdiː piː ˈpiː/, **the (Director of Public Prosecutions, the)** (law) The official who brings criminal proceedings in special or important cases under the superintendence of the *Attorney General*. He also advises government *departments*, *Chief Constable*s and others who are involved in important legal matters.

Dr Barnardo's (Homes) /ˌdɒktə bəˈnaːdəʊz (həʊmz)/ (charities) A charity that runs homes, schools, and other centres for orphans and deprived children, including those with physical or mental handicaps. [founded by an Irish doctor, Thomas John Barnardo (1845-1905) in 1870, who worked among such children in London]

Dr Watson /ˌdɒktə ˈwɒtsn/ (arts) The doctor who is the companion and assistant of Sherlock *Holmes[1]* in the stories by Arthur Conan Doyle. Dr Watson is the person who tells the stories and whose stupidity shows how brilliant the great detective is. It is said that Dr Watson is a self-mocking portrayal of Conan Doyle himself.

draught beer /ˌdraːft ˈbɪə(r)/ (food and drink) A beer stored in a cask or barrel, as distinct from one that is bottled or canned. Such a beer is regarded as purer, and often stronger, by people knowledgeable about the drink. See also *CAMRA*, *real ale*.

dress circle /ˈdres ˌsɜːkl/, **the** (daily life) The first gallery in a theatre, in which *evening dress* formerly had to be worn.

drive /draɪv/ (**1** sport and leisure **2** style) **1** A game of whist or a session of *bingo*. **2** A private road that leads, usually from a gate, up to a person's house.

drop scone /'drɒp skɒn/ (food and drink) A *scone* made by dropping a spoonful of batter on to a hot cooking surface. Also known as a 'Scotch pancake'.

Druids /'druːɪdz/, **the** (1 history 2 life and society) **1** An ancient order of priests in *Britain*, *Ireland* and Gaul in pre-Christian times. **2** One of a number of modern religious societies who aim to revive the ancient order, in particular those who greet the rising of the sun on *Midsummer Day* at *Stonehenge*.

Drury Lane /ˌdrʊərɪ 'leɪn/ (arts) A *London* theatre officially known as the Theatre Royal and famous for its musicals. It is London's oldest theatre still in use, founded in 1663. [named after Drury Lane, a street that runs behind it]

dry /draɪ/ (politics) A term occasionally used, often half-humorously, for a *Conservative Party* politician who supports the 'hard line' policies of Margaret *Thatcher*, as distinct from a *wet*, who opposes them.

duchy /'dʌtʃɪ/ (life and society) The lands or territory held by a duke or duchess. See also *Duchy of Cornwall*, *Duchy of Lancaster*.

Duchy of Cornwall /ˌdʌtʃɪ əv 'kɔːnwəl/, **the** (history) The *duchy* established in *Cornwall* in 1337 by King Edward III for his eldest son, Edward the *Black Prince*. Since this time, the duchy has always passed to the eldest son of the sovereign. See *Duke of Cornwall* and compare *Prince of Wales*.

Duchy of Lancaster /ˌdʌtʃɪ əv 'læŋkəstə(r)/, **the** (history) A duchy established in Lancashire in 1399 and, as crown land, held by the *Chancellor of the Duchy of Lancaster* since this date.

duffle-coat /'dʌfl kəʊt/ (clothing) A short or knee-length outdoor coat, made of strong or heavy wool cloth and usually with a hood. [named after the town Duffel, Belgium, where the cloth for such coats was first made]

Duke of Cornwall /ˌdjuːk əv 'kɔːnwəl/, **the** (royal family) One of the titles of the eldest son of the sovereign as heir to the throne. See *Duchy of Cornwall* and compare *Prince of Wales*.

Duke of Edinburgh /ˌdjuːk əv 'edɪnbrə/, **the** (royal family) The principal title held by Prince Philip, the husband of *Queen Elizabeth*, and the one by which he is usually known. Born in 1926, he served in the *Royal Navy* both before and for some years after his marriage in 1947 to the then Princess Elizabeth. He takes a great deal of interest in industry, in the achievements of young people (see *Duke of Edinburgh's Award Scheme*) and in saving rare wild animals from extinction.

Duke of Edinburgh's Award Scheme /ˌdjuːk əv ˌedɪnbrəz əˈwɔːd skiːm/, **the** (education) A scheme by which a range of awards (Bronze, Silver and Gold medals), are made to young people between the ages of 14 and 21 for enterprise, initiative and achievement shown in such purposeful leisure-time activities as sport, hobbies and excursions, with the voluntary assistance of adults. The scheme was founded by the *Duke of Edinburgh* in 1956.

Duke of Windsor /ˌdjuːk əv ˈwɪnzə(r)/, **the** (royal family) The title given to King Edward VIII (1894-1972) after his *Abdication* in 1936.

Dulwich (College) /ˈdʌlɪdʒ (ˌdʌlɪdʒ ˈkɒlɪdʒ)/ (education) A large *public school*[1] for boys in the district of this name in southeast *London*, founded in 1619. It has 1,350 students.

Dundee cake /dʌnˈdiː keɪk/ (food and drink) A large, round, rich fruit cake containing nuts and spices and decorated with almonds. [first made in Dundee, *Scotland*]

Dunkirk /dʌnˈkɜːk/ (history) The name of the mass evacuation of British troops, and also some French and Belgians, from Dunkirk (Dunkerque), a port in occupied France, in May and June 1940.

Dunlop /ˈdʌnlɒp/ (food and drink) A soft, mild cheese resembling *Cheddar*, originally made at Dunlop, Ayrshire in *Scotland*.

Durex /ˈdjʊəreks/ (medicine) The trade name of a range of contraceptives for men.

Durham Miners' Gala /ˌdʌrəm ˌmaɪnəz ˈɡeɪlə/, **the** (work) An annual parade of miners through the streets of Durham, held on the second Saturday in July, accompanied by brass bands and colourful displays and tableaux. The parade is traditionally led by the leader of the *Labour Party* and the president of the *NUM*. [Note the unusual pronunciation in this name of 'gala'; compare *gala*]

Dutch barn /ˌdʌtʃ ˈbɑːn/ (style) A tall shed for storing hay or straw on a farm. It has no walls, and is usually made of steel with a curved roof.

each way bet /ˌiːtʃ weɪ ˈbet/ (sport and leisure) A bet placed on a horse both for it to win and to be placed, ie, to come first, second or third.

Ealing comedy /ˌiːlɪŋ ˈkɒmədɪ/ (arts) One of a number of comedy films, produced by the Ealing Studios, west *London*, in the period 1948–50. The films were typically 'English' in character and usually featured a group who rebelled against authority.

Earl Marshal /ˌɜːl ˈmɑːʃl/, **the (life and society)** The title of the head of the *College of Arms*, who organizes royal processions and other important state ceremonies.

Earls Court /ˌɜːlz ˈkɔːt/ (London) A large exhibition hall and centre in *London*, where several important annual events are held, including the *Royal Tournament*, *Cruft's* and the *Boat Show*. The centre was built in 1937 (as Earls Court Exhibition Buildings) in the district of London that has the same name.

Early English /ˌɜːlɪ ˈɪŋɡlɪʃ/ (style) A *Gothic style* of architecture flourishing in *England* from the last decade of the 12th century to the end of the 13th century, and characterized by tall, slender, pointed windows with little tracery (open stone work), thick, heavy walls, and the use of columns of stone surrounded by a number of shafts of black marble. Many cathedrals are noted examples of the style, especially those of Salisbury, Wells, Ely and Worcester.

East Anglia /ˌiːst ˈæŋɡlɪə/ (geography) An historic kingdom in the east of *England* that existed in the 6th–8th centuries. Today the term is commonly used to mean the *counties* of Norfolk and Suffolk, and parts of Essex and Cambridgeshire.

East End /ˌiːst ˈend/, **the** (London) An extensive industrial area of *London*, to the east of the *City*, famous for its docks and, formerly, for its poverty.

Easter /ˈiːstə(r)/ (religion) For Christians, the most important Christian festival, traditionally associated with the eating of *Easter eggs*. The season is also closely associated with the coming of spring, and most churches are specially decorated with flowers for the services held on Easter Day. Presents, apart from chocolate eggs and greeting cards, are rarely exchanged. See also *Easter Monday*.

Easter egg /ˈiːstər eg/ (tradition) An egg eaten symbolically at *Easter* to mark the birth of new life and the coming of the spring. The egg may be that of a hen, with a painted or decorated shell, or, more popularly, one made of chocolate (usually large and hollow and often containing individual chocolates or other sweets).

Easter Monday /ˌiːstər ˈmʌndɪ/ (daily life) The day after *Easter* Day (also called Easter Sunday), and a *bank holiday*. It is a traditional date for the start of the summer tourist season.

Eccles cake /ˈeklz keɪk/ (food and drink) A small round pastry cake containing currants and other dried fruit. [originally made in Eccles, Lancashire (now Greater Manchester)]

Economist /ɪˈkɒnəmɪst/**, the** (media) A weekly political, economic and financial magazine influential in industrial and business circles. Its views tend to support the *Conservative Party*. Its circulation in 1981 was over 178,000 and it was founded in 1843.

Edgbaston /ˈedʒbəstən/ (sport and leisure) A well-known *cricket* ground in Birmingham, where *test match*es have been played since 1902.

Edgehill /ˌedʒ ˈhɪl/ **(Battle of Edgehill, the)** (history) The first important battle of the Civil War of the mid-17th century, in which the Parliamentarians fought the Royalists, but neither side won. It took place near the hill so named in Warwickshire in 1642.

Edinburgh /ˈedɪnbrə/ (geography) The capital city of *Scotland*, famous for its fine buildings (especially *Edinburgh Castle*) and for the annual *Edinburgh Festival*. It is a popular tourist centre.

Edinburgh Academy /ˌedɪnbrə əˈkædəmɪ/**, The** (education) A Scottish independent (fee-paying) *secondary school* similar to an English *public school*[1]. It was founded in 1824 and has over 600 students.

Edinburgh Castle /ˌedɪnbrə ˈkɑːsl/ (history) A famous fortress built on a basalt hill (Castle Rock) in the centre of *Edinburgh*, overlooking *Princes Street* and the streets of the old town. The oldest parts of the building date back to about 1100. The *Edinburgh Military Tattoo* is held annually in the grounds of the castle.

Edinburgh Festival /ˌedɪnbrə ˈfestɪvl/**, the** (arts) An annual festival of music and drama held in August and September at various centres in *Edinburgh*. The festival, first held in 1947, has gained international status and has won a reputation for its inclusion of experimental or 'avant-garde' events (the so-called 'Edinburgh *Fringe*').

Edinburgh Military Tattoo /ˌedɪnbrə ˌmɪlɪtrɪ təˈtuː/**, the** (defence) An annual floodlit military parade held for three weeks in August and September on the parade ground of *Edinburgh Castle*. The event is a popular tourist attraction.

Edinburgh rock /ˌedɪnbrə ˈrɒk/ (food and drink) A form of sweet consisting of a hard, brittle, brightly-coloured stick made from sugar. It was first manufactured in *Edinburgh* in 1822. ['rock' is a humorous reference to the rock on which *Edinburgh Castle* stands]

Edward Elgar /ˌedwəd ˈelgɑː(r)/ see *Elgar* (people)

EEC /ˌiː iː ˈsiː/, **the (European Economic Community, the)** (government) The formal name of the *Common Market*.

egg-and-spoon race /ˌeg ən ˈspuːn reɪs/ (sport and leisure) A race in which contestants run a course balancing an egg in a spoon. If a runner's egg falls from the spoon as he is running, he is out of the race. The event is a popular one with children and so often features at *fêtes* and on school sports days.

18 /ˌeɪˈtiːn/ (arts) A category in which a cinema film is placed by the *British Board of Film Censors* to show that no young person under the age of 18 will be admitted. This category replaced the former *X certificate* in 1982. Compare *15* (listed under letter F), *PG* and *U certificate*.

Eights /eɪts/ (sport and leisure) Traditional annual rowing races held between teams of eight people representing individual *colleges*[1] of *Oxford University* on the river *Thames* at *Oxford*[1]. The various races are held over a week (Eights Week) at the end of the academic year in June, and are accompanied by a number of events such as dances and concerts. Compare *Mays*.

eisteddfod /ˌaɪ ˈstedfəd/ (arts) **1** (Eisteddfod) An annual Welsh national bardic (see *bard*) festival of music, literature and drama held alternately in North and South *Wales* during the first week of August. The modern Eisteddfod (Welsh, 'chairing' from the chairing, or seating in a ceremonial chair, of the winning bard) has developed from the gathering of bards held in the 12th century. It is conducted entirely in Welsh and is open to the public. **2** (Eisteddfod) An international festival of folk-dancing and music held annually at Llangollen, North Wales. The festival has no bardic or literary content and is conducted entirely in English. **3** (Eisteddfod) An annual festival for the youth similar to the Welsh national bardic, held alternately in North and South Wales. Its aim is to encourage the evolution of the Welsh language. **4** (eisteddfod) A festival of folk-dancing and music held in *England*, resembling the Eisteddfod[2] at Llangollen.

Elastoplast /ɪˈlæstəplɑːst/ (medicine) The trade name of a make of surgical adhesive dressing for minor wounds, cuts, etc. [from 'elastic' and 'plaster']

Electricity Council /ɪlekˈtrɪsətɪ ˌkaʊnsl/, **the** (science and technology) The central government body that controls the production and distribution of electricity in *England* and *Wales*. Among its members are the chairman of the *CEGB* and representatives of the 12 area electricity boards.

eleven /ɪˈlevn/ (sport and leisure) A team, consisting of 11 players, for football (soccer), hockey or *cricket*.

eisteddfod

eleven-plus /ɪˌlevn ˈplʌs/, **the** (education) An examination formerly used to select school pupils at about the age of 11 for an appropriate secondary education (academic, at a *grammar school*, non-academic, at a *secondary modern school*, or technical, at a *technical school*). The term is still loosely used to apply to a similar selection procedure operated in *Britain* by some *LEA*s.

elevenses /ɪˈlevənzɪz/ (food and drink) A drink or snack (or both) taken in the middle of the morning at about eleven o'clock.

Elgar, Edward /ˈelgɑː(r), ˈedwəd/ (people) Edward Elgar (1857–1934) is generally regarded as the first English composer of international stature since Purcell in the 17th century. His own works encouraged a revival of English music, but his symphonies have been compared to those of Brahms, and his fine 'Dream of Gerontius' (1900), regarded by many as his masterpiece, has been likened to the style of Wagner. Many of Elgar's compositions are popular for their bold melodies, such as the moving slow theme of the much loved 'Enigma Variations' (1899) and the patriotic *Land of Hope and Glory* tune in one of his 'Pomp and Circumstance' marches (1901–7, 1930). He is thought of as a very 'English' composer.

Elgin Marbles /ˌelgɪn ˈmɑːblz/, **the** (arts) A collection of 5th century BC Greek sculptures brought from the Parthenon, Athens, to *England* in 1803 by Thomas Bruce, seventh Earl of Elgin, and now displayed in the *British Museum*. Many people in Greece and some people in *Britain* now believe that the sculptures should be returned to Greece.

Elizabethan /ɪˌlɪzəˈbiːθn/ (style) A style of architecture found in many large houses built in the second half of the 16th century, in the reign of Queen Elizabeth I, and characterized by large, square windows, neoclassical towers and turrets, and elaborate plasterwork in ceilings, as well as the use of oak-panelling.

Embankment /ɪmˈbæŋkmənt/, **the** (London) The short name of the Victoria Embankment, *London*, a street that runs along the north bank of the *Thames*.

employment office /ɪmˈplɔɪmənt ˌɒfɪs/ (work) A public employment office providing details of jobs for people seeking employment. Most of these offices have now been replaced by *jobcentres*.

Encyclopaedia Britannica /ɪnˌsaɪkləˌpiːdɪə brɪˈtænɪkə/, **the** (education) The oldest and largest English language encyclopaedia, first published in *Scotland* in 1768, but from the 11th edition of 1910–11 produced under American ownership and today having a strong American tone.

England /ˈɪŋglənd/ (geography) The largest and most southerly country in *Britain*, with *Wales* to the west and *Scotland* to the north. The name is properly applied only to this land, not to mainland Britain as a whole (and even less to the *United Kingdom*, which includes *Northern Ireland*). England does, however, contain the capital of the United Kingdom, *London*, where the British government is, together with the headquarters of many national and commercial bodies.

English breakfast /ˌɪŋglɪʃ ˈbrekfəst/ (food and drink) A traditional full, cooked breakfast with a hot dish (such as *bacon and eggs*) preceded by *porridge* and followed by *toast* and *marmalade*, the accompanying drink being usually coffee, although also tea. Such breakfasts have in recent years given way to a lighter meal, the so-called *continental breakfast*.

English Chamber Orchestra/ˌɪŋglɪʃ ˈtʃeɪmbər ˌɔːkɪstrə/, **the** (arts) A noted chamber orchestra founded in 1948 by Arnold Goldsbrough and originally (to 1960) called the Goldsbrough Orchestra.

English Civil War /ˌɪŋglɪʃ ˌsɪvl ˈwɔː(r)/, **the** (history) The war between the Cavaliers (supporters of King Charles I) and the Roundheads (supporters of Parliament) in the mid-17th century. A series of battles led to the defeat of the king and his supporters and the establishment of the *Commonwealth*[2].

English National Opera /ˌɪŋglɪʃ ˌnæʃnəl ˈɒprə/, **the (ENO, the)** (arts) A well-known opera company founded in 1931. It is based at the *Coliseum Theatre* in *London* but also goes on tour to different regions of *England*.

English setter /ˌɪŋglɪʃ ˈsetə(r)/ (animal world) A breed of working dog with long, silky coat, usually black and white or brown and white in colour. Compare *Irish setter*. [so-called since, as a gundog, it 'sets' or crouches to mark the position of hunted game]

English-Speaking Union /ˌɪŋglɪʃ ˌspiːkɪŋ ˈjuːnɪən/, **the (ESU, the)** (life and society) A body founded in 1918 to strengthen cultural ties between English-speaking countries. [full title, English-Speaking Union of the *Commonwealth*[1]]

enterprise zone /ˈentəpraɪz ˌzəʊn/ (work) A special urban area, established by the government in 1981–2 to bring new life to a region of economic decay. There are now 25 such zones, located in *London*, the *Midlands*, South *Wales*, northern *England*, central *Scotland* and *Belfast*, *Northern Ireland*. Firms established in the zones receive special financial support and tax exemptions.

Epsom /ˈepsəm/ (sport and leisure) A famous race-course (in full, Epsom Downs) near Epsom, Surrey where, among other horse races, the *Derby* and the Oaks are run annually.

Epsom salts /ˌepsəm ˈsɔːlts/ (medicine) A kind of mineral salt used in medicine as a laxative. [They were originally extracted from a source near Epsom, Surrey]

Equal Opportunities Commission /ˌiːkwəl ɒpəˈtjuːnətɪz kəˌmɪʃn/, **the (EOC, the)** (life and society) A governmental body set up in 1975 (1976 in *Northern Ireland*) to eliminate sex discrimination, and to promote equal opportunities for men and women, in employment, education, training, and the provision of basic facilities and services. The Commission enforces the Equal Pay Act of 1970 and the Sex Discrimination Act of 1975.

Equity /ˈekwɪtɪ/ (work) The trade union to which most actors belong.

Ermine Street /ˈɜːmɪn striːt/ (history) 1 The name of one of the main *Roman roads* in *Britain*, from *London* to York. 2 The name of certain other minor Roman roads or old trackways, mainly in the south of *England*. [named after an old Saxon tribe]

Ernie /ˈɜːnɪ/ (finance) The colloquial name of a special computer unit used by the *Post Office* to select the prize-winning numbers of holders of *Premium Bonds*. [from the initials of Electronic random number indicating equipment, suggested by the man's name Ernie (familiar form of Ernest)]

Eros /ˈɪərɒs/ (London) The colloquial name of the monument to the philanthropist the Earl of Shaftesbury, that stands in the centre of *Piccadilly Circus* in *London*. The monument, formally known as the Shaftesbury Memorial, consists of a fountain topped by a winged archer and his bow, intended to represent the Angel of Christian Charity but popularly taken to be Cupid or Eros. The monument is a traditional meeting place for young people.

Establishment /ɪˈstæblɪʃmənt/, **the** (life and society) A collective term for the top influential sectors of British society, in particular, industrialists and business leaders, the aristocracy (the *peerage*) and the *Church of England*.

estate agent /ɪˈsteɪt ˌeɪdʒənt/ (commerce) A professional firm that deals in the buying and selling of houses, land and other fixed property (though not in *Scotland* where a *solicitor* does all the work that is involved).

estate car /ɪˈsteɪt ˌkɑː(r)/ (transport) A large car designed to carry both passengers and goods (or animals), with a special area behind the seats for the goods and usually with a rear door or doors. Such cars were originally used on farm estates.

Eton (College) /ˈiːtn (ˌiːtn ˈkɒlɪdʒ)/ (education) One of the oldest and best-known *public schools*[1] for boys, at Windsor, Berkshire, on the river *Thames*. Its students (1,250 in number in 1984) are largely from aristocratic and upper-class families, and many former *prime minister*s of *Britain* were educated here. The school was founded in 1440.

Eton suit /ˌiːtn ˈsuːt/ (clothing) A school uniform, or a suit resembling it, worn at *Eton College* and some other schools. It consists of a black jacket (resembling a morning coat without tails), a black waistcoat and tie, black trousers with narrow stripes, a white shirt and a detachable stiff collar, known as an Eton collar.

E-type /ˈiː taɪp/ (transport) An expensive type of *Jaguar* sports car, especially popular in the 1960s.

Euro-MP /ˌjʊərəʊ em ˈpiː/ (government) An *MP* elected to represent his party and his *constituency* (larger than the standard *constituency* for national or local elections) in the European Parliament, the legislative body of the *Common Market*. *Britain* has 81 Euro-MPs sitting in the Parliament, which has a total of 434 members. Elections to the European Parliament have so far been held in 1979 and 1984. Many British electors, however, did not vote because of lack of interest.

Euston /ˈjuːstən/ (transport) A main line railway station in *London*, serving as the terminus for the London Midland Region of *BR*. There is also an Underground station nearby with the same name. See *London Underground*.

evening dress /ˈiːvnɪŋ dres/ (clothing) A formal type of dress for a social function held in the evening, such as a special *dinner* or theatre performance. For men, it consists of a black coat with tails, black trousers, white waistcoat, stiff-fronted white shirt, white wing collar and white bow tie. (A more popular alternative for the coat today, however, is the *dinner jacket*, which is usually worn with a black bow tie.) For women, evening dress is usually a floor-length dress often with a low-cut neck.

Evening News/ ˌiːvnɪŋ ˈnjuːz/, **the** (media) A former *London* daily evening newspaper founded in 1881 and now merged with the *Standard*.

Evening Standard /ˌiːvnɪŋ ˈstændəd/, **the** (media) The former name of the *Standard* newspaper.

eventide home /'iːvəntaɪd ˌhəʊm/ (life and society) A name occasionally used for a *rest home*.

eventing /ɪ'ventɪŋ/ (sport and leisure) An equestrian contest that usually includes dressage, cross-country riding and show jumping, and often lasts for three days. See *three-day event*.

Everton /'evətən/ (sport and leisure) A Liverpool football club with a stadium at *Goodison Park*. [named after the district of Liverpool where it is]

Exchange and Mart /ɪksˌtʃeɪndʒ ən 'mɑːt/ (media) A weekly magazine, consisting entirely of advertisements, that was first published in 1868. In 1981 it had a circulation of over 300,000. It is popular as an easy and cheap way of buying and selling many different kinds of goods.

Exchange Telegraph Company /ɪksˌtʃeɪndʒ 'telɪgrɑːf ˌkʌmpənɪ/, **the (Extel)** (media) An independent news agency supplying financial and sporting news and, together with the *Press Association*, transmitting racing information by telephone and video terminals.

ex-directory /ˌeks daɪ'rektərɪ/ (daily life) A telephone number, usually of a private individual, that is not listed in the official telephone directory published by *British Telecom*. Several public figures and personalities have ex-directory numbers, known only to their immediate friends and business contacts.

Exmoor pony /ˌeksmɔː 'pəʊnɪ/ (animal world) A breed of wild pony found on Exmoor, the high, bleak moorland of Somerset and Devon. When tamed, it is used as a riding pony for children.

Express /ɪk'spres/, **the** (media) The short name of the *Daily Express* newspaper.

Extel /'ekstel/ (media) The short name of the *Exchange Telegraph Company* Ltd.

F W Woolworth /ˌef ˌdʌblju: ˈwʊlwəθ/ see *Woolworth* (commerce)

FA /ˌef ˈeɪ/, **the (Football Association, the)** (sport and leisure) The official body controlling professional and amateur football in *Britain*. In *England* over 350 football clubs are affiliated to the English FA and about 40,000 clubs to regional or district associations. The FA was founded in 1863.

FA Cup /ˌef eɪ ˈkʌp/, **the** (sport and leisure) One of the main annual competitions of the football season, organized on a knock-out basis, with the final match (*Cup Final*) played at *Wembley*. [in full, Football Association Challenge Cup]

Fabian Society /ˈfeɪbɪən səˌsaɪətɪ/, **the** (politics) A political society founded in 1884 and having as its aim the gradual introduction of socialism by democratic means. It was indirectly responsible for the appearance of the *Labour Party*, and has had a number of famous intellectuals and writers among its members, as well as several Labour politicians. Its membership in 1982 was approximately 5,000. [named after the Roman general Fabius Maximus, surnamed Cunctator ('delayer'), famous for his delaying tactics when fighting Hannibal]

Fair Isle /ˈfeər aɪl/ (clothing) A distinctive style of knitting using different colours and designs, particularly for garments such as sweaters and gloves. It was originally developed on Fair Isle, Shetland (see the *Shetlands*).

Farnborough Air Show /ˌfɑːnbrə ˈeə ˌʃəʊ/, **the** (transport) An important international air show held at the *Royal Aircraft Establishment*, Farnborough, Hampshire, once every two years.

farthing /ˈfɑːðɪŋ/ (tradition) For many years the smallest British coin, worth one quarter of a pre-decimal *penny*. It was taken out of circulation in 1961. [from Old English 'feorthing', 'fourth (part)']

Fastnet (Race) /ˈfɑːstnet (ˌfɑːstnet ˈreɪs)/, **the** (sport and leisure) An international yachting race held every two years in August, with the course running from Ryde, *Isle of Wight*, to (and round) the Fastnet Rock, off south-west *Ireland*, and back to Plymouth, Devon. The total length of the course is 1,085 km. See also *Admiral's Cup*.

Fair Isle

Father Christmas /ˌfɑːðə 'krɪsməs/ (tradition) An alternative name for *Santa Claus*.

father of the chapel /ˌfɑːðər əv ðə 'tʃæpl/ (work) The title of the president of a *chapel*[5].

Father of the House /ˌfɑːðər əv ðə 'haʊs/ (government) The traditional title of the *MP* (in the *House of Commons*) or *peer* (in the *House of Lords*) who has served the longest as a member.

Father's Day /'fɑːðəz ˌdeɪ/ (tradition) The third Sunday in June, when presents are traditionally given by children to their father. [based on *Mother's Day*; the tradition was imported to Britain in the 20th century from America]

fellow /'feləʊ/ (**1, 2** education **3** life and society) **1** A senior member (often a professor) of a *college*[1]. **2** A member of a college[1] or university engaged in scientific research and usually combining his work with lecturing. **3** An active or senior member of a scientific or learned society, usually by election or nomination (eg, a Fellow of the *Royal Society*). Such a member has the right to put the appropriate letters after his name, for example, John Smith FRGS (Fellow of the Royal Geographical Society).

Fens /fenz/, **the** (geography) A name used for the low, marshy districts of eastern *England*, especially in Cambridgeshire, Lincolnshire and Norfolk. The districts are noted for their many drains and sluices, built to reclaim the land and to guard against flooding. The name (also Fen District) particularly applies to the rich agricultural land bordering the *Wash*.

Festival Gardens /ˌfestɪvl ˈgɑːdnz/, **the** (London) Pleasure gardens added to Battersea Park in southwest *London* at the time of the *Festival of Britain*, and based on the Tivoli Gardens in Copenhagen, Denmark. Amenities include a concert pavilion, restaurants, bars, tea-rooms and an amusement section with a children's zoo.

Festival of Britain /ˌfestɪvl əv ˈbrɪtn/, **the** (history) A large-scale exhibition opened on the site of the *South Bank, London*, in 1951, to mark the centenary of the *Great Exhibition* of 1851 and to demonstrate British economic and technical progress over the intervening hundred years. A number of buildings put up for the Festival remain in permanent use here, among them the *Royal Festival Hall*. Similar festivals were held throughout *Britain* at the same time.

fête /feɪt/ (daily life) An open-air sale of goods, many of them home-made, and usually accompanied by sports contests, children's entertainments and games and a *raffle*. Fêtes are usually held in summer months, especially at weekends and on *bank holidays*, and are traditionally designed to raise money for a particular cause, such as a local church fund, a charity or a school building fund.

Field /fiːld/, **The** (media) A weekly illustrated magazine printing articles and features on the countryside and country occupations, notably natural history, *field sports*, gardening and farming. It was first published in 1853 and had a circulation in 1981 of over 19,000.

field sports /ˈfiːld spɔːts/ (sport and leisure) The three sports which, together with horse-racing, are traditionally associated with the English *gentry*—hunting (after foxes or hares), shooting (wild or reared animals or birds) and fishing. See also *blood sports*. [so called as taking place 'in the field' rather than on a special course]

15 /ˌfɪfˈtiːn/ (arts) A category in which a cinema film is placed by the *British Board of Film Censors* to show that no child under the age of 15 can be allowed to see the film. Compare *18* (listed under letter E), *PG* and *U certificate*.

fifth form/year /ˈfɪfθ fɔːm/jɪə(r)/ (education) A class in a *secondary school* in the year in which the students will take a school-leaving examination, usually the *GCE* or the *CSE*. Such students will be in their fifth year at the school, having entered at age 11.

Fifth of November /ˌfɪfθ əv nəʊˈvembə(r)/, **the** (history) An alternative name for *Guy Fawkes' Day* (or *Guy Fawkes' Night*), when the failure of the *Gunpowder Plot* (of 5 November 1605) is traditionally celebrated with a bonfire and fireworks.

50 pence (piece) /ˌfɪftɪ 'pens (ˌfɪftɪ ˌpens 'piːs)/ (finance) A seven-sided coin made from a mixture of copper and nickel that looks like silver. It is worth half of the value of a *pound (sterling)*. It replaced the 10/– (ten *shilling*) note in October 1969. See p 376.

finance house /'faɪnæns haʊs/ (finance) A company specializing in lending money, especially to finance hire-purchase agreements.

Financial Times /faɪˌnænʃl 'taɪmz/, **the (FT, the)** (media) A daily national *quality paper* providing up-to-date financial information (in particular regarding company news and the movements of stocks and shares) and also printing articles and features of commercial, industrial and economic interest. It is bought mainly by businessmen, especially in the *City*. The newspaper, traditionally printed on pink paper, was founded in 1888 and had a circulation in 1984 of over 216,000. An edition is also printed in Frankfurt, West Germany.

Financial Weekly /faɪˌnænʃl 'wiːklɪ/, **the** (media) A weekly financial magazine printing articles and features designed mainly for people with business and investment interests, including interviews with business personalities. It was first published in 1979 and had a circulation in 1981 of over 21,000.

financial year /faɪˌnænʃl 'jɪə(r)/, **the** (finance) The annual period ending on 5 April, serving as the income tax year and the period over which the government plans its financial policies and makes its estimates.

Fingal's Cave /ˌfɪŋglz 'keɪv/ (geography) A large cave on the island of Staffa, in the *Hebrides, Scotland*, with six-sided pillars of rock. The same rock formation can be seen at the *Giant's Causeway* in *Northern Ireland*. Fingal's Cave is a popular tourist attraction, although visitors are not now allowed inside the cave because of the danger of falling rock. The cave has been commemorated in the works of a number of poets and musicians, including Keats, Wordsworth, Tennyson and Mendelssohn. ['Fingal' is a shortened form of the name of one of two giants in a folk tale. The tale describes a fight in which the two threw distinctively-shaped rocks at each other]

finishing school /'fɪnɪʃɪŋ skuːl/ (education) A *college²*, usually residential, where some girls complete their education, with the emphasis more on social graces than academic achievement.

first class /ˌfɜːst 'klɑːs/ (1 transport 2 commerce 3 education) 1 The more comfortable, and more expensive, class of seat in a railway train. 2 The higher of two postal rates, providing delivery more rapidly than *second class* mail, and usually the following day, except when that day is Sunday when no post is collected or delivered. 3 The highest class of *honours* *degree*, indicating academic excellence.

first degree /ˌfɜːst dɪˈɡriː/ (education) The degree (usually a *BA* or *BSc*) obtained by most students when graduating from university. At *Cambridge²*, however, the BSc does not exist, while at *Oxford²* it is a *higher degree*. In Scotland the first degree in arts at three of the four older universities is an *MA*.

first floor /ˌfɜːst ˈflɔː(r)/, **the** (daily life) According to the British system of numbering, the floor above the *ground floor* (which is the bottom or lowest floor).

first past the post /ˌfɜːst pɑːst ðə ˈpəʊst/ (politics) A colloquial phrase (from horse-racing) that describes how the British electoral system works. The candidate given the largest number of individual votes, or the party gaining the largest number of seats subsequently, wins an election. See *voting system*.

first reading /ˌfɜːst ˈriːdɪŋ/ (government) The first stage through which a *bill* must pass in its progress through the *House of Commons* (or *House of Lords*). This is thus the official introduction of the bill. Compare *second reading, third reading*.

first school /ˈfɜːst skuːl/ (education) A type of *primary school* for children aged five to eight (or nine, or ten). Compare *middle school*.

fish and chips /ˌfɪʃ ən ˈtʃɪps/ (food and drink) A popular and relatively inexpensive British dish, consisting of plaice or cod fried in batter and served hot with fried, chipped potatoes (known in many restaurants as 'French fries'). The dish is sold in special shops ('fish and chip shops') either to be taken away, wrapped in paper, or if tables are provided to be eaten in the shop. Some young people buy the chips alone to be eaten as a cheap, filling snack. See also *chippy*.

Fitzwilliam Museum /fɪtsˌwɪljəm mjuːˈziːəm/, **the** (arts) A famous museum in Cambridge founded in 1816. Its collections of antiquities, paintings and drawings, coins, ceramics, glass and armour make it one of the most important in the country. [named after its founder, Viscount Fitzwilliam]

5 pence (piece) /ˌfaɪv ˈpens (ˌfaɪv pensˈpiːs)/ (finance) A round coin made from a mixture of copper and nickel that looks like silver. It is worth one-twentieth of the value of a *pound (sterling)* and replaces the old *shilling*, which was the same size and colour and had the same value. See p 376.

fiver /ˈfaɪvə(r)/ (daily life) A colloquial term for a £5 note. Compare *tenner*.

fives /faɪvz/ (sport and leisure) A ball game played on a special court enclosed on three sides, in which two (occasionally four) players throw the ball from a gloved hand so that it bounces off the wall, the aim being to force one's opponent to make a mistake. The game is particularly associated with *Eton College*, and is played at other *public schools¹*. [perhaps originally played by two teams of five players each, or so called with reference to the five fingers of the hand]

flag day /'flæg deɪ/ (charities) A day (usually a Saturday) on which small paper stickers are sold on the street in aid of a particular charity, the buyer placing a sum of money in a tin and wearing the sticker on his or her clothes. [formerly small paper flags, which were pinned tb the clothes, were used]

Flat /flæt/, **the** (sport and leisure) The horse-racing season. [in full, 'flat racing', as distinct from a steeplechase, which has jumps]

Fleet Air Arm /ˌfliːt 'eər ɑːm/, **the** (defence) The branch of the *Royal Navy* concerned with aviation, both shore-based and from aircraft carriers.

Fleet Street /'fliːt striːt/ (1 London 2 media) 1 A street in central *London* where many national newspapers have their editorial offices. 2 The press and the world of journalism generally. [from the river Fleet, now running underground here into the *Thames*]

fly-fishing /'flaɪ ˌfɪʃɪŋ/ (sport and leisure) A special type of fishing using man-made flies instead of hooks with live bait (eg worms). There are both 'dry' and 'wet' flies imitating three main types of real fly: midges, mayflies and sedge flies. The man-made flies are successful because real flies form the main diet of trout and salmon as well as other fish. Experienced fly-fishermen have a special knowledge of the different species of fly normally found in a local area.

flying pickets /ˌflaɪɪŋ 'pɪkɪts/ (work) Mobile *pickets* available to travel to support local pickets during a strike. The first such pickets operated in the miners' strike of 1973.

Flying Squad /'flaɪɪŋ skwɒd/, **the** (law) A department of the *CID*, comprising a group of expert detectives working from *New Scotland Yard* and concentrating on major criminals. [originally a force of police travelling in a motor van to the scene of a smash-and-grab raid]

folk museum /ˌfəʊk mjuːˈzɪəm/ (tradition) A museum that exhibits unique or historic items of everyday domestic use, such as period costumes, cooking utensils, tools, etc. There are such museums in a number of towns and cities, for example, York (Castle Museum), *Cardiff* (Welsh Folk Museum) and *Cambridge[1]* (Cambridge Folk Museum).

folly /'fɒlɪ/ (style) A group of artificially built ruins, or an extravagantly decorated but useless building, designed to improve the landscape in a particular rural area. Such buildings were first put up in the 18th century to improve the view on the estate of a *country house*. [so-called with reference to the folly or foolishness of building a grand structure without thought for the cost]

Fonteyn, Margot /fɒn'teɪn, 'mɑːgəʊ/ (people) Margot Fonteyn (born 1919—real name Margaret Hookham) made her debut in ballet in 1934 and rapidly gained an excellent reputation.

By 1939 she was established as one of *Britain*'s outstanding ballerinas, both in classical ballets such as 'Swan Lake' and 'Sleeping Beauty' and also in modern ballets. She became internationally famous not just because of her technical perfection, but also because of her musical sensitivity and her ability to interpret character through dance. She was still dancing in the late 1970s.

Fontwell Park /ˌfɒntwel ˈpɑːk/ (sport and leisure) A race-course near Bognor Regis, West Sussex.

foolscap /ˈfuːlskæp/ (daily life) A size of paper (usually 17 x 13½ *inch*es) now mostly replaced by the international size A4 (297 x 210 mm). [originally bearing the watermark of a fool's cap and bell]

foot /fʊt/ (daily life) A measure of length still in common use, in particular for the height of a person, comprising 12 *inch*es and equivalent to 30.48 cm. [regarded as the length of a man's foot]

football /ˈfʊtbɔːl/ see *association football* (sport and leisure) and *rugby football* (sport and leisure)

Football League /ˌfʊtbɔːl ˈliːɡ/, **the** (sport and leisure) The organization that controls the principal professional football matches in *Britain*, arranged in four divisions in *England* and *Wales* (three in *Scotland*) with a system of promotion and relegation. In England and Wales, 92 professional clubs belong to the League, while in Scotland 38 clubs belong to the Scottish Football League. The League was formed in 1888.

Footsie /ˈfʊtsɪ/ (finance) A colloquial name for the stocks and shares index introduced in 1984 by the *Stock Exchange*. The index, which operates jointly with the older *FT Index*, records the movements of shares of 100 selected companies, as its full name suggests ('Financial Times-Stock Exchange 100 Index'). [humorous pronunciation of abbreviated title, FT-SE Index]

Foreign and Commonwealth Office /ˌfɒrən ən ˈkɒmənwelθ ˌɒfɪs/, **the (FCO, the)** (government) The government *department* that conducts *Britain*'s relations with countries overseas and which advises the government on all aspects of foreign policy. It is largely staffed by members of the *Diplomatic Service*, and was created in its present form in 1968 from the former Foreign Office and the Commonwealth Office (the latter established in 1964).

Foreign Secretary /ˌfɒrən ˈsekrətrɪ/, **the** (government) The short title of the *Secretary of State* for Foreign and Commonwealth Affairs, otherwise the government *minister*[2], and member of the *Cabinet*, who is the head of the *Foreign and Commonwealth Office*.

forest park /ˌfɒrɪst ˈpɑːk/ (geography) An area of forest land administered by the *Forestry Commission* and having camping and other facilities for the public on the lines of a *national park*. There are seven such parks at present in *Britain* and nine in *Northern Ireland*.

Forestry Commission /ˈfɒrɪstrɪ kəˌmɪʃn/, **the** (government) The government body which administers national (state-owned) forests in *Britain*. Over half the total forest area in Britain is privately owned, and the Commission awards grants to such owners to encourage effective management of their forest land.

Forth /fɔːθ/, **the** (geography) A Scottish river almost 105 miles in length that flows into the North Sea through its well-known large estuary, the Firth of Forth (itself almost 50 miles long), where it is crossed by the two *Forth Bridges*.

Forth Bridge /ˌfɔːθ ˈbrɪdʒ/, **the** (science and technology) **1** The spectacular Forth Rail Bridge, built in the late 19th century west of *Edinburgh, Scotland*, over the Firth of *Forth*, and generally regarded as one of the world's greatest engineering feats. The bridge has a length of 1,710 feet (521 metres) and needs constant painting. Because of this, saying that some task 'is like painting the Forth Bridge' means that it is an apparently endless task or involves unending work. **2** The Forth Road Bridge, built in the mid-20th century across the Firth of Forth just west of the Rail Bridge. It is one of the longest suspension bridges in the world—3,300 feet (1,006 metres).

Fortnum and Mason /ˌfɔːtnəm ən ˌmeɪsn/ (commerce) One of *London*'s leading high-class stores, in *Piccadilly*, famous for its exotic foods. [founded in 1707 by William Fortnum, a footman in the court of Queen Anne, and Hugh Mason, a local shop owner]

Forty-Five /ˌfɔːtɪ ˈfaɪv/, **the** (history) The rising of the Jacobites (supporters of the exiled King James II) led by the Scottish prince Charles Edward Stuart, the *Young Pretender*, in 1745, in an attempt to regain the throne. See also *Culloden*.

Fosse Way /ˌfɒs ˈweɪ/, **the** (history) One of the main *Roman roads* in *Britain*, running from Lincoln to Exeter, Devon. [said to have been named from the 'foss' or ditch that ran next to it]

four-letter word /ˌfɔː letə ˈwɜːd/ (language) A term for a vulgar short word referring to a sexual or excretory organ or function. Many such words are of Germanic origin and today are spelt with four letters. Such words are often called *Anglo-Saxon*[2].

fourth estate /ˌfɔːθ ɪˈsteɪt/, **the** (media) A term for the press, seen as influencing a country's politics (like the *House of Lords*, the 'first estate', the *House of Commons*, the 'second estate', and the clergy of the *Church of England*, the 'third estate').

Fowler /ˈfaʊlə(r)/ (language) The short title of 'A Dictionary of Modern English Usage', first published by Henry Fowler (1858–1933) in 1926 and regarded as a standard reference work on the English language.

Fox-terrier /ˌfɒks ˈterɪə(r)/ (animal world) A breed of dog originally trained to unearth foxes. There are two varieties in

Britain: smooth-haired and wire-haired, with colouring usually white with black or light brown markings.

Foyle's /ˈfɔɪlz/ (commerce) *London*'s largest bookshop, in Charing Cross Road, selling both new and second-hand books. [named after its original owner, William Alfred Foyle]

Fraud Squad /ˈfrɔːd skwɒd/, **the** (law) A special police branch run jointly by the *Metropolitan Police Force* and the *City (of London)* Police to investigate company frauds.

Free Churches /ˌfriː ˈtʃɜːtʃɪz/, **the** (religion) A collective name for all non-*Anglican* and non-*Roman Catholic* Christian *church*es in *Britain*, including the *Methodist Church*, the *Baptists*, the *United Reformed Church* and the *Church of Scotland*. ['free' as they are not 'established', like the *Church of England*]

free house /ˈfriː haʊs/ (daily life) A *pub* that is free to receive its supplies from a number of brewers and is not tied to a single brewer. Compare *tied house*.

freedom of the city /ˈfriːdəm (ˌfriːdəm əv ðə ˈsɪti)/, **the** (life and society) An honorary (nominal) privilege awarded to a person who is a famous resident of a city (or who was born there), or who has performed particular services for a city. Such a person is usually called a 'freeman'.

Freefone /ˈfriːfəʊn/ (commerce) A special telephone service operated by *British Telecom* by which a person can make a telephone call free of charge to commercial organizations, especially when responding to an advertisement.

Freepost /ˈfriːpəʊst/ (commerce) A special mail delivery service operated by the *Post Office* by which a business customer or member of the public can send a letter to a firm or advertiser free of postal charge, with the addressee paying the postage. Such letters travel by *second class* mail only.

freightliner /ˈfreɪtlaɪnə(r)/ (transport) A type of express goods train with specially designed containers. [from 'freight train' and 'liner' as in 'air liner']

French cricket /ˌfrentʃ ˈkrɪkɪt/ (sport and leisure) A simplified version of *cricket*, popular among some children. The game is played with a single bat and ball, with the batsman using his own legs as a wicket. The game is often played with a tennis racket, at the seaside.

fresher /ˈfreʃə(r)/ (education) The name given to first-year students in some universities. [short for 'freshman']

friendly society /ˈfrendli səˌsaɪəti/ (finance) A kind of insurance association, with members' subscriptions providing financial aid in time of need, such as sickness, old age, or widowhood.

Friends of the Earth /ˌfrendz əv di ˈɜːθ/, **the** (politics) A voluntary organization (also a *limited company*) established in 1971 with the aim of conserving the natural resources of the world and discouraging mistreatment of the natural environment. It has 18,000 members worldwide.

Fringe /frɪndʒ//, **the** (arts) The short name of the 'Edinburgh Fringe' at the *Edinburgh Festival*. The term can also apply to any similar festival that has a 'fringe' or unorthodox section.

fringe benefits /ˈfrɪndʒ ˌbenɪfɪts/ (work) Additional benefits or privileges provided with a person's regular salary, such as the use of a car, meals free or at reduced cost, or free insurance.

front bench /ˌfrʌnt ˈbentʃ/, **the** (government) One of the two front benches or rows of seats in the *House of Commons*, to the right and left of the *Speaker*. They are occupied respectively by *ministers*[2] of the current government and equivalent members of the *Opposition* (in particular, of the *Shadow Cabinet*).

front bench

front room /ˌfrʌnt ˈruːm/ (daily life) The main *ground floor* room of a smallish or modest house, often, of a *terraced house*, used either regularly as a sitting-room for relaxation, or only occasionally for receiving guests and visitors. The room is at the front of the house, usually looking onto a road or street.

frontbencher /ˌfrʌnt ˈbentʃə(r)/ (government) An *MP* entitled to sit on one of the *front bench*es in the *House of Commons*. Compare *backbencher* and see also *crossbencher*.

FT /ˌef ˈtiː/, **the** (media) A colloquial name for the *Financial Times*. See also *FT Index* and *Footsie*.

FT Index /ˌef tiː ˈɪndeks/, **the** (finance) The daily record of the movement of shares on the *Stock Exchange*, as provided by the *Financial Times*. See also *Footsie*. [in full, Financial Times Industrial Ordinary Share Index]

Fulham /ˈfʊləm/ (sport and leisure) A popular *London* football club, with a stadium in the district of the same name in southwest London.

fun run /ˈfʌn rʌn/ (sport and leisure) A race in which many people take part, often to raise money for charity. The best known is the annual *London* fun run (also called the London

Marathon), organized by the *Sunday Times* and first held in 1978. See also *sponsored walk*.

Furry Dance /ˈfʌrɪ dɑːns/**, the** (tradition) A traditional massed folk dance held in the streets of Helston, Cornwall, on 8 May annually. [origin of name uncertain: perhaps connected with 'fair' or with 'floral']

Furry Dance

further education /ˌfɜːðər edʒʊˈkeɪʃn/ (education) A term used to apply to any education after *secondary school*, but not including university work (which is *higher education*). See *CFE*.

Fylingdales /ˈfaɪlɪŋdeɪlz/ (defence) A moorland 'site' in North Yorkshire where the Ballistic Early Warning Station of the Ministry of Defence is. The Station is remarkable for its three giant white globes, standing out against the outline of the moors.

GUY FAWKES' NIGHT

G and M /ˌdʒiː ən ˈem/, **the** (work) A colloquial abbreviation for the *GMBATU*, formerly the *GMWU*.

G and S /ˌdʒiː ən ˈes/ (arts) A colloquial abbreviation for the *Gilbert and Sullivan operas*.

Gaelic /ˈɡeɪlɪk/ (language) The Celtic language spoken or understood by about 82,000 people (1984) in the *Highlands* and western coastal regions of *Scotland* and, in an Irish form, by some people in *Ireland*.

> 'Siosleabhar air Breatainn' is Scots Gaelic
> for 'Information Book about Britain'.
> **Gaelic**

Gaelic coffee /ˌɡeɪlɪk ˈkɒfɪ/ (food and drink) A drink, usually served in a glass, consisting of coffee to which cream, sugar and *whisky* have been added. Compare *Irish coffee*.

Gaiety Girls /ˈɡeɪətɪ ˌɡɜːlz/, **the** (history) The title of chorus girls at the Gaiety Theatre, *London*, popular in the 1890s for their beauty. Many of them married members of the *peerage*.

gala /ˈɡɑːlə/ (sport and leisure) **1** A sporting event in which there are a variety of different contests, such as a swimming gala. **2** An annual fair, march or parade, eg, the *Durham Miners' Gala*.

gallon /ˈɡælən/ (daily life) A measure of capacity for liquids and dry goods (such as corn) equal to 4 quarts or 8 *pints* (=4.546 litres in UK, 3.715 litres in USA).

Galloway cattle /ˌɡæləweɪ ˈkætl/ (animal world) A breed of large, hornless cattle with thick black or dark brown coats. [originally bred in the district of Galloway, southwest *Scotland*]

gamekeeper /ˈɡeɪmˌkiːpə(r)/ (sport and leisure) A person employed to look after wild life and game (ie, animals and birds reared for sport, food or profit) on an estate, normally that owned by a member of the *gentry* in the country.

gamesmanship /ˈɡeɪmzmənʃɪp/ (sport and leisure) A term for the art of winning in a game or sport, or of scoring over one's opponent, by the use of various tricks without, however, breaking the rules. One such way might be to speak to one's opponent as he is about to hit the ball. The term was devised by the writer Stephen Potter (1900–1969) for his book (1949) on the subject, whose full title was 'The Theory and Practice of Gamesmanship or the Art of Winning Games Without Actually Cheating'. See *lifemanship*, *one-upmanship*.

Gang Show /'gæŋ ʃəʊ/, **the** (sport and leisure) A variety show staged each year in *London* by the *Scout Association* to raise funds for the Association.

ganger /'gæŋə(r)/ (work) A colloquial term for the foreman of a gang of manual workers.

gangway /'gæŋweɪ/, **the** (government) The cross passage between the seats, about half-way down the chamber of the *House of Commons*. A member sitting 'below the gangway', that is, in that part of the chamber that is further from the *Speaker*, is taken to hold a greater independence of political views than one who sits in the half nearer to him.

garden centre /'gɑːdn ˌsentə(r)/ (commerce) A trading centre where equipment, plants, shrubs, bulbs and seeds for the garden are sold.

garden city /ˌgɑːdn 'sɪtɪ/ (geography) A town laid out with carefully planned parks, gardens and open spaces, and surrounded by a *green belt*, near to an industrial city. The first such town was built (1903) at Letchworth, Hertfordshire, north of *London*. Many *new towns* are garden cities.

Garden of England /ˌgɑːdn əv 'ɪŋglənd/, **the** (geography) A nickname for the *county* of Kent, famous for its picturesque orchards and fields of hops. The name is also used, but less often, for the former county of Worcestershire, famous for its fertile farmland and orchards.

garden party /'gɑːdn ˌpɑːtɪ/ (life and society) An afternoon tea party held on the lawn of a large private house or residence of some kind. Famous garden parties are those held annually (usually in June) by the sovereign at *Buckingham Palace*, to which political, industrial and diplomatic leaders are invited.

garden suburb /ˌgɑːdn 'sʌbɜːb/ (geography) The suburb of a town or city laid out on the same lines as a *garden city*, for example, *Hampstead* Garden Suburb.

garden village /ˌgɑːdn 'vɪlɪdʒ/ (geography) A new village laid out on the lines of a *garden city*.

Garnett, Alf /'gɑːnɪt, ælf/ (media) The name of the leading character in the *BBC* comedy series 'Till Death Us Do Part' which ran on television from 1964 to 1974. Alf Garnett is the *working class* head of a family who constantly gets himself and his family into trouble through his openly expressed views and prejudices about such controversial subjects as race, religion and royalty. In acting his role as a loud-mouthed bigot, however, Alf Garnett actually voices the opinions that are privately held by a number of people, so that his audience, while laughing at him and being openly shocked by him, secretly agree with him. The part of Alf Garnett was played by the actor Warren Mitchell (born 1926).

Garter /'gɑːtə(r)/, **the** (life and society) A colloquial term for the *Order of the Garter*.

Garter ceremony /'gɑːtə ˌserɪmənɪ/, **the** (life and society) The ceremonial installation of new Knights of the Garter at *St. George's Chapel, Windsor*. The route to the Chapel is lined on this occasion by dismounted troopers of the *Household Cavalry*. See also *Order of the Garter*.

gate-leg(ged) table /ˌgeɪt leg(d) 'teɪbl/ (style) A table with one or two hinged flaps that are supported when in use by a hinged leg pulled out from the centre. [the leg opens and closes like a gate]

gate-leg(ged) table

Gatwick /'gætwɪk/ (transport) An international airport, the second largest in Britain (after *Heathrow*), in west Sussex, 24 miles (39 kilometres) south of *London*.

gaudy /'gɔːdɪ/ (life and society) An annual celebratory dinner held in the *colleges[1]* of *Oxford University* and *Cambridge University* to which former students of particular years are invited. [from Latin 'gaudium', 'joy']

Gay Gordons /ˌgeɪ 'gɔːdnz/, **the** (sport and leisure) A Scottish dance popular in ballroom dancing. The name comes from the nickname of the *Gordon Highlanders*.

Gay Liberation Front /ˌgeɪ lɪbə'reɪʃn frʌnt/, **the** (life and society) A movement founded by homosexuals in the 1960s to gain fuller acceptance for homosexuals within the community and in the eyes of the authorities. Colloquial terms for the movement are 'the GLF' and 'Gay Lib'. [from 'gay', a word used to mean 'homosexual']

gazumping /gə'zʌmpɪŋ/ (commerce) The raising of the price of a house by the seller after a verbal agreement has been made but before the sale has been legally completed. [perhaps from Yiddish 'gezumph', 'to swindle']

GC /ˌdʒiː ˈsiː/, **the (George Cross, the)** (life and society) An award for heroism made primarily to civilians and ranking next after the *VC*. The award, instituted in 1940 by King George VI, is in the form of a silver cross on which a representation of St George and the Dragon is surrounded by the words 'For Gallantry'.

GCE /ˌdʒiː siː ˈiː/, **the (General Certificate of Education, the)** (education) The school-leaving examination at *'O' level* or *'A' level*, in various subjects, conducted by eight independent examining boards, most of them connected with a university. The examination can also be taken by candidates at *further education* establishments as well as by candidates entered privately. Compare *CSE* and *GCSE*.

GCHQ /ˌdʒiː siː eɪtʃ ˈkjuː/ **(Government Communications Headquarters, the)** (defence) The top-secret government intelligence-gathering centre at Cheltenham, Gloucestershire. The centre gained notoriety in 1982 when one of its former employees was jailed for 35 years for spying, and again in 1984 when the *Prime Minister* (Margaret *Thatcher*) ordered that all GCHQ employees who belonged to a trade union should either leave their union or get a job elsewhere. It was said that this was necessary to avoid work at GCHQ being disrupted by strike action by the unions.

GCSE /ˌdʒiː siː es ˈiː/, **the (General Certificate of Secondary Education, the)** (education) The new school-leaving examination that will be introduced in 1988. It will replace the two present examinations, the *GCE* and the *CSE*.

Geffrye Museum /ˈdʒefrɪ mjuːˌzɪəm/, **the** (arts) A museum in east *London* opened in 1914. It currently displays the furniture and domestic equipment of a typical *middle class* English home in all periods from 1600 to 1939. There are also displays of costume and a library. The museum is housed in a building erected originally (1715) as an *almshouse* under a bequest from a *Lord Mayor* of London, Sir Robert Geffrye (died 1704).

General Assembly of the Church of Scotland /ˌdʒenrəl əˌsemblɪ əv ðə ˌtʃɜːtʃ əv ˈskɒtlənd/, **the** (religion) The supreme court or governing body of the *Church of Scotland*. It is composed of ministers, elders and other elected members of the Church.

General Council /ˌdʒenrəl ˈkaʊnsl/, **the** (work) The body elected annually by the *TUC* to represent it between Congresses (the important annual meeting of the TUC) and to carry out Congress decisions. It also watches economic and social developments, provides educational and advisory services to unions, and presents trade union viewpoints to the government. It can also help to solve disputes between unions.

general degree /'dʒenrəl dɪˌgriː/ (education) A degree (also known as an ordinary degree or a *pass degree*) obtained in several subjects on a non-specialized course at some universities. Compare *honours degree*.

general election /ˌdʒenrəl ɪ'lekʃn/ (politics) An election held throughout the *United Kingdom* on a particular day to elect a government. Voters cast their votes at a local *polling station* in the *ward* of their particular *constituency* to elect their next *MP*. Compare *by-election*.

general hospital /ˌdʒenrəl 'hɒspɪtl/ (medicine) A hospital that treats a wide range of patients and diseases and does not restrict itself to any one disease or type of patient.

General Medical Council /ˌdʒenrəl 'medɪkl ˌkaʊnsl/, **the** (medicine) A body set up (1858) by *Act (of Parliament)* to control the education, registration and discipline of members of the medical profession.

general practitioner /ˌdʒenrəl præk'tɪʃənə(r)/ see *GP* (medicine)

general science /ˌdʒenrəl 'saɪəns/ (education) A school subject in which basic instruction in physics, chemistry and biology is combined as a single subject.

General Strike /ˌdʒenrəl 'straɪk/, **the** (history) The 'sympathetic' strike of 4–12 May 1926 organized by the *TUC* in support of the miners in their dispute with the coal owners. Although the strike spread to involve workers in the rail, road transport, iron and steel, and building and printing industries, the miners alone stayed on strike for nearly six months.

General Synod /ˌdʒenrəl 'sɪnəd/, **the** (religion) The central governing body of the *Church of England*. It deals with such matters as education, inter-church relations, recruitment of clergy and the care of church buildings.

gentleman /'dʒentlmən/ (life and society) **1** A general term used to refer politely to any man. **2** A man regarded as having the best British characteristics, in particular culture, courtesy and a good education. **3** A man who comes from an aristocratic family, that is, a member of the *gentry*.

gentleman farmer /ˌdʒentlmən 'fɑːmə(r)/ (life and society) **1** A man who runs a farm but does not depend on it for his main income. **2** A man who owns farm land but does not farm it himself.

gentleman-at-arms /ˌdʒentlmən ət 'ɑːmz/ (life and society) A member of one of the two corps forming the dismounted bodyguard of the sovereign (officially the Honourable Corps of Gentlemen-at-Arms), which consists of 40 retired *Army* and *Royal Marines* officers. The other group is the *Yeomen of the Guard*.

gentleman's gentleman /ˌdʒentlmənz 'dʒentlmən/ (life and society) The personal servant of a *gentleman*[3]. An example in literature is Jeeves, a character in the novels of *P G Wodehouse*.

Gentlemen-at-Arms /ˌdʒentlmən ət ˈɑːmz/, **the** (life and society) The short name for the Honourable Corps of Gentlemen-at-Arms (see *gentleman-at-arms*).

gentry /ˈdʒentrɪ/, **the** (life and society) A collective term for members of the aristocracy, individually known as gentlemen and gentlewomen, who rank socially just below the nobility.

Geographical Magazine /ˌdʒɪəˈgræfɪkl mægəˌziːn/, **the** (geography) A monthly illustrated magazine containing articles on people and their environment in all parts of the world and modern geography in all its aspects. The magazine was founded in London in 1935.

Geological Museum /ˌdʒɪə ˈlɒdʒɪkl mjuːˌzɪəm/, **the** (science and technology) The national museum of earth sciences, in *London*, next to the *Science Museum*. It has a large collection of minerals and fossils, and has the largest geological library in the country. It was founded in 1837.

Geordie /ˈdʒɔːdɪ/ (geography) **1** The nickname of an inhabitant of Tyneside, or of a person who comes from there. **2** The English dialect spoken by such a person. [from the dialect version of the name Georgie]

George Cross /ˌdʒɔːdʒ ˈkrɒs/ see *GC* (life and society)

George Medal /ˌdʒɔːdʒ ˈmedl/, **the** (life and society) A medal instituted at the same time as the *GC* to be awarded for acts of heroism which are not considered to merit the Cross. The medal has a representation of St George and the Dragon and the words 'The George Medal'.

Georgian /ˈdʒɔːdʒən/ (history) Relating to one or all the four Kings George I–IV who reigned from 1714 to 1830 or to George V who reigned 1910–36. See also *Georgian poets*, *Georgian style*.

Georgian (style) /ˈdʒɔːdʒən (staɪl)/ (style) A style of architecture and furniture characteristic of the 18th century. In architecture the main features of the style were dignity and restraint and a special regard for symmetry (see *Regency style*). In furniture the designs were typically those of *Chippendale*, *Hepplewhite* and *Sheraton*.

Georgian poets /ˌdʒɔːdʒən ˈpəʊɪts/, **the** (arts) A group of English poets who, in the reign of George V (1910–36), wrote about nature and rural life in the manner of William Wordsworth (1770–1850). Among the main poets in the group were John Masefield (1878–1967), Robert Graves (1895–   ), A.E. Housman (1859–1936), Harold Monro (1879–1932) and Walter de la Mare (1873–1956).

Giant's Causeway /ˌdʒaɪənts ˈkɔːzweɪ/, **the** (geography) A tourist attraction on the north coast of *Northern Ireland*. It is a headland consisting of several thousand pillars of rock, most of them five- or six-sided. The same rock formation can be seen in *Fingal's Cave*. ['giant' comes from a folk tale that tells of a fight between two giants in which they threw distinctively-shaped rocks at each other]

Giant's Causeway

Gielgud, John /ˈgiːlgʊd, dʒɒn/ (people) John Gielgud (born 1904) has shown particular talent as a Shakespearian actor and producer, but has also appeared in non-Shakespearian roles in classic and modern plays. He is famous for his ability to act in very varied roles and for his finely-controlled speaking voice, which he used to great effect in his popular recitations of solo passages from *Shakespeare*. He has appeared in many cinema and television films.

gift token /ˈgɪft ˌtəʊkən/ (commerce) A voucher for a fixed amount bought in a shop and presented as a gift to a person who is then able to select goods to the value of the token in that same shop, or an equivalent branch (where the shop is a chain store). The token looks like a *greetings card*. Some shops make a small charge for the card, while others charge only the value of the token. Compare *book token*.

Gilbert and Sullivan operas /ˌgɪlbət ən ˈsʌlɪvn ˌɒprəz/ (arts) Popular comic operettas by the composer Sir Arthur Seymour Sullivan (1842–1900) and librettist Sir William Schwenck Gilbert (1836–1911). The operettas, which contain elements of satire, were originally staged (1875–1896) at the *Savoy* (*Theatre*), *London*, and have continued to attract a small but enthusiastic following. Among the best known are 'HMS Pinafore' (1878), 'The Pirates of Penzance' (1879) and 'The Mikado' (1885).

Giles cartoons /ˌdʒaɪlz kɑːˈtuːnz/ (media) Cartoons by Carl Ronald Giles (1916–   ) appearing regularly in the *Daily Express*, *Sunday Express* and *Standard*. They show the news of the day in a humorous light, often through the reactions of a fictitious *working class* family.

gill /dʒɪl/ (daily life) A unit of liquid measure equal to one quarter of a *pint* (= 142 millilitres).

gillie /'gɪlɪ/ (sport and leisure) In *Scotland*, an attendant or guide for a person who is hunting or fishing. [from Scottish *Gaelic* 'gille', 'servant']

gilt-edged securities /ˌgɪlt edʒd sɪ'kjʊərətɪz/ (finance) Stocks, usually those issued by the government, that are almost certain to produce interest and can be redeemed (repaid) at face value at almost any time. Such stocks originally had gilt edges.

gin /dʒɪn/ (food and drink) A spirit distilled from grain or malt and flavoured with juniper berries. It is always drunk diluted either with fruit juice or in the form of a cocktail (see *gin and it, gin and tonic*).

gin and it /ˌdʒɪn ən 'ɪt/ (food and drink) A cocktail of *gin* and Italian (sweet) vermouth. ['it' is an abbreviation of 'Italian']

gin and tonic /ˌdʒɪn ən 'tɒnɪk/ (food and drink) A popular drink of *gin* and tonic water, usually with a slice of lemon and chunk of ice added. It is often called 'a g and t'.

ginger biscuit /ˌdʒɪndʒə 'bɪskɪt/ (food and drink) A hard round biscuit flavoured with ginger and usually sprinkled with sugar.

ginger group /'dʒɪndʒə gru:p/ (life and society) A group within a political or other organization that aims to 'activate' its parent body, especially when the latter shows little sign of decisive action. [from colloquial 'ginger' = 'liveliness', 'vigour', from the hot, spicy taste of ginger]

Gipsy Moth /ˌdʒɪpsɪ 'mɒθ/ (sport and leisure) The name of several yachts owned by the famous yachtsman Sir Francis Chichester (1901–72). In 'Gipsy Moth IV' he sailed round the world (1966–7) in 226 sailing days. The yachts were named after the Gipsy Moth aircraft in which he made a solo flight to Australia (1929).

girl Friday /ˌgɜ:l 'fraɪdɪ/ (work) A term for a girl or woman who is a *PA* or secretary, either in a business organization or privately. [from Man Friday, Robinson Crusoe's servant in the novel (1719) by Daniel Defoe]

Girl Guide /ˌgɜ:l 'gaɪd/ (sport and leisure) A term still in use for a member of the *Girl Guides Association* (now officially a *Guide*).

Girl Guides Association /ˌgɜ:l 'gaɪdz əsəʊsɪˌeɪʃn/, **the** (sport and leisure) An organization for girls founded in 1910 as an equivalent to the (present) *Scout Association*. Its members are divided into three groups, the youngest being the *Brownie Guides*, the next youngest the *Guides*, and the oldest the Ranger Guides. In 1982 the Association's membership was about 887,000.

giro /'dʒaɪərəʊ/ (finance) **1** A system of transferring money between one bank and another ('bank giro credit'), introduced when the *Post Office* created its *National Girobank* in 1968. **2** A short name for the National Girobank.

Giro(bank) /'dʒaɪərəʊ(bæŋk)/, **the** (finance) A colloquial name for the *National Girobank*.

Glamis Castle /ˌglɑːmz 'kɑːsl/ (royal family) A picturesque 17th-century castle in *Scotland*, north of Dundee, which was the Scottish family home of the *Queen Mother* before her marriage.

Glasgow /'glɑːzgəʊ/ (geography) An important industrial and commercial city in *Scotland*, and a famous port on the *Clyde*. Its principal industries are ship building and heavy engineering. It is the third largest city in *Britain*.

Glaswegian /glæz'wiːdʒən/ (geography) A native or inhabitant of *Glasgow*.

GLC /ˌdʒiː el 'siː/, **the (Greater London Council, the)** (government) The local government body that was created in 1963, together with 32 *borough*[2] councils, to replace the London County Council and several other councils of different types. This meant that, for the first time, *London* had a clearly-defined *local authority*. The Council consists of 92 *councillors* who are elected to hold office for four years in electoral divisions (districts) that correspond to London's parliamentary *constituencies*. The policies of the Labour controlled GLC in the early 1980s (in the 1981 election, 48 of the councillors belonged to the *Labour Party*) met with increasing opposition from the Conservative government of Margaret *Thatcher* (see *Conservative Party*), and plans were proposed to abolish the Council, as well as the *metropolitan counties* elsewhere in *England*. These plans were approved by *Parliament* in 1985, to come into effect in 1986. See also *County Hall*.

Glencoe Massacre /glen'kəʊ (ˌglenkəʊ 'mæsəkə(r))/, **the** (history) A massacre which took place in 1692 in a valley in west *Scotland* where the Scottish *clan* Campbell, assisted by English troops, massacred the clan Macdonald. [from the name of the valley]

glengarry /glen'gærɪ/ (clothing) A brimless Scottish woollen cap, usually with ribbons hanging at the back. [named after Glen Garry, a valley in the *Highlands*]

Globe (Theatre) /gləʊb (ˌgləʊb 'θɪətə(r))/, **the** (1 history 2 arts) **1** A famous theatre built in 1599 on the south bank of the *Thames*, *London*, in which *Shakespeare*'s greatest plays were first performed. It was burnt down in 1613, rebuilt in 1614, and remained in use until 1644 when it was demolished to make space for new houses. **2** A theatre in *Shaftesbury Avenue*, London, staging mainly light comedies and musicals. It was founded in 1906.

Glorious Goodwood /ˌglɔːrɪəs 'gʊdwʊd/ (sport and leisure) A nickname of the racecourse at *Goodwood*, West Sussex, famous for its attractive setting and for the excellence of its turf. The name is also used of the horse races themselves, especially those held annually in 'Goodwood Week' (July/August).

Glorious Twelfth /ˌglɔːrɪəs 'twelfθ/, **the** (1 history 2 sport and leisure) **1** 12 July 1690, the day (actually 1 July in the old style calendar, and 11 July in the new style) when the Battle of the *Boyne* took place in *Ireland*. The date 12 July is celebrated annually in modern *Northern Ireland* by the Protestants to mark their victory over the Catholics in the Battle. **2** A name for 12 August, when *grouse shooting* begins annually.

Gloucester /'glɒstə(r)/ (geography) The county town of Gloucestershire, whose cathedral is a fine example of *Perpendicular (style)* architecture, with parts in the older *Norman* style.

glue-sniffing /'gluːsnɪfɪŋ/ (life and society) The practice, sometimes fatal, of inhaling the fumes of certain types of glue and other substances in order to achieve a hallucinatory effect. The practice was adopted by some young people in the 1970s, and became more widespread in the 1980s.

Glyndebourne /'glaɪndbɔːn/ (arts) An annual opera festival held at the country house so named near Lewes, East Sussex. The house belonged to John Christie (1882–1962) who founded the festivals here in 1934.

GMBATU /[pronunciation not yet established]/, **the (General, Municipal, Boilermakers and Allied Trades Union, the)** (work) One of the largest trade unions (940,000 members). It is affiliated to the *TUC* and has members in a wide range of employments, mainly non-skilled and industrial.

GMT /ˌdʒiː em 'tiː/ **(Greenwich Mean Time)** (geography) The local time of the 0° meridian that passes through *Greenwich*, and thus the standard time for *Britain* and a basis for other time zones in the world.

GMWU /ˌdʒiː em ˌdʌblju: 'juː/, **the (General and Municipal Workers Union, the)** (work) The former name of the *GMBATU*.

gnome /nəʊm/ (style) A small statue or figure of a gnome, sometimes placed in a front garden as a decoration.

gobstopper /'gɒbstɒpə(r)/ (food and drink) A large, hard, round sweet gradually changing in colour as it is sucked. [from 'gob', a slang term for 'mouth']

God Save the Queen /ˌgɒd seɪv ðə 'kwiːn/ (life and society) The title of the British *national anthem* (in fact the final words of the first verse). In the reign of a king the word 'Queen' changes to 'King'. It is not known who wrote the text of the anthem, but it may have been established in its present form some time in the 18th century.

Gog Magog Hills /ˌgɒg məgɒg 'hɪlz/, **the** (geography) Low hills near *Cambridge*[1] where there is a golf course. The hills are a favourite place for *undergraduates* of *Cambridge University*. The name, which also exists in the form

Gogmagogs, is said to derive from two local legendary giants.
The hills are also known colloquially as the Gogs.

gnome

Gold Cup Day /ˌgəʊld ˈkʌp deɪ/ (sport and leisure) The most
important day of the horse races at *Ascot*, when the prize of
the Ascot Gold Cup is competed for. The prize was
established in 1807.

Gold Stick /ˌgəʊld ˈstɪk/ (life and society) **1** The gilt rod carried
as a badge of office before the sovereign by the colonel of the
Life Guards or the captain of the *Gentlemen-at-Arms*. **2** The
title of the colonel himself when performing this duty.

Golden Age /ˌgəʊldən ˈeɪdʒ/**, the** (history) A term used for the
reign of Queen Elizabeth I, from 1558 to 1603. This was a
period of marked economic progress and of the flowering of
the arts, both largely resulting from Elizabeth's
encouragement and inspiration.

golden bowler /ˌgəʊldən ˈbəʊlə(r)/ (work) A colloquial term
for a post in the *Civil Service* given to a military officer on his
retirement from the services. See *bowler*.

golden handshake /ˌgəʊldən ˈhændʃeɪk/ (work) A colloquial
term for a substantial sum of money paid to an employee,
often a director or other executive, either on his retirement in
recognition of his work, or on his dismissal by way of
compensation.

Golden Hind /ˌgəʊldən ˈhaɪnd/**, the** (1 history 2 transport)
1 The name of the ship in which Sir Francis Drake (?1540–96)
sailed round the world (1577–80). **2** The name of a daily
express train from *London* to Plymouth. (Francis Drake
returned to Plymouth at the end of his voyage and was made
mayor of Plymouth the following year.)

Goldie crew /ˈgəʊldɪ kruː/**, the** (sport and leisure) The reserve
crew of *Cambridge University* for the *Oxford*[2] and *Cambridge*[2]
Boat Race. The name is that of a former Cambridge oarsman.
Compare *Isis*.

Goldsmiths' Company /ˈɡəʊldsmɪθs ˌkʌmpənɪ/, **the** (tradition) One of the oldest *livery companies*, founded in 1327 and the fifth in precedence. Its members, originally goldsmiths, still regulate the manufacture and sale of gold and silver articles.

Goldsmiths' Hall /ˌɡəʊldsmɪθs ˈhɔːl/ (London) The building in the *City (of London)* where the *Goldsmiths' Company* is based. It contains a valuable collection of portraits and goldware.

Good Friday /ˌɡʊd ˈfraɪdɪ/ (religion) The Friday before *Easter* when the Christian church marks the Crucifixion of Christ. In *Britain* it is a *bank holiday* and a day when traditionally *hot cross buns* are eaten.

Good King Wenceslas /ˌɡʊd kɪŋ ˈwensəslæs/ (tradition) The title, and opening words, of a well-known *Christmas* carol (see *carol service*), particularly popular among children. [the carol is of 19th-century origin, but has the 10th-century Bohemian martyr prince Wenceslas as its subject]

good will /ˌɡʊd ˈwɪl/ (commerce) The term for an intangible asset, such as a good reputation or favourable customer connections, taken into account in assessing the value of a deal, particularly the sale of a business.

Goodison Park /ˌɡʊdɪsn ˈpɑːk/ (sport and leisure) The stadium of the football club *Everton* in Liverpool. [from the name of a nearby park]

Goodwin Sands /ˌɡʊdwɪn ˈsændz/, **the** (geography) A dangerous stretch of sand banks at the entrance to the Strait of Dover. [traditionally said to have been an island, belonging to an earl named Godwine, that was washed away by the sea in 1097]

Goodwood /ˈɡʊdwʊd/ (sport and leisure) A fashionable race course near Chichester, West Sussex. See also *Glorious Goodwood*. [from the house and park near which it is]

Goonhilly /ˌɡuːnˈhɪlɪ/ (science and technology) A satellite communications station in *Cornwall*, first operating in 1962. [for Goonhilly Downs, its location]

Goons /ɡuːnz/, **the** (media) The name adopted by a group of radio comedians for their programme 'The Goon Show' in the 1950s. Their humour was a blend of the witty and the near-absurd. The comedians were: Michael Bentine (1922–   ), Spike Milligan (1918–   ), Harry Secombe (1921–   ) and Peter Sellers (1925–80). [name allegedly based on that of a cartoon character]

Goose Fair /ˌɡuːs ˈfeə(r)/, **the** (tradition) An annual fair held in Nottingham, originally one at which geese were sold. The fair takes place on the first Thursday, Friday and Saturday in October.

gooseberry fool /ˌɡʊzbrɪ ˈfuːl/ (food and drink) A sweet dish made with stewed gooseberries which have been sieved and to which whipped cream has been added.

Gorbals /ˈɡɔːblz/, **the** (geography) A suburb of *Glasgow* once notorious for its slums.

Gordon Highlanders /ˌɡɔːdn ˈhaɪləndəz/, **the** (defence) A well-known Scottish army regiment. It was formed in 1881 when the 92nd and 75th regiments were combined, but was originally raised in 1794 by the 5th Duke of Gordon.

Gordonstoun (School) /ˈɡɔːdnstən (ˌɡɔːdnstən ˈskuːl)/ (education) A *public school*[1] (co-educational from 1972) near the coast in north-east *Scotland*. It was founded in 1934 by the German educationalist Kurt Hahn (1886–1974) with the aim of developing a pupil's all-round capabilities, physically as well as academically, so that he should become a good citizen. The school has 460 students. Kurt Hahn also founded the *Outward Bound* (*Trust*).

go-slow /ˌɡəʊˈsləʊ/ (work) A deliberate slowing of the work rate or rate of production by a labour force as a tactic in an industrial dispute. Compare *work-to-rule*.

gossip column /ˈɡɒsɪp ˌkɒləm/ (media) A regular feature in a newspaper (especially a *popular paper*) or magazine in which the latest news and rumours about people in the public eye are given.

Gothic novel /ˌɡɒθɪk ˈnɒvl/ (arts) **1** A mock-romantic horror story, traditionally set in a castle built in the *Gothic (style)*, popularized in the 18th century by the novelist Horace Walpole (1717–97), notably in his novel 'The Castle of Otranto' (1764). **2** A modern version of this, typically with a girl trapped in a castle with unknown dangers, as popularized by Daphne du Maurier (1907–   ) in her novel 'Rebecca' (1938).

Gothic Revival /ˌɡɒθɪk rɪˈvaɪvl/, **the** (style) The revival (1750) of *Gothic (style)* architecture in *England*. A typical example of the style are the *Houses of Parliament*, *London*.

Gothic (style) /ˈɡɒθɪk (staɪl)/ (style) An architectural style in which pointed arches, soaring lines and height predominate. In *Britain* it is typified by the *Early English*, *Decorated* and *Perpendicular (style*s), notably in *church*es and cathedrals.

government health warning /ˌɡʌvənmənt ˈhelθ ˌwɔːnɪŋ/ (medicine) An official warning regarding the danger to health of smoking, printed by law on all cigarette packets and advertisements for cigarettes. The wording usually takes the form: 'Cigarettes can seriously damage your health'.

government training centre /ˌɡʌvənmənt ˈtreɪnɪŋ ˌsentə(r)/ (work) The former name of a *skillcentre*.

governor /ˈɡʌvənə(r)/ (**1** life and society **2** education **3** law) **1** The official title of the head of certain establishments, for example, the Governor of the *Bank of England*. **2** A member of a governing body of a university, *college*[1] or school. **3** The title of the head of a prison.

gown /ɡaʊn/ (**1** clothing **2** education) **1** The loose top garment worn as part of the official dress of certain people, such as a *mayor*, a judge or the students and staff of a university or school. **2** A collective term for the students of a university, as opposed to the inhabitants of the town where the university is located. See *town and gown*.

GP /ˌdʒ ˈpiː/ **(general practitioner)** (medicine) A doctor who is not a specialist but who has a medical practice (a 'general practice') in which he treats all illnesses. He is also sometimes known as a 'family doctor', and often works as a member of a *group practice*.

GPO /ˌdʒiː piː ˈəʊ/**, the (General Post Office, the)** (commerce) The official title of the *Post Office* before 1969.

grace /greɪs/ (religion) A short, usually formal, prayer said before or after a meal, especially in a school or a religious community. Many formal dinners often begin and end with grace, which is said by a clergyman, if one is there, or some other senior person. In some older establishments, such as university *colleges*[1] and *public schools*[1], grace is still said in Latin. A typical English grace runs: 'Bless us, O Lord, and these thy gifts, for Jesus Christ's sake. Amen.'

Grace and Favour residence /ˌgreɪs ən ˈfeɪvə resɪdəns/ (life and society) A house or flat owned by the sovereign and granted free of rent to a person to whom the sovereign wishes to show gratitude. Among such residences are those at *Windsor Castle*, *Hampton Court* and *Kensington Palace*.

grace cup /ˈgreɪs kʌp/ (tradition) A large, usually silver, cup of wine passed round the table at the end of a formal meal for a final toast. [originally such a cup was passed after the *grace*]

graduand /ˈgrædʒʊænd/ (education) A student who is about to graduate, that is, one who has taken his final examinations but not yet been awarded his degree.

graduate /ˈgrædʒʊət/ (education) A person who holds a university degree, normally having attended a university course and passed the final examination.

graduate student /ˈgrædʒʊət ˌstjuːdənt/ (education) An alternative term for a *postgraduate*.

grammar school /ˈgræmə skuːl/ (education) A state or independent (fee-paying) *secondary school* taking pupils aged between 11 and 18. Grammar schools provide a mainly academic education and prepare pupils for *higher education*. Compare *comprehensive school*. The name comes from the fact that Latin grammar formed an important part of the teaching in the original grammar schools, some of which date back to the 15th century. Only 3 per cent of *state school* pupils are at grammar schools. Compare *secondary modern* and *technical school*.

Gramophone /ˈgræməfəʊn/**, The** (media) A monthly magazine containing reviews of recently released gramophone records of classical music, articles on recording artists and technical information on record-playing equipment. It was founded in 1923.

Grampian Television /ˌɡræmpɪən ˈtelɪvɪʒn/ (media) One of the 15 television companies of the *IBA*, transmitting programmes to northeast *Scotland*. [from the *Grampians* in this region]

Grampians /ˈɡræmpɪənz/, **the** (geography) A range of mountains in the *Highlands* of central *Scotland* that includes the *Cairngorms* and is popular with mountain climbers and hill walkers. Many of the high moors in the Grampians are used for *grouse shooting* at the appropriate time of year.

Granada Television /ɡrəˌnɑːdə ˈtelɪvɪʒn/ (media) One of the 15 television companies of the *IBA*, transmitting programmes to Greater Manchester and Lancashire. [company was established in 1954 by the Granada Group]

Grand National /ˌɡrænd ˈnæʃnəl/, **the** (sport and leisure) The most important steeplechase in *Britain*, held annually in the spring at the *Aintree* race course near Liverpool. It was instituted in 1839 and given its present name in 1847. See also *Becher's Brook, Valentine's Brook.*

Grand Old Man /ˌɡrænd əʊld ˈmæn/ (life and society) A title, serious or humorous, for any person who has given long service in some activity. It was originally a nickname of William Ewart Gladstone (1809–98) who was four times *Prime Minister.*

Grand Order of Water Rats /ˌɡrænd ˌɔːdər əv ˈwɔːtə ræts/, **the** (charities) The title of a charitable organization to which many entertainers belong. Officials of the organization have titles such as 'King Rat', 'Scribe Rat' and so on. It was founded in 1930.

Grand Union Canal /ˌɡrænd ˌjuːnɪən kəˈnæl/, **the** (transport) The longest canal in *Britain*, linking *London* with Birmingham and extending for 240 miles (385 km).

Grandstand /ˈɡrændstænd/ (media) A weekly television programme broadcast by *BBC 1* on Saturdays (and occasionally on Sundays). It usually consists of live transmissions of important sports events. The programme was first broadcast in 1958.

Granite City /ˌɡrænɪt ˈsɪtɪ/, **the** (geography) A nickname of Aberdeen, *Scotland*, since many of its buildings are made of local granite, a silver-grey or pink stone.

granny bonds /ˈɡrænɪ ˌbɒndz/ (finance) A colloquial term for the *Savings Certificates* first issued in 1975 to men and women over retirement age (respectively 65 and 60), and having the advantage of being linked to the cost of living index. In 1981 they became available to people below retirement age.

granny flat /ˈɡrænɪ ˌflæt/ (daily life) A flat built onto a house, or made inside it, for an elderly relative (not necessarily a grandmother).

Granta /ˈɡræntə/ (geography) The local name of the river Cam as it flows through *Cambridge*[1]. Compare *Isis.*

Grasmere /ˈɡrɑːsmɪə(r)/ (geography) A picturesque village in the *Lake District* where the poet William Wordsworth

(1770–1850) lived for much of his life and where the *Lake Poets* used to meet.

Gray's 'Elegy' /ˌgreɪz 'elədʒɪ/ (arts) A famous and much quoted poem by Thomas Gray (1716–71). The poem appeared in 1751 and has the full title 'Elegy Written in a Country Churchyard'. The churchyard is traditionally believed to be that of Stoke Poges, Buckinghamshire.

Gray's Inn /ˌgreɪz 'ɪn/ (law) The most recent of the *Inns of Court*, named after the 14th-century family de Gray, who owned the land on which it was built.

Great Britain /ˌgreɪt 'brɪtn/ (geography) The largest island of the *British Isles* and consisting of *England*, *Scotland* and *Wales*. It is often used (incorrectly) to include *Northern Ireland* which is (correctly) part of the *United Kingdom* of Great Britain and Northern Ireland. See map on p 380.

Great Exhibition /ˌgreɪt eksɪ'bɪʃn/, **the** (history) The first international trade fair held in *London* at the *Crystal Palace*[1] in 1851.

Great Fire (of London) /ˌgreɪt 'faɪə(r) (ˌgreɪt faɪər əv 'lʌndən)/, **the** (history) A fire which destroyed more than half the city of *London*, including the old *St Paul's Cathedral*, in 1666.

Great Glen /ˌgreɪt 'glen/, **the** (geography) The name of a long valley, also called Glen More, that runs northeast to southwest across the whole of the north of *Scotland* and includes *Loch Ness*.

Great North Road /ˌgreɪt nɔːθ 'rəʊd/, **the** (transport) The name of the main trunk road that runs from *London* north to *Edinburgh* in *Scotland*, today mainly followed by the A1 route. See *A-road*.

Great Ormond Street /ˌgreɪt 'ɔːmənd striːt/ (medicine) The street in *London* where there is a famous hospital for children, known either as the Great Ormond Street Hospital or the Hospital for Sick Children.

Great Paul /ˌgreɪt 'pɔːl/ (London) The name of the largest bell in *Britain*, in *St Paul's Cathedral*, London. It weighs 16 tons (17,000 kilograms).

Great Plague (of London) /ˌgreɪt 'pleɪg (ˌgreɪt pleɪg əv 'lʌndən)/, **the** (history) An epidemic of bubonic plague in *London* in 1664–5, when more than 70,000 people died, out of an estimated population of 460,000.

Great Seal /ˌgreɪt 'siːl/, **the** (government) The state seal of the *United Kingdom* used on documents of the greatest importance and kept in the office of the *Lord Chancellor*.

Great Tom /ˌgreɪt 'tɒm/ (tradition) The name of the bell over the gate at Christ Church, *Oxford*[1], still traditionally rung 101 times each evening at 9.05. Its original use was to summon students out in the town to return to the *college*[1] at night, 101 being the number of students in residence. [from Tom, a traditional name for a large bell]

Great Train Robbery /ˌɡreɪt 'treɪn ˌrɒbərɪ/, **the** (history) The name used for the robbery of a mail train in Buckinghamshire in 1963. The train was travelling from *Scotland* to *London* and over £2 million in bank notes were stolen from it.

Greater London /ˌɡreɪtə 'lʌndən/ (London) The name of the local government area and *county* set up in 1963 to include *London* and most of the former county of Middlesex together with parts of nearby counties. It is divided into the *City (of London)* and 32 London *boroughs²*. Its area is 610 square miles (1,580 square kilometres) and its population over 6.7 million (1984). See also *GLC*.

Greats /ɡreɪts/ (education) A colloquial term for the final examination at *Oxford University* in Literae Humaniores, the study of Latin and Greek language, literature, history and philosophy.

green belt /'ɡriːn belt/ (geography) A zone of farmland, parks or woodland surrounding a town, especially a *new town*, planned with a view to preventing unnecessary urban development.

Green Cross Code /ˌɡriːn krɒs 'kəʊd/, **the** (daily life) A set of road safety rules for children, first published in 1971. ['Green' for the colour's connotations of safety, 'Cross' to suggest 'crossing the road', 'Code' to suggest the *Highway Code*]

Green Jackets /'ɡriːn ˌdʒækɪts/, **the** (defence) The short form of the name of the army regiment known in full as the Royal Green Jackets, formed in 1866.

Green Line coach /ˌɡriːn laɪn 'kəʊtʃ/ (transport) One of the fleet of green-painted buses operated by London Country Bus Services that serve the area around *London* to a radius of approximately 40 miles (64 kilometres).

green paper /ˌɡriːn 'peɪpə(r)/ (government) A *command paper* setting out proposals for future government policy to be discussed in parliament. [from the colour of the cover]

Green Park /ˌɡriːn 'pɑːk/ (London) A park in *London* extending along the south side of *Piccadilly*. Traditionally no flowers are grown there. [named for its green grass and trees]

Greenham Common /ˌɡriːnəm 'kɒmən/ (defence) An *RAF* base at the village of Greenham Common near Newbury, Berkshire where many United States troops are also stationed. Since 1981, groups of 'peace women' (anti-nuclear protesters) have lived in camps just outside the base. They are protesting against the base being used for nuclear weapons. The women have organized several protest rallies and demonstrations, and their campaign increased considerably when cruise missiles from the United States arrived here in 1983. The women have had several clashes with the police force and military personnel on the base. In spite of attempts to remove them, the women still have camps round the base.

Greensleeves /ˈgriːnsliːvz/ (arts) A popular old love song known from the 16th century and twice mentioned by *Shakespeare*. The song tells of a 'Lady Greensleeves'. It is popularly believed *Henry VIII* wrote the music and the words, though this is not certain.

Greenwich /ˈgrenɪdʒ/ (geography) A southern suburb of *London*, where the *Royal Greenwich Observatory* was until it moved to Herstmonceux in 1958. The 0° meridian that indicates where *GMT* is measured passes through this part of London.

Greenwich Park /ˌgrenɪdʒ ˈpɑːk/ (geography) A large park in *Greenwich* through which passes the 0° meridian that gives *GMT*. From the hill in the centre of the park there is a fine panoramic view of southeast *London*.

greetings card /ˈgriːtɪŋz kɑːd/ (life and society) A decorative card, usually folded in two, with an illustration and wording on the outside and with wording or blank in the middle, sent to greet a person on a special occasion such as *Christmas*, a birthday or the announcement of an engagement to be married.

Grenadier Guards /ˌgrenədɪə ˈgɑːdz/**, the** (defence) The senior regiment of the *Army* in the *Guards Division* of infantry. It was raised in 1685.

Gretna Green /ˌgretnə ˈgriːn/ (tradition) A village in southern *Scotland*, on the border with *England*. Here there is a famous smithy where eloping couples from England could be married by the blacksmith without the usual legal formalities. This tradition operated from 1754 until 1940 when such marriages were declared illegal.

grey area /ˈgreɪ ˌeərɪə/ (work) An unofficial term for an *assisted area* that is relatively high in unemployment but not officially classified as a *development area*. Such areas are located largely in west and southern *Scotland*, the north of *England* and *Wales*.

Greyfriars /ˈgreɪfraɪəz/ (education) An imaginary boys' *public school*[1] that was the setting for a famous series of school stories with *Billy Bunter* as their hero.

greyhound /ˈgreɪhaʊnd/ (animal world) A tall slender fast-moving breed of hunting dog traditionally used in *greyhound racing*. Greyhounds are not necessarily grey in colour: 'grey' comes from an old word for bitch.

Greyhound Derby /ˌgreɪhaʊnd ˈdɑːbɪ/**, the** (sport and leisure) An important annual event in *greyhound racing*, held at the *White City* stadium in *London*. It was first run in 1927.

greyhound racing /ˈgreɪhaʊnd ˌreɪsɪŋ/ (sport and leisure) A popular type of gambling sport in which bets are placed on *greyhounds* racing round a track after a mechanical hare. There are over 100 such tracks in *Britain*.

griddle cake /ˈgrɪdl ˌkeɪk/ (food and drink) An alternative name for a *drop scone*.

Grosvenor House /ˌɡrəʊvnə ˈhaʊs/ (London) The name (in full Grosvenor House Hotel) of a fashionable hotel in *Park Lane, London*.

Grosvenor Square /ˌɡrəʊvnə ˈskweə(r)/ (London) A large square in central *London* where the United States Embassy and other diplomatic offices are. See *Little America*.

ground floor /ˌɡraʊnd ˈflɔː(r)/, **the** (daily life) The bottom floor in a building, corresponding in many other countries to the first floor. The *first floor* in *Britain* is the one above the ground level.

ground floor

ground rent /ˈɡraʊnd rent/ (finance) A rent, traditionally running for 99 years, payable for the lease of a building, in particular a home.

groundsman /ˈɡraʊndzmən/ (sport and leisure) A man responsible for the upkeep of a sports ground or field and for preparing the area of play before a game or match.

group practice /ˌɡruːp ˈpræktɪs/ (medicine) A medical practice in which several *GP*s see their patients in a surgery or clinic shared by all the doctors working there.

grouse shooting /ˈɡraʊs ˌʃuːtɪŋ/ (sport and leisure) A type of shooting popular among the aristocracy, particularly in *Scotland* where there are many moors where grouse live. The sport is restricted to the period 12 August (see *Glorious Twelfth*[2]) to 10 December.

GT /ˌdʒiː ˈtiː/ **(gran turismo)** (transport) The name given to some models of sport car, usually ones capable of high speeds. The term is Italian for 'great touring'.

Guardian /ˈɡɑːdɪən/, **The** (media) A daily *quality paper* of both liberal and *Liberal Party* views. It was founded in 1821 as 'The Manchester Guardian', changing its name in 1961 to 'The Guardian' and from this year printing in both *London* and Manchester. Its circulation is over 473,000 (1984) (1970 — 293,000).

Guards /gɑːdz/, **the** (defence) A general name for any or all of the regiments in the *Guards Division* of the *Army*, and for the *Life Guards* and the *Blues and Royals* in the *Household Cavalry*.

Guards Division /'gɑːdz dɪˌvɪʒn/, **the** (defence) The infantry division of the *Army* that comprises the *Grenadier Guards*, *Coldstream Guards*, *Scots Guards*, *Irish Guards* and *Welsh Guards*. These are the most famous regiments in the Army.

guardsman /'gɑːdzmən/ (defence) A member of any regiment of the *Guards*.

guernsey /'gɜːnzɪ/ (clothing) A thick dark-blue woollen sweater, originally as worn by sailors on Guernsey, in the *Channel Islands*. Compare *jersey*[2].

Guernsey (cow) /'gɜːnzɪ (ˌgɜːnzɪ 'kaʊ)/ (animal world) A breed of dairy cattle, larger than the *Jersey* (cow), producing high-quality creamy milk. Such a cow is usually fawn in colour, occasionally with white markings. Guernsey cows originally came from the island of Guernsey, in the *Channel Islands*; today they are usually found chiefly in the south of *England*, especially *Cornwall*.

guest house /'gesthaʊs/ (daily life) A modest hotel or boarding house, often a private house, offering accommodation to business travellers or holiday makers.

Guide /gaɪd/ (sport and leisure) A member of the *Girl Guides Association*, strictly, one in the *Guides* division. See also *Brownie Guide*.

guide dog /'gaɪd dɒg/ (animal world) A dog specially trained to lead a blind person. Such dogs are trained by the Guide Dogs for the Blind Association, a charity founded in 1933.

guide dog

Guides /gaɪdz/, **the** (sport and leisure) A division of the *Girl Guides Association*, to which girls aged 10 to 15 belong. See also *Brownie Guide*.

guildhall /ˈgɪldhɔːl/ (tradition) The title of a *town hall* in a number of towns and cities. Originally it was the hall belonging to a medieval guild or corporation.

Guildhall /ˈgɪldhɔːl/, **the** (London) The ancient building that serves as the *town hall* for the *City of London*, famous for its large banqueting hall in which official receptions are held on specially important occasions. The Guildhall also contains a library and picture gallery. It was built originally in 1411, with parts rebuilt in 1788.

Guildhall School of Music (and Drama) /ˌgɪldhɔːl ˌskuːl əv ˈmjuːzɪk (ˌgɪldhɔːl ˌskuːl əv ˌmjuːzɪk ən ˈdrɑːmə)/, **the** (education) A private *college²* in *London*, teaching music, stagecraft and the dramatic arts. It was founded in 1880. [from its nearness to the *Guildhall*]

guillotine /ˈgɪlətiːn/ (government) A term for a procedure whereby a *bill* that is going through one of the *Houses of Parliament* is divided into 'compartments', groups of which must be completely dealt with in a day. An alternative term for the procedure is 'closure by compartment'. [after the instrument used for execution by beheading]

guinea /ˈgɪnɪ/ (**1** history **2** finance) **1** A gold coin originally worth one *pound (sterling)*, later worth 21 *shillings*, that was withdrawn from circulation in 1813. **2** A monetary unit of 21 shillings (since 1971, £1.05) used for calculating professional fees and charges although now only rarely. [coin was originally made from gold imported from Guinea]

Guinness /ˈgɪnɪs/ (food and drink) The brand name of a type of strong dark beer (correctly known as *stout*) manufactured by Arthur Guinness Son & Co. Ltd.

Guinness Book of Records /ˌgɪnɪs bʊk əv ˈrekɔːdz/, **the** (media) An annual reference book published by Guinness Superlatives Ltd., a subsidiary company of the firm that manufactures *Guinness*. The book publishes the records that have been broken or achieved in a wide range of activities on a worldwide basis. It was first published in 1955.

gum boots /ˈgʌm buːts/ (clothing) Another name for *wellington boots*.

gun dog /ˈgʌn dɒg/ (sport and leisure) A dog trained to help a shooting party by searching out or retrieving birds and animals.

Gunpowder Plot /ˈgʌnpaʊdə ˌplɒt/, **the** (history) The name of a plot in 1605 when on 5 November Roman Catholics planned to assassinate King James I at the *State Opening of Parliament* by exploding barrels of gunpowder in the vaults of the *Houses of Parliament*. One of the conspirators was Guy Fawkes (see *Guy Fawkes' Night*).

gutter press /ˈɡʌtə pres/, **the** (media) A colloquial term for those *popular papers*, and similar periodicals, that seek sensationalism by means of *gossip columns*, detailed reports of disasters and scandals and erotic features and photographs.

guy /ɡaɪ/ (tradition) A crude model of a human figure, representing Guy Fawkes, made by stuffing old clothes with straw, paper, leaves etc. and burnt on top of a bonfire on *Guy Fawkes' Night*. Such a model may also be carried or displayed by children in the days before Guy Fawkes' Night with the aim of collecting money.

Guy Fawkes' Day /ˈɡaɪ fɔːks deɪ/ (tradition) An alternative name for *Guy Fawkes' Night*.

Guy Fawkes' Night /ˈɡaɪ fɔːks naɪt/ (tradition) A popular celebration annually on the evening of 5 November, the day of the original *Gunpowder Plot*. A bonfire is lit to burn a *guy* and a firework display is arranged. The occasion is usually accompanied by a supper or barbecue and is held both publicly in parks and recreation fields and privately in the gardens of houses. The historic significance of the event has long been ignored. [Guy Fawkes (1570–1606) was one of the Roman Catholic conspirators in the Gunpowder Plot; under torture he revealed the names of the other conspirators and was convicted and executed]

Guy's Hospital /ˌɡaɪz ˈhɒspɪtl/ (medicine) A leading *teaching hospital* in *London*. It was founded in 1721 by Thomas Guy (?1645–1724), a book dealer and philanthropist. The hospital is colloquially known as 'Guy's'.

gymkhana /dʒɪmˈkɑːnə/ (sport and leisure) A popular event, mainly with children taking part, in which horses and their riders display their skill in various races and contests. [from a Hindi word meaning 'ball house', influenced by 'gymnasium']

gyp /dʒɪp/ (tradition) A colloquial term at *Cambridge University* and Durham University for a *college*[1] servant. [perhaps from an old word 'gippo' originally meaning a man's short tunic as worn by a servant]

habeas corpus /ˌheɪbɪəs ˈkɔːpəs/ (law) A writ (legal order) ordering a person who is in custody or prison to be brought before a *court³* or judge so that the court can decide whether the person was legally imprisoned or not. [from the opening words of the Latin writ, 'habeas corpus' ('ad subjiciendum'), 'you should have the body (brought before the judge)']

hackney carriage /ˈhæknɪ ˌkærɪdʒ/ (transport) A term used to apply to a taxi that has been officially licensed to carry fare-paying passengers. [originally used of a carriage drawn by a 'hackney', a type of horse used in harness]

Hadrian's Wall /ˌheɪdrɪənz ˈwɔːl/ (history) An ancient wall, built by order of the Roman emperor Hadrian in the 2nd century AD to defend the northern border of *England* against attacks by Celtic tribes. The wall, which is about 120 km long, crossed England from the river Tyne in the east to the Solway Firth in the west. Long sections of the wall remain today and are a popular tourist attraction. Compare *Antonine Wall*.

haggis /ˈhægɪs/ (food and drink) A traditional Scottish dish made from sheep's or calf's offal (edible internal organs), suet, oatmeal and onions, and boiled in a bag. The bag was originally made from a sheep's stomach but is now made from a synthetic substance. See also *Burns' Night*.

halfpenny /ˈheɪpnɪ/ (finance) A small bronze coin worth half a *penny* (pre-decimal or decimal, see *D-day²*). The decimal halfpenny was withdrawn from circulation in 1985.

hall /hɔːl/ (1 life and society 2, 3, 4, 5 education) 1 The name often given to *country houses* in many parts of the country, especially the *Midlands* and north of *England*. 2 The name of some *colleges¹* in a university, such as Trinity Hall, *Cambridge²*. 3 The short title of a *hall of residence*. 4 The dining room in a college¹. 5 An assembly room in a school.

hall of residence /ˌhɔːl əv ˈrezɪdəns/ (education) A term used in some *colleges¹* and universities for a student hostel.

Hallé (Orchestra) /ˈhæleɪ (ˌɔːkɪstrə)/, **the** (arts) A leading British symphony orchestra, founded by Charles Hallé in Manchester in 1857.

Hallowe'en /ˌhæləʊˈiːn/ (tradition) A name for 31 October, the eve of All Saints Day, when according to an old tradition girls would use certain 'magic' rites to foresee who they would marry. Today the day is usually marked by costume or fancy-dress parties, and is a popular occasion with young people and children (see *trick or treat*). [from an alternative name for All Saints Day, 'All Hallows', and 'even' ('eve')]

Hampden Park /ˌhæmdən 'pɑːk/ (sport and leisure) A *football* stadium in *Glasgow*, *Scotland*, where a number of international football matches are played, as well as the annual Scottish Cup Final (the equivalent of the English *Cup Final*).

Hampden roar /ˌhæmdən 'rɔː(r)/, **the** (sport and leisure) The loud massed cheering and chanting at *Hampden Park* during football matches, and in particular during the Scottish Cup Final.

Hampstead /'hæmpstɪd/ (London) A fashionable residential district of northwest *London*, in places still keeping the character of a picturesque village, which it originally was. In the 20th century it came to be associated with left-wing intellectualism and the unorthodox life-style of some of its residents.

Hampton Court /ˌhæmptən 'kɔːt/ (history) A great palace with gardens on the banks of the *Thames*, west of *London*, and one of the finest historical monuments in *Britain*. The palace was first built by Cardinal Wolsey in the early 16th century, and was later enlarged and improved by *Henry VIII* and a number of famous architects and sculptors. The palace gardens contain a well-known maze. [in full Hampton Court Palace, named after the village of Hampton here]

Handybank /'hændɪbæŋk/, **the** (finance) A branch of the Co-operative Bank (run by the *Co-operative Wholesale Society*). [handy since it is open on days and at times when most banks are closed]

Hansard /'hænsɑːd/ (government) The short title of the daily publication that gives a word-for-word report of proceedings in the *House of Commons* (properly the Official Report of Parliamentary Debates). [named after Luke Hansard, who first printed the journals of the House of Commons in 1774]

happy hour /'hæpɪ aʊə(r)/ (daily life) A time (usually in the early evening, and not necessarily an hour) when alcoholic drinks are sold at reduced prices in a *bar[1]*, *club* or other establishment.

hare and hounds /ˌheər ən 'haʊndz/ (sport and leisure) A children's game in which one group of players tries to find and capture the other group. The chased group ('hares') leaves a trail of some kind for the chasers ('hounds') to follow.

Harley Street /'hɑːlɪ striːt/ (medicine) A street in central *London* famous for its many private medical specialists and consultants.

Harris tweed /ˌhærɪs 'twiːd/ (clothing) The name of a type of tweed (thick woollen cloth) used for men's suits and other clothing, made on the Scottish island of Harris, Outer *Hebrides*.

Harrods /'hærədz/ (commerce) A fashionable *London* department store, one of the largest in Europe. The store, in *Knightsbridge*, claims to be able to supply any article and provide any service. Henry Harrod owned a small grocer's shop on the same site in the 1840s, and, in 1861, his son Charles turned it into a shop selling many different kinds of article.

Harrogate /'hærəgɪt/ (geography) A fashionable resort in North Yorkshire, famous as a conference and trade fair centre, and for its annual International Festival of the Arts and Sciences.

Harrovian /hə'rəʊvɪən/ (education) A member of *Harrow School*.

Harrow (School) /'hærəʊ (ˌhærəʊ 'skuːl)/ (education) One of the leading *public schools¹* for boys, in the *Greater London borough²* of the same name (formerly in Middlesex). It was founded in 1571 and has 740 students.

Hartnell, Norman /'hɑːtnəl, ˌnɔːmən/ (people) Norman Hartnell (1901–79) was the longest-established couture dress designer in *Britain*, opening his fashion house in 1924. He was famous for his beautifully embroidered dresses, designed to be worn on grand occasions, and in particular for the dresses he designed for *Queen Elizabeth* and *Queen Elizabeth, the Queen Mother*. His most magnificent creation was the Queen's *Coronation* dress.

harvest festival /ˌhɑːvɪst 'festɪvl/ (religion) A special annual church service held in the autumn to give thanks for the gathering in of the harvest. On the day of the service, the church is usually decorated with fruit, vegetables, loaves of bread and other produce.

Harvey Smith /ˌhɑːvɪ 'smɪθ/ (daily life) A colloquial term for a *V-sign²*. [from an occasion when the show jumper, Harvey Smith, made this sign in public]

Harwell /'hɑːwel/ (science and technology) A short name used for the Atomic Energy Research Establishment, the chief nuclear energy research establishment of the *United Kingdom Atomic Energy Authority*, near the village of this name in Oxfordshire.

Hastings /'heɪstɪŋz/ (geography) A popular seaside resort in East Sussex, and one of the *Cinque Ports*, where a well-known annual international chess contest is held. See also *Hastings, Battle of*.

Hastings /'heɪstɪŋz/ (**Battle of Hastings, the**) (history) A famous battle in English history, in which William the *Conqueror* defeated the Anglo-Saxon King Harold near Hastings in 1066, thus beginning the *Norman Conquest* of *Britain*.

hat trick /'hæt trɪk/ (sport and leisure) The scoring of three

goals in football or hockey by the same player, or the
dismissing of three batsmen in *cricket* by the same bowler.
[from the special hat formerly awarded a player for this
achievement]

hatches, matches and dispatches /ˌhætʃɪz, ˌmætʃɪz ən dɪˈspætʃɪz/
(daily life) A semi-humorous term for the advertisements in
the *personal columns* of a newspaper that announce,
respectively, births, marriages and deaths.

Haymarket (Theatre) /ˈheɪmɑːkɪt (ˌheɪmɑːkɪt ˈθɪətə(r))/, **the**
(arts) A famous *London* theatre built in 1820 in the
Haymarket (where *Her Majesty's Theatre* is also), and
officially named the 'Theatre Royal, Haymarket'.

Hayward Gallery /ˌheɪwəd ˈgælərɪ/, **the** (arts) An art gallery
opened in 1968 on the *South Bank, London*, where special
exhibitions are held. The Gallery also has open air sculpture
displays. [named after Isaac Hayward, leader of the London
County Council (see *GLC*) from 1947 to 1965]

H-blocks /ˈeɪtʃ blɒks/, **the** (law) The main prison blocks of the
Maze Prison, near *Belfast*, which are built in the form of a
letter 'H'.

H-blocks

Head of the River Race /ˌhed əv ðə ˈrɪvə reɪs/, **the** (sport and
leisure) An annual race between the eights of various rowing
clubs held on the river *Thames* in *London* over the same
course as that followed by the crews of the *Boat Race*, but in
the opposite direction.

Heal's /hiːlʃ/ (commerce) A large modern furniture store in
London. [founded by John Heal in 1810]

health centre /ˈhelθ ˌsentə(r)/ (medicine) A centre for medical
and administrative health welfare work, where a *group
practice* is operated.

health visitor /ˈhelθ ˌvɪzɪtə(r)/ (medicine) A medical worker
who visits families needing preventive care and health
education, especially those with young children and babies.

She is appointed by the state and works closely with *GPs* and *district nurses*.

Heart of Midlothian /ˌhɑːt əv mɪdˈləʊðɪən/ (sport and leisure) A Scottish *football club* founded in 1875, with a stadium in *Edinburgh*. [probably named after the Edinburgh prison that also gave its name to a novel by Walter Scott]

Heart of Oak /ˌhɑːt əv ˈəʊk/ (tradition) A well-known sailors' song and march, written in 1770 by the English actor David Garrick (1771–79). [title of the song, which contains the lines, 'Heart of oak are our ships, Heart of oak are our men']

Hearts /hɑːts/ (sport and leisure) The short name of *Heart of Midlothian football club.*

Heath Robinson /ˌhiːθ ˈrɒbɪnsn/ (daily life) A term used to refer to a machine or contrivance that is over complicated for the simple task it is supposed to perform. [from William Heath Robinson (1872–1944), the cartoonist and illustrator who drew such mechanical contrivances]

heather mixture /ˈheðə ˌmɪkstʃə(r)/ (clothing) A woollen cloth of mixed colours speckled like heather (ie, with mixed threads of green, purple and brown).

Heathrow /ˌhiːθ ˈrəʊ/ (transport) *Britain*'s largest international airport, west of *London* and linked with the capital by the Underground (see *London Underground*). It was opened in 1946 and is officially known as *London Airport*.

heavies /ˈhevɪz/, **the** (media) A colloquial term for the *quality papers*.

Hebrides /ˈhebrədiːz/, **the** (geography) A group of islands off the north-west coast of *Scotland*, divided into the Outer Hebrides and Inner Hebrides. The main islands of the Outer Hebrides are Lewis and Harris (the northern and southern parts of the same island), North Uist and South Uist. In the Inner Hebrides the largest islands are Skye, Mull, Jura and Islay. All the islands are popular with tourists seeking a remote summer holiday in *Britain*.

Hell's Angels /ˌhelz ˈeɪndʒlz/ (life and society) One of a number of groups of young motor-cyclists, usually dressed in black, and notorious for their unruly and destructive behaviour. Such groups originated in the United States in the 1950s.

Help the Aged /ˌhelp ðɪ ˈeɪdʒɪd/ (charities) A charity that aims to provide financial and material aid for poor and disadvantaged elderly people, both in the *United Kingdom* and overseas.

Henley Regatta /ˌhenlɪ rɪˈɡætə/ (sport and leisure) An important international rowing contest (officially Henley Royal Regatta) held annually over five days in late June and early July on the river *Thames* at Henley, Oxfordshire. The Regatta was established in 1834 and by the end of the 19th century had become, as it still is, a very fashionable event.

Henry VIII /ˌhenrɪ ðɪ 'eɪtθ/ (people) The king of *England* (1491–1547) who rejected the belief that the Pope was head of the Church and had himself declared to be the supreme head of the Church in England. Today he is often more popularly remembered for his six wives. He divorced two of his wives and had two others executed.

Hepplewhite /'heplwaɪt/ (style) A style of elegant and graceful wooden furniture, with distinctive heart-shaped chair-backs, designed in the 18th century by George Hepplewhite. Compare *Chippendale* and *Sheraton*.

* **Her Majesty** /hɜː 'mædʒəstɪ/ **(HM)** (royal family) The title used when referring to the sovereign as *queen*, in full, 'Her Majesty the Queen'.

* **Her Majesty's Theatre** /hɜː ˌmædʒəstɪz 'θɪətə(r)/ (arts) A leading *London* theatre in the Haymarket. It opened in 1705 as the Queen's Theatre, was renamed the King's Theatre in 1714, and Her Majesty's Theatre, in honour of *Queen Victoria*, in 1837. Since then it has traditionally changed 'Her' to 'His' in the reign of a king (eg, during the years 1902 to 1952).

hereditary peer /hɪˌredɪtrɪ 'pɪə(r)/ see *peer*[1] (life and society)

Hereford (cow) /'herɪfəd (ˌherɪfəd 'kaʊ)/ (animal world) One of the most common breeds of beef cattle, usually brown with a white head. [originally bred in Herefordshire]

Heriot-Watt University /ˌherɪət ˌwɒt juːnɪ'vɜːsətɪ/ (education) A university in *Edinburgh, Scotland*, founded in 1966. [originally the Heriot-Watt Institution and School of Arts; named after the jeweller and educational benefactor George Heriot (1563–1624) and the engineer and inventor James Watt (1736–1819)]

heritage coast /'herɪtɪdʒ kəʊst/ (geography) A stretch of undeveloped coast officially declared to be of scenic beauty and so to be protected against exploitation by commercial, industrial or touristic enterprise. Such coasts, at present (1984) 37 in number, are defined by the *Countryside Commission*.

HGV /ˌeɪtʃ dʒiː 'viː/ **(heavy goods vehicle)** (transport) **1** A large or heavy lorry (truck) or commercial vehicle, whose driver must possess a special driving licence. **2** The licence itself, obtained by passing a special driving test.

Hibernian /hɪ'bɜːnɪən/ (sport and leisure) A Scottish *football club* founded in 1875, with a stadium in *Edinburgh*. [from Hibernia, the Roman name for *Ireland*, as club was founded by an Irishman]

High Church /ˌhaɪ 'tʃɜːtʃ/ (religion) A member of the *Church of England* who attaches much importance to the authority of the priesthood, the spiritual power of the sacraments, and the observance of ritual. Compare *Low Church* and *Anglo-Catholic*.

* In the reign of a king, 'Her' in these titles changes to 'His'.

High Court (of Justice) /ˌhaɪ ˈkɔːt (ˌhaɪ kɔːt əv ˈdʒʌstɪs)/, **the**
(law) A part of the *Supreme Court* that covers all civil cases
and some criminal ones. It is divided into the *Chancery[1]*
Division, the *Queen's Bench Division*, and the Family Division
(the latter being concerned with all jurisdiction affecting the
family, such as adoption and guardianship). The High Court
has 80 or so judges who are attached to a particular division
within it. Each judge sits alone (without a *jury*) when first
hearing a case.

high school /ˈhaɪ skuːl/ (education) A term used for some
grammar schools for boys and in particular for many *secondary
schools* for girls. (Over 20 girls' *public schools[1]* operated by the
Girls' Public Day School Trust have 'High School' as part of
their name.)

High Street /ˈhaɪ striːt/ (daily life) The name of one of the
central streets, with many shops, in a town or *city*. The High
Street was originally the most important street; today it may
be considerably shorter and (because of traffic restrictions)
quieter than many other streets in a town.

high tea /ˌhaɪ ˈtiː/ (food and drink) An early evening meal
similar to a light supper, usually with a cooked dish or
sandwiches, and accompanied by a pot of tea. The meal is
particularly popular in the north of *England* and in *Scotland*.

higher degree /ˌhaɪə dɪˈɡriː/ (education) A more advanced
degree than a *first degree*, such as an *MA*, or a doctoral degree
such as a Doctor of Philosophy (PhD).

higher education /ˌhaɪər edʒʊˈkeɪʃn/ (education) Education at
a university or *polytechnic*, at degree level or higher, as
distinct from *further education*.

Highland fling /ˌhaɪlənd ˈflɪŋ/, **the** (sport and leisure) A kind
of energetic Scottish reel (dance), typically one danced by a
highlander[1]. The reel is danced by one person alone. [said to
be named from the lively actions of the dance, when the arms
are flung in the air]

Highland games /ˌhaɪlənd ˈɡeɪmz/, **the** (sport and leisure) An
alternative name for a *Highland Gathering*.

Highland Gathering /ˌhaɪlənd ˈɡæðərɪŋ/ (sport and leisure) A
traditional annual festival of Scottish sports and music held at
a centre in the *Highlands*. The best known is the *Braemar
Gathering*, first held in 1832, but other Gatherings (or Games)
are also held at Aboyne, Lonach, Blackford, Alloa, Markinch
and Leslie, even though not all of these towns are in the
Highlands.

highlander /ˈhaɪləndə(r)/ (**1** geography **2** defence) **1** A native
of the *Highlands* of *Scotland*. **2** A soldier in a Scottish
Highland Regiment, such as the Royal Highland Fusiliers or
the *Gordon Highlanders*.

Highlands /ˈhaɪləndz/, **the** (geography) A mountainous region
of northern *Scotland*, in particular the area north of the
Grampians, famous for its *Gaelic* speakers.

Highlands and Islands /ˌhaɪləndz ən ˈaɪləndz/, **the**
(geography) **1** The administrative region of northern *Scotland*
that comprises the *Highlands* and the islands of the Inner
Hebrides. **2** A general term for the whole of northern Scotland
including the mainland Highlands and the major island
groups, the Hebrides, the *Orkneys* and the *Shetlands*.

Highway Code /ˌhaɪweɪ ˈkəʊd/, **the** (transport) A government
publication setting out the main rules and regulations
applying to road users, whether pedestrians, riders or
drivers. It was first published in 1931.

Hilton /ˈhɪltən/, **the** (London) An American-style modern
multi-storey hotel in *Park Lane*, *London*, owned by Hilton
International UK. There are also Hilton hotels elsewhere in
Britain. [in full, Hilton International London Hotel, named
after the American parent company founded by Conrad
Hilton (1887–1979) in 1919]

* **HMG** /ˌeɪtʃ em ˈdʒiː/ **(Her Majesty's Government)**
(government) An abbreviation for the official title of the
government of the day.

* **HMS** /ˌeɪtʃ em ˈes/ **(Her Majesty's Ship)** (defence) The official
designation of all *Royal Navy* ships, followed by the name of
the ship, as in 'HMS Invincible'.

* **HMSO** /ˌeɪtʃ em es ˈəʊ/ **(Her Majesty's Stationery Office)**
(government) The government publishing house, founded in
1786. It publishes only material sponsored by parliament,
government *department*s, and other official bodies. Most of its
wide-ranging books and booklets are informational, and
include school textbooks, guidebooks, year books and naval
and military publications.

HMV /ˌeɪtʃ em ˈviː/ **(His Master's Voice)** (commerce) A well-
known gramophone record company, with the name now
used as a record label by EMI Records Ltd. The label shows a
dog listening to an old-style gramophone.

Hogmanay /ˈhɒgməneɪ/ (tradition) A name used in *Scotland*
for *New Year's Eve* (31 December), and in particular for the
traditional annual celebration held on this day. [said to be
derived from an old French dialect word meaning 'a gift at
the New Year']

holding company /ˈhəʊldɪŋ ˌkʌmpəni/ (finance) A company
having controlling shareholdings in other companies.

Holloway (Prison) /ˈhɒləweɪ (ˌhɒləweɪ ˈprɪzn)/ (law) A large
prison for women, in north *London*. [named after district
where it is]

holly /ˈhɒli/ (tradition) A tree with bright red berries and
shiny, dark green, prickly leaves. In *Britain* the tree is
associated with *Christmas*, and small pieces of holly are often
used for decoration in houses and churches. A piece of holly,
too, is often used to decorate the top of a *Christmas pudding*.

---

* In the reign of a king, 'Her' in these titles changes to 'His'.

At Christmas time pictures of holly are used on greetings cards and in advertisements. Holly is mentioned in the words of several Christmas carols. Some people still believe that it is unlucky to bring holly into a house before *Christmas Eve*.

Holmes, Sherlock /həʊmz ˈʃɜːlɒk/ (**1** arts **2** London) **1** The famous detective in the stories by Arthur Conan Doyle (1859–1930). **2** A popular *pub* in central *London*, containing a reconstruction of Sherlock Holmes's fictional residence in *Baker Street*.

Holy Island /ˈhəʊlɪ ˌaɪlənd/ (geography) An island off the coast of north-east *England*, famous as one of the earliest Christian communities in England. It is also known as Lindisfarne, and has a small resident population.

Holy Loch /ˌhəʊlɪ ˈlɒk/ (defence) An inlet of the river *Clyde*, *Scotland*, used as a base (since 1961) for American nuclear submarines.

Holyrood House /ˌhɒlɪruːd ˈhaʊs/ (royal family) A large mansion (properly, the Palace of Holyrood House) in *Edinburgh, Scotland*, used as a residence by members of the *royal family* when visiting Scotland. The house, which stands in a park beside a ruined abbey, was built in the early 16th century. [house was named after abbey, itself dedicated to the 'Holy Rood', or cross of Christ]

Home Counties /ˌhəʊm ˈkaʊntɪz/**, the** (geography) A general name for the *counties* surrounding *London*, especially Essex, Kent, and Surrey, and also including the former county of Middlesex (now mostly in *Greater London*).

Home Guard /ˌhəʊm ˈɡɑːd/**, the** (history) A part-time army defence force recruited in the Second World War to fight a possible German invasion of *Britain*. Enlistment was at first voluntary, but later (for younger men) compulsory. Although disbanded in 1945, the Home Guard was again formed for the period 1951–6. [originally called Local Defence Volunteers; name changed to Home Guard by Winston *Churchill* in 1940]

home help /ˌhəʊm ˈhelp/ (daily life) A person appointed by a *local authority* to provide practical assistance in the home for disadvantaged people such as the sick, the disabled and the elderly.

Home Office /ˈhəʊm ˌɒfɪs/**, the** (government) The government *department* responsible for internal affairs in *Britain*, in particular the administration of law and order, immigration, community and race relations, broadcasting and the conduct of political elections.

Home Rule /ˌhəʊm ˈruːl/ (politics) The self-government of *Ireland*, unsuccessfully campaigned for by Irish nationalists from the 1870s to the 1920s, when the cause was taken up in a new form by *Sinn Féin* and the *IRA* after the creation of *Northern Ireland* and the Republic of Ireland. The Home Rule campaign might have succeeded in the early 1900s if it had not been for the First World War and the constant opposition of the *Ulster* Unionists. See *Ulster Democratic Unionist Party*, *Ulster Unionist Party*.

Home Secretary /ˌhəʊm ˈsekrətrɪ/, **the** (government) The minister responsible for the *Home Office* (in full *Secretary of State* for the Home Department).

Home, Sweet Home /ˌhəʊm swiːt ˈhəʊm/ (tradition) The title of a popular song of 1823 used to express an Englishman's traditional love of his home.

Homelink /ˈhəʊmlɪŋk/ (commerce) A domestic telecommunications system introduced jointly in 1983 by the Nottingham Building Society (see *building society*), *British Telecom* and the *Bank of Scotland*. It enables a member of the Society to carry out a number of business or financial transactions at home (eg, transfer money from his building society account to his bank) by using the *Prestel* service linked to his television set.

Honourable /ˈɒnərəbl/, **the (Hon, the)** (life and society) A courtesy title placed before the names of various members of the *peerage*, including the children of viscounts and barons and the younger sons of earls, for example 'The Honourable William Fraser' ('The Hon. William Fraser'). The title is also used in the *House of Commons* by one *MP* when speaking of another, as 'the honourable member for Swindon' or 'my honourable friend'.

honours degree /ˈɒnəz dɪˌgriː/ (education) A *first degree* at a university obtained with distinction, with the student obtaining a 'class I', 'class II' or 'class III' degree, as distinct from a *pass degree*.

Hooray Henry /ˌhuːreɪ ˈhenrɪ/ (life and society) A term used for a male *Sloane Ranger*, especially someone who has a loud voice or is unusually jolly.

hopscotch /ˈhɒpskɒtʃ/ (sport and leisure) A game popular among young children. A player throws a stone or other small object into one of a number of squares chalked or scratched on the ground in a particular arrangement, and then hops to it through the other squares to pick it up. [from 'hop' and 'scotch', the latter word meaning 'trace (a line)']

hornpipe /ˈhɔːnpaɪp/ (sport and leisure) A lively traditional sailors' dance, performed by one person, originally to a hornpipe (an old instrument like a clarinet) but today to any solo instrument.

Horse Guards /ˈhɔːs gɑːdz/, **the (1 defence 2 London) 1** A cavalry regiment of the *Army* which, together with the *Life Guards*, forms the *Household Cavalry* (today as part of the *Blues and Royals*). **2** The building in *Whitehall[1]*, *London*, where the daily *Changing of the Guard* by the mounted guards of the Household Cavalry is a popular tourist attraction. See also *Horse Guards Parade*.

Horse Guards Parade /ˌhɔːs gɑːdz pəˈreɪd/ (London) A parade-ground behind the *Horse Guards[2]* where the annual ceremony of *Trooping the Colour* takes place on the sovereign's *Official Birthday*.

Horse of the Year Show /ˌhɔːs əv ðə ˈjɪə ˈʃəʊ/, **the** (sport and leisure) An annual show-jumping contest held in October, usually at *Wembley* or the *White City* in London. The contest, which decides the leading show jumpers of the year, was first held in 1949.

hopscotch

horse's neck /ˌhɔːsɪz ˈnek/ (food and drink) A colloquial term for an alcoholic drink of brandy and ginger ale.

hospice /ˈhɒspɪs/ (medicine) A hospital or home for the care of the terminally ill.

hot cross bun /ˌhɒt krɒs ˈbʌn/ (food and drink) A bun containing currants or candied peel, marked on top with a cross and traditionally eaten hot (toasted) with butter on *Good Friday*.

hotpot /ˈhɒtpɒt/ (food and drink) A hot dish especially popular in the north of *England*, consisting of a stew or casserole of meat (less often, fish) cooked with sliced potatoes. A common version is the Lancashire hotpot.

house /haʊs/ (education) In a school such as a *preparatory school* or *public school¹*, a building where a group of pupils lives. Each group of pupils is seen as having a distinctive group identity especially in competitions within the school. The term 'house' is also used in some day schools for such a group of pupils.

House /haʊs/, **the** (1 government 2 finance) 1 A short name for the *House of Commons* (less often, the *House of Lords*) 2 A short name for the *Stock Exchange* in *London*.

House of Commons /ˌhaʊs əv ˈkɒmənz/, **the** (government) The lower house of the British parliament, consisting of 650 elected *MPs*: 523 for *England*, 38 for *Wales*, 72 for *Scotland* and 17 for *Northern Ireland*. The main purpose of the House of Commons is to make the laws of the land by passing various *Acts (of Parliament)*, as well as to discuss current political issues. The House sits for five days each week. Each 'sitting' starts in the afternoon and may go on throughout the night. The House sits for about 175 days in the year and has a maximum term of five years, at the end of which a *General Election* must be held. Compare *House of Lords*.

House of Lords /ˌhaʊs əv ˈlɔːdz/, **the** (government) The upper house of the British parliament, consisting of over 1,000 non-elected members (*Lords Spiritual* and *Lords Temporal*). Its work is largely complementary to that of the *House of Commons* and includes examining and revising *bills* from the Commons, and discussing important matters which the Commons cannot find time to debate. It also acts in a legal capacity as a final court of appeal (see *Law Lords*). The House usually sits for four days a week (on average, 150 days in the year) and has an average daily attendance of about 300 *peers*.

housefather/housemother /ˈhaʊsˌfɑːðə(r)/ˈhaʊsˌmʌðə(r)/ (education) A man/woman in charge of a boarding house in a *special school* or a residential establishment for children such as a children's home or *community home*.

Household Cavalry /ˌhaʊshəʊld ˈkævlrɪ/, **the** (defence) A section of the *Army*, comprising the two regiments of the *Life Guards* and the *Blues and Royals*, that among other duties attends the sovereign and carries out special ceremonial functions in *London*. See also *Horse Guards*.

Household Troops /ˌhaʊshəʊld ˈtruːps/, **the** (defence) A general term for the cavalry regiments of the *Army* (the *Household Cavalry*) who with the five infantry regiments of the *Guards Division* carry out special escort and guard duties for the sovereign.

housemaster /ˈhaʊsˌmɑːstə(r)/ (education) A teacher in charge of a *house*, especially in a boys' boarding school.

housemistress /ˈhaʊsˌmɪstrɪs/ (education) A teacher in charge of a *house*, especially in a girls' boarding school.

Houses of Parliament /ˌhaʊzɪz əv ˈpɑːləmənt/, **the** (government) The buildings in *London* in which the *House of Commons* and the *House of Lords* assemble. The modern buildings stand on the site of the Royal *Palace of Westminster[1]*, which was built by Edward the Confessor in the 14th century. The Palace was very badly damaged by fire in 1834 and all that could be saved was *Westminster Hall*. The present Houses of Parliament were built on the site between 1840 and 1867 from designs by Sir Charles Barry and Augustus Pugin. The House of Commons was bombed during the Second World War but was completely rebuilt by 1950.

housing association /'haʊzɪŋ əsəʊsɪˌeɪʃn/ (finance) A local
organization that provides rented homes for poorer families
and in particular for elderly, disabled and single people. It
also shares ownership of a house with people who cannot
afford to buy a house without considerable financial help.

housing estate /'haʊzɪŋ ɪˌsteɪt/ (daily life) A planned area of
housing, either of private houses or *council houses*, usually
having its own shops and other amenities.

housing estate

hovercraft /'hɒvəkrɑːft/ (transport) The name of a vehicle able
to travel over land or sea on a 'cushion' of air beneath it, and
otherwise known as an 'air cushion vehicle'. The vehicle is
used in the *Hoverspeed* service of *BR*.

hoverport /'hɒvəpɔːt/ (transport) A port from which *hovercraft*
travel on a regular route, for example, Dover, Kent (to
Boulogne, France), and Ramsgate, Kent (to Calais, France).

Hoverspeed /'hɒvəspiːd/ (transport) A cross-Channel (*England*
to France) *hovercraft* passenger company, with routes
between Dover and Boulogne, and Dover and Calais.

Hoylake /'hɔɪleɪk/ (sport and leisure) A holiday resort on the
Irish Sea in Merseyside, with a famous golf course (the Royal
Liverpool Golf Club).

HTV /ˌeɪtʃ tiː 'viː/ (media) One of the 15 television companies
of the *IBA*, transmitting programmes to *Wales* and the *West
Country*. The company combines HTV Wales and HTV West.
HTV is the abbreviation of Harlech Television.

Humpty Dumpty /ˌhʌmptɪ 'dʌmptɪ/ (tradition) An egg-shaped
character in a popular nursery rhyme, who also features in
Lewis *Carroll*'s 'Through the Looking Glass' (1872). The name
is used figuratively for a person or thing that cannot be
restored or mended once overthrown, since in the nursery
rhyme Humpty Dumpty 'had a great fall' and 'all the king's

horses and all the king's men/Couldn't put Humpty Dumpty together again'.

Humpty Dumpty

hundred /'hʌndrəd/ (history) A former division of a *county* in *England*, having its own court and supposed to contain a hundred families. Hundreds had become established administrative units by the 10th century, and existed, though with less importance, down to the 20th century. Compare *Chiltern Hundreds*.

hundreds and thousands /ˌhʌndrədz ən 'θaʊzəndz/ (food and drink) Tiny pieces of coloured sugar, used for decorating cakes and sweets.

hunt /hʌnt/ (sport and leisure) A *club* or association of men and women who hunt animals on horseback or, less frequently, on foot. The traditionally established hunts are those that hunt foxes on horseback, using packs of hounds, with the members of the hunt wearing a special uniform (often, scarlet coats, but also green, and other colours) and having a base in a particular *county* or district. Hunting is a sport followed mainly by the *gentry*, as well as by large landowners and *gentlemen farmers*, and has in recent years come increasingly under attack from movements such as the *League Against Cruel Sports*. Animals hunted, apart from the fox, are the deer, the hare, the otter and the badger. See also *blood sports*, *field sports*, *master of foxhounds*.

hunt the thimble /ˌhʌnt ðə 'θɪmbl/ (sport and leisure) A children's game in which players in turn try to find a thimble (or other object) hidden in an unlikely place.

Hyde Park /ˌhaɪd ˈpɑːk/ (London) *London*'s best-known public
park, extending (with neighbouring *Kensington Gardens*) to
an area of 360 acres (250 hectares). It includes the *Serpentine*,
Speakers' Corner and *Rotten Row*, and has become a centre for
massed meetings and demonstrations. It was first open to the
public in 1635, and the *Great Exhibition* was held here in 1851.
[name said to derive from 'hide', a former area of land]

Hyde Park Corner /ˌhaɪd pɑːk ˈkɔːnə(r)/ (London) A road
junction at the south-east corner of *Hyde Park, London*,
regarded as one of the busiest and noisiest in *Britain*.

Hymns Ancient and Modern /ˌhɪmz ˌeɪnʃənt ən ˈmɒdn/ (**Hymns
A and M)** (religion) A well-known collection of hymns used
by the *Church of England* and first published in 1861.

INTER-CITY TRAIN

Ian Paisley /ˌiːən ˈpeɪzlɪ/ see *Paisley* (people)
IBA /ˌaɪ biː ˈeɪ/, **the (Independent Broadcasting Authority, the)**
(media) The body set up in 1972 (before this, the
Independent Television Authority) to appoint and co-
ordinate the television and radio stations that operate
independently of those managed by the *BBC*. The Authority
operates 15 regional television companies and 43 *local radio*
stations. Finance for the running of all television and radio
stations is provided solely by commercial advertising (ie, by
the fees paid by the companies whose advertisements are
broadcast on television and radio). See also *Channel Four, ILR,
IRN, ITN, TV-am*.
Ibrox Park /ˌaɪbrɒks ˈpɑːk/ (sport and leisure) The stadium in
Glasgow, Scotland, of *Rangers* football club.
ICI /ˌaɪ siː ˈaɪ/ **(Imperial Chemical Industries)** (science and
technology) The largest chemical concern in *Britain*, formed
in 1926 from four other chemical companies. Among the
group's principal products are pharmaceuticals, paints,
plastics and petrochemicals.
Ideal Home Exhibition /ˌaɪdiːl ˈhəʊm eksɪˌbɪʃn/, **the**
(commerce) An annual exhibition of house interiors,
furniture, and a wide range of household items, sponsored
by the *Daily Mail* and held in Spring at *Earls Court, London*.
Illustrated London News /ˌɪləstreɪtɪd ˌlʌndən ˈnjuːz/, **the**
(media) A monthly news magazine with high-quality
photographs illustrating topical and cultural affairs of British
and international interest and with a series of regular articles
on a wide range of subjects, from politics to archaeology.
ILR /ˌaɪ el ˈɑː(r)/ **(Independent Local Radio)** (media) The *IBA*
body that provides the services for the companies that
operate the IBA's *local radio* stations. The first stations were
introduced in 1973 (see *Capital Radio, LBC*), and their
programmes are similar to those operated by the *BBC*. News
is supplied to the ILR companies by *IRN*.
Imperial War Museum /ɪmˌpɪərɪəl ˈwɔː mjuːˌzɪəm/, **the**
(defence) A military museum in *London*, founded in 1917. It
illustrates all aspects of the two world wars and other military

operations in which *Britain* and the *Commonwealth* have been involved since 1914.

inch /ɪntʃ/ (daily life) A measure of length still in common use, together with the *foot*, for a person's height and certain other regular measurements. There are twelve inches in a foot, with one inch equal to 2.54 cm.

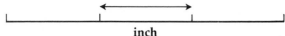

inch

income tax /ˈɪŋkəm ˌtæks/ (finance) A personal tax which is levied on the amount of money a person earns in a year or on the amount of money a person receives from investments in a year. The higher the amount of money earned, the higher the tax charged. See *Inland Revenue, PAYE*.

independent school /ɪndɪˈpendənt skuːl/ (education) A fee-paying school, usually a *public school*[1] or *preparatory school*, that operates outside the state system. Many such schools are long established and have gained a reputation for their high standards; however, only approximately 6% of all school children attend independent schools. See also *private school.*

industrial action /ɪnˌdʌstrɪəl ˈækʃn/ (work) A term used for a strike or an industrial protest of some kind, such as a *go-slow* or *work-to-rule*.

industrial council /ɪnˌdʌstrɪəl ˈkaʊnsl/ (work) A general name for a *Whitley council.*

industrial estate /ɪnˈdʌstrɪəl ɪˌsteɪt/ (work) An area of a town, usually on the outskirts, set aside for factories or the commercial premises of various firms.

Industrial Revolution /ɪnˌdʌstrɪəl revəˈluːʃn/, **the** (history) The great economic and social change that happened in *Britain* starting in the second half of the 18th century. Agricultural and home-based trades and industries gradually gave way to factory-based industries with complex machinery. As a result, many people who had previously been employed in agriculture moved to towns and cities. Britain was the first country to become industrialized in this way.

infant school /ˈɪnfənt skuːl/ (education) A school for very young children from the age of five, when compulsory education begins, to seven. See also *first school.*

Inland Revenue /ˌɪnlənd ˈrevənjuː/, **the** (finance) The government *department* (in full, Board of Inland Revenue) that administers the tax laws and is responsible for collecting *income tax* from employees. See also *PAYE*.

in-laws /ˈɪn lɔːz/, **the** (life and society) A colloquial term for the close relatives of a person's wife or husband. [short for 'mother-in-law', 'brother-in-law', etc.]

inn /ɪn/ (daily life) An alternative term for a *pub* or (usually small) hotel, often occurring in the name of the house, as the 'New Inn', the 'Market Inn'. The term suggests an old or historic building with 'character'.

inn sign /ˈɪn saɪn/ (daily life) A painted signboard outside a *pub* illustrating its name.

Inner Temple /ˌɪnə ˈtempl/, **the** (law) The oldest and best known of the *Inns of Court*. See also *Temple[1]*.

Inns of Court /ˌɪnz əv ˈkɔːt/, **the** (law) The four societies, and their buildings, to one or other of which all *barristers* and judges belong. The societies (*Lincoln's Inn, Inner Temple, Middle Temple, Gray's Inn*) are in central *London* and have been in existence at least since the 14th century. Today their buildings are largely used as offices (*chambers[1]*) where about 2,000 barristers practise, although there are also flats there where people live.

Institute of Directors /ˌɪnstɪtjuːt əv dɪˈrektəz/, **the** (work) One of the largest organizations for businessmen, founded in 1903. Its members are mainly company directors, *stockbrokers* and lawyers.

insurance broker /ɪnˈʃɔːrəns ˌbrəʊkə(r)/ (finance) An agent who arranges various types of insurance for other people and who charges commission for doing this.

Intelpost /ˈɪntelpəʊst/ (commerce) An international transmission service of the *Post Office*, by which letters and other documents are sent in facsimile copies by satellite. [from 'international satellite *post*']

InterCity train /ˌɪntəˌsɪtɪ ˈtreɪn/ (transport) A fast main line train of *BR* that runs between major cities, for example, *London*—Cardiff, Birmingham—Manchester, Newcastle— *Edinburgh*. Some InterCity trains are officially known as 'InterCity 125 High Speed Trains'. These trains have special diesel engines (one at each end). The engines and carriages are modern and streamlined in design and, because of this, the '125' trains have a maximum speed of 125 miles an hour (201 km an hour).

intermediate area /ɪntəˈmiːdɪət ˌeərɪə/ (work) An *assisted area* where the government encourages industrial investment. Of the two types of assisted area, the intermediate area is regarded as being in least urgent need of aid. Compare *development area* and see also *special development area*.

Inverness /ˌɪnvəˈnes/ (geography) A town in northern *Scotland* that is a popular tourist centre and 'capital' of the *Highlands*.

investment trust /ɪnˈvestmənt trʌst/ (finance) An organization that invests its members' money and distributes the profits among them.

Iona /aɪˈəʊnə/ (geography) A small, historic island off the west coast of *Scotland*, close to Mull in the *Hebrides*. It has many important early Christian monuments, and several Scottish, Irish and Norwegian kings of this period are buried here. The island is popular with tourists in the summer.

IOU /ˌaɪ əʊ ˈjuː/ (finance) A note of a debt given by a borrower to a person who has lent him a sum of money. [pronunciation of 'I owe you']

IRA /ˌaɪ ɑːr 'eɪ/, **the (Irish Republican Army, the)** (politics) A militant organization of Irish nationalists aiming to establish a united Irish Republic by campaigns of violence and terror. Since 1969 they have been increasingly active in mainland *Britain*, as well as in *Northern Ireland*.

Ireland /'aɪələnd/ (geography) The most westerly country of the *British Isles*, separated from mainland *Britain* by St George's Channel and the Irish Sea. The name Ireland can be used to apply to the island as a geographical entity, but is normally used to mean the Republic of Ireland, as distinct from *Northern Ireland*, which is part of the *United Kingdom*.

Irish coffee /ˌaɪərɪʃ 'kɒfɪ/ (food and drink) An alcoholic drink consisting of a mixture of Irish *whiskey* with coffee, sugar, and cream. Compare *Gaelic coffee*.

Irish Guards /ˌaɪərɪʃ 'gɑːdz/, **the** (defence) The fourth oldest regiment of the *Guards Division* of the *Army* formed in 1900.

Irish Republican Army /ˌaɪərɪʃ rɪˌpʌblɪkən 'ɑːmɪ/ see *IRA* (politics)

Irish setter /ˌaɪərɪʃ 'setə(r)/ (animal world) A breed of working dog with smooth, silky coat, always chestnut in colour. Compare *English setter*.

Irish stew /ˌaɪərɪʃ 'stjuː/ (food and drink) A stew of mutton (less often, lamb or beef), onions and potatoes. [said to have been originally a meatless stew, as the only kind poor Irish peasants could afford]

IRN /ˌaɪ ɑːr 'en/ **(Independent Radio News)** (media) A national and international news service provided by *LBC* for all the radio stations operated by the *IBA*.

Isis /'aɪsɪs/ (**1** geography **2** sport and leisure) **1** The name of the river *Thames* as it flows through *Oxford¹*. Compare *Granta*. **2** The reserve crew of *Oxford University* for the *Oxford²* and *Cambridge²* Boat Race. Compare *Goldie crew*.

Isle of Man /ˌaɪl əv 'mæn/, **the** (geography) An island of the *British Isles* between *England* and *Northern Ireland*, in the Irish Sea. The Isle of Man is not part of the *United Kingdom*, but is a self-governing crown dependency, with the monarch represented by a lieutenant-governor. It thus has its own parliament (the *Tynwald*), and its own system of local administration, with its own law courts. It is popular with tourists from *Britain* and some Britons come here to live, partly because of its low tax rate. It is famous for the annual *TT* motorcycle races held here. See also *Manx* and compare *Channel Islands*.

Isle of Wight /ˌaɪl əv 'waɪt/, **the** (geography) An island off the south coast of *England*, and an English *county* in its own right. It is popular with tourists and has a sunny climate and mostly mild weather. It is well known for its many seaside resorts, at one of which *Cowes Week* is held.

I-spy /ˌaɪ 'spaɪ/ (sport and leisure) A children's guessing game. One player names the first letter of an object he can see (with the rhyming formula, 'I spy, with my little eye, something beginning with P'), and the others have to guess what the object is.

ITA /ˌaɪ tiː ˈeɪ/, **the (Initial Teaching Alphabet, the)** (language) A special alphabet of 44 characters, sometimes used for teaching children to read. Each character corresponds to a sound in the English language.

ITN /ˌaɪ tiː ˈen/ **(Independent Television News)** (media) A company (non profit-making) that provides a common news service for all the 15 television companies operated by the *IBA*. See *News at Ten*.

It's a Long Way to Tipperary /ɪts ə ˌlɒŋ weɪ tə tɪpəˈreərɪ/ (tradition) A popular marching song, originally composed in 1912, and sung by troops embarking for France in the First World War. [referring to the girl left behind in Tipperary, *Ireland*]

ITV /ˌaɪ tiː ˈviː/ **(Independent Television)** (media) A general term used for the television programmes broadcast by the 15 companies appointed by the *IBA*.

Jack Russell (terrier) /ˌdʒæk ˈrʌsl (ˌdʒæk ˌrʌsl ˈterɪə(r))/ (animal world) One of a number of breeds of small terrier. The original breed, introduced by John Russell, a 19th-century clergyman, is now extinct. [from Jack, a familiar form of the name John]

Jack the Giant-Killer /ˌdʒæk ðə ˈdʒaɪənt ˌkɪlə(r)/ (tradition) The legendary Cornish hero of a tale of *King Arthur*. He had a cap that made him invisible, seven-league boots and a magic sword, and went round the country killing troublesome giants.

Jack the Ripper /ˌdʒæk ðə ˈrɪpə(r)/ (history) The nickname given to the undiscovered murderer of at least seven women in *London* in 1888. See also *Yorkshire Ripper*. ['ripper' meaning 'cutter': all the victims had their throats cut]

Jackie /ˈdʒækɪ/ (media) A weekly comic for teenage girls containing love stories in photographs, and features on romance, pop music and fashion.

Jack-in-the-box /ˈdʒæk ɪn ðə ˌbɒks/ (tradition) A toy consisting of a box containing a doll that springs out when the box is opened.

Jacobean /ˌdʒækəˈbiːən/ (style) **1** A furniture style of the 17th century, characterized by the use of dark oak with rich carving, particularly in wooden armchairs with high backs and straight seats and arms. **2** An architectural style of the same period, characterized by its straight lines and symmetry and similar to the *Elizabethan* style but with curved arches. [found in the reign of James I (1603–25) whose Latin name was 'Jacobus']

Jaguar /ˈdʒæɡjʊə(r)/ (transport) An expensive make of car manufactured by *BL*, colloquially known as a 'Jag'.

jamboree /ˌdʒæmbəˈriː/ (sport and leisure) **1** A large rally of *Scouts* or *Guides*. **2** A slightly dated term for a party or large gathering.

Jane Austen /ˌdʒeɪn ˈɒstɪn/ see *Austen* (people)

Jayne Torvill and Christopher Dean /ˌdʒeɪn ˈtɔːvɪl ən ˌkrɪstəfə ˈdiːn/ see *Torvill and Dean* (people)

jersey /ˈdʒɜːzɪ/ (clothing) **1** A warm knitted long-sleeved garment, originally woollen but now often of man-made fibre, for the upper part of the body. **2** A fine machine-knitted fabric (of wool, cotton, nylon, etc) used for clothing. [from the sweaters traditionally worn by the fishermen of Jersey, *Channel Islands*; compare *guernsey*]

Jersey (cow) /ˈdʒɜːzɪ (ˌdʒɜːzɪ ˈkaʊ)/ (animal world) A breed of dairy cow with dark red or light brown colouring, famous for its rich milk. [originally bred in Jersey, *Channel Islands*]

Jerusalem /dʒəˈruːsələm/ (tradition) The title of a hymn with words by William Blake (1757–1827) traditionally sung at the end of a meeting by members of the *WI*. [from the reference in the hymn to building 'Jerusalem in England's green and pleasant land']

Jerusalem Bible /dʒəˌruːsələm ˈbaɪbl/**, the** (religion) A translation of the Bible into modern English by Roman Catholic scholars, first published in 1966. [translated in Jerusalem]

Jiffybag /ˈdʒɪfɪ ˌbæg/ (daily life) The trade name of a type of padded envelope used for sending books and other articles through the post. [from 'jiffy', a colloquial term for 'moment', 'instant': the envelopes are designed to pack articles 'in a jiffy']

job release scheme /ˌdʒɒb rɪˈliːs skiːm/ (work) A scheme introduced in the 1980s to encourage older employees to retire early and so release jobs for younger unemployed people.

jobber /ˈdʒɒbə(r)/ (finance) A short term for a *stock-jobber*.

Jobcentre /ˈdʒɒbˌsentə(r)/ (work) A local government office in a town where notices of job vacancies are on display and where a person wanting advice about a job can consult an employment adviser. The surroundings in a Jobcentre are more informal than in the older *employment offices*.

jobs for the boys /ˌdʒɒbz fə ðə ˈbɔɪz/ (work) A term used to describe jobs or posts given to a person's close friends or associates.

Jock /dʒɒk/ (tradition) A colloquial name for a Scotsman, especially a soldier in the *Scots Guards*. [Scottish form of 'Jack', itself a general name for a man]

Jockey Club /ˈdʒɒkɪ ˌklʌb/**, the** (sport and leisure) The governing body of horse racing, founded in the 1750s.

jodhpurs /ˈdʒɒdpəz/ (clothing) A type of riding breeches worn by men and women, loose-fitting round the hips and tight-fitting from the thighs down to the ankles.

Jodrell Bank /ˌdʒɒdrəl ˈbæŋk/ (science and technology) The astronomical laboratory near Macclesfield, Cheshire, that is officially called the Nuffield Radio Astronomy Laboratories of Manchester University. It is famous for its giant radio telescope, which was first used in 1957. The Observatory itself was founded in 1947. [local name for land on which the laboratory was built]

John Bull /ˌdʒɒn 'bʊl/ (tradition) A personification of *England* or the English, originally represented (in a political satire of 1712 by John Arbuthnot) as a bluff, kind-hearted, bull-headed farmer.

John Gielgud /ˌdʒɒn 'giːlgʊd/ see *Gielgud* (people)

John Milton /ˌdʒɒn 'mɪltən/ see *Milton* (people)

John o'Groats /ˌdʒɒn ə'grəʊts/ (geography) A village in the extreme north west of the Scottish mainland, traditionally regarded as the northernmost point of mainland *Britain* (compare *Land's End*). [said to be named after a Dutchman, Jan de Groot, who built a house here in the late 15th century]

Joneses /'dʒəʊnzɪz/, **the** (life and society) A term used to refer to one's neighbours in the phrase, 'to keep up with the Joneses', meaning 'to be (seen to be) socially and materially equal to one's neighbours'. [Jones is one of the most common British surnames; the phrase originated in an American comic strip cartoon before the First World War]

JP /ˌdʒeɪ 'piː/ **(Justice of the Peace)** (law) An unpaid *magistrate* appointed by the *Lord Chancellor* to 'keep the peace' in a particular area, or deal with minor criminal offences (without a *jury*) in a court of law.

Judy /'dʒuːdɪ/ (media) A weekly *comic* for schoolgirls.

jugged hare /ˌdʒʌgd 'heə(r)/ (food and drink) A stew of hare cooked in an earthenware pot or casserole, usually with wine and seasoning, and served with red currant sauce. [special use of 'jug']

juggernaut /'dʒʌgənɔːt/ (transport) A word for any large, heavy lorry or truck, especially one driven along narrow roads or through a town and threatening other road users or local residents. [from the Hindi name, meaning 'lord of the world', of the god Vishnu, whose idol was pulled through the town of Puri, India, on a gigantic chariot, with worshippers throwing themselves under the chariot's wheels as a form of self-sacrifice]

jumble sale /'dʒʌmbl ˌseɪl/ (daily life) A sale of varied, cheap, secondhand goods or home-made wares, with the profit usually going to a charity.

jury /'dʒʊərɪ/ (law) A group of twelve people sworn to deliver a verdict ('guilty' or 'not guilty') according to the evidence put before them in a criminal case in a *court*[3] of law. Normally, their verdict is a unanimous one; but it may also be a majority verdict, provided that there are not more than two people who disagree. If agreement cannot be reached, there must be a retrial.

juvenile court /ˌdʒuːvənaɪl 'kɔːt/ (law) A *court*[3] of law that hears the case of a young person aged 10 to 16.

KEW GARDENS

Kelly's (Directories) /ˈkelɪz (ˌkelɪz daɪˈrektərɪz)/ (media) A series of *county* and town directories of *England* giving commercial and private addresses, details of local authorities and postal information. They were first published in 1799.

Kempton Park /ˌkemptən ˈpɑːk/ (sport and leisure) A race course in Surrey near Sunbury, southwest *London*. [named after park here]

Kennel Club /ˈkenl ˌklʌb/, **the** (animal world) A *London club* for dog breeders and showers, founded in 1873.

Kensington /ˈkenzɪŋtən/ (London) A fashionable district of southwest central *London*, famous for its high-class shops and stores, its luxury homes and its foreign embassies.

Kensington Gardens /ˌkenzɪŋtən ˈgɑːdnz/ (London) A park extending to the west of *Hyde Park*, and originally the private gardens of *Kensington Palace*. The Gardens are famous for the *Round Pond*, and for the statue of *Peter Pan*[3].

Kensington Palace /ˌkenzɪŋtən ˈpælɪs/ (London) A royal palace in *Kensington, London*, originally known as Nottingham House (as the home of the Earl of Nottingham) but bought in 1689 by King William III and from then until 1760 the main private residence of the sovereign. *Queen Victoria* was born here in 1819, and Queen Mary, wife of George V, in 1867. Today part of the building is still occupied by relations of the *royal family* and certain aristocratic pensioners. The *London Museum* was here until 1976. See *Museum of London*.

Kentish Man /ˌkentɪʃ ˈmæn/ (geography) A traditional name for a native of west Kent (strictly, one born west of the river Medway). Compare *Man of Kent*.

Kenwood /ˈkenwʊd/ (London) A fine mansion house, open to the public, in *Hampstead*, northwest *London*. The house is famous for its art collection and for its park, in which open air concerts are held in the summer.

Kew Gardens /ˌkjuː ˈgɑːdnz/ (London) The name usually used for the Royal Botanical Gardens which are beside the river *Thames* at Kew in west *London*. The Gardens are mainly a centre for botanical research, but are open to the public and are famous for their hothouses, landscaped park, lake and water garden and their interesting buildings.

Kidderminster (carpet) /ˈkɪdəmɪnstə(r) (ˌkɪdəmɪnstə ˈkɑːpɪt)/ (style) A type of reversible carpet made from wool fibres that are dyed before they are spun into yarn. [as originally manufactured at Kidderminster, in the county of Hereford and Worcester]

kilt /kɪlt/ (clothing) Part of the traditional dress of a Scotsman: a heavy pleated woollen skirt, usually of *tartan¹*, in front of which is worn a *sporran*. The kilt is part of the uniform of a *highlander²*.

kilt

kindergarten /ˈkɪndəgɑːtn/ (education) An alternative term for a *nursery school*, especially a private one.

king /kɪŋ/ (royal family) The title of a male sovereign. The last king of the *United Kingdom* was George VI (reigned 1936–52). Compare *queen*.

King Arthur /ˌkɪŋ ˈɑːθə(r)/ (people) King Arthur is a half-legendary, half-historical king of *Britain* and the hero of several tales of medieval romance, the so-called 'Arthurian cycle' with the famous *Knights of the Round Table* and the magician Merlin. The historical King Arthur may have been a Briton who fought against the invading Anglo-Saxons in the 5th century. His 'kingdom' is traditionally set in the *West Country*, with his 'capital' in the Somerset town of Glastonbury. Stories about King Arthur and his knights have been constantly told for many centuries. The name of King Arthur is still preserved in popular affection as that of a national hero and king.

King Charles spaniel /ˌkɪŋ tʃɑːlz ˈspænjəl/ (animal world) One of four breeds of toy spaniel (King Charles, Tricolour, Ruby, Blenheim). The King Charles has a black coat with bright tan markings. [the breed was popularized by King Charles II]

King James Bible /ˌkɪŋ dʒeɪmz ˈbaɪbl/, **the** (religion) An alternative name for the *Authorized Version* of the Bible, whose translation was authorized by King James I.

King's College Hospital /ˌkɪŋz ˌkɒlɪdʒ ˈhɒspɪtl/ (medicine) A teaching hospital in south *London* that was originally part of King's *College[1]*, which itself is part of *London University*.

King's Cross /ˌkɪŋz ˈkrɒs/ (transport) **1** A main line railway station in north central *London*, a terminus of the Eastern Region of *BR*. **2** An Underground station in the same place as the main line station. See *London Underground*. [from crossroads here, where a statue of King George IV stood for the 15 years from 1833]

King's School /ˌkɪŋz ˈskuːl/ (education) The name of certain *public schools[1]*, especially former *cathedral schools* that were reorganized by King *Henry VIII* during the Reformation. Some of the schools are still in cathedral cities, including those of *Canterbury*, Chester, and Worcester.

Kinnock, Neil /ˈkɪnək, niːl/ (people) Neil Kinnock (born 1942) was elected leader of the *Labour Party* and *Leader of the Opposition* in 1983, having been an *MP* in *Wales* since 1970. A Welshman with a *working class* background, he represents the left wing of his party, and has shown himself to be an articulate and eloquent speaker and a man of principle, without being autocratic. After his election, public opinion polls showed a sharp swing back to the Labour Party, whose popularity had decreased since the *Conservative Party* came to power in 1979. Many of Neil Kinnock's supporters believe that he will be the next *Prime Minister* after Margaret *Thatcher*.

kirk /kɜːk/, **the** (religion) **1** A word sometimes used for a Scottish church, especially one belonging to the *Church of Scotland*. **2** A colloquial term sometimes used for the Church of Scotland itself, especially by people who do not belong to it.

kitemark /ˈkaɪtmɑːk/ (daily life) An official mark, representing a stylized toy kite, on products that conform to the safety standards set by the *BSI*. [mark is formed as monogram of letters BSI enclosed in a triangle]

kitemark

knees-up /'niːz ʌp/ (daily life) A colloquial term for a (lively) party or gathering. [from the opening words of the popular song of the 1930s, 'Knees up, Mother Brown!']

Knights of the Round Table /ˌnaɪts əv ðə ˌraʊnd 'teɪbl/**, the** (tradition) The legendary group of knights, 150 in number, created by *King Arthur*. Among the best known are Sir Lancelot, Sir Galahad, Sir Gawain and Sir Tristram. See also *Round Table*.

Knightsbridge /'naɪtsbrɪdʒ/ (London) A fashionable district in *London*'s *West End*, well-known for its high-class shops and in particular for its jewellers' shops and antique shops.

Labour Party /'leɪbə ˌpɑːtɪ/, **the** (politics) One of the two largest political parties in *Britain* (together with the *Conservative Party*). It claims to represent the interests of the *working class* (ie, labour) as against the interests of the employers (who represent capital). It grew up at the end of the 19th century, first taking the name Labour Party in 1906. It draws most of its support from highly urban and industrialized areas, particularly in the *Midlands* and the north of *England*, and, as well as being the main party for working class people, it is also supported by a significant number of *middle class* people, especially intellectuals. Its policies are closely connected with those of the trade union movement (see *TUC*). Compare *Liberal Party* and *SDP*.

lady /'leɪdɪ/ (life and society) **1** A general term used to refer to any woman, and now much more acceptable than 'woman' which many people think is less polite. 'Lady' is often used with another word to describe a particular job, for example, *dinner lady* and *lollipop lady*. **2** A woman regarded as possessing the best British characteristics, in particular culture, courtesy and consideration for the needs of others. Compare *gentleman*². **3** (Lady) A title of honour borne by various classes of women of the *peerage*. **4** A woman who comes from an *upper class* or aristocratic family, whether officially having the title 'Lady' or not.

Lady Chapel /'leɪdɪ ˌtʃæpl/ (religion) In most cathedrals and some large churches, a *chapel*¹ dedicated to the Virgin Mary, usually situated behind the high altar.

Lady Day /'leɪdɪ ˌdeɪ/ (religion) 25 March, the day of the feast of the Annunciation of the Virgin Mary, celebrated in many *Anglican* and all *Roman Catholic Church*es with a special service. It is not a *bank holiday*.

lady-in-waiting /ˌleɪdɪ ɪn 'weɪtɪŋ/ (royal family) A woman, often a member of the *gentry*, appointed to be a personal attendant to the sovereign or to some other member of the *royal family*.

laird /leəd/ (life and society) The title of a landowner in *Scotland*. [form of 'lord']

Lake District /'leɪk ˌdɪstrɪkt/, **the** (geography) A picturesque district of northeast *England* in Cumbria, popular with tourists and famous for its lakes and mountain peaks. It is a *national park*.

Lake Poets /ˌleɪk 'pəʊɪts/, **the** (arts) The name used for the poets William Wordsworth, Samuel Taylor Coleridge and Robert Southey, who lived in the *Lake District* in the 19th century and drew inspiration for much of their poetry from the scenery there.

Lake School /'leɪk skuːl/, **the** (arts) A collective term for the *Lake Poets*.

Lambeth Conference /ˌlæmbəθ 'kɒnfərəns/, **the** (religion) A conference of bishops of the *Church of England* held every ten years (since 1867) at *Lambeth Palace, London*.

Lambeth Palace /ˌlæmbəθ 'pælɪs/ (religion) The *London* residence of the *Archbishop of Canterbury*, in the district of Lambeth, south of the *Thames*.

Lambeth walk /ˌlæmbəθ 'wɔːk/, **the** (tradition) A popular *cockney*[2] dance, traditionally performed on a street with all the dancers in line. It was specially popular in the 1930s. It is also the name of a song. [named after Lambeth Walk, a street in Lambeth, south *London*]

Lancashire (cheese) /'læŋkəʃə(r) (ˌlæŋkəʃə 'tʃiːz)/ (food and drink) A type of crumbly, white cheese with a mild flavour. [originally from Lancashire]

Lancaster House /ˌlæŋkəstə 'haʊs/ (government) A grand house in central *London* used mainly for government conferences. It was built in 1825 for the Duke of York (as York House) but was bought in 1912 by Sir William Lever (later Lord Leverhulme) who changed its name to that of the county where he grew up and presented it to the nation. The *London Museum* was housed in it until 1946.

Lancet /'lɑːnsɪt/, **The** (medicine) A weekly journal for doctors and members of the medical profession. It was first published in 1823 and had a circulation in 1981 of over 28,000.

Land of Hope and Glory /ˌlænd əv ˌhəʊp ən 'glɔːrɪ/ (tradition) A popular patriotic song, originally glorifying the *British Empire* when first sung in 1902 (words by A C Benson (1862–1925), music by Edward *Elgar* (1857–1934)), but still sung on special occasions, and traditionally performed at the *Last Night of the Proms*.

Land of my Fathers /ˌlænd əv maɪ 'fɑːðəz/ (tradition) The (unofficial) national anthem of the Welsh, first published in 1860. [Welsh, 'Hen Wlad fy Nhadau']

landlady /'lændleɪdɪ/ (daily life) A woman who owns or runs a boarding house or lodgings, or who rents out a *bedsit(ter)*.

Land's End /ˌlændz 'end/ (geography) The extreme southwest point of *England*, in *Cornwall*, and a popular tourist attraction. The total length of *Britain* is traditionally expressed as 'from Land's End to *John o'Groats*', a distance of 603 miles

(970.4 km) in a straight line, or 900 miles (1448.4 km) by road.

landslide (victory) /'lændslaɪd (ˌlændslaɪd 'vɪktərɪ)/ (politics) In an election, especially a *general election*, either a massive change of votes from one party to another, or a considerably increased majority for a party already in power.

lardy cake /'lɑːdɪ keɪk/ (food and drink) A rich, sweet cake or loaf made of bread dough, with lard, dried fruit and other ingredients. The cake is traditionally found in the south of *England*.

Last Night of the Proms /ˌlɑːst ˌnaɪt əv ðə 'prɒmz/, **the** (arts) The final performance of the annual *Promenade Concerts*, when the audience is traditionally very lively (eg, waving flags and banners, joining in the chorus of the songs) and when favourite musical compositions are usually performed, among them a version of the *hornpipe* and the accompanied song *Land of Hope and Glory*. At the end of the performance, the conductor usually makes a speech to the audience. See *promenader*.

latchkey child /'lætʃkiː ˌtʃaɪld/ (life and society) A child who returns from school to let himself in with his own key to an empty house or flat, since his parents are both out at work.

Law Lords /'lɔː lɔːdz/, **the** (law) *Peer*s in the *House of Lords* who sit as the highest *court*[3] of appeal in *England*. They include the *Lord Chancellor* and any peers who have held high judicial office or have themselves been Lord Chancellor. See *peer*[3].

Law Society /'lɔː səˌsaɪətɪ/, **the** (law) The professional body, founded in 1825, that registers *solicitors* and investigates complaints about the conduct of any solicitor.

Laxton's Superb /ˌlækstənz suː'pɜːb/ (food and drink) A variety of late eating apple with large, red-skinned fruit. [after the firm of Laxton Brothers, who first bred it in the 1920s]

lay reader /'leɪ ˌriːdə(r)/ (religion) A person who, although not a member of the clergy, has been authorized to conduct certain religious services in a church.

LBC /ˌel biː 'siː/ **(London Broadcasting Company, the)** (media) A *local radio* station run by the *IBA*. It opened in 1973 and broadcasts 24 hours a day, transmitting mainly information programmes such as news bulletins, weather and traffic reports, as well as talks, discussions and reviews.

L-driver /'el ˌdraɪvə(r)/ (transport) A person who is learning to drive a road vehicle such as a car or motor-cycle. See also *L-plates*. ['L' for 'learner']

LEA /ˌel iː 'eɪ/ **(local education authority)** (education) The local government body that is responsible for the state schools in a district, but also *further education*, and that engages teachers, maintains school buildings and supplies school equipment and materials.

Leader of the House /ˌliːdər əv ðə ˈhaʊs/, **the** (government)
1 In the *House of Commons*, an *MP* chosen from the political
party with the highest number of seats. He is given the
responsibility of planning and supervising the government's
legislative programme and of arranging the business of the
House. In particular, he advises when any difficulty arises. It
is not an official government post so he receives no special
salary. **2** In the *House of Lords*, the chief spokesman for the
government, with functions similar to those of the Leader of
the House of Commons.

Leader of the Opposition /ˌliːdər əv ðə ɒpəˈzɪʃn/, **the**
(government) The leader of the main opposing party in the
House of Commons who, if his party wins the next *general
election*, will become *Prime Minister*. See also *Shadow Cabinet*.

League Against Cruel Sports /ˌliːg əˌgenst ˌkruəl ˈspɔːts/, **the**
(sport and leisure) An organization actively campaigning for
the abolition of all *blood sports*. The group was founded in
1924 and in recent years has become increasingly militant,
with 12,000 members in 1982.

leap year /ˈliːp jɪə(r)/ (tradition) A calendar year that has 366
days instead of the usual 365 days. This happens every fourth
year. According to popular tradition, a woman has the right
to ask a man to marry her (instead of the other way round,
which is more usual) on the 'extra' day, 29 February.

leek /liːk/ (tradition) The vegetable that is the national
emblem of *Wales*. See *daffodil*.

Leicester (cheese) /ˈlestə(r) (ˌlestə ˈtʃiːz)/ (food and drink) A
·type of rich, orange-coloured cheese with a flaky texture and
a mild flavour. [originally from Leicester]

Leicester Square /ˌlestə ˈskweə(r)/ (London) A square in
central *London* where, round a public garden, there are
several cinemas, theatres, and restaurants. [from the former
residence here of the Earl of Leicester in the 17th century]

Lent /lent/ (religion) The most solemn period of the Christian
year. It lasts for 40 days from *Ash Wednesday* to the day before
Easter, with its climax in Holy Week (the week before Easter)
which includes *Palm Sunday, Maundy Thursday* and *Good
Friday*. Traditionally, people did not eat meat or other rich
food during Lent. Today, very few Christians follow the
tradition strictly, preferring to make a smaller sacrifice, such
as not eating sweets, or giving up some minor luxury.

Levin, Bernard /ˈlevɪn, ˈbɜːnəd/ (people) Bernard Levin (born
1928), a well-known journalist, critic and broadcaster, began
his career with the *Daily Mail*, moving to *The Times* in 1971.
His writing is known for its wit, originality, depth of feeling
and enthusiasm. The subjects he chooses vary from the
serious (the murder of millions of people in Cambodia) to the
light-hearted (his liking for cheese) but they all show the
Englishman's love of talking passionately about something
that is important to him. Bernard Levin will speak out openly

against any person or practice that he feels is wrong or immoral.

Lewis Carroll /ˌluːɪs ˈkærəl/ see *Carroll* (people)

Liberal Party /ˈlɪbərəl ˌpɑːtɪ/, **the** (politics) The third largest political party in *Britain*, after the *Conservative Party* and the *Labour Party*. It began in the 19th century as a party that campaigned for the removal of unnecessary restrictions on freedom of thought and action, and that advocated the control of government in the hands of the people instead of a single class. With the appearance of the Labour Party, however, much of the considerable influence of the Liberals declined, and by the 1970s there were only a very few Liberal *MP*s. In 1981, however, it joined forces with the newly-formed *SDP* (see *Liberal-SDP Alliance*) and its position was strengthened. The Liberal Party has traditionally found most of its support in the *Celtic fringe*, but more recently in some urban areas.

Liberal-SDP Alliance /ˌlɪbərəl ˌes diː ˌpiː əˈlaɪəns/, **the** (politics) An official alliance between the *Liberal Party* and the *SDP* formed in 1981, with the aim of gaining more *seats* at a *general election* and so increasing the influence of both parties.

Liberty's /ˈlɪbətɪz/ (commerce) A large fashion store in *Regent Street, London*, founded in 1875 by Arthur Liberty. The store is famous for the distinctive design of its fabrics.

licensing hours /ˈlaɪsənsɪŋ ˌaʊəz/ (daily life) The hours when *pubs* are open for the sale of alcoholic drink. The hours vary from one part of the country to another, but are on average 11.30 am to 2.30 pm and 6.00 pm to 10.30 pm.

Life Guards /ˈlaɪf gɑːdz/, **the** (defence) The premier regiment of the British army (see *Army*), together with the *Blues and Royals*. They were first formed in 1656 and are now part of the *Household Cavalry*.

life peer /ˌlaɪf ˈpɪə(r)/ see *peer*[2] (life and society)

lifemanship /ˈlaɪfmənʃɪp/ (life and society) A term used to describe the skill in obtaining an advantage over another person or persons. [term invented in 1950 by Stephen Potter; see *gamesmanship, one-upmanship*]

light ale /ˌlaɪt ˈeɪl/ (food and drink) A general term for a light-coloured beer. Compare *bitter*.

Lilliburlero/Lillibullero /ˌlɪlɪbəˈleərəʊ/ (arts) The signature tune of the *BBC World Service*, once attributed to Purcell but now known to have existed earlier (in the 16th century). The word itself is part of a meaningless refrain in a 17th-century political ballad mocking the Irish Roman Catholic supporters of James II.

limerick /ˈlɪmərɪk/ (language) A short poem, usually about something funny or improbable. It is always five lines long and has a characteristic rhyming scheme. Limericks have been popular since the end of the 19th century and in modern times have often been indecent or vulgar. Some of the best known limericks were written by Edward Lear (1812–1888), including this one:

'There was an old man with a beard,
Who said, "It is just as I feared—
   Two owls and a hen
   Four larks and a wren
Have all built their nests in my beard!" '

limited company /ˌlɪmɪtɪd ˈkʌmpənɪ/ (finance) A company owned by the individuals and organizations who have bought shares in it, in particular a public limited company (see *PLC*). If the company gets into debt, the amount that the shareholder will be called on to pay is limited by law, and will be related to the amount of shares the shareholder has. See also *Ltd.*

Lincoln's Inn /ˌlɪŋkənz ˈɪn/ (law) One of the four *Inns of Court* in *London*. [named after the original owner of the inn here, Thomas de Lincoln]

lion /ˈlaɪən/ (tradition) The lion, the 'king of beasts', has been used as a symbol of national strength and of the British monarchy for many centuries.

Lions Club /ˈlaɪənz klʌb/ (charities) A local branch of an international association (in full, International Association of Lions Clubs) devoted to community service work. There are 750 branches in *Britain* (1982), with a total membership of about 20,000. The Association was founded in 1917.

liquorice allsorts /ˌlɪkərɪs ˈɔːlsɔːts/ (food and drink) A type of confectionery consisting of black and white or brightly coloured sweets containing liquorice. ['all sorts' for the different colours and shapes of the sweets]

listed building /ˌlɪstɪd ˈbɪldɪŋ/ (history) A building officially listed as being of architectural or historic interest, and thus one that cannot be pulled down or altered without the approval of the *local authority*.

Listener /ˈlɪsnə(r)/, **The** (media) A weekly magazine published by the *BBC* and containing articles mainly about BBC television and radio broadcasts. There are also articles about *ITV* programmes as well as book reviews, poems and reviews of the arts. It was first published in 1929 and has a circulation (1981) of over 33,000.

Little America /ˌlɪtl əˈmerɪkə/ (London) A nickname for *Grosvenor Square, London*, where the American Embassy is located.

Little Neddy /ˌlɪtl ˈnedɪ/ (government) A colloquial name for a local industrial or agricultural committee meeting of the *NEDC*. Compare *Neddy*.

Littlewoods /ˈlɪtlwʊdz/ (commerce) A leading mail order and chain store company, with branches in several larger towns and cities.

Liver bird /ˈlaɪvə bɜːd/ (tradition) A name for an inhabitant of

Liverpool. [from a mythical bird invented in the 17th century to explain the origin of the name Liverpool, and now adopted as the city's emblem]

Liverpool Street /ˈlɪvəpuːl striːt/ (transport) **1** A main line railway station in east *London*, a terminus of the Eastern Region of *BR*, especially for trains from *East Anglia*. **2** An Underground railway station here. See *London Underground*. [street named in honour of Lord Liverpool, a 19th-century *Prime Minister*]

Liverpudlian /ˌlɪvəˈpʌdlɪən/ (geography) A native or resident of Liverpool. ['pool' of Liverpool humorously altered to 'puddle']

livery company /ˈlɪvərɪ ˌkʌmpənɪ/ (tradition) One of the 83 guilds of the *City (of London)*. Such guilds are mostly descended from medieval associations of craftsmen (goldsmiths, tailors, basketmakers, etc.) and today not only maintain associations with their craft or trade but make grants to education and charity. [named for their 'livery' or special uniform worn on ceremonial occasions]

living room /ˈlɪvɪŋ ˌruːm/ (daily life) The main *ground floor* room in a house used for relaxation and for entertaining guests. Compare *front room*.

Lloyd's /lɔɪdz/ (finance) An association of *London underwriters* established in 1688. It was originally mainly concerned with marine insurance and the publication of shipping news, but today deals in a wide range of insurance policies as well as issuing a daily bulletin ('Lloyd's List') of shipping information. [named after Edward Lloyd, in whose coffee house the underwriters originally carried on their business]

Lloyds (Bank) /lɔɪdz (ˈbæŋk)/ (finance) One of the four main English banks, founded in 1865 and with branches in most towns and cities. It was first established under the name of Taylor and Lloyd, and adopted its present name in 1889.

Lloyd's Register /ˌlɔɪdz ˈredʒɪstə(r)/ (transport) A society formed in 1760 to classify ships. Today it is managed by a large committee of shipowners, shipbuilders and *underwriters*, and publishes 'Lloyd's Register Book', with details of all sea-going vessels and 'Lloyd's Register of Yachts'. [named after the coffee house where *Lloyd's* originated]

local /ˈləʊkl/ (daily life) A familiar name for a *pub*, especially one regularly visited by a person since it is close to his home or place of work.

local authority /ˌləʊkl ɔːˈθɒrətɪ/ (government) A body elected for the local government of a district such as a town or *county*, as distinct from a national government body. Examples of local authorities are a *county council, town council* or *district council*.

local radio /ˌləʊkl ˈreɪdɪəʊ/ (media) A radio station operated either by the *BBC* or the *IBA* (see *ILR*). It serves a small area, often a single city and its neighbourhood, and its programmes contain much information and material of local interest. The BBC currently operates 30 local radio stations in *England* and the *Channel Islands,* while the IBA has 43 stations throughout *Britain.* Local radio has its largest audience in the early morning, when people are having breakfast and preparing to go to work. Generally, most local radio stations broadcast news bulletins and programmes of light or popular music. Audience participation, either in the studio or by telephone, is also popular on local radio.

Loch Lomond /ˌlɒk ˈləʊmənd/ (geography) The largest lake in *Britain,* north west of *Glasgow* in south central *Scotland.* Its attractive setting among green hills and wooded mountains make it popular with tourists, who also like to visit the nature reserve at its southeast corner. 'Loch' is the Scottish word for 'lake'.

Loch Ness /ˌlɒk ˈnes/ (geography) Probably *Britain*'s best-known lake, because of the *Loch Ness monster* which may live in the deep water. It is a long lake in northern *Scotland,* where it forms part of the *Caledonian Canal.* It extends for 23 miles (36 km) and in places is over 700 feet (213 metres) in depth. 'Loch' is the Scottish word for 'lake'.

Loch Ness Monster /ˌlɒk nes ˈmɒnstə(r)/, **the** (tradition) A large prehistoric creature said to be living in the deep waters of *Loch Ness, Scotland,* but as yet, in spite of various 'sightings', not scientifically proved to exist. See also *Nessie.*

lockout /ˈlɒkaʊt/ (work) The closure of a place of employment, such as a factory, by an employer, in an attempt to persuade employees to accept terms offered during a time of dispute.

locum /ˈləʊkəm/ (medicine) A doctor or clergyman who stands in temporarily in the absence of the regular doctor (clergyman). [short for Latin 'locum tenens', 'holding the place']

lodge /lɒdʒ/ (**1** daily life **2, 3** education) **1** A small house at the entrance of the *drive²* to a *country house,* usually occupied by a *gamekeeper* or gardener. **2** The residence of the head of a *college¹* at *Cambridge University.* **3** An office for porters or other domestic staff at the entrance to a college¹ or university.

lollipop /ˈlɒlɪpɒp/ (food and drink) A large boiled sweet or toffee stuck on a short stick to be sucked.

lollipop lady/man /ˈlɒlɪpɒp ˌleɪdɪ/mæn/ (daily life) A woman or man employed by a *local authority* to help children across a busy street on their way to or from school. She or he carries a pole with a disc on the end (resembling a *lollipop*) and holds it up as a sign to stop traffic.

Lombard Street /ˈlɒmbɑːd striːt/ (finance) **1** A street in the *City (of London)* traditionally associated with banking. **2** The *London* money market in general. [named after the money-dealers from Lombardy, Italy, who came here in medieval times]

lollipop lady

London /'lʌndən/ (London) The capital of *Britain* and its
largest city, with a population of 6.7 million (1984). The
Houses of Parliament are here, as is the Queen's (see *Queen
Elizabeth*) most important residence, *Buckingham Palace*.
London stands on the river *Thames* and is an important port.
The docks and main industrial sites are in the *East End* while
the *West End* is famous for its theatres (eg, the *Palladium*) and
shops (eg, *Harrods*). The *City (of London)* is one of the most
important financial centres in the world. There are many
historical buildings in London (eg, the *Tower of London*), as
well as famous art galleries, concert halls and opera houses
(eg, the *National Gallery*, the *Royal Festival Hall* and the *Royal
Opera House*). There are several large and attractive public
parks within the city (eg, *Hyde Park*). The administrative area
of London (which consists of the City plus 32 *boroughs*[2]) is
currently managed by the *GLC*.

London Airport /ˌlʌndən 'eəpɔːt/ (transport) The official name
of *Heathrow*.

London Bridge /ˌlʌndən 'brɪdʒ/ (transport) **1** Until 1747 the
only bridge across the river *Thames* in *London*. It was rebuilt
in 1824–31, and in 1968 taken down and sold to the USA, with
a new bridge being opened on the site in 1973. **2** An
Underground railway station south of the bridge. See *London
Underground*.

London Festival Ballet /ˌlʌndən ˌfestɪvl 'bæleɪ/, **the** (arts) A
well-known ballet company performing both classical and
modern works, founded in 1950 immediately before the
Festival of Britain. The Company has no home theatre and
most of its performances are held either at major *London*
theatres such as the *Coliseum*, the *Royal Festival Hall* or
Sadler's Wells Theatre, or else at theatres round *Britain* while
on tour.

London Gazette /ˌlʌndən gəˈzet/, **the** (government) The bulletin of the British government, publishing mainly official announcements and legal advertisements, but also armed forces promotions and the *New Year Honours* and *Birthday Honours*. It first appeared (as the 'Oxford Gazette') in 1665, and today is published four times a week (including *bank holidays*).

London Library /ˌlʌndən ˈlaɪbrərɪ/, **the** (arts) *Britain*'s largest private subscription library, in central *London*. It was founded in 1841 and currently contains nearly one million books on all subjects except medical, legal and scientific.

London Mozart Players /ˌlʌndən ˈməʊtsɑːt ˌpleɪəz/, **the** (arts) A leading chamber orchestra, performing mainly the works of Mozart and Haydn.

London Museum /ˌlʌndən mjuːˈzɪəm/, **the** (London) The name of the *Museum of London* before it was reorganized and expanded in 1976.

London Philharmonic Orchestra /ˌlʌndən ˌfɪləmɒnɪk ˈɔːkɪstrə/, **the (LPO, the)** (arts) A leading British symphony orchestra, founded in 1932.

London Regional Transport /ˌlʌndən ˌriːdʒənl ˈtrænspɔːt/ **(LRT)** (transport) The body responsible for the management and operation of public transport (including the Underground (see *London Underground*)) in *Greater London*. Since 1970 the *GLC* has held responsibility for the overall policy and financial control of transport in London.

London Symphony Orchestra /ˌlʌndən ˈsɪmfənɪ ˌɔːkɪstrə/, **the (LSO, the)** (arts) A leading symphony orchestra founded in 1904. It is based at the *Barbican*.

London Tourist Board /ˌlʌndən ˈtʊərɪst bɔːd/, **the (LTB, the)** (London) A tourist service set up in *London* in 1963 to provide information for tourists visiting both London and *Britain* in general.

London Transport /ˌlʌndən ˈtrænspɔːt/ (transport) The short name of the *London Regional Transport*.

London Underground /ˌlʌndən ˈʌndəgraʊnd/, **the** (transport) The main underground railway in *Britain*, evolving in *London* in the 19th century, and now providing an extensive network of lines (not all of them underground) to most parts of *Greater London* and even areas of the *Home Counties*. The routes of the nine named lines frequently cross and, at these places, there are stations where passengers can cross from one line to another. The nine lines are: the Bakerloo Line, the Central Line, the Circle Line, the District Line, the Jubilee Line, the Metropolitan Line, the Northern Line, the Piccadilly Line and the Victoria Line. A special service operates on the *Waterloo and City Line* between *Waterloo*[1] and the *City* to provide transport for business people who come daily to London from the south of *England*. Trains on the London Underground run every day at frequent intervals from early morning to about midnight, and are usually very crowded in the 'rush hour' (between about 8.0 and 9.30 am and 4.30 and 6.30 pm). Apart from the Waterloo and City Line, which is operated by the Southern Region of *BR*, the whole of the London Underground is run by *London Regional Transport*.

London Underground

London University /ˌlʌndən juːnɪˈvɜːsətɪ/ (education) One of the largest universities in *Britain*, founded in 1836. It has over 30 independent *colleges*[1] and institutes located both in *London* and in the *Home Counties*. It had no students of its own before 1900 and awarded degrees to students of other universities who had successfully passed their final examinations (in cases where universities could not award their own degrees). Many of its students live in other areas of the country and study by means of a *correspondence course.*

London Zoo /ˌlʌndən ˈzuː/, **the** (London) The short name of the Zoological Gardens, *Britain*'s best-known zoo, opened in *Regent's Park, London*, in 1826 by the Zoological Society of London.

Londonderry Air /ˌlʌndəndərɪ ˈeə(r)/, **the** (arts) A popular Irish folk tune, first published in 1885 and since then arranged and recorded in a variety of ways, by various instruments. The tune is popular as much for its slow, haunting melody as for its words.

long distance footpath /ˌlɒŋ dɪstəns ˈfʊtpɑːθ/ (sport and leisure) An extended route for tourists who like walking. At present there are 13 approved long distance footpaths and *bridleways* in *England* and *Wales* with a total length of about 1,600 miles (2,580 km). Among the best known long distance footpaths are: the *Pennine Way*, the Cotswold Way, about 100 miles long, from Chipping Campden, Gloucestershire to Bath, Avon, and the South Downs Way, from Petersfield, Hampshire to Eastbourne, East Sussex.

Long Man of Wilmington /ˌlɒŋ mæn əv ˈwɪlmɪŋtən/, **the** (history) An ancient landmark near the village of Wilmington, East Sussex, consisting of the giant outline of a man, holding an upright stick in each hand, cut out of the turf on a chalk hill. The origin of the figure is unknown.

long vacation /ˌlɒŋ vəˈkeɪʃn/ (education) The summer vacation at a university, which usually extends for at least three months, from July to September.

Lonsdale Belt /ˌlɒnzdeɪl 'belt/, **the** (sport and leisure) The highest award in professional boxing, a richly decorated belt awarded to a British champion, and kept by him if won three times running. [originally given by the Earl of Lonsdale in 1909]

lord /lɔːd/ (**1** government **2** religion **3** law) **1** A *peer* who is a member of the *House of Lords*. **2** The title of a bishop, especially if a member of the House of Lords. **3** The title of certain senior judges.

Lord Chamberlain /ˌlɔːd 'tʃeɪmbəlɪn/, **the** (life and society) The chief official of the royal household. He is responsible for all royal ceremonial, except important state functions, which are arranged by the *Earl Marshal*.

Lord Chancellor /ˌlɔːd 'tʃɑːnsələ(r)/, **the** (government) The title (in full, Lord High Chancellor) of the chief legal officer in *England*. He is a member of the *Cabinet* and of the *Privy Council* and he is the *Speaker²* of the *House of Lords* (where he sits on the *woolsack*).

Lord Chief Justice /ˌlɔːd tʃiːf 'dʒʌstɪs/, **the** (law) The title of the judge who presides over the *Queen's Bench Division* in the *High Court of Justice*. He ranks next after the *Lord Chancellor* and is a *peer*.

Lord High Chancellor /ˌlɔːd haɪ 'tʃɑːnsələ(r)/ see *Lord Chancellor* (government)

Lord Lieutenant /ˌlɔːd lef'tenənt/, **the** (government) The representative of the sovereign in a *county*. The title was created in the 16th century, and originally carried many responsibilities. Today the position is mainly ceremonial, although the holder does make recommendations for appointments as a *JP*. The title is an honorary one and the holder (who can be a woman) is not necessarily a *peer*.

Lord Mayor /ˌlɔːd 'meə(r)/, **the** (government) The title given to the *mayor* of *London* and of certain other large *cities*. It can be borne by a man or woman (see *mayoress*).

Lord Mayor's Banquet /ˌlɔːd meəz 'bæŋkwɪt/, **the** (London) An annual ceremonial dinner held in the *Guildhall, London*, after the election of a new *Lord Mayor* of London. The *Prime Minister* traditionally makes an important speech at the dinner.

Lord Mayor's Show /ˌlɔːd meəz 'ʃəʊ/, **the** (London) A ceremony held each year on the second Saturday in November, when the newly elected *Lord Mayor* of *London* rides in a horse-drawn carriage through the streets of London to be presented to the *Lord Chief Justice* at the Royal Courts of Justice. His carriage is accompanied by a procession of other vehicles, arranged to make a colourful display on a particular theme chosen personally by the Lord Mayor. In 1981, for example, the theme was 'Transport'.

Lord Mountbatten /ˌlɔːd maʊntˈbætn/ (royal family) Lord Mountbatten (1900–79, full name and title, 1st Earl Louis Mountbatten of Burma) was a cousin of *Queen Elizabeth* and one of *Britain*'s outstanding military leaders of the 20th century. He was promoted through all the officer ranks of the *Royal Navy* to become vice-admiral in 1942 and supreme commander in South-East Asia, with the acting rank of admiral, in 1943. In 1947, he was appointed viceroy of India and played a prominent part in the transfer of power from Britain to India and Pakistan. For the next two years he was governor-general in India, after which he again returned to the Navy. In 1979, while he was on holiday in *Ireland*, he was assassinated by the Provisional *IRA*.

Lord President of the Council /ˌlɔːd ˌprezɪdənt əv ðə ˈkaʊnsl/, **the** (government) The title of the peer who presides at meetings of the *Privy Council*. He is responsible for presenting the business of the Council to the sovereign, and is also *Leader of the House*[1] of Commons and a member of the *Cabinet*.

Lord Privy Seal /ˌlɔːd ˌprɪvɪ ˈsiːl/, **the** (government) The senior member of the *Cabinet* without any special duties. He is usually, however, the *Leader of the House*[2] of Lords, and until 1884 had the special responsibility of keeping the *Privy Seal*.

Lord Provost /ˌlɔːd ˈprɒvəst/, **the** (government) The title of the provost (equivalent to the English *mayor*) of five Scottish cities: Aberdeen, Dundee, *Edinburgh, Glasgow* and Perth.

Lord's /lɔːdz/ (sport and leisure) A famous cricket ground in north *London*, the headquarters of the *MCC*. [named in honour of Thomas Lord, who bought the ground for this Club in 1814]

Lord's Day Observance Society /ˌlɔːdz ˌdeɪ əbˈzɜːvəns səˌsaɪətɪ/, **the** (life and society) A society founded in 1831 to promote the religious observance of *Sunday* ('the Lord's Day') as the Christian Sabbath. The Society today is most active in campaigning against the introduction of laws that permit commercial or sporting activities on Sundays.

Lords Spiritual /ˌlɔːdz ˈspɪrɪtʃʊəl/, **the** (government) A collective term for those bishops in the *Church of England* who are members of the *House of Lords*. Compare *Lords Temporal*.

Lord's Taverners /ˌlɔːdz ˈtævənəz/, **the** (sport and leisure) A cricket team consisting of stage personalities who take part in matches at *Lord*'s and elsewhere in order to raise money for charity. [named after the Tavern, the club at Lord's where the team was first planned in 1950]

Lords Temporal /ˌlɔːdz ˈtempərəl/, **the** (government) A collective name for all those *peers* in the *House of Lords* who are not *Lords Spiritual*.

Lough Neagh /ˌlɒk ˈneɪ/ (geography) The largest lake in the *British Isles*, in *Northern Ireland* west of *Belfast*. It is popular with yachtsmen and walkers. 'Lough' is the Irish word for 'lake'.

lounge bar /'laʊndʒ bɑː(r)/ (daily life) A *bar*[1] in a *pub*, hotel or restaurant, which is more comfortable than a *public bar*, and where the drinks are more expensive.

Low Church /ˌləʊ 'tʃɜːtʃ/ (religion) A member of the *Church of England* who attaches greater importance to the literal interpretation of the Bible and to evangelism generally than to ritual or the value of the sacraments. Compare *High Church*.

Low Sunday /'ləʊ ˌsʌndɪ/ (religion) The *Sunday* after *Easter*.

lower class /ˌləʊə 'klɑːs/ (life and society) The sector of society that has the lowest position in the social scale. The term is in many ways similar to *working class* and is regarded by many, because of its implication of inferiority, as critical or patronizing. Compare *middle class, upper class*.

lower middle class /ˌləʊə 'mɪdl klɑːs/ (life and society) The sector of society that is midway between *lower class* and *middle class* and that is usually considered to be made up of shopkeepers, minor *civil servants*, etc.

lower school /'ləʊə skuːl/ (education) A term occasionally used for the junior classes of a *secondary school*. Today such classes are often organized as a *middle school*.

Lowlands /'ləʊləndz/**, the** (geography) The relatively flat region of central *Scotland*, in the valleys of the *Clyde* and the *Forth*, as distinct from the *Highlands* to the north.

loyal toast /ˌlɔɪəl 'təʊst/ (tradition) A toast to the sovereign proposed at the end of an official *dinner* or banquet. Traditionally, diners are not permitted to smoke until the toast has been drunk.

Loyalists /'lɔɪəlɪsts/**, the** (politics) The Protestants in *Northern Ireland* who wish *Ulster* to retain her links with *Britain*.

L-plates /'el pleɪts/ (transport) The metal or plastic plates attached to the front and rear of a vehicle driven by an *L-driver*. The plates are square in shape and contain a red letter 'L' on a white background.

LSE /ˌel es 'iː/**, the (London School of Economics, the)** (education) A *college*[1] of *London University* founded in 1895 (full name, London School of Economics and Political Science) to provide courses leading to degrees in economics, political science and related subjects. The college has gained a reputation in recent times for the strongly radical opinions of its students and staff.

Ltd /'lɪmɪtɪd/ **(Limited)** (finance) An abbreviation following the name of a firm or company to show that it is a *private limited company*, not a public limited **company** (which has the letters *PLC* after its name).

lucky dip /ˌlʌkɪ 'dɪp/ (sport and leisure) A box or container of some kind holding small prizes, buried in sawdust or

something similar, to be searched for by children. The game
is a common attraction at a *fête*.

L-plates

ludo /'lu:dəʊ/ (sport and leisure) A board game in which
players move counters over the squares of a straight course
by throwing a dice. The player who reaches the centre of the
board first is the winner. [Latin, 'I play']

lump /lʌmp/, **the** (work) A colloquial term for workers in the
construction trade, especially with reference to their non-
payment of *income tax* and *national insurance*. [such workers
are paid a 'lump sum' that is, in cash with no deductions]

lunch /lʌntʃ/ (food and drink) A midday meal, usually eaten
between 12.00 and 2.00. For those who have supper in the
evening, it will usually be the main meal of the day; for those
who have dinner in the evening as their main meal, it will
usually be a light meal. See also *dinner* as an alternative name
for lunch.

luncheon /'lʌntʃən/ (food and drink) A formal name for *lunch*,
especially as printed on an invitation card, a menu, etc.

Luncheon Voucher /'lʌntʃən ˌvaʊtʃə(r)/ **(LV)** (commerce) A
voucher worth a particular sum of money that can be
exchanged for a *lunch* or for food in a café, restaurant, buffet,
etc by the employee to whom it has been issued.

Lutine bell /ˌlu:ti:n 'bel/, **the** (tradition) A bell in the building
of *Lloyd's*, *London*, rung before the announcement of the loss
of a ship. The bell is the ship's bell of the French frigate
'Lutine' sunk in 1799: the vessel was insured with Lloyd's for
the sum of half a million *pounds* (*sterling*).

LWT /ˌel ˌdʌblju: 'ti:/ **(London Weekend Television)**
(media) One of the 15 television companies of the *IBA*. It
broadcasts programmes to the *London* area at the weekends

168

(Friday evening to Sunday night), while *Thames Television* broadcasts on weekdays.

Lyonesse /ˌlaɪə'nes/ (tradition) In the stories about *King Arthur*, the mythical country that was the birthplace of Sir Tristram, one of the *Knights of the Round Table*. It was said to have been somewhere in southwest *England* and to have been covered by the sea (perhaps between *Land's End* and the *Scilly Isles*).

MA /ˌem ˈeɪ/ **(Master of Arts)** (education) **1** The commonest type of *higher degree* awarded by an English university, usually for studying a non-scientific subject. Unusually, *Oxford University* awards an MA to anyone who has an *Oxford² BA* degree, who has been a member of the university for at least 21 terms and who pays £5. Similarly, *Cambridge University* awards an MA degree to anyone who has had a *Cambridge²* BA degree for at least two years and who requests it (no fee is paid). **2** A *first degree* (equivalent to an English BA) awarded at the Scottish Universities.

ma'am /mæm/ (life and society) A title of respect used to speak to a female member of the *royal family* and certain other women of rank. [conventional abbreviation of *madam*]

madam /ˈmædəm/ (life and society) A polite way of addressing a woman, especially when the speaker does not know her well enough to use her name or wants to show a formal, respectful relationship. Compare *sir*.

Madame Tussaud's /ˌmædəm təˈsɔːdz/ (London) A famous waxworks museum in *London*, opened in 1835 by Marie Tussaud (1760–1850). The museum contains wax figures of famous and notorious characters in both history and contemporary life, and is also noted for its displays of particularly horrifying events in the *Chamber of Horrors*.

Madeira cake /məˈdɪərə keɪk/ (food and drink) A kind of rich sponge case, round in shape and decorated with lemon peel. [formerly eaten with Madeira wine]

Magic Circle /ˌmædʒɪk ˈsɜːkl/**, the** (arts) A professional association of conjurors and illusionists, founded in 1905. Its *London* headquarters possess a museum and a library of publications on magic and conjuring. Its membership is currently (1982) 1,500.

magistrate /ˈmædʒɪstreɪt/ (law) A general term used for a minor legal officer, in particular a *JP* in *England*.

Magna Carta /ˌmægnə ˈkɑːtə/ (history) **1** The charter granted by King John in 1215, which recognized the rights and privileges of the barons, the church and the freemen, and which is traditionally regarded as the basis of English liberties. [Latin, 'Great Charter'] **2** An original copy of this charter, especially the ones in Lincoln Cathedral and Salisbury Cathedral, and the two copies in the *British Museum*.

magnum /ˈmægnəm/ (food and drink) A large bottle of wine holding the equivalent of two normal bottles, otherwise one and half litres.

maid of honour /ˌmeɪd əv ˈɒnə(r)/ (food and drink) A small tart with an almond flavoured filling. [apparently originally a fancy name for a type of cheese cake sold at Richmond, Surrey, in the 18th century]

maiden speech /ˌmeɪdn ˈspiːtʃ/ (government) The first speech of an *MP* in the *House of Commons*, or of a *peer* in the *House of Lords*.

Mail /meɪl/, **the** (media) The short name of the *Daily Mail* newspaper.

Mail on Sunday /ˌmeɪl ɒn ˈsʌndɪ/, **The** (media) A Sunday *popular paper* first published in 1982 and controlled by the same company as that owning the *Daily Mail*. The paper has developed a reputation for its 'scoops' and for its exposure of scandals. Its current circulation is 1.6 million. It is accompanied by a colour magazine ('You').

Mallory Park /ˌmælərɪ ˈpɑːk/ (sport and leisure) A motor-cycle and motor-car racing circuit near Hinckley, Leicestershire, where international motor-cycle races are held.

Malvern Festival /ˌmɔːlvən ˈfestɪvl/, **the** (arts) An annual drama festival held in August at Great Malvern, Hereford and Worcester.

Man Alive /ˌmæn əˈlaɪv/ (media) A weekly television series of programmes about various people's professions and special vocations, broadcast at irregular intervals on *BBC 2* since 1965.

Man of Kent /ˌmæn əv ˈkent/ (geography) A traditional name for someone born in east Kent (strictly, one born east of the river Medway). Compare *Kentish Man*.

Manchester City /ˌmæntʃɪstə ˈsɪtɪ/ (sport and leisure) A popular *football club* founded in 1887 (originally as Ardwick Football Club) with a stadium in south Manchester.

Manchester United /ˌmæntʃɪstə juːˈnaɪtɪd/ (sport and leisure) A leading English *football club* founded in 1878 with a stadium in southwest Manchester near *Old Trafford*.

Mancunian /mæŋˈkjuːnɪən/ (geography) A native or inhabitant of Manchester. [from the supposed medieval Latin name of Manchester, 'Mancunium', actually 'Mamucium']

Mandy /ˈmændɪ/ (media) A *comic* for schoolgirls first published in 1967. [from the popular girl's name Mandy, itself a short form of Amanda]

Mansion House /ˈmænʃn ˌhaʊs/, **the** (1 London 2 transport) 1 The official residence of the *Lord Mayor* of *London*, with a large banqueting hall (the so-called Egyptian Hall) where official banquets and receptions are held. The house was built in the mid-18th century. **2** An Underground railway station nearby. See *London Underground*.

Manx /mæŋks/ (language) A former Celtic language of the *Isle of Man*, not now used for everyday speech except by a few enthusiasts.

Manx cat /ˌmæŋks 'kæt/ (animal world) A breed of tailless cat, believed to have originated on the *Isle of Man*.

Manx cat

Mappin Terraces /ˌmæpɪn 'terəsɪz/, **the** (animal world) An enclosure of man-made cliffs and caves in the *London Zoo*, where polar bears and mountain sheep, among other animals, are housed. [named after the benefactor, Jonathan Mappin, who gave money for the Terraces to be opened in 1914]

Marble Arch /ˌmɑːbl 'ɑːtʃ/ (London) A triumphal arch in *London* originally built in 1828 to form the main entrance to *Buckingham Palace*. It was found to be too narrow for the royal carriage, so was re-erected on its present site, northeast of *Hyde Park*, in 1851, where it served for some years as a gateway to the Park.

Margaret Thatcher /ˌmɑːgrɪt 'θætʃə(r)/ see *Thatcher* (people)

marginal constituency /ˌmɑːdʒɪnl kən'stɪtjuənsɪ/ (politics) A *constituency* whose *MP* was elected by a narrow majority in a *by-election* or *general election*.

marginal seat /ˌmɑːdʒɪnl 'siːt/ see *marginal constituency* (politics) and *seat* (politics)

Margot Fonteyn /ˌmɑːgəʊ fɒn'teɪn/ see *Fonteyn* (people)

market day /'mɑːkɪt deɪ/ (daily life) A day, once weekly or twice weekly, when a market is held in a *market town*.

market garden /ˌmɑːkɪt ˈɡɑːdn/ (commerce) A special garden where fruit and vegetables are grown for sale.

market town /ˈmɑːkɪt taʊn/ (geography) A town, especially one in a rural area, that holds a regular market on a *market day*. The market consists of individual stalls selling agricultural produce and cheap manufactured goods (often, clothes and domestic products), and is usually held on a central square or along central streets.

Marks & Spencer /ˌmɑːks ən ˈspensə(r)/ (commerce) A chain store selling high-quality clothing and food products, founded in 1884 by Michael Marks (who took Thomas Spencer into partnership in 1894). The store is known colloquially as 'Marks and Sparks'.

Marlborough (College) /ˈmɔːlbrə (ˌmɔːlbrə ˈkɒlɪdʒ)/ (education) A leading *public school*[1], founded in 1843 in Marlborough, Wiltshire, and having 900 students.

Marlborough House /ˌmɔːlbrə ˈhaʊs/ (London) A large house in *Pall Mall, London*, built in the early 18th century for the Duchess of Marlborough and serving until 1953 as a residence for members of the *royal family*. In 1962 it became a centre for conferences of the heads of countries to the *Commonwealth*[1].

marmalade /ˈmɑːməleɪd/ (food and drink) A type of jam made from the pulp and peel of oranges, or other citrus fruits, and usually eaten at breakfast, spread on buttered bread, rolls or toast.

Marplan /ˈmɑːplæn/ (media) An organization that conducts public opinion polls, founded in 1959. It publishes its results in *quality papers*, mostly the *Financial Times* and the *Guardian*. [abbreviation of '*mar*ket research *plan*']

Martello tower /mɑːˌteləʊ ˈtaʊə(r)/ (history) A type of small circular tower by the sea. Such towers were originally built in *Britain* in about 1803 for coastal defence against a possible invasion by Napoleon's forces, and they can still be found in southeast *England*. [named after Mortella Point, Corsica, where the British navy captured a similar tower in 1794]

Mary Quant /ˌmeərɪ ˈkwɒnt/ see *Quant* (people)

Mary Rose /ˌmeərɪ ˈrəʊz/**, the** (history) The most important ship in *Henry VIII*'s navy, which capsized and sank off Portsmouth, Hampshire in 1545. Almost all its crew of 700 men were drowned. In 1982, after many difficulties, the wreck was raised from the sea bed. The remains of the ship, together with articles found on board, are now on display in Portsmouth in a special museum.

Mary Whitehouse /ˌmeərɪ ˈwaɪthaʊs/ see *Whitehouse* (people)

Marylebone /ˈmærələbən/ (transport) 1 A main line *London* railway station, and a terminus of the Western Region of *BR* (for trains from Banbury, Oxfordshire and Aylesbury, Buckinghamshire). 2 An Underground railway station here. See *London Underground*.

master /ˈmɑːstə(r)/ (education) **1** A short title of a person holding an *MA* degree, or some other *higher degree*. **2** The title of the head of some *colleges*[1], in particular those of *Cambridge University*.

Master /ˈmɑːstə(r)/ (life and society) A written, and occasionally spoken, form of address for a boy, placed before his first name (eg, Master Peter Jones). The usage is becoming increasingly old-fashioned.

master of foxhounds /ˌmɑːstər əv ˈfɒkshaʊndz/ (**MFH**) (sport and leisure) A man or woman in charge of a pack of foxhounds, as used for a *hunt*, and responsible for various administrative duties in connection with the hunt.

master of hounds /ˌmɑːstər əv ˈhaʊndz/ (sport and leisure) A short term for a *master of foxhounds*, or a term used when the hounds are not foxhounds.

Master of the Horse /ˌmɑːstər əv ðə ˈhɔːs/, **the** (royal family) An official responsible for the personal safety of the sovereign. At the ceremony of *Trooping the Colour* he rides immediately behind the sovereign, and when the sovereign is in procession to the *State Opening of Parliament*, or on any other occasion, he rides in the next carriage.

Master of the Queen's Music /ˌmɑːstər əv ðə ˌkwiːnz ˈmjuːzɪk/, **the** (royal family) The title of the musician, usually a well-known composer, appointed to attend members of the *royal family* on musical occasions such as special concerts, to organize the music for coronations, royal weddings and similar state occasions, and to compose music for such occasions. The post is an honorary one, and when the sovereign is a *king* changes in title to 'Master of the King's Music'. ['Music' in the title was until recently traditionally spelt 'Musick']

Master of the Rolls /ˌmɑːstər əv ðə ˈrəʊlz/, **the** (law) The senior civil judge in *England*. He presides over the Court of Appeal in the *Supreme Court of Judicature*, is keeper of the records at the *Public Record Office*, and is a member of the *Privy Council*. He ranks third in importance after the *Lord Chancellor* and the *Lord Chief Justice*.

Mastermind /ˈmɑːstəmaɪnd/ (media) A weekly television quiz programme on *BBC 1*. Contestants answer both specialized questions (on a theme of their own choice) and general questions, with the winner proceeding to further rounds, until the final contestant, with the highest score, wins the title of 'Mastermind' for the year.

matron /ˈmeɪtrən/ (medicine) **1** The head of the nursing staff and medical facilities in a school or other residential institution such as a *rest home*. **2** The title (now no longer official) of the administrative head of the nursing staff in a hospital.

mature student /məˌtjʊə ˈstjuːdənt/ (education) An adult student, in particular one entering a university some years after leaving school, or enrolling on a course of evening classes.

Maundy money /ˈmɔːndɪ ˌmʌnɪ/ (tradition) Coins specially minted for presentation by the sovereign to specially chosen elderly people on *Maundy Thursday*. At present (1985) there are four such coins, value 4p, 3p, 2p and 1p.

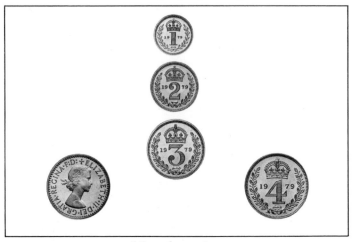

Maundy money

Maundy Thursday /ˌmɔːndɪ ˈθɜːzdɪ/ (tradition) The Thursday before *Easter*, when in a selected cathedral *city* the sovereign traditionally presents small purses of *Maundy money* to specially chosen people, the number of people being the same as the sovereign's age in years. Originally the sovereign also washed the feet of the old people, in memory of the washing of the disciples' feet by Christ.

May Day /ˈmeɪ deɪ/ (tradition) 1 May, traditionally a celebration of the coming of spring, when *fêtes* and other outdoor events are held, and at which a *May Queen* may be elected. The first Monday after it has been an official *bank holiday* since 1978. In some cities, as elsewhere in Europe, the day is marked by political or industrial meetings and rallies.

May Queen /ˈmeɪ kwiːn/ (tradition) A girl selected as being the most beautiful on *May Day*. She is usually crowned with a garland of flowers and often driven in procession through the streets.

Mayfair /ˈmeɪfeə(r)/ (London) A fashionable and expensive area of *London*'s *West End*, containing a number of high-class hotels, restaurants and shops. It extends over the area bounded by *Oxford Street* (to the north), *Regent Street* (east), *Piccadilly* (south) and *Park Lane* (west) and was formerly the site of an annual summer fair.

mayor /meə(r)/ (government) In *England* and *Wales*, the chief municipal officer of a town or *city*, and especially a *borough*[1]. He is the chairman of the council and carries out a number of honorary functions such as entertaining an important guest, opening a new building and attending special church services. He is formally addressed as 'The Worshipful (the Mayor of . . .)' (in a city, 'The Right Worshipful'), and his wife is known as the *mayoress*. A mayor may be a woman, in which case she is still (usually) called 'mayor'. In *Scotland* the function of a mayor is carried out by a *provost*. See also *Lord Mayor*.

mayoress /meə'res/ (life and society) The wife (or other official female companion, such as the daughter) of a *mayor*. She usually accompanies the mayor on his official engagements, but she is not formally addressed as 'The Worshipful'. The word is also occasionally used for a female mayor.

maypole /'meɪpəʊl/ (tradition) A tall pole fixed upright in the ground and traditionally danced round on *May Day*, each dancer holding a ribbon attached to the top of the pole.

maypole

Mays /meɪz/, **the** (**1** education **2** sport and leisure) **1** The final examinations at *Cambridge University*, held in May. **2** The rowing races held after these examinations, originally in May but now in June. Compare *Eights*.

Maze (Prison) /meɪz ('prɪzn)/, **the** (law) A prison near Lisburn, *Northern Ireland*, which became widely known when *IRA* terrorists held prisoner there went on hunger strike as a protest because they were not treated as political prisoners. In 1981 several of the hunger strikers died. [English form of Irish name meaning 'the plain']

MCC /ˌem si: 'si:/, **the (Marylebone Cricket Club, the)** (sport and leisure) *Britain*'s leading professional *cricket club*, and until 1969 the governing body of cricket (now controlled by the Cricket Council). It was founded in 1787 in the village of Marylebone, northwest of *London* (now a district of London), and has its home ground at *Lord*'s.

McNaughten Rules /məkˌnɔːtn 'ruːlz/, **the** (law) A set of rules stating that a person can be said to have been insane when committing a crime only if he can prove that he did not know what he was doing, or that he did not realize that what he was doing was wrong. The rules date from the case of *Regina* v. McNaughten in 1843. (Also spelt as McNaghten Rules.)

meals on wheels /ˌmiːlz ɒn 'wiːlz/ (daily life) A system organized by the *WRVS* to deliver hot meals by car to old people and invalids. Some *local authorities* organize this sort of system as well.

Meccano /məˈkɑːnəʊ/ (daily life) The trade name of a construction kit for children (or adults) consisting of miniature metal or plastic parts (rods, wheels, etc.) from which a working model can be made. The kits were manufactured until the 1980s by the firm of the same name.

Medical Research Council /ˌmedɪkl rɪˈsɜːtʃ ˌkaʊnsl/, **the (MRC, the)** (medicine) The main government agency for the support of biomedical research. It has over 50 research units, mostly in universities, medical schools and hospitals, and was established in 1920.

Melba toast /ˌmelbə 'təʊst/ (food and drink) A type of very thin, crisp toast. [said to have been a favourite of Dame Nellie Melba (1861–1931), the Australian opera singer]

Melody Maker /'melədɪ ˌmeɪkə(r)/ (**MM, the**) (media) A weekly magazine devoted to jazz and pop music, founded in 1926 and having a circulation in 1981 of just under 100,000.

Melton Mowbray pie /ˌmeltən ˌməʊbreɪ 'paɪ/ (food and drink) A high-quality type of pork pie, originally manufactured in Melton Mowbray, Leicestershire.

Men of Harlech /ˌmen əv 'hɑːlek/ (tradition) An old Welsh marching song, originally sung by soldiers marching into battle. [properly, Welsh 'Rhyfelgyrch Gwŷr Harlech', 'March of the men of Harlech'; Harlech is an ancient coastal town with a castle in northwest *Wales*]

Men of the Trees /ˌmen əv ðə 'triːz/, **the** (life and society) An organization founded in 1924 to campaign for the appreciation of trees as a part of the ecological environment and to encourage their planting and protection. The association has about 3,000 members.

Mensa /'mensə/ (life and society) A social organization (now international) whose members are able to score, in an intelligence test, a result higher than 98% of people in general. The British society was founded in 1946 and has a membership of nearly 6,000. [Latin, 'table': the organization operates on the principle of a 'round table', with all members having equal status]

merchant bank /ˌmɜːtʃənt ˈbæŋk/ (finance) A special kind of bank whose functions include financing the transit of goods and providing financial and commercial advice to business.

Mercury /ˈmɜːkjʊrɪ/ (commerce) An independent business telecommunications system, first operating in 1983 to compete with *British Telecom* and formed as a joint venture (Mercury Communications) in 1982 between the firms Cable and Wireless, *BP* and *Barclays (Bank)*. [named after the messenger of the gods in Roman mythology]

Merlin /ˈmɜːlɪn/ (tradition) In the stories about *King Arthur*, a famous wizard and Arthur's advizer.

Mermaid Theatre /ˌmɜːmeɪd ˈθɪətə(r)/, **the** (arts) A *London* theatre, opened in 1959, that originally staged mainly classic productions but today covers a wide repertoire of modern and traditional plays. [named after the Mermaid Tavern where writers met in the time of *Shakespeare*]

Merry England /ˌmerɪ ˈɪŋglənd/ (tradition) A traditional concept of 'good old England', in particular the *England* of *Elizabethan* times (the 16th century), when life is imagined to have been generally pleasant and the national mood one of optimism. ['merry', now meaning 'cheerful', 'jolly', meant 'pleasant' in the 16th century]

Merry Monarch /ˌmerɪ ˈmɒnək/, **the** (history) A nickname of Charles II (1630–85), mainly on account of his many mistresses (including the famous actress and seller of oranges, Nell Gwynn) and his extravagant way of life.

Mersey sound /ˌmɜːzɪ ˈsaʊnd/, **the** (arts) The characteristic pop music of the *Beatles* and other groups performing in Liverpool (on the river Mersey) in the 1960s.

Messrs /ˈmesəz/ (life and society) The plural of Mr, used in particular for the names of firms, as 'Messrs J Smith & Sons'. [contraction of 'Messieurs', of French origin]

Methodist /ˈmeθədɪst/ (religion) A member of the *Methodist Church*.

Methodist Church /ˌmeθədɪst ˈtʃɜːtʃ/ (religion) The largest of the *Free Churches*, founded in 1729 by the preacher John Wesley (1703–91) as an evangelical revivalist movement. The present Church is based on a union in 1932 of most of the separate Methodist Churches that had developed by then. In 1984 it had nearly half a million adult full members.

Metro /ˈmetrəʊ/, **the** (transport) The urban electric railway (its full name is the Tyne and Wear Metro) that operates on Tyneside, northeast *England*, to link Newcastle-upon-Tyne and Gateshead. The service, a light rapid transport system, was constructed in the early 1980s using special new tunnels under the River Tyne and a new bridge over it. Trains run every day at ten minute intervals on four routes called 'Metrolines'.

metropolitan county /ˌmetrəpɒlɪtən ˈkaʊntɪ/ (geography) One of the six conurbations named as *counties* in the reorganization of local government boundaries in 1974. The six are: Merseyside (centred on Liverpool), Greater Manchester, West *Midlands* (centred on Birmingham), West Yorkshire (centred on Leeds and Bradford), South Yorkshire (centred on Sheffield) and Tyne and Wear (centred on Newcastle). In 1985, the Conservative government (see *Conservative Party*) passed legislation in the *House of Commons* to abolish the Metropolitan counties. See also *GLC*.

Metropolitan Police Force /ˌmetrəpɒlɪtən pəˈliːs fɔːs/**, the** (law) The police force responsible for *London*, with its headquarters at *New Scotland Yard*. (The *City (of London)*, however, has its own separate force.)

MG /ˌem ˈdʒiː/ (transport) The name of a make of popular sports car, originally produced in the 1920s by the firm of Morris Garages, near *Oxford¹*.

Michaelmas /ˈmɪklməs/ (tradition) 29 September, and a *quarter day*. In the *Church of England* and the *Roman Catholic Church*, the day is celebrated as that of St Michael and All Angels. The name is still used for the academic term that starts about this time in some schools and universities. A traditional dish for Michaelmas Day was roast goose. The day is not a *bank holiday*.

middle class /ˌmɪdl ˈklɑːs/ (life and society) A social class not clearly defined but generally regarded as above *lower class* and below *upper class*. To this class belong a wide range of businessmen and professional people, although the term is frequently used in a critical sense to mean 'bourgeois', 'materialistic', 'petty-minded'.

middle school /ˈmɪdl skuːl/ (education) **1** A school for pupils aged (usually) between nine and 14, this being a separately organized stage between *primary school* and *secondary school*. See also *first school*. **2** The fourth and fifth years in some *secondary schools*, when students are preparing for the *GCE* or *CSE* examination. ['middle' since between the junior or *lower school* and senior or *upper school*]

Middle Temple /ˌmɪdl ˈtempl/**, the** (law) One of the four *Inns of Court* in *London*. [so named as between the *Inner Temple* and a site known as the 'Outer Temple']

Middlesex Hospital /ˌmɪdlseks ˈhɒspɪtl/**, the** (medicine) A *teaching hospital* in *London*, founded in 1745. [named after the *county* of Middlesex in which London was situated until the separate County of London was formed in 1888]

Midland (Bank) /ˈmɪdlənd (ˌmɪdlənd ˈbæŋk)/**, the** (finance) One of the four main English banks, with branches in many towns and *cities*. [founded in 1836 as the Birmingham and Midland Bank; see *Midlands*]

Midlands /ˈmɪdləndz/**, the** (geography) The central *counties* of *England*, including Warwickshire, Northamptonshire,

Leicestershire, Nottinghamshire, Derbyshire, Staffordshire, the *metropolitan county* of West Midlands and the eastern part of the county of Hereford and Worcester.

Midsummer Day /ˌmɪdsʌmə 'deɪ/ (tradition) 24 June, and a *quarter day*. In the *Church of England*, the day is celebrated as that of St John the Baptist. At dawn on this day *Druids*² greet the sunrise at *Stonehenge*.

MI5 /ˌem aɪ 'faɪv/ (defence) The former name, still popularly used, of the counter-intelligence agency of the British government. Compare *MI6*. [initials of 'Military Intelligence', section five]

mild /maɪld/ (food and drink) A kind of beer that is darker in colour than *bitter* and contains fewer hops.

Militant Tendency /ˌmɪlɪtənt 'tendənsɪ/, **the** (politics) An extreme *Trotskyite* or left-wing group within the *Labour Party*, whose leaders were expelled from the Party in 1982 on the grounds that they had formed a 'party within a party' and had, therefore, acted against the constitution of the Labour Party. The group started to become unpopular in 1980 when its members were said to have tried to gain control of various political organizations and trade union branches.

Milk Cup /ˌmɪlk 'kʌp/, **the** (sport and leisure) The trophy that is the prize given to the team that wins the annual *Football League Cup Final* which is played at *Wembley*. The cup is given by the *Milk Marketing Board*. Compare *Milk Race*.

Milk Marketing Board /ˌmɪlk 'mɑːkɪtɪŋ bɔːd/, **the** (commerce) The body that, through nine regional boards in the *United Kingdom*, administers a system (Milk Marketing Scheme) by which milk is sold from farms to dairies, depots and creameries and then to distributors and consumers.

Milk Race /'mɪlk reɪs/ (sport and leisure) An annual international cycle race for amateurs (in 1983, both professionals and amateurs) held since 1951. Initially the race, round a road course of some 1,500 miles (2,410 km) and lasting 13–15 days, was known as the Tour of Britain and was a professional contest sponsored by the *Daily Express*. From 1953 it was sponsored by the *Milk Marketing Board* and given its present name.

milkman /'mɪlkmən/ (daily life) A man who delivers bottled milk every day, including *bank holidays* (in most regions of *Britain*), to private houses and business premises such as shops and offices. He makes his deliveries in the early morning, often so that the milk is fresh for breakfast, and, although in rural areas he uses conventional transport such as a van, in towns and cities he makes deliveries mostly by means of a 'milk float', a small electrically-powered vehicle. The customer normally pays for the milk each week.

Millbank /'mɪlbæŋk/ (London) An embankment on the north bank of the *Thames*, *London*, on which are situated the *Tate*

Gallery and the *Millbank Tower*. [named after a former watermill on the bank here]

milkman

Millbank Tower /ˌmɪlbæŋk ˈtaʊə(r)/, **the** (London) A modern tower block, 34 storeys high, on *Millbank, London*, built in 1963 and currently occupied by the offices of various commercial companies, in particular the engineering firm of Vickers, for whom it was originally designed.

Millionaires' Row /ˌmɪliəneəz ˈrəʊ/ (London) A nickname for the street of Kensington Palace Gardens, *London*, famous for its houses belonging to rich people.

Milton, John /ˈmɪltən, dʒɒn/ (people) John Milton (1608–74) is best known for his great poem 'Paradise Lost' (1667), written when he had already gone blind. It is based on the Old Testament theme of man's disobedience in the Garden of Eden, with Satan as the main character. Milton's two other best-known works are 'Paradise Regained' (1671) and 'Samson Agonistes' (1671). Milton has had his imitators in more recent times, but none has matched the rich style and heroic characterization of his greatest epic poem.

mince pie /mɪns ˈpaɪ/ (food and drink) A small round pastry pie filled with *mincemeat¹* and traditionally eaten at *Christmas*.

mincemeat /ˈmɪnsmiːt/ (food and drink) **1** A rich mixture of dried fruit, spices and other ingredients used for making *mince pies*. **2** Minced meat.

MIND /maɪnd/ (charities) A charitable organization founded in 1946 to promote the mental health and welfare of people who are mentally ill. Its official title is the National Association for Mental Health, but with the aim of publicizing its objectives it adopted the name MIND after a campaign in 1971.

Mini /'mɪnɪ/ (transport) The name of a series of small cars manufactured by *BL*, since the 1960s, when they were particularly popular among young people.

mini-budget /'mɪnɪ ˌbʌdʒɪt/ (government) A minor *Budget* between two annual ones, often announced in the autumn.

minister /'mɪnɪstə(r)/ (**1** religion **2, 3, 4** government) **1** A clergyman in any one of the *Free Churches*. **2** The head of a government *department*. Most of these are formally called *Secretaries of State*. **3** A minister of state who is a government minister appointed to help a Secretary of State (see *minister²*) with the work of his department. **4** A non-departmental office-holder in the government, such as the *Chancellor of the Duchy of Lancaster* or the *Paymaster General*.

ministry /'mɪnɪstrɪ/ (government) **1** A collective term for all the *ministers²,³,⁴* in a government. **2** A government *department* headed by a minister² or a *Secretary of State*. **3** The building where such a department operates.

minor /'maɪnə(r)/ (law) For legal purposes, a young person under the age of 18.

minster /'mɪnstə(r)/ (religion) A name used for certain cathedrals and large churches, especially ones originally part of a monastery. Among the best known are York Minster and Beverley Minster (Humberside).

Minton /'mɪntən/ (style) A fine-quality chinaware manufactured in Stoke-on-Trent, Staffordshire, since 1798. [first produced by the potter Thomas Minton (1765-1836)]

MIRAS /'maɪræs/ (finance) A system introduced in 1983 that changed the way in which a person who holds a *mortgage* gets the tax relief allowed on the interest payable on the money loaned. The *building society* or other institution making the loan makes adjustments to each borrower's repayments to allow for the tax relief and then reclaims the money from government funds. [abbreviation of 'Mortgage Interest Relief *At* Source']

Mirror /'mɪrə(r)/, **the** (media) A daily *popular paper* with a circulation in 1985 of about 3.4 million (1970, 4.7 million). It carries many photographs and is noted for being outspoken on topical matters and for explaining political issues in easily understandable language. It is regarded as being left of centre politically and was founded in 1903. Up until 1985, it was known as the *Daily Mirror*.

M16 /ˌem aɪ 'sɪks/ (defence) The former name, still popularly used, of the intelligence and espionage agency of the British government. Compare *MI5*.

Miss /mɪs/ (life and society) **1** A title sometimes used, in speech and writing, for an unmarried woman or girl, placed either before the first name (as 'Miss Jane Brown') or before the surname ('Miss Brown'). **2** A form of address sometimes used by schoolchildren to a female teacher and, less often, by a customer to attract the attention of a female assistant in a shop, café, etc.

M'lud /məˈlʌd/ (law) A conventional written formula used to represent the pronunciation of *'My Lord'* when addressing a judge in a court of law. See *lord³*.

mock turtle soup /ˌmɒk ˌtɜːtl ˈsuːp/ (food and drink) A kind of imitation turtle soup made from a calf's head.

mod /mɒd/, **the** (arts) An annual meeting in the *Highlands* of *Scotland* with musical and literary contests in which *Gaelic*, not English, is the language used. [Gaelic, 'assembly']

Mods /mɒdz/, **the** (life and society) **1** A name for teenagers who in the 1960s aimed to rival the *Rockers*. Mods were neatly dressed, with short hair, and drove motor scooters. There were frequent fights between the two groups, especially on *bank holidays* at seaside resorts such as *Brighton*. **2** A name for teenagers and young adults who go on motorcycles to seaside resorts as the earlier Mods had done. They do not usually fight with rival groups, since there are now no Rockers, but they do sometimes fight with other young people who live locally or are on holiday there. [short for 'modern']

Monopolies Commission /məˈnɒpəlɪz kəˌmɪʃn/, **the** (government) The Monopolies and Mergers Commission is a government body first set up in 1948 to investigate and report on any possibly unlawful monopoly or merger referred to it, usually by the *Secretary of State* for Trade and Industry or the Director General of Fair Trading. A monopoly is a situation where at least 25% of particular goods or services is supplied by or to a single person, or by two or more people, in a way which prevents competition, or restricts or distorts it. A merger is the common ownership of two or more companies. The Commission can prevent a merger, or obtain an undertaking that any harmful effects should be remedied, or, if the merger has already taken place, order that it should be reversed. The Monopolies Commission deals with both state-owned industries and bodies as well as private companies.

Montagu Motor Museum /ˌmɒntəgjuː ˈməʊtə mjuːˌzɪəm/, **the** (transport) A private museum of old motor-cars (especially *veteran cars* and *vintage cars*) in the grounds of Palace House, *Beaulieu*, Hampshire, a *country house* that is the home of Lord Montagu (born 1936). The museum, formally known as the National Motor Museum, was founded by Lord Montagu in 1952 in memory of his father, an early motor-car enthusiast.

Monument /ˈmɒnjʊmənt/, **the** (London) A stone column in east central *London* commemorating the *Great Fire* of 1666. The column was built in 1671–7, and is 202 feet (61.5 metres) high—popularly regarded as the exact distance of the column from the baker's shop where the Great Fire started.

Moonraker /ˈmuːnreɪkə(r)/ (tradition) A nickname for a native or inhabitant of the *county* of Wiltshire. According to an old tale, some Wiltshiremen, who had smuggled casks of brandy into the county, were caught one evening by a customs officer just as they were trying to rake the casks out of a pond. When asked what they were doing, they replied that they were 'raking for the moon'. The customs officer, pitying such apparent stupidity, passed on, leaving the quick-thinking men with their brandy.

Moor /mɔː(r)/, **the** (law) A colloquial name for *Dartmoor*[2].

Moor Park /ˌmɔː ˈpɑːk/ (sport and leisure) A well-known golf course near Rickmansworth, Hertfordshire.

MORI /ˈmɒrɪ/ (life and society) An organization that conducts public opinion polls, established in 1969 as a joint Anglo-American enterprise. [initials of *M*arket and *O*pinion *R*esearch *I*nternational]

morning coat /ˈmɔːnɪŋ kəʊt/ (clothing) A type of frock coat with broad, rounded tails, forming part of *morning dress*.

morning dress /ˈmɔːnɪŋ dres/ (clothing) A formal type of dress for men, consisting of *morning coat*, dark grey trousers, and (usually) grey top hat. It is worn for formal occasions in the early part of the day, as distinct from *evening dress*.

Morning Star /ˌmɔːnɪŋ ˈstɑː(r)/, **the** (media) A daily *popular paper* that supports the *Communist Party*, who founded it in 1930. Until 1966 it was called the 'Daily Worker'. Its circulation is under 30,000.

morris dance /ˈmɒrɪs dɑːns/ (sport and leisure) An old English folk dance usually performed by a group of men wearing a distinctive costume which includes knee-straps covered in small bells. [according to some, 'morris' denotes the Moorish origin of the dance]

morris dance

mortarboard /ˈmɔːtəbɔːd/ (education) A black academic *cap*[5] with a tassell on top, worn by the students and members of the teaching staff of some universities and schools. [cap has flat, square top resembling the square board used by builders for carrying mortar]

mortarboard

mortage /'mɔːɡɪdʒ/ (finance) An agreement by which a person can buy a house by means of a loan from a *building society* or other source. The buyer must pay back the loan in instalments, usually monthly. If he fails to do this, the loaner can legally claim the house. [Old French, 'dead pledge']

Moss Bros /'mɒs brɒs/ (clothing) A firm with branches in several towns and cities where men's clothes, in particular *evening dress* and *morning dress*, can be bought or hired. The firm was founded in 1881. [abbreviation for 'Moss Brothers']

MOT (test) /ˌem əʊ 'tiː (test)/, **the (Ministry of Transport test)** (transport). The popular name for the annual test of a motor vehicle to make sure that it is working properly and is mechanically safe. In *Great Britain* private cars and light vans which are three or more years old must be tested (at private garages authorized to do the test); in *Northern Ireland* private cars seven or more years old must be tested (at official vehicle inspection centres). Heavy goods vehicles (see *HGV*[1]) are also subject to annual tests at special testing stations.

Mothering Sunday /'mʌðərɪŋ ˌsʌndɪ/ (tradition) The fourth *Sunday* in *Lent*, when formerly mothers traditionally received presents from their children. The day, originally regarded as a church festival, has now been mainly superseded by *Mother's Day*.

Mother's Day /'mʌðəz deɪ/ (tradition) The second *Sunday* in May, when presents are traditionally given by children to their mothers. The special day is a relatively modern commercial import from the United States.

Motor /'məʊtə(r)/, **The** (media) A weekly magazine for motor-car owners and drivers, first published in 1902 and having a circulation in 1981 of nearly 32,000.

Motor Show /ˈməʊtə ʃəʊ/, **the** (transport) An international exhibition of the latest motor-car models, held every two years at the *National Exhibition Centre*, Birmingham.

Motorail /ˈməʊtəreɪl/ (transport) A service operated by *BR* to transport motor-cars and their passengers on special trains over certain long-distance routes (mainly from the south of *England* to *Scotland*). [blend of 'motor' and 'rail']

motorway /ˈməʊtəweɪ/ (transport) A major road for fast-moving traffic, usually having two or three lanes in each direction and linking large cities. All motorways have facilities that most other roads do not have, in particular *service areas*, while access to motorways from other roads is carefully regulated and is made by special linking roads (*slip roads*). Motorways have their own regulations: they must not be used, for example, by pedestrians, learner drivers or cyclists. They also have special signs and signals. All motorways are designated by a particular number, and among the best known are the M1 (*London* to the north of *England*) and the M4 (London to South *Wales*). Most motorways are currently being gradually extended.

motorway

Mountbatten /maʊntˈbætn/ see *Lord Mountbatten* (royal family)

MP /ˌem ˈpiː/ **(Member of Parliament)** (government) A member of the *House of Commons* elected by the voters of his *constituency* to represent them in *Parliament* and to pursue the policies of his particular political party.

Mr /ˈmɪstə(r)/ (life and society) **1** A title used in spoken and written form of a man, either before the first name (as 'Mr James Green') or before the surname ('Mr Green'). **2** A form of address used in the same way. **3** A form of address conventionally used, normally before the surname alone, for a senior warrant officer in the *Royal Navy*, for the officers of a merchant ship (except the captain), for a surgeon, and for the holders of certain posts in authority (as 'Mr Chairman', 'Mr *Speaker*'). **4** A form of address occasionally used alone, especially by a younger man to an older (although such usage is considered over-familiar). In this use it is always written 'Mister'.

Mrs /'mɪsɪz/ (life and society) **1** A title used in spoken and written form of married women, either before the first name ('Mrs Anne Hodgson') or before the surname ('Mrs Hodgson'). **2** A form of address used the same way. **3** A form of address occasionally used alone, especially familiarly or jokingly (and usually written as 'Missis'). [in origin an abbreviation of 'mistress']

Mrs Beeton /ˌmɪsɪz 'biːtn/ (food and drink) The short name of a popular cookery book, still published, which originally appeared in 1861 as 'The Book of Household Management', by Mrs Isabella Beeton (1836–65).

Ms /məz/ (life and society) A title in use in *Britain* from the 1970s (although earlier in the United States) for a woman regardless of her marital status, largely in order to avoid the use of *Miss¹* (unmarried) or *Mrs¹* (married). The title is by no means universally accepted, and many women prefer either the older titles or no title at all. [artificially devised to be an abbreviation of both 'Miss' and 'Mrs']

muffin /'mʌfɪn/ (food and drink) A thick round yeast cake somewhat resembling a large *crumpet* (although not as porous) and also served toasted and spread with butter.

Muppets /'mʌpɪts/**, the** (media) The glove puppets that were the central characters in the popular *ITV* series 'The Muppet Show', running from 1976 to 1980. The puppets had grotesque appearance, and they chiefly represented animal characters such as Miss Piggy, Kermit the Frog and Fozzie Bear. The humour and entertainment of the programmes lay largely in a variety of good, old jokes and songs. Although the series was British in origin, the general presentation was American in style. [blend of 'marionette' and 'puppet']

Murder Squad /'mɜːdə skwɒd/**, the** (law) A colloquial name for the *CID*, the detective branch of the police force. [based on *Fraud Squad*]

Murrayfield /'mʌrɪfiːld/ (sport and leisure) The ground of the Scottish *Rugby Union* in *Edinburgh*.

Museum of London /mjuːˌzɪəm əv 'lʌndən/**, the** (London) A museum of the history of *London* from prehistoric times to the present day, opened in the *City (of London)* in 1976 as an amalgamation of the former Guildhall Museum (on the site of the present *Barbican*) and the *London Museum*.

musical chairs /ˌmjuːzɪkl ˈtʃeəz/ (sport and leisure) A popular children's game. While music is played children run round a group of chairs placed back to back and numbering one fewer than the number of players. When the music suddenly stops, the children race to sit down on the chairs, the last player being out of the game, since he has no chair to sit on. The number of chairs is then progressively reduced by one until only one chair is left. The winner is the first of the two remaining players to sit on this chair when the music finally stops.

Muzak /ˈmjuːzæk/ (commerce) The trade name of a system of background music relayed to restaurants, shops, clubs and other public buildings. The term is also used as a general name for any recorded light music played in shops, restaurants, *pubs* or factories.

My Lady /maɪ ˈleɪdɪ/ (life and society) A form of address used to a woman who bears the official title of *Lady*[3]. Compare *My Lord*.

My Lord /maɪ ˈlɔːd/ (life and society) A form of address used to a man who bears the official title of *Lord*[1,2,3]. See also *M'lud*.

mystery tour /ˈmɪstərɪ ˌtʊə(r)/ (transport) A commercially organized coach tour to a destination known only to the driver.

NAAFI /'næfɪ/ (defence) One of a number of canteens and shops providing services for the armed forces both in *Britain* and overseas. [abbreviation of *Navy, Army and Air Force Institutes*]

Naffy /'næfɪ/ (defence) A colloquial spelling for a *NAAFI* or the organization that runs them.

NALGO /'nælgəʊ/ **(National and Local Government Officers' Association, the)** (work) A trade union for professional, technical and administrative staff in the local government service, including the *NHS*, the nationalized gas and electricity industries and road passenger transport. The union was formed in 1905 and is *Britain*'s largest non-manual workers' trade union, with a membership of 726,000.

National /'næʃnəl/**, the** (sport and leisure) A short title for the *Grand National*.

national anthem /ˌnæʃnəl 'ænθəm/ see *God Save the Queen* (life and society)

National Bus Company /ˌnæʃnəl 'bʌs ˌkʌmpənɪ/**, the (NBC, the)** (transport) The largest state bus and coach operating company in *England* and *Wales* with over 40 regional subsidiaries and a network of long-distance coach services. It was established in 1968.

National Coal Board /ˌnæʃnəl 'kəʊl bɔːd/ see *NCB* (work)

National Council for Civil Liberties /ˌnæʃnəl ˌkaʊnsl fə ˌsɪvl 'lɪbətɪz/**, the (NCCL, the)** (life and society) A voluntary body founded in 1934 to promote the rights of the individual citizen and to oppose discrimination of all kinds and the abuse of power. Some people have recently criticised it because they feel it is becoming too openly political.

National Exhibition Centre /ˌnæʃnəl eksɪ'bɪʃn ˌsentə(r)/**, the (NEC, the)** (commerce) A large exhibition complex east of Birmingham, opened in 1976 to house many major exhibitions, including some, such as the *Motor Show*, that were previously held only in *London*.

National Film Theatre /ˌnæʃnəl 'fɪlm ˌθɪətə(r)/**, the (NFT, the)** (arts) A cinema theatre founded in 1951 on the *South Bank* complex, *London*, as an extension of the *British Film Institute*. It runs a daily showing of important or historic films of all kinds and nationalities in two auditoriums, and holds the annual London Film Festival.

National Front /ˌnæʃnəl 'frʌnt/, **the (NF, the)** (politics) A small extreme right-wing political party founded in 1966 and campaigning, among other radical policies, for the expulsion of coloured immigrants from *Britain*, and for the introduction of *corporal punishment* and *capital punishment* for certain criminal offences.

National Gallery /ˌnæʃnəl 'gælərɪ/, **the** (arts) One of *London*'s best known art galleries, in *Trafalgar Square*. It was founded in 1824 and houses one of the most important collection of Italian paintings outside Italy.

National Girobank /ˌnæʃnəl 'dʒaɪərəʊbæŋk/, **the** (finance) A low-cost banking and money transfer service run by the *Post Office*, with facilities available to both private and business customers. It was established in 1968 and operates through all *Britain*'s post offices.

national grid /ˌnæʃnəl 'grɪd/, **the** (geography) **1** The national network of transmission lines, pipes, etc that distributes electricity, gas and water (or any of these individually) throughout *Britain*. **2** The network of horizontal and vertical lines used on maps published by the *Ordnance Survey* to help people using the maps to find places marked on them. The origin of the grid lies to the west of the *Scilly Isles* at a point whose true co-ordinates are 2°W, 49°N.

national insurance /ˌnæʃnəl ɪn'ʃɔːrəns/ (finance) A system of compulsory contributions by employees and employers to provide state financial assistance in sickness, retirement, unemployment and certain other cases.

National Marriage Guidance Council /ˌnæʃnəl ˌmærɪdʒ 'gaɪdəns ˌkaʊnsl/, **the** (charities) A voluntary organization that provides practical advice, through a network of marriage guidance centres, to men and women whose marriage is threatened or has broken up, and to young men and women contemplating marriage for the first time.

national park /ˌnæʃnəl 'pɑːk/ (geography) One of ten large rural areas in *England* and *Wales* named by the *Countryside Commission* as districts where the countryside is to be preserved and protected, but also where facilities for the public, such as car parks and camping sites, are to be provided at certain points. All the parks are in areas of hill or mountain country, moorland or forest.

National Physical Laboratory /ˌnæʃnəl 'fɪzɪkl ləˌbɒrətrɪ/, **the (NPL, the)** (science and technology) The research station of the *Department* of Trade and Industry, based mainly at Teddington, *Greater London*, where it is the national standards laboratory of the *United Kingdom*. Its work includes establishing internationally acceptable basic standards of measurement, and research in mathematics and computer usage and in marine and offshore technology.

National Portrait Gallery /ˌnæʃnəl ˈpɔːtreɪt ˌgælərɪ/, **the**
(arts) *Britain*'s leading art gallery of portraits of famous
people in British history. It is next to the *National Gallery* in
London. It was founded in 1856 and in 1984 contained over
8,000 original portraits and more than 500,000 photographs.

National Railway Museum /ˌnæʃnəl ˈreɪlweɪ mjuːˌzɪəm/, **the**
(transport) A museum of railway relics, locomotives and
rolling stock opened in York in 1975 as a department of the
Science Museum, London.

National Savings Bank /ˌnæʃnəl ˈseɪvɪŋz bæŋk/, **the (NSB, the)**
(finance) A savings bank operated by the *Post Office* and
offering a wide range of investment schemes, among them
National Savings Certificates and *Premium Bonds*.

National Savings Certificates /ˌnæʃnəl ˈseɪvɪŋz səˈtɪfɪkəts/
(finance) Certificates, offered for sale by the *Post Office*
through the *National Savings Bank*, that give an increasing
rate of interest to the purchaser until they are sold back,
usually after a fixed number of years. No *income tax* is
payable on the interest of the certificates, which were first
issued in 1916 to raise money for the First World War. There
is a fixed upper limit to the number of certificates an
individual may hold.

national service /ˌnæʃnəl ˈsɜːvɪs/ (history) A compulsory
period of service in the armed forces introduced during the
Second World War (for men aged 18 to 41), from 1948 to 1951
(for 21 months for men aged 19 to 25), and from 1951 to 1960
(for two years for men aged 18½ to 25).

National Theatre /ˌnæʃnəl ˈθɪətə(r)/, **the** (arts) **1** A *London*
theatre opened on the *South Bank* site in 1976 and staging
both classical and modern plays in its three auditoriums.
2 The theatre company based now at the National Theatre
and formerly at the *Old Vic* (from 1963).

National Trust /ˌnæʃnəl ˈtrʌst/, **the (NT, the)** (life and
society) A non-governmental organization founded in 1895
to protect and preserve historic buildings and monuments,
and countryside areas of natural beauty in *England, Wales* and
Northern Ireland. The Trust preserves several *country houses*
and in 1984 had over one million members. See also *National
Trust for Scotland*. [full title, National Trust for Places of
Historic Interest or Natural Beauty]

National Trust for Scotland /ˌnæʃnəl ˌtrʌst fə ˈskɒtlənd/, **the
(NTS, the)** (life and society) A sister organization of the
National Trust, founded in 1931 and carrying out in *Scotland*
work similar to that undertaken by the National Trust in
England, Wales and *Northern Ireland*. It has over 100,000
members.

National Westminster (Bank) /ˌnæʃnəl ˈwestmɪnstə(r) (ˌnæʃnəl
ˌwestmɪnstə ˈbæŋk)/, **the** (finance) One of the four main
banks in *England*, with branches in many towns and cities. It
was formed in 1968 as the result of a merger between the

National Provincial Bank and the Westminster Bank. The Bank introduced the *Access* credit card in 1972, in association with *Lloyds (Bank)* and the *Midland (Bank)*.

National Youth Orchestra /ˌnæʃnəl ˈjuːθ ˌɔːkɪstrə/**, the (NYO, the)** (arts) The leading orchestra of young professional musicians and music students in *Britain*, organized through a system of local youth orchestras.

National Youth Theatre /ˌnæʃnəl ˈjuːθ ˌθɪətə(r)/**, the** (arts) A company of young professional stage actors based at the Shaw Theatre in northwest *London*.

nationalized industries /ˌnæʃnəlaɪzd ˈɪndəstrɪz/**, the** (commerce) *Britain*'s present nationalized (state-owned) industries are largely those created by the Labour government (see *Labour Party*) after 1945, and include the *Bank of England, British Airways, BR,* the *NCB,* the *BSC, British Shipbuilders,* the *Post Office* and the gas and electricity boards. However, the Conservative government (see *Conservative Party*) of Margaret *Thatcher,* elected in 1979, embarked on a policy of 'privatization', or transferring many state-owned industries to private enterprise. Among such former nationalized industries are the now privately owned *British Aerospace, Britoil, British Telecom* and *Sealink,* once a subsidiary of *BR.*

nativity play /nəˈtɪvəti pleɪ/ (tradition) A play performed by young children, usually before *Christmas,* showing the biblical story of the birth of Jesus Christ.

nativity play

NATO /ˈneɪtəʊ/ (defence) The basic purpose of NATO, as established in 1952, is to enable its member countries to maintain peace with freedom by persuading any potential enemy that the use of force will cause the countries who are members to fight back in self-defence. At the same time, NATO countries are continuously negotiating to reduce the level of nuclear and conventional arms. The defence policy of *Britain* is based on that of NATO and is fully committed to it. [abbreviation of 'North Atlantic Treaty Organization']

Natural History Museum /ˌnætrəl 'hɪstrɪ mjuː ˌzɪəm/, **the** (education) *London*'s leading natural history museum. It houses five major departments (zoology, entomology, palaeontology with anthropology, botany and mineralogy) and has an extensive educational programme. It was founded as part of the *British Museum*, although housed separately since 1862. [official title British Museum (Natural History), although separated administratively from the Museum in 1963]

Nature /'neɪtʃə(r)/ (media) A scientific journal published weekly since 1879 and having a circulation in 1980 of over 23,000.

NatWest /ˌnæt'west/, **the** (finance) A popular abbreviation of the name of the *National Westminster Bank*.

naughty postcard /ˌnɔːtɪ 'pəʊstkɑːd/ (daily life) A picture postcard traditionally sold at seaside resorts and showing a brightly coloured illustration with an amusing 'naughty' (usually punning) caption. ['naughty' in the sense, 'mildly indecent']

NBL /ˌen biː 'el/, **the (National Book League, the)** (life and society) A charitable trust founded in 1945 to increase interest in, and use of books. Many teachers, writers, and booksellers are members of the league, and most public libraries are corporate members.

NCB /ˌen siː 'biː/, **the (National Coal Board, the)** (work) The state body set up in 1947 to manage *Britain*'s coal mines, which were formerly privately owned. In 1984 there were 170 collieries operated by the NCB (compared with nearly 300 in the early 1970s), mainly in South *Wales*, Nottinghamshire, Derbyshire, South Yorkshire and West Yorkshire, but also with some mines in the West *Midlands*, Merseyside, Kent, Durham and the *Lowlands* of *Scotland*. In 1984 proposals made by the NCB to close many unprofitable or nearly exhausted mines resulted in a lengthy miners' strike called by the *NUM*, with some other industries giving support. See also *General Strike*, Arthur *Scargill*.

NCP /ˌen siː 'piː/ **(National Car Parks)** (commerce) A *London*-based commercial company that operates many paying car parks throughout *Britain*.

NEB /ˌen iː 'biː/, **the (National Enterprise Board, the)** (work) A public corporation established in 1975 to promote the expansion of private industry. In 1981 it joined with the National Research Development Corporation to form the *British Technology Group*.

NEDC /ˌen iː diː 'siː/, **the (National Economic Development Council, the)** (work) A government organization set up in 1962 with the aim of improving the efficiency of the nation's economy. Representatives of government, management and trade unions meet monthly under the chairmanship of the *Chancellor of the Exchequer* or the *Prime Minister*. See also *Little Neddy*.

Neddy /'nedɪ/ (work) A colloquial abbreviation for the *NEDC*. [abbreviation NEDC spoken as short form of man's name Edward]

Neil Kinnock /ˌniːl 'kɪnək/ see *Kinnock* (people)

Nelson's Column /ˌnelsnz 'kɒləm/ (London) A tall column nearly 185 feet (44 m) high in *Trafalgar Square, London*, with a statue of Admiral Nelson (1758–1805). It was put up here in 1840–3 with Trafalgar Square itself planned as a memorial to Nelson. The Column is also famous for the bronze lions by the sculptor Landseer added at its base in 1867.

Nessie /'nesɪ/ (tradition) A popular nickname for the *Loch Ness Monster*.

New Commonwealth /ˌnjuː 'kɒmənwelθ/, **the** (geography) A term sometimes used for all *Commonwealth[1]* countries apart from the older countries of Canada, Australia and New Zealand.

New Covent Garden (Market) /ˌnjuː ˌkɒvənt 'gɑːdn (ˌnjuː ˌkɒvənt ˌgɑːdn 'mɑːkɪt)/ (London) The present official name of *Covent Garden[1]* since its move to its new premises in 1974.

New Forest pony /ˌnjuː fɒrɪst 'pəʊnɪ/ (animal world) A breed of pony living in semi-wild conditions in the New Forest, Hampshire. When tamed, such ponies are popular as safe mounts for children, since they have already become used to motor traffic on roads running through the Forest.

New Musical Express /ˌnjuː ˌmjuːzɪkl ɪk'spres/, **the (NME, the)** (media) A weekly magazine about British and American rock music and personalities. It was founded in 1952 and has the largest circulation of all popular music periodicals, over 176,000.

New Sadler's Wells Opera /ˌnjuː ˌsædləz ˌwelz 'ɒprə/, **the** (arts) An opera company founded in 1982 and giving performances of light operas at *Sadler's Wells, London*.

New Scientist /ˌnjuː 'saɪəntɪst/, **the** (media) A weekly magazine of information and articles on the latest developments in science and technology. It was first published in 1956 and has a circulation of nearly 86,000.

New Scotland Yard /ˌnjuː skɒtlənd 'jɑːd/ (law) The headquarters of the *London Metropolitan Police Force*, housing the *Flying Squad*, the *Murder Squad* (see *CID*), the Criminal Record Office and the Traffic Control Department. The original headquarters was at *Scotland Yard*, off *Whitehall[1]*, and the name became New Scotland Yard when the headquarters moved first to a site by the *Thames* in 1890, then to its present building in *Westminster[1]* in 1966.

New Society /ˌnjuː sə'saɪətɪ/ (media) A weekly magazine of the social sciences and social policies, first published in 1962 and having a circulation of over 32,000.

New Statesman /ˌnjuː ˈsteɪtsmən/, **the** (media) A left-wing weekly political and literary magazine with a 'progressive' attitude to its readers. The periodical has a particular interest in matters of scandal and concern, startling literary disclosures and new intellectual movements. It was founded in 1931 and has a circulation of just over 40,000. Compare the *Spectator*, its 'opposite number'.

new town /ˈnjuː taʊn/ (geography) A planned town built since 1900 by the government with the aim of encouraging the move of industry and population from crowded cities to new areas. The term particularly applies to the 32 new towns named as such since 1946 (21 in *England*, two in *Wales*, five in *Scotland*, four in *Northern Ireland*).

New Year Honours /ˌnjuː jɪər ˈɒnəz/, **the** (life and society) The announcement of honorary titles, orders and medals awarded annually by the sovereign on *New Year's Day*. Compare *Birthday Honours*.

New Year's Day /ˌnjuː jɪəz ˈdeɪ/ (tradition) 1 January, and a *bank holiday* (held on the Monday following if the day falls on a Saturday or *Sunday*). The holiday is not marked with any particular custom in *Britain*, largely because it comes so soon after *Christmas*. Compare *New Year's Eve*.

New Year's Eve /ˌnjuː jɪəz ˈiːv/ (tradition) 31 December, when traditionally parties and dances are held and when, in *Scotland*, *Hogmanay* is celebrated. In many large towns and cities there is a public gathering to 'see the New Year in', the largest and liveliest usually being held in *Trafalgar Square, London*. The day is not a *bank holiday*.

News At Ten /ˌnjuːz ət ˈten/ (media) A nightly television news programme broadcast at 10.00 by *ITN* since 1964. Compare *Nine O'Clock News*.

News of the World /ˌnjuːz əv ðə ˈwɜːld/, **the** (media) A Sunday *popular paper* founded in 1843 and having a circulation of over four million, the highest of any *Sunday* newspaper. The paper specializes in crime and court reporting, and its accounts of scandals and sexual offences are the most detailed of any national newspaper. It is politically independent.

NHS /ˌen eɪtʃ ˈes/, **the (National Health Service, the)** (medicine) The system of national medical services throughout *Britain* that is largely financed by taxation, and that enables people, especially the young, the elderly and the needy, to obtain medical prescriptions and hospital and other treatment either free of charge or at reduced cost. The service was established in 1948.

Nightrider /ˈnaɪt ˌraɪdə(r)/, **the** (transport) Two express trains running nightly without sleeping cars. One goes from *London* to *Glasgow* and the other from London to Aberdeen.

999 /ˌnaɪn naɪn ˈnaɪn/ **nine-nine-nine** (daily life) The emergency telephone number to be dialled if the fire brigade, the police or an ambulance are needed.

Nine O'Clock News /ˌnaɪn əklɒk ˈnjuːz/, **the** (media) **1** A nightly television news programme broadcast at 9.00 by *BBC 1* since 1970. **2** The nightly radio news broadcast made at this time by the *BBC* from 1927 to 1960.

nineteenth hole /ˌnaɪntiːnθ ˈhəʊl/, **the** (sport and leisure) A humorous name among golf players for the *bar¹* in the clubhouse, to which players go after playing the eighteenth (and final) hole on the course.

nine-to-five-job /ˌnaɪn tə ˈfaɪv dʒɒb/ (work) In many offices, a standard working day of eight hours, from 9.00 am to 5.00 pm.

Ninian Park /ˌnɪnɪən ˈpɑːk/ (sport and leisure) The stadium of *Cardiff City* football club, in west *Cardiff*. [after park here]

Nonconformists /ˌnɒnkənˈfɔːmɪsts/ (religion) The members of any Protestant church except the *Church of England*, including the *Methodists*, the *Baptists*, the *United Reformed Church* and the *Church of Scotland*. Compare *Free Churches*. [so called because they do not conform to the established church, ie, the Church of England]

non-U /ˌnɒn ˈjuː/ (life and society) A somewhat old-fashioned term used half-humorously to describe a word or action that is felt to show social inferiority, for example, saying 'toilet' instead of 'lavatory', or tucking a serviette (also regarded as a non-U word) into one's collar when dining. Compare *U*.

Norfolk Broads /ˌnɔːfək ˈbrɔːdz/, **the** (geography) Another name for the *Broads*, specifically the ones in Norfolk.

Norman /ˈnɔːmən/ (style) The Romanesque style of architecture found mainly in *Britain*, especially in churches and castles from the time of the *Norman Conquest* to the 12th century. It is characterized chiefly by rounded arches, round pillars, square towers and massive stone walls.

Norman Conquest /ˌnɔːmən ˈkɒŋkwest/, **the** (history) The invasion and settlement of *England* by the Normans, led by William the *Conqueror* after the Battle of *Hastings* in 1066.

Norman Hartnell /ˌnɔːmən ˈhɑːtnəl/ see *Hartnell* (people)

North (Country) /ˈnɔːθ (ˌkʌntrɪ)/, **the** (geography) The northern part of *England*, whose inhabitants are popularly well known for their friendliness, directness and shrewdness, especially in business, as distinct from the more reserved and elusive character of those who live in the south.

North Sea gas /ˌnɔːθ siː ˈgæs/ (science and technology) Natural gas obtained from gas fields beneath the North Sea, mainly off the coast of East Anglia and off the east coast of *Scotland*. *Britain*'s gas supply was formerly produced from coal, but natural gas from the North Sea is now the sole source of all the country's gas (since the late 1960s).

North Sea oil /ˌnɔːθ siː ˈɔɪl/ (science and technology) Crude oil obtained from oil fields beneath the North Sea, mainly off the east coast of *Scotland* and the northeast coast of *England*.

Britain formerly imported almost all its oil supplies, but from the mid-1970s itself became an oil producer.

Northern Ireland /ˌnɔːðən ˈaɪələnd/ (geography) Before the early 20th century, Northern Ireland was part of *Ireland* as a whole, having developed in the middle ages as the Kingdom of *Ulster*, later the Province of Ulster. After many English and Scots people settled here in the 16th century, Northern Ireland became mainly Protestant (two out of three people were Protestant), unlike the rest of Ireland which remained, as before, mainly Roman Catholic. By the terms of an Anglo-Irish treaty of 1921, Northern Ireland was granted its own parliament in which a Protestant government was formed after successive elections. Roman Catholics, who were excluded from political office, came increasingly to resent the continuing Protestant domination, and, as a result, a vigorous civil rights movement emerged in the late 1960s. The sectarian (Catholic against Protestant) disturbances which followed were exploited by extremists of both faiths, and in particular by the Provisional *IRA* (which broke away from the Official IRA in 1970). Consequently, British troops were sent to Northern Ireland in 1969 to help to keep the peace. The Northern Ireland government was unable to introduce satisfactory reforms. Consequently, the British government imposed *direct rule* (of Northern Ireland from *Westminster*[2]) in 1972. Since then, in spite of the efforts of the British government, the police force in Northern Ireland and the British *Army* units there, violence and terrorism has continued, with the IRA also taking its campaign of violence to mainland *Britain* (especially *London* and British military bases). The continuing unrest has not been helped by rising unemployment in Northern Ireland, and, although terrorism continues, the level of violence is now lower than it was in the 1970s. See also *Northern Ireland Assembly*, *Troubles*.

Northern Ireland Assembly/ˌnɔːðən ˌaɪələnd əˈsemblɪ/, **the** (government) The elected assembly that was restored in *Northern Ireland* in 1982. Although it only has consultative powers at present, it should regain administrative and legislative powers in the future. The Protestant political parties won a large majority in the election, and the minority Roman Catholic parties refused to take their seats. *Sinn Féin* won five of the 78 seats. The election of the Assembly did not affect *direct rule*, which continued as before.

Norwich City /ˌnɒrɪdʒ ˈsɪtɪ/ (sport and leisure) The professional football club of Norwich, Norfolk, with its own stadium in the city. It was founded in 1905.

Norwich School /ˈnɒrɪdʒ skuːl/, **the** (arts) A group of early 19th-century painters, led by John Crome (1768–1821), who were based in Norwich, Norfolk, and represented *England*'s most distinctive regional school of painting. Followers of the group found most of their subjects in the countryside of

Norfolk and *East Anglia* with their style in turn influenced by Dutch 17th-century painters.

not proven /ˌnɒt ˈpruːvn/ (law) In *Scotland*, the verdict given by a *jury* when the evidence presented in *court³* neither proves nor disproves the case against the person accused. The verdicts 'guilty' and 'not guilty' are also used in Scotland, as well as in *England*, *Wales* and *Northern Ireland*. 'Not proven' is used only in Scotland.

Notting Hill /ˌnɒtɪŋ ˈhɪl/ (London) A district of west *London* with a large coloured immigrant population, noted for its racial riots and clashes from the 1950s. Now it is best known for the lively *Notting Hill Carnival*.

Notting Hill Carnival /ˌnɒtɪŋ hɪl ˈkɑːnɪvl/, **the** (life and society) An annual West Indian carnival held over the *August Bank Holiday* in the streets of *Notting Hill*, west *London*, since 1966, when it was founded as a purely local fair. Some Carnivals of the 1970s were marred by clashes between whites and blacks, and between participants and the police.

Notting Hill Carnival

NSPCA /ˌen es ˌpiː siː ˈeɪ/, **the (National Society for the Prevention of Cruelty to Animals, the)** (charities) The former name of the *RSPCA*.

NSPCC /ˌen es ˌpiː siː ˈsiː/, **the (National Society for the Prevention of Cruelty to Children, the)** (charities) A voluntary organization founded in 1884 to prevent the ill-treatment of children, in private or in public, and the corruption of their morals. The Society had in 1982, 50,000 voluntary workers who investigated reported cases of cruelty or neglect.

nuclear power /ˌnjuːklɪə ˈpaʊə(r)/ (science and technology)
Britain has been developing nuclear power for several years,
and in 1956 the country's first large-scale nuclear power
station at Calder Hall (now part of *Sellafield*) began to supply
electricity to the *national grid*[2]. There are currently 11 nuclear
power stations in operation controlled by the electricity
authorities, while four others also feed electricity to the
national grid. The first two Advanced Gas-cooled Reactors (in
Somerset and Strathclyde) began operating in 1976, and three
more came into production in 1984. Further reactors of this
type are planned. See also *British Nuclear Fuels*.

NUJ /ˌen juː ˈdʒeɪ/, **the (National Union of Journalists, the)**
(work) The leading journalists' trade union, with (in 1984)
over 32,000 members.

NUM /ˌen juː ˈem/, **the (National Union of Mineworkers, the)**
(work) An influential trade union for coal miners, formed in
1945 from the former Miners' Federation of *Great Britain*, an
association of coal miners' unions founded in 1880. The
Union, with a membership of 208,000, was under Communist
leadership for a long time. It has been very active in
campaigning for its members' rights. In March 1984, it started
a prolonged strike because it disagreed with government
plans for the coal industry. The strike lasted nearly a year. See
also Arthur *Scargill*.

Number Ten/No 10 /ˌnʌmbə ˈten/ (government) The official
residence of the *Prime Minister* in *Downing Street, London*.

Number/No 10

NUPE /ˈnjuːpɪ/ **(National Union of Public Employees, the)**
(work) A trade union founded in 1888 (as the Employees'
Protection Association of the London County Council),
whose members do a wide range of jobs, although many are
local authority manual workers and *NHS* employees. The

Union, with a membership of over 689,000, has more women members than any other trade union.

NUR /ˌen juː ˈɑː(r)/, **the (National Union of Railwaymen, the)** (work) The largest of the trade unions to which railway workers belong, with 143,000 members. Compare *ASLEF*. The Union was founded in 1871 (as the Amalgamated Society of Railway Servants) and has long had strong ties with the *Labour Party*, which it was indirectly involved in forming.

nursery rhyme /ˈnɜːsərɪ raɪm/ (tradition) A short traditional verse or song popular with children. Many such rhymes have a historic or satirical background, the meaning of which is mostly lost today.

nursery school /ˈnɜːsərɪ skuːl/ (education) A school for very young children, usually three or four years old (before compulsory education, which begins at the age of five).

nursery stakes /ˈnɜːsərɪ steɪks/, **the** (sport and leisure) A race for two-year-old horses.

nursing home /ˈnɜːsɪŋ həʊm/ (medical) A private hospital or home usually for old or invalid people.

NUS /ˌen juː ˈes/, **the (National Union of Students, the)** (education) A voluntary organization for students in *further education* and *higher education*, founded in 1922, and operating through local branches in *colleges*[1,2] and universities. It promotes the educational, social and general interests of students and in 1982 had a membership of approximately one million.

NUT /ˌen juː tiː/, **the (National Union of Teachers, the)** (education) The largest professional organization for teachers in *England* and *Wales*, to which teachers in both state and *independent schools* can belong. It aims to improve the professional status and conditions of employment of its members and to promote the cause of education in the interests of schoolchildren. The Union belongs to the *TUC* and has about 210,000 members. In recent years it has been vigorously campaigning for better pay for teachers. It was founded in 1870.

THE OVAL

O Come, All Ye Faithful /ˌəʊ ˌkʌm ɔːl jiː ˈfeɪθfl/ (tradition) The
title, and opening words, of a popular *Christmas* carol, often
sung as the final hymn in a *carol service*. [19th-century
English translation of Latin hymn, 'Adeste, fideles']

'O' Level /ˈəʊ ˌlevl/ (**Ordinary Level**) (education) The basic
school-leaving examination of the *GCE*, usually taken in one
or more subjects at age 15 or 16. Compare *'A' level*, *CSE*,
GCSE.

OAP /ˌəʊ eɪ ˈpiː/ (**old age pensioner**) (life and society) A
retired man or woman of pensionable age (see *old age
pension*). Such pensioners are entitled to certain services at
reduced rates, for example, rail travel at half-price (if the
ticket-holder has a *Railcard*), cheaper admission fees to
cinemas, exhibitions, etc, and in some cases free goods or
services such as free bus travel in some areas, and also free
medical services. See *NHS*, also *meals on wheels*, *Senior
Citizen*.

oatcake /ˈəʊtkeɪk/ (food and drink) A type of thin, brittle cake
or biscuit of oatmeal, popular in *Scotland*.

Observer /əbˈzɜːvə(r)/, **The** (media) A Sunday *quality paper*
first published in 1791 and having a circulation of 773,000 in
1984. The newspaper is politically independent and is noted
for the high quality of its writing, its authority, and, in recent
years, its increasing originality.

Offa's Dyke /ˌɒfəz ˈdaɪk/ (history) A long, ancient earthwork
extending (with some gaps) from north *Wales* to south. It was
built in the 8th century by Offa, King of Mercia (died 796), as
a boundary between the English (to the east) and the Welsh
(to the west), and today still more or less follows the modern
border between the two countries.

office party /ˌɒfɪs ˈpɑːtɪ/ (daily life) A party, especially one on
or just before *Christmas Eve*, held in the office of a commercial
or government organization. Alcoholic drinks are usually
served, and the normal formality of the workplace changes to
a much more relaxed atmosphere. The usual business
relationship between employers and employees is

deliberately ignored. The office party has thus become a suitable subject for a number of jokes and tales of amorous indiscretions.

Official Birthday /əˌfɪʃl ˈbɜːθdeɪ/, **the** (royal family) The official birthday of the sovereign, at present the second Saturday in June. It is marked by *Trooping the Colour* and by the announcement of the *Birthday Honours*. The day is not the sovereign's true birthday, and is not a *bank holiday*, although many *civil servants* are given a day off.

off-licence /ˈɒf laɪsəns/ (commerce) A shop licensed to sell alcoholic drink (to people aged 18 and over) to be drunk off its premises, as distinct from a *bar¹* or restaurant, where such drink is drunk on the premises.

old age pension /ˌəʊld eɪdʒ ˈpenʃn/, **the** (finance) The state pension which all men get when they retire at the age of 65. A woman who has worked gets a pension when she retires at 60. A woman who has not had paid employment does not get a pension herself but her husband gets a joint pension for them both. The money is raised from the *national insurance* contributions paid during the person's working life.

Old Bailey /ˌəʊld ˈbeɪlɪ/, **the** (law) The popular name of the *Central Criminal Court*, in *London*. [after the street where it is situated, itself named after an 'old bailey', or former outer castle wall here]

old boy /ˈəʊld bɔɪ/ (education) A former student of a *secondary school*, especially a *public school¹*. He may well belong to a society or association of former students run by the school and thus keep in touch with its progress. See also *old boy network*, *old school tie*.

old boy network /ˌəʊld ˈbɔɪ ˌnetwɜːk/ (life and society) An informal 'closed' community of *old boys*, including former university students, used by one individual to gain status in a job or other situation by means of the influence of one or more of the others in the network.

Old Contemptibles /əʊld kənˈtemptəblz/, **the** (history) A nickname for the survivors of the British Expeditionary Force who fought with the French and Belgians against the Germans in the First World War. After the war, the men held regular annual parades, the last of which took place in 1974. [name said, on doubtful authority, to have come from an order issued by the German Emperor, referring to the British force as a 'contemptible little army'; as used by the veterans, the term lost its critical sense]

Old English sheepdog /ˌəʊld ɪŋglɪʃ ˈʃiːpdɒg/ (animal world) A breed of sheepdog formerly used as a working dog by shepherds in southern *England* and *Wales*, but now mostly kept as a domestic pet. It is distinguished by its long grey and white hair, which traditionally falls over its eyes.

Old English sheepdog

old girl /ˈəʊld ɡɜːl/ (education) A former female student of a *secondary school*, especially a *public school[1]* (whether for girls only or not). She may well belong to an association of past students, in the same way as an *old boy*.

Old Lady of Threadneedle Street /ˌəʊld ˌleɪdɪ əʊ θredˈniːdl striːt/, **the** (finance) A nickname for the *Bank of England*, which is in the street of this name. The Bank was itself nicknamed the 'Old Lady' in the late 18th century. [street name said to be a corruption of 'three needles', from the signboard of a Needlemakers' Company here showing three needles]

Old Moore's Almanack /ˌəʊld mɔːz ˈɔːlmənæk/ (media) A popular annual publication which claims to forecast important events for the particular year. The periodical takes its title from the almanac published in 1699 by the physician and astrologer Francis Moore (1657–1715), which predicted the weather as a commercial promotion for the pills he manufactured.

old school tie /ˌəʊld skuːl ˈtaɪ/ (education) A distinctive (often striped or crested) tie worn by an *old boy* as a member of an association of former students. The tie is regarded as typifying the attitudes and values held, or thought to be held, by *public school[1]* students, in particular loyalty, superiority, snobbishness and sportsmanship.

Old Trafford /ˌəʊld ˈtræfəd/ (sport and leisure) A well-known football stadium and cricket ground in southwest Manchester. The stadium is the home ground of *Manchester United*, and the cricket ground is used for *test matches* and other important matches. [named after the district]

Old Vic /ˌəʊld ˈvɪk/, **the** (arts) A well-known *London* theatre opened in 1818, originally as the Royal Coburg, but in 1833 renamed the Royal Victoria Theatre in honour of the 14-year-old princess (later *Queen*) *Victoria*. From 1963 the theatre became the temporary home of the *National Theatre* company, and from 1976 was used by the *Young Vic*, who later made their home nearby. In 1980 the Old Vic closed, due to the collapse of the Old Vic company, but the theatre was reopened in 1982. [name arose as affectionate nickname]

Old woman who lived in a shoe /ˌəʊld ˌwʊmən huː ˌlɪvd ɪn ə ˈʃuː/, **the** (tradition) A character in a nursery rhyme who 'had so many children she didn't know what to do'. The phrase is sometimes used half-seriously for a large family or for a large gathering of people in a restricted space.

Olympia /əˈlɪmpɪə/ (commerce) A large exhibition complex in west *London*, opened in 1886. A number of well-known annual events are held here, including (until recently) *Cruft's* and the *Ideal Home Exhibition*.

ombudsman /ˈɒmbʊdzmən/, **the** (government) The popular name for the *Parliamentary Commissioner*, a state-appointed official who investigates complaints referred to him by *MP*s from members of the public who claim to have been unfairly or wrongly treated by a government *department*. Since 1972 the ombudsman has also held the post of Health Service Commissioner, and in his role investigates complaints against the *NHS* authorities. [Swedish, 'commissioner'; Sweden was the first country to appoint such an official]

one-upmanship /ˌwʌn ˈʌpmənʃɪp/ (life and society) A semi-humorous term used to define the 'art' of gaining an advantage, usually by cunning or bluff, over others, especially with reference to social or intellectual superiority. The term was invented by the comic author Stephen Potter for his book of that name (1952). Compare *gamesmanship*, *lifemanship*. [from 'one up', in sense 'one point higher', 'one point ahead']

open day /ˈəʊpən deɪ/ (daily life) A day when members of the public are admitted to a normally private or professional establishment such as a school, factory or military base. On such an occasion special displays, tours and exhibits are usually arranged to explain the operation and aims of the establishment.

open shop /ˌəʊpən ˈʃɒp/ (work) An arrangement in a factory or other place of employment by which employees can work whether or not they belong to a trade union. Compare *closed shop*.

Open University /ˌəʊpən juːnɪˈvɜːsətɪ/, **the (OU, the)** (education) A non-residential university based in the new town of Milton Keynes, Buckinghamshire. Students do not need to have any formal qualifications to study for a degree and many *mature students* enrol. Study is by means of a *correspondence course* linked to radio and television programmes. For some of the OU courses students have to attend one-week *summer schools* that are held in many of

Britain's traditional universities. The University was founded in 1969 and began its first courses in 1971. [so named because it is 'open' to all to become students]

Opposition /ˌɒpə'zɪʃn/**, the** (government) The major political party (in *Britain* at present, either the *Conservative Party* or *Labour Party*) that is opposed to the government of the day, and whose *ministers*[2] sit opposite (facing) the government benches in the *House of Commons*. See also *Leader of the Opposition, Shadow Cabinet*. [officially known as Her Majesty's Loyal Opposition]

Oracle /'ɒrəkl/ (media) A teletext service provided by the *IBA*. Compare *Ceefax*. [from 'oracle' in its basic sense of 'one who announces information', but later interpreted as initials of 'optical reception of announcements by coded line electronics']

Orangemen /'ɒrɪndʒmən/ (politics) Members of the Orange Society, an Irish political society aiming to preserve Protestantism, especially in *Northern Ireland*, and thus to gain supremacy over Roman Catholics and Irish nationalists. The Society was founded in 1795, and took its name from King William III of Orange (1650–1702) who defeated James II and his Catholic supporters at the Battle of the *Boyne* (1690). The Orangemen still hold an annual parade in Northern Ireland cities on the anniversary of the Battle (12 July). See also *Apprentice Boys' Parade*.

oranges and lemons /ˌɒrɪndʒɪz ən 'lemənz/ (tradition) A game popular among young children in which two players (an 'orange' and a 'lemon') form an arch by joining hands and, singing a *nursery rhyme*, suddenly trap one of the other players in their arms as he runs under the arch, the trapping occurring when the two singers have reached the word 'chop' (repeated) at the end of the rhyme. The nursery rhyme, whose opening words are 'Oranges and lemons', is said to have a historic origin and to refer to executions in *London*.

order in council /ˌɔːdər ɪn 'kaʊnsl/ (government) An order made in theory by the sovereign with the advice of the *Privy Council*, but in practice a decree of the *Cabinet*.

Order of Merit /ˌɔːdər əv 'merɪt/**, the (OM, the)** (life and society) An order given to both civilians and military personnel who are outstanding in any field. It was instituted in 1902 and is limited in number to 24 men and women.

Order of the Bath /ˌɔːdər əv ðə 'bɑːθ/**, the** (life and society) One of the highest orders of knighthood, in three classes, each divided into two divisions, military and civil. The order was traditionally founded in 1399, and originally admission to it was characterized by a ritual bathing, among other ceremonies. Women became eligible for the order in 1971. [full title, 'The Most Honourable Order of the Bath']

Order of the Garter /ˌɔːdər əv ðə 'gɑːtə(r)/**, the** (life and society) The highest order of knighthood, together with the

Order of the Thistle. According to tradition, the Order was founded in 1348 by King Edward III, who is said to have picked up a garter dropped by the Countess of Salisbury at a court festival and gallantly tied it round his own knee, saying, 'Honi soit qui mal y pense' ('Shame on him who thinks evil of it'), words which today form the motto of the Order. The Order holds its special services in *St George's Chapel, Windsor Castle.* A Knight of the Order places the initials KG after his name. [full title, 'The Most Noble Order of the Garter']

Order of the Thistle /ˌɔːdər əv ðə ˈθɪsl/, **the** (life and society) The highest order of knighthood, together with the *Order of the Garter.* It was founded in 1687, and is mainly given to Scottish noblemen (limited to 16 in number), hence its name (see *thistle*). A Knight of the Order places the initials KT after his name. [full title, 'The Most Ancient and Most Noble Order of the Thistle']

order paper /ˈɔːdə ˌpeɪpə(r)/ (government) A publication listing the order in which business is to be conducted in the *House of Commons.*

ordinary shares /ˌɔːdənrɪ ˈʃeəz/ (finance) Shares issued by a company and entitling their holders to a share of the company's profits after the payment of *preference shares* to other holders.

Ordnance Survey /ˌɔːdnəns ˈsɜːveɪ/, **the** (geography) The official map-making body of the government, founded in 1791 under the Board of Ordnance (military supplies). It became well-known for its 'inch to a mile' maps of *Britain,* first published in the mid-19th century. From the early 1970s these were succeeded by the metric '2 cm to 1 km' maps, on a slightly enlarged scale.

Orkneys /ˈɔːknɪz/, **the** (geography) A sizeable group of islands lying to the north of mainland *Scotland* with Mainland their largest island. The islands are rich in Scandinavian remains and are popular with tourists. Compare the *Shetlands.*

Oulton Park /ˌəʊltən ˈpɑːk/ (sport and leisure) A motor-racing track east of Chester, Cheshire. [originally the park of Oulton Hall, a country house here]

Outward Bound (Trust) /ˌaʊtwəd ˈbaʊnd (ˌaʊtwəd ˌbaʊnd ˈtrʌst)/, **the** (education) An organization that arranges outdoor enterprises for young people, including sailing, canoeing, rock climbing and orienteering. The Trust was formed in 1946 by the head of *Gordonstoun School.* [from 'outward bound', term used of a ship leaving port for a particular destination]

Oval /ˈəʊvl/, **the** (sport and leisure) A well-known *cricket* ground in southeast *London,* officially the home ground of the Surrey County Cricket Club. [from its shape]

Ovaltine /ˈəʊvltiːn/ (food and drink) The brand name of a nourishing drink made from a powder containing malt extract, milk and eggs, to which hot milk is added. [originally 'Ovomaltine', from Latin 'ovum', 'egg' and 'malt']

Owen, David /'əʊɪn, 'deɪvɪd/ (people) Originally a right-wing member of the *Labour Party*, and *Foreign Secretary* from 1977 to 1979 in the Labour government, David Owen (born 1938) resigned from the party in 1981, together with Roy Jenkins, Shirley Williams and William Rodgers (the 'gang of four'), to found the *SDP*. In the contest for the leadership of this new party, he first lost to Roy Jenkins in the election of 1981, but was then successful in 1983. Trained as a doctor of medicine, David Owen is well-known for his able and determined manner and his 'common-sense' style leadership.

Oxbridge /'ɒksbrɪdʒ/ (education) A colloquial term for the universities of *Oxford²* and *Cambridge²*, jointly regarded as being academically superior to other universities and as enjoying and giving special privilege and prestige.

Oxfam/OXFAM /'ɒksfæm/'ɒksfæm/ (charities) A well-known charity providing practical relief in developing countries, founded in *Oxford¹* in 1942 and still having its head office there. It runs many shops in towns round *Britain* in which second-hand goods, as well as goods specially made in developing countries, are sold, to raise funds for its work. [abbreviation of *Ox*ford Committee for *Fam*ine Relief]

Oxford /'ɒksfəd/ (1 geography 2 education) 1 A historic city in Oxfordshire, and its *county town*, famed for its university and its fine medieval architecture. It is a major tourist centre. 2 A short name for *Oxford University*. Compare *Cambridge²*.

Oxford accent /ˌɒksfəd 'æksənt/ (language) As popularly used, an informal name for *RP*. However, some people use it as a name for an exaggerated form of RP that is traditionally believed to be associated with *Oxford University*.

Oxford blue /ˌɒksfəd 'bluː/ (1 daily life 2 sport and leisure) 1 A dark blue colour. Compare *Cambridge blue¹*. 2 A *blue³* at *Oxford University*.

Oxford Group /'ɒksfəd gruːp/, **the** (life and society) The original name of the worldwide movement for moral and spiritual renewal now known as Moral Rearmament. This was founded in *Oxford¹* in 1921.

Oxford Movement /'ɒksfəd ˌmuːvmənt/, **the** (religion) A movement towards *High Church* doctrine and practice in the *Church of England*, begun in *Oxford¹* in 1833.

Oxford Street /'ɒksfəd striːt/ (London) One of *London*'s most popular shopping streets, especially known for its department stores and varied clothing shops. [originally the road out of London leading to *Oxford¹*]

Oxford University /ˌɒksfəd juːnɪ'vɜːsɪtɪ/ (education) One of the two oldest and most famous universities in *Britain*, the other being *Cambridge University*. It was founded in the 12th century. There are at present 35 colleges: three are for women only and the rest take both men and women. Among the best known are: Christ Church, founded in 1546, with its large front *quadrangle* and its famous *chapel*[2] (which is also Oxford Cathedral); Magdalen College, founded in 1458, with its tall bell-tower in the *Perpendicular (style)* (on which the chapel *choir* sings at dawn on *May Day*); All Souls College, founded in 1437, which is unique in having no *undergraduates* but only *fellows*[2]; and New College, founded in 1379, with its fine chapel and well-known choir. There are at present approximately 9,400 students in residence, of whom over a third are women. The city of *Oxford*[1], although considerably more industrialized than *Cambridge*[1], is popular with tourists because of the University's many beautiful medieval buildings. See also *Ashmolean Museum, Blackwell's, Bodleian Library, Eights, Greats, Radcliffe Camera, Sheldonian Theatre.*

oyez /əʊˈjez/ (tradition) The traditional cry used by a *town crier*[1], and called three times to attract the attention of his hearers before he makes his announcement. [from Old French, 'hear!']

PANDA CAR

P & O /ˌpiː ən ˈəʊ/ **(Peninsular and Oriental (Steam Navigation Company), the** (transport) A famous shipping company, one of the largest in the world, founded in 1837, originally as a mail shipping route to the Iberian peninsula. It received its present name when its contract was extended to Egypt (the 'Orient') in 1840. Today it is the world's largest cruise operator.

P G Wodehouse /ˌpiː dʒi ˈwʊdhaʊs/ see *Wodehouse* (people)

PA /ˌpiː ˈeɪ/ **(personal assistant)** (work) A woman (less often, a man) who assists a businessman, writer, etc in his work. She acts as secretary, receives clients and visitors, deals with telephone calls, keeps his engagement diary and generally ensures the smooth running of her employer's office or daily routine. Compare *girl Friday*.

Paddington /ˈpædɪŋtən/ (transport) **1** A main line railway station in west *London*, and a terminus of the Western Region of *BR*. **2** An Underground railway station here. See *London Underground*.

Paddy /ˈpædɪ/ (tradition) An informal name for an Irishman. [from St Patrick, the patron saint of *Ireland* and the common Irish forename Patrick]

page three /ˌpeɪdʒ ˈθriː/ (media) A colloquial reference to page 3 of the *Sun* newspaper, on which a photograph of a partly or entirely nude female model appears every day.

Paisley, Ian /ˈpeɪzlɪ, ˌiːən/ (people) Ian Paisley (born 1926) is a moderator (leader) of the Free Presbyterian Church of Ulster in *Northern Ireland* and a prominent member of the Protestant community. As a politician he has been a vigorous campaigner against any possible union of Northern Ireland with the Republic of *Ireland* and a staunch supporter of *Ulster* (ie, Northern Ireland) remaining part of the *United Kingdom*. In 1970 he was elected as Protestant Unionist *MP* for the *constituency* of North Antrim, and in 1971 with others formed the United Ulster Unionist Council. Subsequently he became leader of the *Ulster Democratic Unionist Party*.

paisley pattern /ˈpeɪzlɪ ˌpætn/ (style) A distinctive abstract coloured pattern resembling an elaborate curving teardrop or tree cone, today found on the fabric used for a variety of clothes such as dresses and ties, but originally found on the *paisley shawl*.

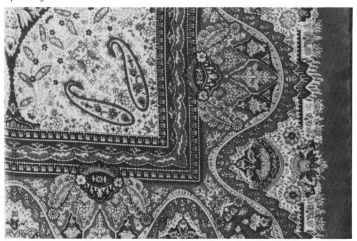

paisley pattern

paisley shawl /ˌpeɪzlɪ ˈʃɔːl/ (clothing) Properly, a shawl of soft, fine wool printed with a *paisley pattern*, originally made in Paisley, *Scotland*, in the 19th century.

Paisleyites /ˈpeɪzlɪaɪts/ (politics) A nickname for followers or supporters of Ian *Paisley*.

Palace /ˈpælɪs/, **the** (royal family) A colloquial term for *Buckingham Palace*.

Palace of Westminster /ˌpælɪs əv ˈwestmɪnstə(r)/, **the** (1 London 2 government) **1** A former royal palace in *London* (now officially known as the Old Palace of Westminster) on the site of which the present *Houses of Parliament* stand. The palace was largely destroyed by fire in the early 19th century, and the best known surviving part today is *Westminster Hall*. **2** The official name (in full, New Palace of Westminster) of the *Houses of Parliament*.

Pall Mall /ˌpæl ˈmæl/ (London) A street in central *London*, noted for its many *clubs*. [where pall-mall was formerly played, a now obsolete game in which a ball (Italian 'palla') was driven along an alley by a mallet (Italian 'maglio')]

Palladium /pəˈleɪdɪəm/, **the** (arts) A well-known *London* musical and variety theatre (also known as the London Palladium). [name apparently derived from the Palladium, or statue of Pallas Athene, in classical mythology, by confusion, or false association, with the Colosseum, the great amphitheatre in Rome]

Palm Sunday /ˌpaːm ˈsʌndɪ/ (religion) In the Christian church, the *Sunday* before *Easter*. In some *Church of England* churches and in the *Roman Catholic Church* small crosses made of palm leaves are given to members of the congregation. [from the Bible story in which palm branches were thrown on the ground in front of Christ as he entered Jerusalem]

Pancake Day /ˈpæŋkeɪk deɪ/ (tradition) A popular name for
Shrove Tuesday.

pancake race /ˈpæŋkeɪk reɪs/ (tradition) A traditional annual
race on *Shrove Tuesday*, in which (usually) women run with
pancakes. Each runner has a pancake in a pan. As she runs,
she tosses the pancake up and over in the air and catches it
again in the pan. See also *tossing the pancake*.

pancake race

pancakes /ˈpæŋkeɪks/ (food and drink) Cakes traditionally
eaten on *Shrove Tuesday*. They are thin and flat and made
from eggs, flour and milk, fried on both sides in fat in a pan
and usually served as a dessert, rolled and sprinkled with
lemon juice and sugar.

panda car /ˈpændə kɑː(r)/ (law) A name for a police car,
especially a blue and white or black and white one. [because
it is imagined to look like the black and white stripes of a
panda]

Panorama /ˌpænəˈrɑːmə/ (media) A weekly socio-political documentary television programme on *BBC 1*, devoted to topical subjects or current controversial matters, at home and abroad. It was first broadcast in 1953.

pantomime /ˈpæntəmaɪm/ (tradition) A type of musical play given annually at *Christmas* in theatres and elsewhere by professionals and amateurs. It has a traditional 'fairy tale' story (eg, 'Babes in the Wood', 'Cinderella') and is usually very lively and colourful with music and songs (in which the audience join) and dancing. Traditionally a man plays the *dame*, the older female, often the hero's mother, while the hero or *principal boy* is played by a young woman. Pantomimes are particularly popular with children, and a visit to one is one of the traditional treats of the Christmas season.

paperboy/girl /ˈpeɪpəbɔɪ/gɜːl/ (daily life) A schoolboy or schoolgirl who delivers newspapers and magazines daily to private houses and commercial premises such as offices and shops. The customer orders his papers through a newsagent, and pays his bills there, usually on a weekly basis, with the newsagent often making a special extra charge for the delivery. The paperboy or papergirl makes the delivery in the early morning, before going to school. He or she normally has to sort and 'mark up' (indicate the address on) the papers before beginning the round. The paperboy or papergirl is paid a small sum of money for this work.

parish church /ˌpærɪʃ ˈtʃɜːtʃ/ (religion) The church of a parish (church district) attended by churchgoers living in the parish (or in a neighbouring parish). In a village the parish church will often be the only one; in a town it will usually be one of several.

parish council /ˌpærɪʃ ˈkaʊnsl/ (government) In *England* and, formerly, *Wales*, the smallest body involved in local government in rural areas.

parish magazine /ˌpærɪʃ mægəˈziːn/ (religion) A regular (usually monthly) magazine published by the priest and *PCC* of a *parish church*, for members of the congregation. It contains a timetable of church services, announcements of births, baptisms, marriages and deaths, reports by members of the parish council and articles of topical, social or religious interest.

parish register /ˌpærɪʃ ˈredʒɪstə(r)/ (religion) A book in which the baptisms, marriages and burials in a particular parish are recorded.

Park Lane /ˌpɑːk ˈleɪn/ (London) A street in central *London* bordering the eastern side of *Hyde Park* and long famous for its wealth and fine buildings. Today it is best known for its top-class hotels, such as the *Dorchester* and *Grosvenor House* and its tall office buildings. It is one of the borders of *Mayfair*.

Parkhurst (prison) /'pɑːkhɜːst (ˌpɑːkhɜːst 'prɪzn)/ (law) A prison on the *Isle of Wight* for men serving long sentences. It is noted for its severe regime. [name of village and former forest ('hurst') here]

parking ticket /'pɑːkɪŋ ˌtɪkɪt/ (transport) A notice left on an incorrectly parked car by a *traffic warden*, informing the car owner that he must pay a fine or be summoned to a *court[3]* of law.

Parkinson's law /'pɑːkɪnsnz lɔː/ (work) A humorous law, expressed as a law of economics, saying that in official employment, such as the *Civil Service*, work expands to fill the time available for its completion. [formulated by C. Northcote Parkinson (born 1909), in a book of the same name published in 1958]

Parliament /'pɑːləmənt/ (government) The most important law-making body of the British people consisting of the *House of Commons*, the *House of Lords* and the sovereign (ie, *king* or *queen*).

Parliamentary Commissioner /ˌpɑːləmentrɪ kəˈmɪʃənə(r)/, **the** (government) The official name of the *ombudsman*.

parliamentary private secretary /ˌpɑːləmentrɪ ˌpraɪvɪt 'sekrətrɪ/ **(PPS)** (government) An *MP* (a *backbencher*) who is appointed by a *minister[3]* to help him in his contacts with other backbenchers, and who generally acts as his personal secretary and adviser. Compare *parliamentary secretary*.

parliamentary secretary /ˌpɑːləmentrɪ 'sekrətrɪ/ (government) An *MP* appointed, usually as a junior *minister[2]*, to act as a deputy for a senior minister who is not a *Secretary of State*. He shares in his senior's parliamentary and departmental duties and may be given special areas of responsibility in the *department*. Compare *parliamentary under-secretary of state*, *parliamentary private secretary*.

parliamentary under-secretary of state /ˌpɑːləmentrɪ ˌʌndə sekrətrɪ əv 'steɪt/ (government) The equivalent of a *parliamentary secretary* when the senior *minister[2]* is a *Secretary of State*.

parson /'pɑːsn/ (religion) **1** A term either for the priest in charge of a parish or for any clergyman. **2** A form of address occasionally used to a clergyman.

pass (degree) /'pɑːs (dɪˌgriː)/ (education) A *college[1]* or university final examination passed satisfactorily but not at such a high standard as that of an *honours degree*.

Passion Sunday /ˌpæʃn 'sʌndɪ/ (religion) The second *Sunday* before *Easter* (the fifth Sunday in Lent), when the solemn preparation for Easter begins in the Christian church. The day is marked with special prayers and hymns.

Patent Office /'peɪtnt ˌɒfɪs/, **the** (government) The government *department* responsible for issuing patents to firms and organizations and individual inventors.

patrial /'peɪtrɪəl/ (law) An official term used from the 1970s for a citizen of the *United Kingdom*, or of a British colony, or the *Commonwealth¹*, who has a legal right to enter and stay in *Britain* because either he, or his father or his father's father, was born there. [Latin, 'patria', 'fatherland']

Paul Jones /ˌpɔːl 'dʒəʊnz/ (sport and leisure) An old-time dance which begins with the women dancing round in an inner circle, the men circling the opposite way. When the music stops, a dancer's partner for the coming dance is the person opposite him or her. The Paul Jones always has the same music, but the intervening dances vary, and can be a waltz, quickstep, etc. [said to be named after the 18th-century Scottish naval adventurer John Paul Jones, who captured many pirate ships]

pavement artist /'peɪvmənt ˌɑːtɪst/ (daily life) A person who attempts to earn a living by drawing pictures (usually in coloured chalks) on the pavements, especially in *London*.

PAYE /ˌpiː eɪ waɪ 'iː/ **(Pay As You Earn)** (finance) A state scheme by which an employee's *income tax* is deducted direct from his pay by his employer, who in turn sends the money to the *Inland Revenue*. [implying 'pay when you earn']

paying guest /ˌpeɪɪŋ 'gest/ **(PG)** (daily life) A person who lives as a lodger in a private house, paying rent to the owner of the house.

Paymaster General /ˌpeɪmɑːstə 'dʒenrəl/**, the** (government) The government *minister⁴* who acts as a banker for *departments* other than the *Inland Revenue* and Customs and Excise, and who is responsible for the payment of many public service pensions, including those of *civil servants*, teachers, members of the *NHS* and members of the armed forces.

Payphone /'peɪfəʊn/ (commerce) A coin-operated telephone used by several people, in a public or private building such as a *pub* or a student hostel.

PCC /ˌpiː siː 'siː/ **(parochial church council)** (religion) The administrative body of a *parish church*, usually consisting of responsible members of the church's congregation. Most of the members are elected to the council by members of the parish.

PDSA /ˌpiː diː es 'eɪ/**, the (People's Dispensary for Sick Animals, the)** (charities) A voluntary organization, founded in 1917, that provides free veterinary treatment for animals, and through leaflets and films promotes the correct care of domestic pets.

Peak District /'piːk ˌdɪstrɪkt/**, the** (geography) A picturesque region of north central *England* in north Derbyshire, with hills, valleys, moorlands and caves. The area, popular for the climbing, walking and pot-holing it offers, is a *national park*. [named not only for its hill peaks but for the summit of High Peak, 603 m high]

pearly king/queen /ˌpɜːlɪ ˈkɪŋ/ˈkwiːn/ (London) A *London* market trader who on special occasions wears a traditional suit of dark clothes covered with pearl buttons. The pearly king or queen is the man or woman whose clothes have the most lavish design of pearl buttons.

pearly king/queen

pease pudding /ˌpiːz ˈpʊdɪŋ/ (food and drink) A hot savoury dish of boiled peas with ham or pork.

pebble dash /ˈpebl dæʃ/ (style) A kind of finish on the exterior walls of some houses, consisting of small stones set in plaster. [originally pebbles were dashed (thrown) against wet plaster to form the wall covering]

peer /pɪə(r)/ (life and society) **1** (hereditary peer) A titled member of the aristocracy (see p 379) who has the right to speak and vote in the *House of Lords* provided he is 21 or older. When a peer dies, the title is inherited by his closest male relation, usually his son. Occasionally, a woman can inherit a title. Since 1963 a peer has had the right to renounce his title during his lifetime, although this does not prevent that peer's heir from inheriting the title in the ordinary way. Most hereditary peers are men. Women peers are called 'lady peers' or, sometimes, 'peeresses'. **2** (life peer) A person who is given a title during his or her lifetime, usually as a reward for public service. Life peers have the right to speak and vote in the House of Lords. Women life peers are addressed in the same way as a hereditary peer.   A small number of peers have the right to sit in the House of Lords because of the office they hold. Amongst them are some bishops of the

Church of England (eg, the *Archbishop of Canterbury* and the *Archbishop of York*) and the *Law Lords* (eg, the *Lord Chancellor*).

peerage /ˈpɪərɪdʒ/ (life and society) A collective term for all the *peer*s or their titles in their different ranks (see p 379). There are technically five separate peerages in *Britain*: of *England*, *Scotland*, *Ireland*, *Great Britain* (since 1707); and the *United Kingdom* (since 1801). Peers of Ireland are not entitled to sit in the *House of Lords* unless they also hold one of the non-Irish titles.

peeress /ˈpɪəres/ (life and society) **1** A woman who holds an hereditary or a life peerage in her own right (usually called 'lady peer'). **2** The widely-used term for the wife or widow of a *peer*[1] (though a peeress is officially only a woman who holds a title in her own right). She may not sit or vote in the *House of Lords*.

pelican crossing /ˌpelɪkən ˈkrɒsɪŋ/ (transport) A type of road crossing for the use of pedestrians. It is marked with black and white stripes or rows of metal studs, and has traffic lights that can be set to stop traffic by people who wish to cross. Compare *zebra crossing* and see *Belisha beacon*. [based on '*pe*destrian *li*ght *con*trolled crossing' assimilated to 'pelican']

pelican crossing

penal system /ˈpiːnl ˌsɪstəm/ (law) *Britain*'s penal system is basically divided into non-custodial (without imprisonment) and custodial (with imprisonment). Non-custodial sentences take the form of fines, probation (going free but living under supervision) and absolute discharge (going free with no conditions of any kind). Custodial sentences, for more serious crimes, order imprisonment for any stated period, ranging from a few days to life. Most prisoners serving sentences of more than 18 months become eligible for release on parole after completing one third of their sentence or 12 months, whichever is the longer, and even prisoners serving life sentences are eligible for release on licence, after consideration by the *Home Secretary* or the *Secretary of State for Scotland* in the case of Scottish prisoners.

Penguin /ˈpeŋgwɪn/ (arts) A paperback book published by *Penguin Books*.

Penguin Books /ˌpeŋgwɪn ˈbʊks/ (commerce) A well-known publisher of paperback books, founded in 1935. From the beginning, their aim has been to publish good books at a price that anyone can afford. They were the first publisher to do so.

Pennine Way /ˌpenaɪn ˈweɪ/, **the** (geography) A *long distance footpath* extending for some 250 miles (400 km) along the *Pennines*, opened in 1965. It begins west of Sheffield, in north Derbyshire, and runs north to a point just north of the Cheviot Hills, in southern *Scotland*. On its route, it passes through three *national parks*, including the *Peak District*.

Pennines /ˈpenaɪnz/, **the** (geography) England's main mountain chain, extending southwards from Northumberland to the middle of Derbyshire and the north part of Staffordshire. The so-called 'backbone of *England*' is really more a series of uplands. The highest point of the Pennines is Cross Fell (2,930 feet (893 m)). See also *Pennine Way*.

penny /ˈpenɪ/ (finance) A low-value bronze coin worth (since 1971) one-hundredth of a *pound (sterling)*. Before 1971 (when it was made of copper) it had a value of one-twelfth of a *shilling*, or one two-hundred-and-fortieth of a pound. (The plural of 'penny' is 'pennies' to refer to individual coins, 'pence' to refer to a total sum of money, as 5p (five pence).) See p 376.

Penny Black /ˌpenɪ ˈblæk/ (history) The first British postage stamp, and also the first adhesive stamp in general use. It was issued in 1840 and has a profile of Queen Victoria on a dark background. It is not the rarest British stamp but is still highly valued today by many collectors.

penny-farthing /ˌpenɪ ˈfaːðɪŋ/ (transport) An early type of bicycle with a very large front wheel (resembling an old *penny*) and a very small rear one (resembling a *farthing*). The pedals were fastened to the front wheel.

Pentonville (prison) /ˈpentənvɪl (ˌpentənvɪl ˈprɪzn)/ (law) A large prison for men, opened in 1842 in north *London*. [named after district]

People /ˈpiːpl/, **the** (media) The former name (to 1972), still in colloquial use, for the *Sunday People* newspaper.

Perpendicular (style) /ˌpɜːpənˈdɪkjʊlə(r) (staɪl)/ (style) A *Gothic style* of architecture of the 14th and 15th centuries, characterized chiefly by large windows with vertical lines of tracery, and fan vaulting. Examples of the style are the *chapel*[2] of King's College, *Cambridge²*, St George's Chapel at *Windsor Castle* and several of the older *colleges¹* at *Oxford²* and Cambridge².

penny-farthing

personal column /ˈpɜːsənl ˌkɒləm/ (media) A column of advertisements in a newspaper or magazine, where people can make personal announcements, send private messages and make requests for friends or companions, etc.

Peter Pan /ˌpiːtə ˈpæn/ (1 arts 2 life and society 3 London)
1 The boy hero of a play of the same name by J M Barrie, first staged in 1904 ('the boy who wouldn't grow up'). **2** A boyish, youthful or immature man. **3** A statue of Peter Pan¹ in *Kensington Gardens, London*, erected in 1912.

Peter Pan collar /ˌpiːtə pæn ˈkɒlə(r)/ (clothing) A close-fitting collar on a girl's or woman's dress, with rounded ends at the front.

Petticoat Lane /ˌpetɪkəʊt ˈleɪn/ (London) A street in *London*'s *East End* where a weekly market is held on *Sunday* mornings. The market is famous for the variety of goods on sale there. Formerly these were mainly clothes (including petticoats), hence the name of the street, which is officially Middlesex Street.

PG /ˌpiː ˈdʒiː/ (arts) A category in which a cinema film is placed by the *British Board of Film Censors* to indicate that, in their judgement, the film contains some scenes that may be unsuitable for children. Compare *15* (listed under letter F), *18* (listed under letter E) and *U certificate*. ['PG' for the initials of 'parental guidance']

Philharmonia Orchestra /ˌfɪləməʊnɪə 'ɔːkɪstrə/, **the** (arts) A leading *London* symphony orchestra founded in 1945 and until 1977 called the New Philharmonia Orchestra.

Piccadilly /ˌpɪkə'dɪlɪ/ (London) A central shopping street in *London*, with a wide variety of shops, stores, hotels, tourist offices and showrooms. [said to be named after the 'piccadills' or fancy collars sold here formerly]

Piccadilly Circus /ˌpɪkədɪlɪ 'sɜːkəs/ (**1, 2** transport **3** language) **1** A well-known road junction in central *London* where a number of famous streets meet, including *Piccadilly*, *Regent Street* and *Shaftesbury Avenue*. The junction is famous for its brightly lit neon advertisements at night. In the centre of the junction stands the memorial popularly known as *Eros*. **2** An Underground railway station here. See *London Underground*. **3** A humorous name for any crowded or busy place, such as a *High Street*, a public swimming pool in summer or a noisy school yard.

pickets /'pɪkɪts/ (work) A group of workers stationed outside a workplace such as a factory or a coalmine during a strike or other dispute. Usually their aim is to prevent or dissuade employees or clients from entering, or commercial suppliers from delivering, goods. Pickets frequently display placards showing the name of the trade union and stating their demands. See also *flying pickets, secondary picketing*.

pickets

pidgin English /ˌpɪdʒɪn 'ɪŋglɪʃ/ (language) **1** A language made up of elements of English and some other foreign language, especially Chinese or Japanese, originally developing as a means of verbal communication when trading. **2** Loosely, any kind of English spoken with the elements of another language, whether for genuine communication or for comic effect. [perhaps Chinese pronunciation of English word 'business']

pig in the middle /ˌpɪg ɪn ðə 'mɪdl/ (sport and leisure) A children's game in which one player, in between two others, tries to catch a ball that they throw to each other past him. When he succeeds (in catching the ball), he changes places with the player who threw it.

piggy bank /'pɪgɪ bæŋk/ (daily life) A child's money-box in the shape of a pig, with a slot in the top (the back of the pig) for the coins. [apparently from 'pig' or 'piggin', an old word for a pot or jar, not related to 'pig' the animal]

Pilgrims' Way /ˌpɪlgrɪmz 'weɪ/, **the** (geography) A track running from Winchester, Hampshire, to *Canterbury*, Kent, today used as a footpath but originally the route of medieval pilgrims travelling to the shrine of Thomas à Becket (1118-70) in Canterbury Cathedral.

Pinewood Studios /ˌpaɪnwʊd 'stjuːdɪəʊz/, **the** (arts) A large film studio near Slough, Buckinghamshire, opened in 1936 and now owned by the Rank Organization.

pinstripe suit /ˌpɪnstraɪp 'suːt/ (clothing) A formal or business suit for men made of dark cloth with very narrow contrasting stripes.

pint /paɪnt/ (daily life) A liquid measure equal to 0.568 litres, still used for selling milk and beer.

pinta /'paɪntə/ (food and drink) A colloquial word for a pint of milk. [corruption of 'pint of']

pips /pɪps/, **the** (media) The radio time signal broadcast on the hour by the *BBC*, consisting of five short high-pitched sounds ('pips') and a final longer one. Time is measured from the end of the sixth pip.

plaid /plæd/ (clothing) A long piece of cloth with a *tartan[1]* pattern, worn over the shoulder as part of the traditional dress of a Scotsman, especially a *highlander[1]*.

Plaid Cymru /ˌplaɪd 'kʌmrɪ/ (politics) A Welsh nationalist party founded in 1925 and campaigning for the separation of *Wales* from the *United Kingdom* in order to preserve the country's culture, language and economic life. [Welsh, 'party of Wales']

planning permission /'plænɪŋ pəˌmɪʃn/ (law) The necessary permission that must be obtained from a *local authority* by a person planning to make alterations to his building.

play street /'pleɪ striːt/ (daily life) In the residential district of a city, a street that is closed to traffic and used as a play area by children, especially when there is no other play area (such as a park or playground) available in the neighbourhood.

playgroup /'pleɪ gruːp/ (education) A regular organized gathering of pre-school age children, often supervised by the mother of one of them, in which the children play games and are guided in other activities for a morning or afternoon.

playschool /'pleɪ skuːl/ (education) Another name for a *playgroup* or *nursery school*.

PLC/Plc/plc /ˌpiː el 'siː/ˌpiː el 'siː/ˌpiː el 'siː/ **(public limited company)** (finance) A commercial, usually large, company, whose shares can be bought and sold by the public on the *Stock Exchange*. Such companies must be registered under the Companies Act of 1980 and must place the words 'public limited company' or its abbreviation after their name. Compare *private limited company*.

ploughman's lunch /ˌplaʊmənz 'lʌntʃ/ (food and drink) A snack *lunch* of cheese, bread and butter, usually accompanied by tomatoes, lettuce, celery, or other salad and pickles. Such a meal has been popular in *pub*s as a midday snack since the early 1970s. [suggesting the midday meal that ploughmen used to have in the field]

plum pudding /ˌplʌm 'pʊdɪŋ/ (food and drink) A traditional rich, dark-coloured steamed or boiled pudding made with flour, suet and eggs, and containing raisins, currants, or other dried fruit (but not plums), spices and often alcohol. Compare *Christmas pudding*. [from 'plum' in former and now special sense of 'raisin', 'dried fruit', since raisins were used instead of dried plums in puddings]

plus-fours /ˌplʌs 'fɔːz/ (clothing) A kind of loose, baggy breeches (strictly knickerbockers) coming down to below the knee, that used to be worn by golfers (from the 1920s) and are still worn by some sportsmen. [so named from the extra four inches of cloth needed for the distinctive 'overhang' over the knee]

Plymouth Brethren /ˌplɪməθ 'breðrɪn/, **the** (religion) A puritanical religious sect founded in Dublin in about 1825, largely as a reaction against *High Church* principles. Members of the sect aim at strict piety, regard the Bible as infallible and reject a formal ordained priesthood. [from one of the first congregations, established at Plymouth, Devon, in 1831]

Poet Laureate /ˌpəʊɪt 'lɒrɪət/, **the** (arts) The title of the poet appointed for life as an officer of the royal household. He usually produces verse for formal or state occasions such as a coronation or state funeral, but is not obliged to do so. The first Poet Laureate is usually regarded as Ben Jonson (in 1616). [from the laurel crown or wreath originally awarded as a sign of honour]

Poets' Corner /ˌpəʊɪts 'kɔːnə(r)/ (arts) An area of *Westminster Abbey* where several famous poets and writers are buried, or where monuments to them are raised. Among those buried here are Chaucer (1340–1400), Browning (1812–89), Tennyson (1809–92), Dickens (1812–70), Hardy (1840–1928) and Kipling (1865–1936).

point-to-point /ˌpɔɪnt tə 'pɔɪnt/ (sport and leisure) A horse race over fences (steeplechase) organized by a *hunt* or other local group, and usually restricted to amateurs riding horses that they have ridden regularly in the hunt. [originally run over the countryside, not on a course, from one point to another]

police /pə'liːs/ (law) The police force of *Britain* is relatively small in relation to the population, with about one policeman or policewoman to every 400 people. At present there are 52 regional police forces, each headed by a *Chief Constable*, with *London* looked after by the *Metropolitan Police Force* (with its headquarters at *New Scotland Yard*) and the *City* (*of London*) force. The British police are normally not armed, but policemen do carry a truncheon (a short thick club). Their duties range from everyday tasks such as protecting people and property, patrolling roads and streets (see *bobby*) and controlling traffic, to preventing and investigating crimes and arresting offenders. See also *CID, Fraud Squad, Vice Squad, special constable.*

polling booth /'pəʊlɪŋ buːð/ (politics) One of a number of enclosed compartments in a *polling station* where an elector marks his vote on the *ballot paper* in an election such as a *by-election* or *general election.*

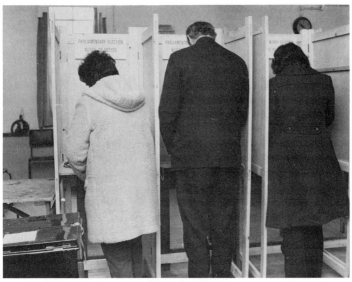

polling booth

polling day /'pəʊlɪŋ deɪ/ (politics) A day appointed for electors to cast their votes (at *polling stations*) in an election such as a *by-election* or *general election*. The day is usually a Thursday.

polling station /'pəʊlɪŋ ˌsteɪʃn/ (politics) A building, often a public hall or a school, where electors vote on *polling day*. In a *by-election* or *general election*, polling stations are usually open from 7 am to 9 or 10 pm.

polls /pəʊlz/, **the** (politics) A collective term for the *polling stations* in an election.

polytechnic /ˌpɒlɪ ˈteknɪk/ (education) One of 30 *colleges*[2] in *England* and *Wales* that provide a wide range of courses at *further education* or *higher education* level, with some courses leading to a degree. Many polytechnics run courses that still have a greater technical or vocational bias than that of a university.

Pony Club /ˈpəʊnɪ klʌb/, **the** (sport and leisure) A club for young pony riders, holding a wide range of meetings, shows and contests. It was founded in 1929 and currently (1984) has about 50,000 members.

pony-trekking /ˈpəʊnɪ ˌtrekɪŋ/ (sport and leisure) A type of holiday activity in which ponies are ridden cross-country, especially over rough country such as moorland and hill country. The sport became popular from the 1970s.

pools /puːlz/, **the** (sport and leisure) A weekly gambling contest, organized by various firms throughout the country, in which bets are placed on the results of football matches. The contest is conducted mainly by predicted results being sent on a special form ('pools coupon') through the post, although some firms also arrange for collectors to call for the forms at people's private houses. [also called 'football pools': 'pool' in sense of 'combined stake']

Poppy Day /ˈpɒpɪ deɪ/ (tradition) A popular name for *Remembrance Sunday*, when people wear an artificial poppy in memory of those who fell in the two world wars. The poppies represent those that grew in the cornfields of Flanders in the First World War, and symbolize the soldiers who died in that war (and now, also, the Second World War). They are made by ex-servicemen and are sold by representatives of the *Royal British Legion*, who gain much of their income from the proceeds.

popular paper /ˌpɒpjʊlə ˈpeɪpə(r)/ (media) A daily or *Sunday* newspaper whose format and content is designed for the undemanding reader. Most popular papers are *tabloids*, and have brief and direct news reports and a large number of photographs. Emphasis is put on personal stories (especially when sensational, or involving a figure in the public eye such as a member of the *royal family*), and importance is also given to sport and to entertaining features such as cartoons and contests (eg, *bingo*). The style of English is often colloquial or conversational, with much use of slang, nicknames and catchy headlines (often in large, bold letters). Leading daily popular papers are the *Daily Express*, the *Daily Mail*, the *Mirror*, the *Daily Star* and The *Sun*. Leading Sunday popular papers are the *Sunday Express*, the *Mail on Sunday*, the *Sunday Mirror*, the *News of the World* and the *Sunday People*. Most popular papers have a *lower class* or *lower middle class* readership, compared with the *middle class* and *upper class* readership of the *quality papers*.

pork-pie hat /ˌpɔːk paɪ ˈhæt/ (clothing) A man's hat with a round, flat crown and a brim that can be turned down as well as up. [from its resemblance to the top layer of pastry crust on a pork pie]

porridge /ˈpɒrɪdʒ/ (food and drink) A once popular dish in an *English breakfast*—oatmeal cooked in water or milk until as thick as required. It is eaten hot with a spoon, usually with sugar (or salt) and milk (or cream) added on top. The dish is traditionally popular in *Scotland*, but in *England* has largely been replaced by other prepared cereals that do not need cooking.

Port of London Authority /ˌpɔːt əv ˈlʌndən ɔːˌθɒrəti/, **the (PLA, the)** (transport) The independent (non-governmental) body that operates the port and docks of *London*. The Authority is technically a public trust, and similar trusts control other major ports in *Britain*, although many are also operated as nationalized (state-owned) bodies or are managed by a *local authority*. Some other port authorities function as companies, including the one at Liverpool.

Portobello Road /ˌpɔːtəbeləʊ ˈrəʊd/ (London) A street in west *London* famous for its daily market, especially the one held on Saturday. The market is famous for its variety, but its greatest attractions are its antiques, boutique clothes, *Victoriana* and 'junk' (discarded or second-hand objects, some occasionally found to be valuable). [street named after former farm here, named in turn after British capture of Portobello, Panama, in 1739]

Porton Down /ˌpɔːtn ˈdaʊn/ (science and technology) The short name of the Centre for Applied Microbiology and Research, which has its laboratories at Porton, northeast of Salisbury, Wiltshire. The Centre has been the subject of public protest in recent years, both for its work in connection with biological and chemical warfare and for its use of live animals for scientific research. The Centre is a state-owned body.

positive vetting /ˌpɒzətɪv ˈvetɪŋ/ **(PV)** (government) The process by which government and armed forces personnel engaged in sensitive or high-security work are examined, and their background and personal contacts investigated, so that they can be officially cleared for their duties. ['positive' in sense 'having necessary qualities and reliability'; 'vetting' from colloquial verb 'to vet', meaning 'to examine' (as a *vet*erinary surgeon or 'vet' examines animals)]

Post Office /ˈpəʊst ˌɒfɪs/, **the (PO, the)** (commerce) The public corporation (until 1969, government *department*) responsible for the delivery of mail as well as the operation of a number of other services, notably the *National Savings Bank*.

Post Office Tower /ˌpəʊst ɒfɪs ˈtaʊə(r)/, **the** (London) The former name, still popularly used, of the *Telecom Tower*, *London*.

postal district /ˈpəʊstl ˌdɪstrɪkt/ (geography) The district of a large town or city for postal delivery, usually given as a combination of letters and figures, for example (in *London*) EC3 ('east central district number three'), N4 ('north four'). All postal districts have now become part of a *postcode*.

postal order /ˈpəʊstl ˌɔːdə(r)/ (finance) A printed order to pay a named person or company a stated sum of money, bought at a post office. Postal orders are mostly for small amounts and are chiefly used by people who do not have a bank account (and therefore cannot send a cheque). At present (1985) they are issued in values from 25p to £10.

postal vote /ˈpəʊstl vəʊt/ (politics) A vote sent by post in a *by-election* or *general election* by a voter who has to be away from his *constituency* on *polling day*. Compare *proxy vote*.

Postbus /ˈpəʊstbʌs/ (transport) A *Post Office* minibus transporting both mail and passengers in some rural areas.

postcode /ˈpəʊstkəʊd/ (daily life) A combination of letters and figures forming the final item in a postal address and used by the *Post Office* to sort and deliver mail. In *Britain* the postcode is written in two halves: the first group gives the initials of the town or city where the area head post office is situated, plus the number of the district in that area; the second half gives the *postman*'s delivery area or 'walk' in the form of a figure and letter combination. Thus the postcode GU31 4LN indicates the area head post office of Guildford, Surrey (GU), the district of Petersfield (and an area round the town), Hampshire (31), the street named The Causeway (4) and the section of houses on this street numbered 125 to 209 (LN). All addresses in Britain officially have a postcode, but some people prefer not to use it in their address.

postgraduate /ˌpəʊst ˈɡrædʒʊət/ (education) A student who has completed a university course and who is continuing to study for a more advanced qualification such as a *higher degree*. See also *graduate student*.

postman /ˈpəʊstmən/ (daily life) An employee of the *Post Office* who delivers mail daily (except on *Sunday*) to private and public buildings. In towns he usually makes his deliveries on foot or by bicycle; in rural areas he will deliver the post by van. There are normally three deliveries a day, two of letters and one of parcels. The first, main delivery is usually in the early morning, and the second in the late morning. Parcels are normally delivered in the morning. On Saturdays there is only one delivery of letters (and one of parcels). There are no deliveries on *bank holidays*. In a few isolated or remote areas the postman will also collect mail as well as deliver it.

postman's knock /ˌpəʊstmənz ˈnɒk/ (sport and leisure) A children's game (or, on occasions, adults' game) in which one of the players goes outside and knocks on the door of the room where the other players are as a 'postman' delivering a 'letter' which has to be 'paid for' with a kiss.

Potteries /'pɒtərɪz/**, the** (geography) A name for the six towns of Burslem, Hanley, Longton, Fenton, Tunstall and Stoke-on-Trent, Staffordshire (the first five officially became part of Stoke-on-Trent in 1910). The area has long been famous for its china and earthenware industries.

pound (sterling) /paʊnd ('stɜːlɪŋ)/ (finance) The basic unit of British currency, divided into 100 pence (before decimalization, 240 pence) (see *penny*), and circulating either as a banknote ('pound note') or, from 1983, a coin ('pound coin'). Its written symbol, placed before the number of pounds, is £, as £5 ('five pounds'). In colloquial speech, many people do not add an 's' to 'pound' in the plural ('five pound'), especially when an amount in pence follows ('five pound fifty'). From the end of 1984, pound notes were gradually taken out of circulation and now pound coins are increasingly used. See p 376.

PPP /ˌpiː piː 'piː/ **(Private Patients Plan)** (medicine) An insurance organization similar to *BUPA* by which financial cover can be provided for private medical treatment outside the *NHS* for regular subscribers.

prefect /'priːfekt/ (education) In some schools, a senior boy or girl in a position of authority, for example, in charge of a class.

preference shares /'prefrəns ʃeəz/ (finance) Shares that entitle their holders to preference (priority) when *dividends* are paid. The rate of the dividend, however, is usually lower than that of *ordinary shares*.

Premium (Savings) Bonds /'priːmɪəm bɒndz (ˌpriːmɪəm 'seɪvɪŋz bɒndz)/ (finance) Bonds (certificates of a loan) issued by the *Treasury* since 1956 for sale to members of the public. Many bonds pay interest to the lender, but Premium Bonds, instead of earning interest, enter a monthly draw for cash prizes. They are usually bought at a *Post Office*. See *Ernie*.

prep school /'prep skuːl/ (education) A colloquial abbreviation for a *preparatory school*.

preparatory school /prɪ'pærətrɪ skuːl/ (education) An independent (fee-paying) school for children aged (usually) 7 to 13. Many are boarding schools and for boys only (aged 7–13) or girls only (7–11) and some form a junior department of a *public school*[1]. Most pupils go on from a preparatory school to a public school by taking the *Common Entrance* examination. [providing education 'preparatory' to a public school]

pre-preparatory school /ˌpriː prɪ'pærətrɪ skuːl/ (education) An independent school that prepares children aged 5 to 7 for entry to a *preparatory school*.

Pre-Raphaelites /ˌpriː 'ræfəlaɪts/**, the** (arts) A group of painters (full name, the Pre-Raphaelite Brotherhood) founded in 1848 with the aim of restoring to painting the vivid colours,

attention to detail, and naturalistic subjects that they
regarded as typical (and best) of the early Italian Renaissance
masters, who were painting before Raphael. Many of the
group chose biblical and romantic subjects for their themes.
Among leading members were Dante Gabriel Rossetti
(1828–82), Holman Hunt (1827–1910), John Millais (1829–96)
and Edward Burne-Jones (1833–98).

presbytery /'prezbɪtrɪ/ (religion) **1** In some *Church of England*
churches and cathedrals, the name used for the area where
the main altar is. **2** In the *Roman Catholic Church*, the
residence of a priest. **3** In a Presbyterian church, a local
church court of *ministers*[1] and elders.

pre-school playgroup /ˌpriːskuːl 'pleɪgruːp/ (education) An
alternative name for a *playgroup*.

prescription /prɪ'skrɪpʃn/ (medicine) An official order for a
patient's medicines or medical appliances, made by a doctor
or dentist. The patient usually takes his prescription to a
chemist (known as a 'dispensing chemist'), where it will be
prepared according to the directions of the doctor. The
amount of medicine to be taken and the correct way to take it
is always written on a label stuck to the medicine container.
There is a standard charge for the *NHS* dispensing of a
prescription but some patients obtain theirs free, including
all children under 16, expectant mothers, *OAP*s and patients
suffering from certain permanent conditions. Private
patients, who are not treated through the NHS, are also given
prescriptions by their doctor, but they must pay the full cost
of any medicine or appliance.

presiding officer /prɪˌzaɪdɪŋ 'ɒfɪsə(r)/ (politics) A person
appointed to be in charge of a *polling station* during a *by-
election* or *general election*.

Press Association /'pres əsəʊsɪˌeɪʃn/, **the (PA, the)** (media) A
leading British news agency, founded in 1868 and providing
a full service of home news to national and regional
newspapers, the *BBC*, *ITN* and other subscribers.

Press Council /'pres ˌkaʊnsl/, **the** (media) An independent
organization founded by the press in 1953 with the aim of
preserving the traditional freedom of the British press. It
judges complaints made by members of the public about the
behaviour of newspapers and magazines and obliges the
press to publish the results of its findings, even in a
newspaper that itself has been found guilty of unprofessional
conduct.

Prestel /'prestel/ (media) A viewdata service started in 1979,
and now operated by *British Telecom*. It transmits information
and messages from a computer over the telephone network
and displays them in the form of coloured words, figures and
graphics on a suitably equipped television set. See also
Homelink. [apparently a blend of '*pres*s' and '*tele*phone']

Prestwick /ˈprestwɪk/ (transport) An international airport near Prestwick, southwest *Scotland*.

primary school /ˈpraɪmərɪ skuːl/ (education) A junior state school for children aged (usually) 5 to 11, after which they pass to a *secondary school*. Some children in this age group, however, attend a *first school* or *middle school*.

primate /ˈpraɪmeɪt/ (religion) An alternative title for an archbishop. See *Primate of All England*, *Primate of England*.

Primate of All England /ˌpraɪmeɪt əv ɔːl ˈɪŋglənd/, **the** (religion) The official title of the *Archbishop of Canterbury*. Compare *Primate of England*.

Primate of England /ˌpraɪmeɪt əv ˈɪŋglənd/, **the** (religion) The official title of the *Archbishop of York*. Compare *Primate of All England*.

Prime Minister /ˌpraɪm ˈmɪnɪstə(r)/, **the (PM, the)** (government) The head of the government, who presides over the *Cabinet* and gives posts to *ministers²*. The Prime Minister sits in the *House of Commons* and, among other responsibilities, recommends a number of appointments to the sovereign, including senior clergy in the *Church of England*; high legal offices such as the *Lord Chief Justice*, *Privy Councillors*, *Lords-Lieutenant* and the *Poet Laureate*. He or she is also, by tradition, Minister for the *Civil Service*. ['Prime' as the first or chief minister of state]

Primrose League /ˌprɪmrəʊz ˈliːg/, **the** (politics) An organization for promoting *Conservative Party* principles, founded in 1883 in memory of Benjamin Disraeli (1804–81), a Conservative British *Prime Minister*. The aims of the League are 'the maintenance of religion, of the constitution of the realm, and of the unity of the British *Commonwealth*¹ and Empire'. In the early 1970s it still had over two million members. [named after what was said to be Disraeli's favourite flower]

prince /prɪns/ (royal family) The title of the sons of the sovereign, of the sons of his or her sons, and of the husband of a *queen*. It is used together with the prince's name, as in 'Prince Charles', 'Prince William'. See also *Prince of Wales*.

Prince of Wales /ˌprɪns əv ˈweɪlz/, **the** (royal family) The title of 'Prince of Wales' is traditionally given by the British sovereign to his or her eldest son, who is heir to the throne. The earliest recorded bearer of the title was Edward II in the early 14th century. The present Prince of Wales is Prince Charles (born 1948), eldest son of *Queen Elizabeth*. Prince Charles was invested with the title of Prince of Wales at Caernarfon Castle, as all his predecessors have been. He is one of the most popular members of the *royal family* and is well-known as a keen promoter of British interests. In 1981 he married Lady Diana Spencer, now the *Princess of Wales*.

Prince Regent /ˌprɪns ˈriːdʒənt/, **the** (history) The title of King George IV as regent (ruler) of *Great Britain* and *Ireland* while his father, George III, was insane from 1811–20.

Princes in the Tower /ˌprɪnsɪz ɪn ðə ˈtaʊə(r)/, **the** (history) A popular name for the boy king Edward V (1470–83) and his younger brother Richard, Duke of York (1472–83), both (perhaps) murdered in the *Tower of London*, allegedly by order of their uncle, the Duke of Gloucester, so that he could succeed to the throne as Richard III (1452–85).

Princes Street /ˈprɪnsɪz striːt/ (geography) A central street of *Edinburgh, Scotland*, with fashionable shops and restaurants, and with gardens running along its south side. In the gardens are a memorial to the Scottish author Sir Walter Scott and a famous floral clock. [named after the princes who were the sons of George III (1738–1820)]

princess /prɪnˈses/ (royal family) The title of the daughters of the sovereign and of the daughters of his or her sons. It is used together with the princess's name, as in 'Princess Anne'.

Princess of Wales /ˌprɪnses əv ˈweɪlz/, **the** (royal family) The title of 'Princess of Wales' is traditionally given by the British sovereign to the wife of the *Prince of Wales*. The present Princess of Wales (the former Lady Diana Spencer) married the Prince of Wales in 1981. She has won the affection of many people by her modesty, shyness and beauty. The wedding of the royal couple in 1981 was one of the great public events of the year, and subsequently the Princess became a setter of fashion, admired for her dazzling evening clothes and fine jewels. Her broad hats and low heels were widely copied in 1983. In 1982 she gave birth to her first child, Prince William, and two years later to her second son, Prince Henry.

principal boy /ˌprɪnsəpl ˈbɔɪ/ (tradition) The young 'hero' in a *pantomime*, traditionally played by a female actor. In 'Cinderella' the part is that of Prince Charming; in 'Jack and the Beanstalk', that of Jack; in 'Aladdin and his Wonderful Lamp', that of Aladdin; in 'Dick Whittington', that of Dick.

Printing House Square /ˌprɪntɪŋ haʊs ˈskweə(r)/ (media) **1** A square south of *Fleet Street[1]*, *London* where the royal printers had their premises in the 17th century and where the offices of The *Times* were from its foundation in 1785. (In 1974 the newspaper moved its offices to new buildings in Gray's Inn Road, calling them 'New Printing House Square'. This, however, is not an official name, but an informal transfer of the former name.) **2** A nickname of 'The Times', or of its London offices.

private bar /ˌpraɪvɪt ˈbɑː(r)/ (daily life) An additional *bar[1]* in a *pub*, similar to a *lounge bar*.

private bill /ˌpraɪvɪt ˈbɪl/ (government) A bill presented to parliament on behalf of a private individual or group of people (eg, the shareholders of a company), as distinct from a *public bill*. Compare also *private member's bill*.

private company /ˌpraɪvɪt ˈkʌmpənɪ/ see *private limited company* (finance)

Private Eye /ˌpraɪvɪt ˈaɪ/ (media) A weekly satirical magazine, first published in 1962. It aims to expose scandals and corrupt practices, especially those involving public figures such as politicians and leading businessmen, and on more than one occasion has been sued (sometimes successfully) for libel. [from the nickname for a private detective]

private hotel /ˌpraɪvɪt həʊˈtel/ (daily life) A hotel where the owner has the right to refuse admission to a guest, especially one who arrives without having previously booked.

private income /ˌpraɪvɪt ˈɪŋkʌm/ (finance) Income not from regular work but from other sources, such as investment or gambling.

private limited company /ˌpraɪvɪt ˌlɪmɪtɪd ˈkʌmpənɪ/ (finance) A commercial, often small, company, that is legally defined as any company that is not a public limited company (see *PLC*), and so is one that cannot offer shares to the public. Such companies are in the majority, and the distinction between the two types was introduced with the passing of the Companies Act of 1980. A private limited company usually puts the abbreviation 'Ltd' (Limited) after its name to indicate that it is legally a *limited company*.

private means /ˌpraɪvɪt ˈmiːnz/ (finance) An alternative term for *private income*.

private member /ˌpraɪvɪt ˈmembə(r)/ (government) An *MP* who is not a member of the government (ie, a *minister*[2]) or of the *Shadow Cabinet*.

private member's bill /ˌpraɪvɪt ˈmembəz bɪl/ (government) A *public bill* introduced in the *House of Commons* by a *private member*. Compare also *private bill*.

private patient /ˌpraɪvɪt ˈpeɪʃnt/ (medicine) A patient who pays for his medical treatment and does not receive it through the *NHS*. Most private patients subscribe to a special insurance scheme operated by a *provident society* or *friendly society* such as *BUPA* or *PPP*.

private practice /ˌpraɪvɪt ˈpræktɪs/ (medicine) A doctor's practice where *private patients* are treated.

private road /ˌpraɪvɪt ˈrəʊd/ (transport) A road running over private property, such as the estate of a *country house*. It is usually open to the public but may be closed. Private roads must be closed to the public at least once a year in order to remain private.

private school /ˌpraɪvɪt ˈskuːl/ (education) An *independent* (fee-paying) *school* such as a *preparatory school*, as distinct from a *state* (non-fee-paying) *school*. The finances of such schools are often controlled by a charitable trust. Most *public schools*[1] are in fact private schools, although the term is not generally used in order to avoid confusion.

private treaty /ˌpraɪvɪt ˈtriːtɪ/ (law) An arrangement by which the price of a house to be sold is agreed directly between seller and buyer, not through an *estate agent*.

Privy Council /ˌprɪvɪ ˈkaʊnsl/, **the** (government) The private council of the sovereign. Its main function today is to advise the sovereign to approve certain government decrees (so-called *orders in council*) and to issue royal proclamations. All *Cabinet ministers*[2,4] are members of the Privy Council, as are eminent people in *Commonwealth*[1] countries, as appointed by the sovereign. In 1984 the total membership was about 380. A full meeting of the Council is called only when a sovereign dies or announces his or her intention to marry.

Privy Councillor/Counsellor /ˌprɪvɪ ˈkaʊnsələ(r)/ (government) A member of the *Privy Council*.

Privy Seal /ˌprɪvɪ ˈsiːl/, **the** (government) A seal fastened on certain royal documents that are not important enough for the *Great Seal*, or on documents that later receive the Great Seal.

probate /ˈprəʊbeɪt/ (law) The process of officially proving that a will is genuine and that what it says is valid. This process is carried out in the *High Court of Justice*.

probation /prəˈbeɪʃn/ (law) A scheme whereby a criminal offender is placed under the supervision of a *probation officer* for a period of between six months (12 months in *Scotland*) and three years. The aim is to rehabilitate the offender by allowing him to lead a normal life rather than be put in prison. An offender being supervised in this way is said to be 'on probation'.

probation officer /prəˈbeɪʃn ˌɒfɪsə(r)/ (law) An officer appointed by a court to supervise, advise and befriend a *probationer*[2].

probationer /prəˈbeɪʃənə(r)/ (1 work 2 law) 1 Someone who is training to do a particular job, for example a trainee teacher. 2 A criminal offender who is on *probation*.

proctor /ˈprɒktə(r)/ (education) A *don* or member of the teaching staff appointed at some universities to supervise examinations, enforce discipline, and carry out other administrative duties.

procurator fiscal /ˌprɒkjʊreɪtə ˈfɪskl/ (law) In *Scotland*, an officer of a *sheriff*[2] court who acts as a public prosecutor and who carries out the duties that a *coroner* would carry out in *England*.

progressive school /prəˈɡresɪv skuːl/ (education) Usually an *independent* (fee-paying) *school*, where so-called pupil-centred methods are used, so that the children are encouraged to develop social, cultural and practical abilities as well as academic ones. Such schools developed in the late 19th and early 20th centuries, one example being *Dartington Hall*.

Promenade Concerts /ˌprɒməˈnɑːd ˌkɒnsəts/, **the** (arts) An annual series of summer concerts sponsored by the *BBC* and

held at the *Albert Hall, London*. The Concerts are particularly
popular with younger music-lovers, many of whom stand (as
promenaders) in the arena in front of the orchestra and fill the
Hall on the *Last Night of the Proms*. The Concerts were first
held in 1895, originally in the Queen's Hall (a building
destroyed in 1941). The programmes are always of classical
music but have become more adventurous and original in
recent years. ['Promenade' since originally members of the
audience 'promenaded' or walked about during the concert,
whereas they now stand]

promenader /ˌprɒməˈnɑːdə(r)/ (arts) A person, especially a
young concert-goer, who attends *Promenade Concerts* and
who stands in the arena (floor of the hall) during the
performace.

promenader

Proms /prɒmz/**, the** (arts) A colloquial abbreviation for the
Promenade Concerts.

proportional representation /prəˌpɔːʃənl ˌreprɪzenˈteɪʃn/
(politics) The system whereby a political party secures seats
in an election in proportion to the actual numbers of people
that voted for it. Proportional representation is not used in
British political elections. In recent years there has been a
growing demand for some form of this system, but so far
neither the *Conservative Party* nor the *Labour Party* has been
willing to commit itself to it. See also *voting system*.

prorogation /ˌprəʊrəˈgeɪʃn/ (government) The act by which
the sovereign ends a session of parliament, usually when a
general election is announced. The *House of Commons* closes
completely, but the *House of Lords* may sit when prorogued in
order to hear legal appeals.

provident society /ˈprɒvɪdənt səˌsaɪətɪ/ (finance) Another name
for a *friendly society*.

provisional licence /prəˌvɪʒənl ˈlaɪsns/ (transport) A licence granted provisionally to the driver of a motor vehicle while he is learning to drive (ie, as an *L-driver*).

Provisionals /prəˈvɪʒənlz/, **the** (politics) The faction of *Sinn Féin* and the *IRA* that has existed since 1969 when the split into the 'Official' and the 'Provisional' IRA was made. The Provisionals (or 'Provos') follow a policy of terrorism in their aim of achieving a united *Ireland*.

provost /ˈprɒvəst/ (**1** education **2, 3** religion) **1** The title of the head of some *colleges[1]* and schools. **2** A senior official of a cathedral in the *Church of England*, especially one of the newer ones. **3** The head of a cathedral chapter in the *Roman Catholic Church* in *England*.

proxy vote /ˈprɒksɪ vəʊt/ (politics) A vote at an election, such as a *by-election* or a *general election*, that is made by a person on behalf of a voter when that voter is unable to go to the *polling station* for some reason (eg, disability or long-term illness). Official permission must be given before a proxy vote can be used. Compare *postal vote*.

PSBR /ˌpiː es biː ˈɑː(r)/ (finance) The term used (in full, *public sector borrowing requirement*) to indicate the money that the government needs to borrow to supplement what it receives through tax revenue and other sources. It obtains it by selling government stock and *Treasury* bills and by encouraging various forms of national savings which are designed to attract the smaller saver. The Conservative government (see *Conservative Party*) of Margaret *Thatcher* announced its intention to reduce PSBR gradually.

PTA /ˌpiː tiː ˈeɪ/ (**parent-teacher association**) (education) An association organized by an individual school to enable parents of children at the school and their teachers to meet and discuss the school's policies and the children's progress. Most schools have a PTA meeting at the school once a *term[1]*.

pub /pʌb/ (**public house**) (daily life) An establishment where alcoholic (and non-alcoholic) drinks and, usually, snacks or meals are sold. The pub is a traditional feature of almost all towns and villages, and is often a building of 'character' or even historic interest (see *inn*). For many people, it is a kind of *club*, where one can relax, talk with friends, listen to music, play games (such as *darts* or *bar billiards*) and enjoy drinking and eating. Most pubs are open twice daily (see *licensing hours*), and many have a garden where food and drink can be consumed in the summer (see *beer garden*). Inside the building, there are almost always both a *public bar* and *lounge bar*, and possibly also a *saloon bar* and *private bar*. There may also be a separate restaurant or dining area. Children under 16 are not admitted to a pub, although they may sit outside with adults in the garden. Children under 18 may not buy or drink alcohol. As a rule, most pubs are owned by a particular brewery (see *tied house*), but some are not (see *free house*).

Some of the larger or better furnished pubs also provide overnight accommodation, and thus are like small hotels. All pubs have distinctive names (see *inn sign*), many of which reflect their historic origin. See also *ploughman's lunch*.

public bar /ˌpʌblɪk 'bɑː(r)/ (daily life) The most popular *bar[1]* in a *pub*, where drinks are cheapest and the atmosphere usually liveliest. If *darts* is played in the pub, it will be in the public bar.

public bill /ˌpʌblɪk 'bɪl/ (government) A *bill* that affects the general public, as distinct from a *private bill*. See also *private member's bill*.

Public Lending Right /ˌpʌblɪk 'lendɪŋ raɪt/ **(PLR)** (law) A government scheme, first operating in 1984, by which payment is made from public funds to authors (both writers and illustrators) whose books are lent out from public libraries. At present (1984) no author can earn more than £5,000 from the scheme in any one year.

public limited company /ˌpʌblɪk ˌlɪmɪtɪd 'kʌmpənɪ/ see *PLC* (finance)

Public Record Office /ˌpʌblɪk 'rekɔːd ˌɒfɪs/, **the** (government) An office in *London* that holds official (government) records, including those of *courts[3]* of law and of most government *departments*. Many of the documents it holds are of great national interest, such as the *Domesday Book* and the papers of the *Gunpowder Plot*. The office is open to members of the public.

public school /ˌpʌblɪk 'skuːl/ (education) **1** An *independent* (usually fee-paying) *school* for students aged 11 (or 13) to 18. Many of *Britain*'s public schools are long-established and have gained a reputation for their high academic standards, as well as their exclusiveness and snobbery. The boys' schools include such well-known schools as *Eton*, *Harrow*, *Westminster* and *Winchester*. (Many traditional boys' schools now take some girls, if only in the *sixth form*.) Among leading girls' public schools are *Roedean* and Cheltenham Ladies' College (see *Cheltenham*). Most of the members of the British *Establishment* were educated at a public school. See also *preparatory school*. ['public' since originally students could enter the school from anywhere in *England* and not just from the immediate neighbourhood]. **2** The title occasionally used for a school in *Scotland* that is supported from public funds (ie, is non-fee-paying). It should not be confused with the better-known public school[1], which is an independent (fee-paying) school.

pudding /'pʊdɪŋ/ (food and drink) **1** A sweet dish cooked with flour, milk, eggs, fruit and other ingredients, and usually served hot. Examples are *Christmas pudding* and *plum pudding*. **2** A term for any sweet course or dessert at *lunch* or *dinner*. **3** A savoury dish usually made of pastry or batter and containing meat. Examples are *steak and kidney pudding* and *pease pudding*.

Pullman (train) /ˈpʊlmən (treɪn)/ (transport) A luxury *Inter-City train* with *first class[1]* seats only and with special comfort and facilities, such as meals and drinks served at a passenger's seat. [name ultimately derives from American railcar designer George M Pullman (1831–97)]

Punch /pʌntʃ/ (media) A weekly humorous and satirical magazine, founded in 1841 and having a circulation of nearly 90,000. It has a reputation for the high standard of its literary and dramatic criticism. [named after character in *Punch and Judy* play]

Punch and Judy /ˌpʌntʃ ən ˈdʒuːdɪ/ (tradition) A traditional play for puppets, popular with children and traditionally performed at seaside and other holiday resorts. The play, today usually performed by glove or hand puppets, has historic origins in European popular comedies, notably the Italian 'commedia dell'arte' (with the character Punchinello). Its main characters are the hunch-backed, hook-nosed Punch, full of optimism, his wife Judy, with whom he quarrels and their dog, Toby.

Punch and Judy

punks /pʌŋks/ (life and society) Young people who from the mid-1970s cultivated an extravagent and 'anarchic' form of dress and hairstyle, and who were devotees of punk rock music. They usually wore gaudy, ragged clothes, often fastened with chains or safety pins. They had spiky, brightly dyed hair and a few pierced their noses and ears with pins. In *Britain*, the punk movement was considerably boosted by the Sex Pistols rock group. From the 1980s punks became more stylized, while punk rock music moved into a less frenetic phase ('post-punk').

punt /pʌnt/ (sport and leisure) An open, flat-bottomed boat that is broad and square at both ends. It is used on shallow rivers and is propelled by someone standing at one end pushing against the river bed with a long pole. Punts are very popular at *Cambridge University* and *Oxford University*.

punt

punter /'pʌntə(r)/ (sport and leisure) A person who bets on the results of horse races, *greyhound racing* and other sporting events in a *betting shop*, either on the course itself or by post from home (especially in the *pools*).

Purcell Room /'pɜːsel ruːm/, **the** (arts) A recital hall on the *South Bank* site, *London*, used mainly for performances of chamber music. It is in the same complex as the *Queen Elizabeth Hall*, the *Royal Festival Hall* and the *Hayward Gallery*. [named after English classical composer Henry Purcell (?1659–95)]

putting /'pʌtɪŋ/ (sport and leisure) A simplified game of golf popular in public parks and at seaside resorts, where it is played on a course known as a 'putting green'. Compare *clock golf*.

Pytchley (Hunt) /'paɪtʃlɪ (ˌpaɪtʃlɪ 'hʌnt)/, **the** (sport and leisure) One of the best known *hunts*, founded about 1750 in the village of Pytchley, near Kettering, Northamptonshire.

QUEENSBERRY RULES

* QC /ˌkjuː ˈsiː/ **(Queen's Counsel)** (law) A senior *barrister* appointed on the recommendation of the *Lord Chancellor* and taking precedence after the *Attorney General* and *Solicitor General*. Such barristers wear silk gowns and in *court³* sit 'within the *bar²*', (in the special area reserved for the judge or magistrate). [originally appointed by the *queen* (see *Queen Elizabeth*), and still officially called 'Her Majesty's Counsel Learned in the Law']

QE2 /ˌkjuː iː ˈtuː/**, the (Queen Elizabeth 2, the)** (transport) A large liner built by *Cunard* to operate as a cruise liner in the winter and as a passenger liner between Southampton and New York in the summer. The ship was launched in 1967 and entered service in 1969, replacing an earlier 'Queen Elizabeth' liner withdrawn from service in 1970.

QPR /ˌkjuː piː ˈɑː(r)/ (sport and leisure) The nickname of *Queen's Park Rangers football club*.

quadrangle /ˈkwɒdræŋgl/ (style) An inner courtyard of a *college¹*, especially one at *Oxford University*. Compare *court²*.

Quakers /ˈkweɪkəz/ (religion) The popular name of members of the *Society of Friends*, a religious body founded in *England* in 1668. Quakers are unlike other Protestants since they have no officiating *ministers¹* or order of service in their worship, which takes place in the form of 'meetings'. At these, anyone can offer spoken prayer, ministry or reading. All men and women Quakers are equal. Quakers are noted for their pacifism, their high but not rigid moral standards, their association with charity work and education and their endeavours to abolish persecution and to aid the poor. [originally a derogatory nickname: their founder, George Fox, had told a judge that he and others should 'quake at the word of the Lord']

quality paper /ˌkwɒlətɪ ˈpeɪpə(r)/ (media) A daily or *Sunday* newspaper that aims at the educated reader. Quality papers contain detailed news coverage and comment, authoritative editorials, a wide range of topical features written by experts in their field, arts and literary reviews and much professional

* In the reign of a king, 'Queen's' in these titles becomes 'King's' and 'QC' becomes 'KC'.

advertising. The three Sunday quality papers have an accompanying colour supplement, with many photographs and advertisements. The daily quality papers are the *Daily Telegraph*, the *Financial Times*, The *Guardian* and The *Times*. The three Sunday papers are the *Sunday Telegraph*, The *Observer* and the *Sunday Times*. Compare *popular paper*.

quadrangle

quango /ˈkwæŋgəʊ/ (government) A term for what is officially known as a 'non-departmental public body' (with the term itself usually understood to be an abbreviation of '*quasi-autonomous non-governmental organization*'). Such bodies are mainly funded by central government, and oversee and develop activities in areas of public interest. Examples of quangos are the British Waterways Board (which controls navigation on *Britain*'s rivers and canals), the Police Complaints Board (set up to deal with complaints by members of the public against police officers) and the Centre for Information on Language Teaching and Research (which provides information services to language teachers in Britain and researchers in European countries). Quangos were first established in the mid-1970s but, after a government review in 1979, several have been abolished.

Quant, Mary /kwɒnt, ˈmeərɪ/ (people) The dress styles introduced by Mary Quant (born 1934) in the 1960s were so influential that for a time *London* replaced Paris as an important fashion centre. Mary Quant's designs were very much aimed at young people and her main creation, the miniskirt, contributed to the liberated feeling of the 1960s. Mary Quant's fashion shop in *Chelsea* soon grew into a flourishing wholesale business, and she exported clothes all over the world. Subsequently she has worked in other fields of fashion and design, including household textiles and cosmetics.

quarter day /ˈkwɔːtə deɪ/ (law) One of four days in the year when certain payments such as rent and interest are due. In *England, Wales* and *Northern Ireland* they are 25 March (the church festival of the Annunciation of the Blessed Virgin Mary, more commonly known as Lady Day), 24 June (St John the Baptist's Day, often called *Midsummer Day*), 29 September (St Michael and All Angels' Day, more commonly known as *Michaelmas Day*) and 25 December (*Christmas Day*). In *Scotland* they are 2 February (Candlemas), 15 May (*Whit Sunday*), 1 August (Lammas) and 11 November (Martinmas).

queen /kwiːn/ (royal family) The title of a female sovereign and at present that of *Queen Elizabeth*. The queen is the official head of state, the head of the legal system of *Britain*, the commander-in-chief of all armed forces and the head ('supreme governor') of the *Church of England*. Many important government processes require the participation of the queen, including the summoning, *prorogation* and dissolution of parliament. Several *bills*, too, require her official approval (so-called *royal assent*). She also gives many important honours and awards, mostly on the advice of the *Prime Minister*, although she herself personally selects the people who receive the *Order of the Garter*, the *Order of the Thistle*, the *Order of Merit* and the Royal Victorian Order. By convention she invites the leader of a party winning a *general election* to form a government. In international affairs, the queen has the power to declare war and make peace, as well as to recognize foreign states and governments, conclude treaties and annex or cede territory. The queen also appoints many important office holders, including government *ministers*[2], judges, diplomats and bishops in the Church of England. She also has the power to remit all or part of the sentence passed on a criminal (by granting a 'royal pardon').

Queen Anne (style) /ˌkwiːn ˈæn (staɪl)/ (style) 1 A style of furniture popular in the early 18th century and characterized by the use of walnut veneer, curved legs on chairs and an overall simplicity and elegance. 2 An architectural style similarly popular in this period, characterized by the use of red brick and simple, classical lines. [both typical of the reign of Queen Anne (1665–1714)]

Queen Elizabeth /ˌkwiːn ɪˈlɪzəbəθ/ (royal family) Queen Elizabeth II (born 1926) has been *queen* since 1953. Among her many royal duties are the regular visits she makes to foreign countries, and especially those of the *Commonwealth*[1], whose interests and welfare are very important to her. The Queen has done much to simplify the formalities of the monarchy, including allowing the *BBC* to make an unprecedented documentary film about the everyday life of the *royal family*. She also instituted the tradition of the 'walkabout', an informal feature of an otherwise formal royal visit, when she walks about among the public crowds and stops to talk to some people. The Queen has long been regarded with considerable respect and affection by many of her subjects. The annual *Christmas* broadcast made by the Queen on radio and television has become a traditional and popular feature of the season, and there were widespread celebrations and special programmes of events in 1977 to mark her Silver Jubilee. The Queen's husband is the *Duke of Edinburgh*, and her four children are the *Prince of Wales* (born 1948), Princess Anne (born 1950), Prince Andrew (born 1960) and Prince Edward (born 1964). The Queen's mother is *Queen Elizabeth, the Queen Mother*.

Queen Elizabeth Hall /ˌkwiːn ɪˌlɪzəbəθ ˈhɔːl/, **the** (arts) A concert hall in *London* on the *South Bank* site, used chiefly for performances of classical music. It is in the same complex (built 1967) as the smaller *Purcell Room* and the nearby *Hayward Gallery* and *Royal Festival Hall*.

Queen Elizabeth, the Queen Mother /ˌkwiːn ɪˌlɪzəbəθ ðə ˌkwiːnˈmʌðə(r)/ (royal family) The mother of *Queen Elizabeth* and widow of King George VI (died 1952). The Queen Mother (born 1900), is a very popular member of the *royal family*, greatly respected for her sympathy for and interest in her people. She holds many honorary titles, both civilian and military, and is still remembered by many for the morale-raising visits she made to many parts of *Britain*, together with her husband, in the Second World War. See also *queen mother*.

Queen Elizabeth 2 /ˌkwiːn ɪˌlɪzəbəθ ðə ˈsekənd/ see *QE2* (transport)

queen mother /ˌkwiːn ˈmʌðə(r)/ (royal family) The title of the widow of a former *king* who is also the mother of the reigning sovereign. The present queen mother is *Queen Elizabeth, the Queen Mother*. See also *queen*.

Queen of the South /ˌkwiːn əv ðə ˈsaʊθ/ (sport and leisure) A Scottish *football club* founded in 1919, with a stadium in Dumfries, southern *Scotland*.

Queen Victoria /ˌkwiːn vɪkˈtɔːrɪə/ (royal family) The queen who had the longest reign in British history and who did much to make the monarchy respectable after the unpopular reigns of a number of monarchs. Queen Victoria (1819–1901) came to be a unique symbol of the British monarchy in modern times, with a high sense of duty and loyalty to her people, and a genuine sympathy for her poorer subjects. She came to the throne in 1837 and three years later married her cousin, Albert. After her husband's death in 1861, she mourned him constantly, and although at first her tragic widowhood attracted increased public affection and sympathy, her continuing avoidance of public appearances made her less popular with her people. The adjective 'Victorian', which had come to be used in her lifetime to mean 'flourishing', 'potentially great', came to acquire the sense of 'over-strict', 'censorious', much as it means today. Victoria herself, too, is now remembered as a humourless, unsmiling queen (she is said to have replied 'We are not amused' when a groom playfully imitated her), instead of the happy, dutiful and popular sovereign and mother that she had originally been.

Queen Victoria Memorial /ˌkwiːn vɪkˌtɔːrɪə məˈmɔːrɪəl/, **the** (London) A monument to *Queen Victoria* built in front of *Buckingham Palace, London,* in 1911.

* **Queen's Bench Division** /ˌkwiːnz ˈbentʃ dɪˌvɪʒn/, **the** (law) One of the three main divisions of the *High Court of Justice,* having the *Lord Chief Justice* as its president. It deals chiefly with actions for damages for breach of contract, actions for recovery of land or goods, election petitions and cases regarding the registration of electors.

* **Queen's Birthday** /ˌkwiːnz ˈbɜːθdeɪ/, **the** (royal family) At present (1985), either the date of the true birthday of *Queen Elizabeth* II, 21 April, or of her *Official Birthday,* on the second Saturday in June. The *Union Jack* is flown on public buildings and the *national anthem* played on the Queen's true birthday, but it is not a *bank holiday* and no particular annual ceremony is held.

Queen's Club /ˌkwiːnz ˈklʌb/, **the** (sport and leisure) A leading tennis club in west *London,* equally well-known as a centre for *real tennis* and *rackets*. It was founded in 1886.

* **Queen's English** /ˌkwiːnz ˈɪŋglɪʃ/, **the** (language) Standard, correct English, as traditionally spoken by an educated southerner.

* **Queen's Gallery** /ˌkwiːnz ˈgælərɪ/, **the** (arts) An art gallery open to the public inside *Buckingham Palace, London,* where a (changing) selection of paintings and other works of art from the royal collections is on display. The Gallery was opened in 1962 and is housed in what used to be the private *chapel*[2] of Buckingham Palace.

Queen's Park Rangers /ˌkwiːnz pɑːk ˈreɪndʒəz/ **(QPR)** (sport and leisure) A popular *London football club,* founded in 1885 and having a stadium near White City in west London. [named after former stadium at Queen's Park, northwest London]

---

* In the reign of a king, 'Queen's' in these titles becomes 'King's'.

Queen's Prize /ˌkwiːnz ˈpraɪz/, **the** (sport and leisure) The main prize for rifle shooting at *Bisley*, founded by *Queen Victoria* in 1860.

* **Queen's Speech** /ˌkwiːnz ˈspiːtʃ/, **the** (government) The speech made by the sovereign (when a *queen*) at the opening of a session of *Parliament*, in which the government outlines its planned programme and the policies it intends to follow. The speech is prepared for the sovereign to read by the *ministers*[2] of the government in power.

Queen's University /ˌkwiːnz juːnɪˈvɜːsətɪ/, **The** (education) The oldest university of *Northern Ireland*, founded in *Belfast* in 1845 as Queen's College, part of the Queen's University of Ireland, and operating as a separate university from 1908. It has over 6,000 students.

Queensberry Rules /ˌkwiːnzbərɪ ˈruːlz/, **the** (sport and leisure) The code of rules followed in modern boxing, relating to the length of rounds, composition of gloves, types of blows allowed and other similar matters. [rules originated by Marquess of Queensberry in 1869]

quid /kwɪd/ (daily life) A colloquial term for a *pound (sterling)*. The word does not take an 's' in the plural so that 'five pounds', for example, would be 'five quid'.

Quorn /kwɔːn/, **the** (sport and leisure) A well-known *hunt* in Leicestershire. [founded in the mid-18th century at Quornden Hall, a *country house* near Loughborough]

---

* In the reign of a king, 'Queen's' in these titles becomes 'King's'.

RAC /ˌɑːr eɪ ˈsiː/, **the (Royal Automobile Club, the)**
(transport) One of two leading motoring organizations in
Britain, the other being the *AA*. It was founded in 1897 and
today offers a wide range of touring and mechanical services
to its members as well as publishing a number of guides and
motoring books.

race meeting /ˈreɪs ˌmiːtɪŋ/ (sport and leisure) A sporting event
at which horses or *greyhounds* race over a set course at set
times.

race relations /ˌreɪs rɪˈleɪʃnz/ (life and society) *Britain* has long
had ethnic and national minority groups, and a variety of
people have settled in the country, either to escape political
or religious persecution or simply to seek a better life. The
largest single minority group in Britain are the Irish, while
many Jews have also settled in this country. After the Second
World War a large number of Eastern European and other
refugees came to Britain, and were followed during the 1950s
and early 1960s by large communities from the West Indies,
India and Pakistan. There are also sizeable communities of
Chinese, Greek and Turkish Cypriots, and Italians and
Spaniards now in Britain, besides Americans and
Australians. The difficulties that many minorities face are
partly dealt with by a range of social programmes, and the
legal rights of such people were officially recognized by the
passing of the Race Relations Act of 1976, which established
the *Commission for Racial Equality*.

rackets /ˈrækɪts/ (sport and leisure) A game rather like *squash*
played in an enclosed court with a hard ball by two or four
people. The game was officially adopted at *Harrow School* in
the early 19th century, and one of its main centres in *Britain*
today is at the *Queen's Club, London*. [named from the racket
with which the ball is hit in the game]

RADA /ˈrɑːdə/ **(Royal Academy of Dramatic Art, the)**
(education) A school that trains professional actors and
actresses. It was founded in 1904 and has its headquarters in
central *London*. The public are admitted to performances
staged by its students in the Vanbrugh Theatre here (named
after the 18th-century dramatist Sir John Vanbrugh).

Radcliffe Camera /ˌrædklɪf ˈkæmrə/, **the** (education) The main reading room of the *Bodleian Library* at *Oxford University*, founded by the physician John Radcliffe (1650–1714). The domed building of the Camera is one of the landmarks of central *Oxford¹*. ['Camera' here in basic sense of 'vaulted room']

Radio 4 /ˌreɪdɪəʊ ˈfɔː(r)/ (media) A national radio channel of the *BBC* providing a varied service. It has many programmes on news and current affairs as well as plays, music, talks and educational broadcasts for schools. It transmits these programmes from 6 am to soon after midnight. Certain educational programmes, for the *Open University* and for schools to record for later use, are also broadcast on a special wavelength from 11.30 pm to a similar late night closing time.

Radio 1 /ˌreɪdɪəʊ ˈwʌn/ (media) A national radio channel of the *BBC*, providing a service mainly of pop and rock music plus news bulletins. It broadcasts from 6 am to midnight.

Radio 3 /ˌreɪdɪəʊ ˈθriː/ (media) A national radio channel of the *BBC*, broadcasting programmes mainly of classical music, from 7 am to midnight. In the early morning or late at night, however, it also broadcasts programmes for the *Open University* on a special wavelength.

Radio Times /ˌreɪdɪəʊ ˈtaɪmz/, **the** (media) A weekly magazine published by the *BBC* to give the detailed schedules of television and radio programmes for a particular week, starting on Saturday. The schedules are accompanied by features and photographs. The magazine, first published in 1923, has a circulation of about 3.3 million. Compare *TV Times*.

Radio 2 /ˌreɪdɪəʊ ˈtuː/ (media) A national radio channel of the *BBC*, broadcasting light entertainment, music and sports programmes for 24 hours a day. At certain times its broadcasts combine with those of *Radio 1*.

RAF /ˌɑːr eɪ ˈef/, **the (Royal Air Force, the)** (defence) The British air force, arising in 1912 with the formation of the Royal Flying Corps and officially formed in 1918 with the amalgamation of the RFC and the Royal Naval Air Service. Fighter pilots of the RAF gained a high reputation for their achievement in the Second World War. In 1964 the RAF was placed under the Ministry of Defence (see *ministry²*), together with the *Army* and the *Royal Navy*. The total number of its service men and women is currently just over 92,000.

raffle /ˈræfl/ (sport and leisure) A type of lottery held at *fêtes*, etc, in which the prizes are goods rather than money. Most raffles are held to raise money for a particular charity, or to help pay for the building of a new *club* or the buying of sports equipment for a school.

rag (week) /ˈræg (wiːk)/ (education) A special week of entertainments arranged in some universities to raise money for charity. The highlight of the week is traditionally a procession through the streets of the town or city, in which open vehicles carry colourful scenes performed by students, while other students with collecting boxes collect money from the crowds lining the route.

Railcard /'reɪlkɑːd/ (transport) A card sold by *BR* to certain groups of rail travellers, enabling them to travel at half-price or at specially reduced rates. Among such travellers are *OAP*s, young people aged under 24 and disabled people. The Railcard is valid for one year only.

Ralph Vaughan Williams /ˌreɪf ˌvɔːn 'wɪljəmz/ see *Vaughan Williams* (people)

Rangers /'reɪndʒəz/ (sport and leisure) A popular Scottish *football club* with its stadium at *Ibrox Park* in *Glasgow*. It draws support especially from among the local Protestant community and its traditional rivals are *Celtic*.

rates /reɪts/ (finance) Local taxes paid by landowners and property owners (and in particular those who own houses and commercial premises) to contribute towards the cost of local services, such as education (schools and *colleges*[2]), transport, police, waste disposal, libraries and *courts*[3] of law. Each payment is calculated annually by the *local authority*. Government property is not subject to rates, although special payments are required.

reader /'riːdə(r)/ (education) The title of certain senior lecturers at some universities. [originally, in 16th century, one who read learned works and explained them to pupils and students]

real ale /ˌrɪəl 'eɪl/ (food and drink) Another term for *draught beer*, especially beer which has been brewed and stored in the traditional way and which has continued to ferment in its cask before being drawn. See also *CAMRA*.

real tennis /ˌrɪəl 'tenɪs/ (sport and leisure) An old form of (lawn) tennis played in a four-walled indoor court with a special hard ball and racket. The game is still played today by enthusiasts, and has one of its main centres at the *Queen's Club, London*. [originally 'royal' tennis; the name was not widely used until the 20th century, when lawn tennis, on open, outdoor courts, became the much more popular version of the game]

receiver /rɪ'siːvə(r)/ (law) An official appointed to manage the property or business of a person who has been declared bankrupt or insane.

recess /rɪ'ses/ (government) 1 The temporary closure of parliament over a holiday or vacation period, such as the 'summer recess'. 2 The suspension of parliament between a *prorogation* and the start of the next session.

Record Mirror /'rekɔːd ˌmɪrə(r)/, **the** (media) A weekly magazine devoted to pop music. It was first published in 1954 and has a circulation of over 113,000.

recorded delivery /rɪˌkɔːdɪd dɪˈlɪvərɪ/ (commerce) A service operated by the *Post Office* in which, for a fee, a record of posting and delivery is made, and limited compensation given if an item is lost or damaged in the post. Compare *registered post*.

recorder /rɪˈkɔːdə(r)/ (law) A *barrister* or *solicitor* who has been qualified for at least ten years and who is appointed to act as a judge in a *crown court*.

rector /ˈrektə(r)/ (**1** religion **2** education) **1** A clergyman in charge of a parish, originally one entitled to receive the whole of the tithes (income from the parish). **2** The title of the head of some schools, *colleges*[1,2] and universities.

rectory /ˈrektərɪ/ (religion) The residence of a *rector*[1].

red /ˌred/, **the** (finance) A colloquial term for a money account such as a bank account that is overdrawn or in debit. Compare *black*. [such accounts were originally made in red ink, whereas credit accounts were written in black]

Red Arrow (bus) /ˌred ˈærəʊ (bʌs)/ (transport) A single-deck bus operated by *London Regional Transport* to run between the main *London* railway termini and the chief shopping and business areas. [from the colour of such buses]

Red Arrows /ˌred ˈærəʊz/, **the** (defence) A special aerobatics squadron of the *RAF* performing in red aircraft.

red biddy /ˌred ˈbɪdɪ/ (food and drink) A colloquial term for an alcoholic drink made from cheap red wine and methylated spirits. It is an unpleasant and dangerous drink. [apparently from 'Biddy', a nickname for an old woman, since some female tramps enjoy the drink]

red book /ˈred bʊk/ (media) A colloquial term for one of a number of official directories of people, which are bound in red. Among such books are *Who's Who*, *Burke('s Peerage)*, the various *Kelly's* (*Directories*) and handbooks and similar annual or regular publications.

Red Bus Rover /ˌred bʌs ˈrəʊvə(r)/ (transport) A ticket that gives unlimited travel for one day on any of the red (city) buses operated by *London Regional Transport*. [*London*'s red buses run chiefly in the urban areas of London, while green buses (see *Green Line coach*) travel on routes out into the country]

Red Devils /ˌred ˈdevlz/, **the** (defence) **1** The semi-official nickname of the Parachute Regiment of the British army. [apparently first called this by the Germans in the Second World War] **2** A special team from the *Army* who give displays of sky-diving and parachuting.

Red Ensign /ˌred ˈensən/, **the** (transport) The ensign (flag) of the Merchant Navy, having a red background with the *Union Jack* in the top left quarter (nearest the flagpole).

Red Flag /ˌred ˈflæg/, **the** (politics) The hymn or official song of the *Labour Party*, sung at the end of party conferences and other big meetings. [from, 'We'll keep the Red Flag flying here!', the last line of the song, composed in 1889 by the socialist James Connell]

Red Devils

Red Hand of Ulster /ˌred hænd əv ˈʌlstə(r)/, **the** (tradition) The badge of *Northern Ireland*, in origin that of the O'Neill *clan*. It is shown heraldically as an upright red hand severed at the wrist (hence its alternative name of 'Bloody Hand'). See also *shamrock*.

redbrick university /ˌredbrɪk juːnɪˈvɜːsətɪ/ (education) One of the universities founded in the late 19th century and the first half of the 20th century, as distinct from the older *Oxford University* and *Cambridge University*. Many such universities were built in red brick, contrasting with the mellow grey stone of the old foundations.

redcoat /ˈredkəʊt/ (sport and leisure) A steward and entertainer at a *Butlin's* holiday camp, who wears a red coat as part of his uniform.

Regency (style) /ˈriːdʒənsɪ (staɪl)/ (style) A style of furniture and architecture found in *England* at the end of the 18th century and beginning of the 19th. It was the equivalent of the French Empire style and was characterized by neo-classical designs and, in furniture, the use of rosewood and brass inlay work. [period overlapped 1811–20 when the future King George IV was *Prince Regent*]

Regent Street /ˈriːdʒənt striːt/ (London) A central shopping street in *London*, originally built as a processional way for the *Prince Regent* in the 19th century. Its fashionable stores include a range of jewellery, clothing, china and gift shops.

Regent's Park /ˌriːdʒənts ˈpɑːk/ (London) A large park in northwest *London*, laid out in 1811 for the *Prince Regent*. It contains a boating lake, an open-air theatre, a large number of sports fields, tracks and courts, flower gardens and a central refreshment pavilion. On its north side is the *London Zoo*.

Regina /rɪˈdʒaɪnə/ (law) The term used for the prosecution in criminal proceedings during the reign of a queen, as in 'Regina v. Jones', since the *queen* is nominally the prosecutor in all criminal cases. The corresponding term in the reign of a king is 'Rex'. [Latin, 'queen']

registered post /ˌredʒɪstəd ˈpəʊst/ (commerce) A *Post Office* service for sending valuable items, including money, through the post (in specially strengthened envelopes or in special packing). A fee is paid, and compensation paid if the item is lost or damaged in the post. Any *first class*[2] letter can be sent by registered post, but on the whole the service is intended to provide compensation at a higher rate, for items of value, than for items sent by *recorded delivery*.

registration number /redʒɪˈstreɪʃn ˌnʌmbə(r)/ (transport) The official number given to a motor vehicle when it is first registered. The number is shown on plates ('number plates') at the front and back of the vehicle (at the back only, on motorcycles and other two-wheeled vehicles). Many vehicles on the roads of *Britain* in 1986 still have a registration number consisting of three letters (chosen to indicate the licensing authority of the area where the car is registered), three numbers (less often one or two, indicating the serial number of the car with the licensing authority) and a final letter (which indicates the year of registration). From 1 August 1983 the letter indicating the year of registration was placed in front, followed first by the numbers and then by the letters.

registration number

registry /'redʒɪstrɪ/ (religion) A place or room in a church where registers are kept, especially the register signed by a bride and groom immediately after their marriage ceremony in the church.

registry office /'redʒɪstrɪ ˌɒfɪs/ (government) An office where civil marriages are performed (as distinct from marriages performed in a *church*) and where births and deaths are recorded.

Regius professor /ˌriːdʒɪəs prə'fesə(r)/ (education) A person appointed by the sovereign to a university chair (professorship) founded by a royal patron. [Latin 'regius', 'royal']

Reith lectures /ˌriːθ 'lektʃəz/, **the** (media) An annual series of lectures on a political, economic, scientific or other subject, broadcast on radio or television by the *BBC* and published in The *Listener*. The lectures were founded in 1947 by Lord Reith (1889–1971), first general manager of the BBC.

remand centre /rɪ'mɑːnd ˌsentə(r)/ (law) Another name for a *remand home*.

remand home /rɪ'mɑːnd həʊm/ (law) A place of detention to which young offenders are sent while awaiting trial in court. At present there are seven such centres.

Remembrance Sunday /rɪ'membrəns ˌsʌndɪ/ (tradition) The *Sunday* nearest to 11 November, *Armistice Day*. On this Sunday the dead of both world wars are remembered in special *church* services and civic ceremonies, the chief of which is the laying of wreaths at the *Cenotaph, London* by members of the *royal family* in the presence of leading statesmen and politicians (including the *Prime Minister* and *Leader of the Opposition*). See also *two-minute silence*, *Poppy Day*.

Remembrance Sunday

Remploy /'remplɔɪ/ (work) A non-commercial state company operating various workshops and centres where practical work is undertaken by people with physical handicaps. Much of their work is making simple furniture and fittings for use in government and armed services establishments. [from 're-employ']

rest home /'rest həʊm/ (life and society) A common term for an old people's home.

restrictive practice /rɪˌstrɪktɪv 'præktɪs/ (1 commerce 2 work) 1 A trading agreement against the public interest, for example, an agreement to sell to certain buyers only. 2 A practice of some trade unions, such as a *closed shop* or *work-to-rule*, that similarly limits trading.

retirement age /rɪ'taɪəmənt eɪdʒ/ (work) The age at which employed people normally retire from work, at present 65 for men, 60 for women. See also *OAP*, *old age pension*.

returning officer /rɪ'tɜːnɪŋ ˌɒfɪsə(r)/ (government) The officer who presides at a *by-election* or, in a particular *constituency*, at a *general election*.

Reuters /'rɔɪtəz/ (media) The principal British world news agency, formerly owned jointly by a number of press organizations including the *Press Association* and the Newspaper Publishers Association. It was founded by the German telegraph promoter Baron Paul Julius de Reuter (1816–99), who opened his *London* office in 1851. In 1984 Reuters became a *PLC*.

Reverend, Rev. /'revərənd/, **the** (religion) The traditional title of a clergyman in the *Church of England*, and in most of the *Free Churches*. It is usually put before the first name, as 'the Reverend Peter Marshall' (or written, 'the Rev. Peter Marshall'), but also used (incorrectly, according to some) before the surname alone ('the Reverend Marshall') or even (also incorrectly) alone ('the Reverend'). See also *Right Reverend*, *Very Reverend*.

Revised Version /rɪˌvaɪzd 'vɜːʃn/, **the (RV, the)** (religion) A revision of the *Authorized Version* of the Bible, prepared by two committees of British scholars, with American collaborators. The New Testament was produced in 1881, the Old Testament in 1885, and the Apocrypha in 1895. The older Authorized Version still remains popular in many *churches* and with many *Anglicans*.

rhyming slang /'raɪmɪŋ slæŋ/ (language) The slang way of speaking, originally popular among *cockneys*[2], in which a rhyming phrase, or part of it, is substituted for a standard word. An example is 'loaf of bread' (or simply 'loaf') for 'head', or 'apples and pears' (or simply 'apples') for 'stairs'. Some examples of rhyming slang have passed into spoken English generally, for example, 'use your loaf' means 'use your intelligence', 'think effectively'.

Right Honourable, Rt Hon /raɪt ˈɒnərəbl/, **the** (life and
society) The form of address used for people holding a
number of titles or offices, among them an earl, a viscount, a
baron, a *Lord Mayor* (also a *Lord Provost*) and a *Privy
Councillor* (see p 379). The full title appears in the form 'The
Rt Hon the Earl of Derby'. Compare *Honourable*.

Right Reverend, Rt Rev /raɪt ˈrevərənd/, **the** (religion) The
formal title of a bishop in the *Church of England*, appearing in
the form 'The Rt Rev the (Lord) Bishop of Oxford'.

Ritz /rɪts/, **the** (London) A fashionable *London* hotel and
restaurant in *Piccadilly*, founded in 1906 by the Swiss hotelier
César Ritz.

Robin Hood /ˌrɒbɪn ˈhʊd/ (tradition) A semi-legendary outlaw
hero of English and Scottish ballads, said to have lived in the
12th or 13th century. He is still popular for his life-long policy
of taking from the rich (by force, if necessary) and giving to
the poor. According to tradition, he lived with his 'Merry
Men' (companions) in Sherwood forest, Nottinghamshire.

Robin Hood

rock /rɒk/ (food and drink) A type of sweet in the form of a round, hard, brittle stick of peppermint sugar, with a white centre and a coloured edible coating. Such sticks are traditionally sold at seaside or other tourist resorts, where they often have the name of the resort inside in pink sugar, running from one end of the stick to the other. The sweet appears to have been first produced commercially in *Edinburgh*. See *Edinburgh rock*.

rock cake /'rɒk keɪk/ (food and drink) A small individual cake containing dried fruit, and thought to look like a rock.

Rockers /'rɒkəz/ (life and society) Groups of teenagers who rivalled the *Mods* in the 1960s. Rockers wore leather jackets, had long hair, and rode motorcycles. [from their addiction to *rock* music]

Roedean (School) /'rəʊdiːn (ˌrəʊdiːn 'skuːl)/ (education) A famous *public school*[1] for girls, near *Brighton*, East Sussex. It was founded in 1885 and has 435 students, all boarders. [named after a place here, meaning 'rough valley']

Rogation Days /rəʊ'geɪʃn deɪz/ (religion) Special days set aside in the *Church of England* for solemn prayers asking for a good harvest. The days are the four days before *Ascension Day*, with the *Sunday* known as 'Rogation Sunday'. In some *church*es a special service is accompanied by a procession outside the church building, and the ceremony of *beating the bounds* may also be held (instead of on Ascension Day). [literally 'asking days', from the prayers offered]

Roget /'rɒʒeɪ/ **(Roget's Thesaurus)** (language) A well-known dictionary of synonyms of the English language, arranged in classified lists. The dictionary, which now exists in several different editions, was first published in 1853 by an English physician, Peter Mark Roget (1779–1869). [full title is 'Roget's Thesaurus of English Words and Phrases', with 'thesaurus' used in sense 'treasury', 'store-house' (ie, of synonyms)]

Rolling Stones /ˌrəʊlɪŋ 'stəʊnz/, **the** (people) Together with the *Beatles*, the Rolling Stones were one of the most important British pop groups of the 1960s. The group formed in 1963, and the initial established line-up was Mick Jagger (vocals) (born 1943), Keith Richard (guitar, vocals) (born 1943), Brian Jones (guitar, vocals) (1942–69), Bill Wyman (bass) (born 1936) and Charlie Watts (drums) (born 1941). The group arose from the members' mutual interest in blues and rhythm-and-blues. The Rolling Stones were deliberately brash, anti-establishment and provocative. Their public behaviour was severely criticized by some sections of the media for their alleged decadence. This 'shock effect' was precisely what they wished to achieve, and their powerful and uninhibited music was a major factor in the development of *Britain*'s 'alternative society'. The group's two most popular hits were 'Satisfaction' (1965)—'I Can't Get No Satisfaction', the full title, summarized their philosophy of frustration and ferocity—and 'Jumpin' Jack Flash' (1968). [name taken from a song by the American black singer Muddy Waters]

Rolls (-Royce) /rəʊlz (ˌrəʊlz 'rɔɪs)/ (transport) A well-known make of expensive motor-car famous for its luxury and its reliability. [firm founded in 1906 by Charles Stewart Rolls and Henry Royce]

roly-poly /ˌrəʊlɪ 'pəʊlɪ/ (food and drink) A roll of baked or steamed suet pastry filled with jam or fruit, eaten as a dessert for *lunch* or *dinner*. The dish is a variety of *suet pudding* and is popular with children. [name, based on 'roll', suggests something round and fat]

Roman Catholic Church /ˌrəʊmən ˌkæθəlɪk 'tʃɜːtʃ/, **the** (religion) The Roman Catholic Church became established in *Britain* in medieval times and its influence increased considerably after the *Norman Conquest*. However, after the Reformation and *Henry VIII*'s break with the church of Rome (he took the title of Supreme Head of the Church and Clergy of England), the position of the Roman Catholic Church in Britain altered dramatically, so that it was outlawed for a time and was no longer the sole Christian church. For many years, British Roman Catholics were served by missionary priests (Englishmen who had trained abroad) and had no bishops or archbishops. Today there are both bishops and archbishops, and many of the old religious orders, previously banned, have been restored. Even so, many of the highest posts in the country are still closed to Roman Catholics, and no member of the Church can become sovereign, regent or *Lord Chancellor*. The Republic of *Ireland* is a strongly Roman Catholic country and there are still many Roman Catholics in *Northern Ireland*, although the majority of the population there are Protestants. In the *United Kingdom* as a whole Roman Catholics are the second largest religious community (after the *Church of England*).

Roman road /ˌrəʊmən 'rəʊd/ (history) One of a number of roads or trackways in *England*, built by the Romans during their occupation of *Britain* in the 1st–4th centuries AD. Sections of the roads still survive, whether in their original form or as stretches of modern roads. They were particularly noted for their length and straightness. Among the best known Roman roads are the *Fosse Way*, *Ermine Street*[1] and *Watling Street*.

Ronnie Scott's /ˌrɒnɪ 'skɒts/ (arts) A well-known jazz *club* in Soho, *London*. [named after its owner, the jazz player (saxophonist) Ronnie Scott (born 1927), who has owned it since 1959]

rose /rəʊz/ (tradition) The national emblem of *England* from the time of the *Wars of the Roses*. Compare *leek*, *thistle*, *daffodil*.

Rotary Club /'rəʊtərɪ klʌb/, **the** (life and society) One of the *clubs* in *Britain* that belong to Rotary International, a world

organization of business and professional men, founded in
the United States in 1905. The organization has the self-stated
aim to 'provide humanitarian service, encourage high ethical
standards, and help build goodwill and peace in the world'.
In Britain there are over 54,000 members known as Rotarians,
in over 1,000 clubs. [members originally met at one another's
houses, in rotation]

Rotten Row /ˌrɒtn ˈrəʊ/ (London) A horse-riding track
running along the south side of *Hyde Park, London*, from *Hyde
Park Corner* to *Kensington Gardens*. [popularly supposed to be
a corruption of French 'route du roi', 'road of the king', but
probably meaning what it says, with 'rotten' in sense 'soft']

Round House /ˌraʊnd ˈhaʊs/, **the** (arts) A modern theatre in
Hampstead, London, opened in 1967 in what was formerly a
'roundhouse', a circular building for servicing railway
locomotives. In its early years it had a reputation as a centre
for young people, who attended rock concerts, film shows
and other modern entertainments here. The building today
also contains a cinema, library and art gallery. There is now a
scheme to develop the Round House as a centre for black
performing arts.

Round Pond /ˌraʊnd ˈpɒnd/, **the** (London) A pond in
Kensington Gardens, London where both children and adults
traditionally sail toy boats and yachts.

Round Table /ˌraʊnd ˈteɪbl/, **the** (1 tradition 2 life and society)
1 In the stories about *King Arthur*, the table at which the
Knights of the Round Table sat. A round table was deliberately
chosen so that none of the knights sat in a more important
place than any of the others. **2** One of a number of *club*s for
young business and professional people, aged between 18
and 40, where discussions, debates and other meetings are
held with the aim of undertaking community service and
promoting international understanding. Such clubs were first
organized in 1972.

rounders /ˈraʊndəz/ (sport and leisure) A ball game
resembling American baseball, in which the players strike a
hard leather ball the size of a tennis ball with a wooden bat,
shorter than a baseball bat. They then try to run round four
bases (making a 'rounder') before the ball is returned to the
thrower ('bowler', as in *cricket*). If a player cannot complete
the round, he or she must then stop at one of the bases, and
can only move on when the next player hits the ball. The
game is particularly popular with children.

Row /rəʊ/, **the** (London) A colloquial name for *Rotten Row*.

Royal Academy (of Arts) /ˌrɔɪəl əˈkædəmɪ (ˌrɔɪəl əˌkædəmɪ əv
ˈɑːts)/, **the** (arts) The oldest society in *Britain* devoted
entirely to the fine arts, founded in 1768 and well-known for
its annual summer exhibition of contemporary art held at its
headquarters, *Burlington House*, in *Piccadilly, London*.

Royal Academy of Music /ˌrɔɪəl əˌkædəmɪ əv ˈmjuːzɪk/, **the (RAM, the)** (education) A school training professional musicians, founded in 1822 and having its headquarters in west *London*.

Royal Aircraft Establishment /ˌrɔɪəl ˈeəkrɑːft ɪˌstæblɪʃmənt/, **the (RAE, the)** (defence) An aircraft design and test establishment at Farnborough, Hampshire, under the control of the *RAF*. See also *Farnborough Air Show*.

Royal Albert Hall /ˌrɔɪəl ˌælbət ˈhɔːl/, **the** (London) The full name of the *Albert Hall, London*.

Royal and Ancient /ˌrɔɪəl ən ˈeɪnʃənt/, **the (R and A, the)** (sport and leisure) A leading golf *club* in St Andrews, *Scotland*, recognized (except in the United States) as the international headquarters of golf. It was founded in 1754 and adopted its present name in 1834 by permission of King William IV (in full, 'Royal and Ancient Golf Club of St Andrews').

Royal Ascot /ˌrɔɪəl ˈæskət/ (sport and leisure) A four-day horse-racing meeting held at *Ascot* each year in June. The event is one of the most important racing occasions in *Britain* and members of the *royal family* always attend.

royal assent /ˌrɔɪəl əˈsent/ (law) The official signing of an *Act (of Parliament)* by the sovereign, as a result of which it becomes law.

Royal Ballet /ˌrɔɪəl ˈbæleɪ/, **the** (arts) *Britain*'s national ballet company, with its centre at the *Royal Opera House, London*. It was founded in 1931, renamed the Sadler's Wells Ballet in 1941 (see *Sadler's Wells*), and became the Royal Ballet in 1956, when it merged with the Sadler's Wells Theatre Ballet, which had been formed in 1946. It performs both classical and English works.

Royal Ballet School /ˌrɔɪəl ˈbæleɪ skuːl/, **the** (education) The school for young professional ballet dancers entering the *Royal Ballet*. It is in west *London* in two separate centres, junior (residential) and senior.

Royal Bank of Scotland /ˌrɔɪəl ˌbæŋk əv ˈskɒtlənd/, **the** (finance) The largest Scottish bank, founded in 1727 and with branches in many Scottish towns and cities and with an increasing number in *England* (through its ownership of Williams and Glyn's, one of the smaller English banks).

Royal British Legion /ˌrɔɪəl ˌbrɪtɪʃ ˈliːdʒən/, **the** (charities) An organization of ex-service men and women, founded in 1921 and with membership open to all British men and women who have served in the armed forces. Its aim is to assist all ex-service personnel and their families both financially and materially. It gains most of its income from *Poppy Day*. Its current membership is over 700,000.

Royal College of Art /ˌrɔɪəl ˌkɒlɪdʒ əv ˈɑːt/, **the (RCA, the)** (education) A *college*² in central *London* that offers art students a professional course at *postgraduate* level and awards *higher degrees* such as Doctor of Philosophy (PhD) and *MA*. It was founded in 1837.

Royal College of Music /ˌrɔɪəl ˌkɒlɪdʒ əv ˈmjuːzɪk/, **the (RCM, the)** (education) A *college²* in central *London* that offers professional training to students intending to take up music as a career, and makes academic awards in music. It was founded in 1883.

Royal Court (Theatre) /ˌrɔɪəl ˈkɔːt (ˌrɔɪəl ˌkɔːt ˈθɪətə(r))/, **the** (arts) A theatre in southwest *London* originally opened in 1870 and, after a series of closures, reopened in its present form in 1965. It gained a reputation for its experimental productions (by the English Stage Company), and today stages mainly contemporary plays.

royal duke /ˌrɔɪəl ˈdjuːk/ (royal family) A duke who is also a *prince*, since he is a member of the *royal family*. There are at present four royal dukes: *the Duke of Edinburgh*, the *Duke of Cornwall*, the Duke of Gloucester and the Duke of Kent.

Royal Enclosure /ˌrɔɪəl ɪnˈkləʊʒə(r)/, **the** (sport and leisure) A special area of the stands at *Ascot*. To gain a ticket for this enclosure one must apply well in advance to the Ascot office, who check every applicant, and their sponsors, for suitability. [in full, Royal Ascot Enclosure]

royal family /ˌrɔɪəl ˈfæməlɪ/ (royal family) The British sovereign and his or her immediate family, regarded as representing the highest aristocratic presence in the land, with each member attracting much popular interest and the constant attention of the media. At present the royal family is headed by *Queen Elizabeth*, and directly includes the *Duke of Edinburgh*, *Queen Elizabeth, the Queen Mother*, the *Prince* and *Princess of Wales*, the Queen's other three children (see *Queen Elizabeth*) and the Queen's sister, Princess Margaret (born 1930). Outside this immediate circle, the royal family also includes the Queen's cousins, the Dukes of Gloucester and Kent (see *royal duke*), and the spouses and children of these and other relations apart from those already mentioned. When members of the royal family attend an official ceremony the *national anthem* is played and the *Union Jack* may be flown.

Royal Festival Hall /ˌrɔɪəl ˌfestɪvl ˈhɔːl/ (arts) A concert hall on the *South Bank* site, *London*, built in 1948–51 for the *Festival of Britain*. See also *Queen Elizabeth Hall, Purcell Room*.

Royal Greenwich Observatory /ˌrɔɪəl ˌɡrenɪdʒ əbˈzɜːvətrɪ/, **the** (science and technology) An astronomical observatory established at *Greenwich, London*, in 1675, originally for improving methods of navigation. The growth of London, with its smoke and bright lights, had a bad effect on the work of the Observatory, and in 1946 the decision was made to move it to Herstmonceux Castle north of Eastbourne, East Sussex. The move was completed in 1958. The Observatory is responsible for accurate time measurement for *Britain*, and the time zones of the world are based on *GMT*.

royal family

Royal Highland Regiment /ˌrɔɪəl ˈhaɪlənd ˌredʒɪmənt/ see *Black Watch* (defence)

Royal Highness /ˌrɔɪəl ˈhaɪnɪs/ (royal family) The form of address used for a member of the *royal family* (other than the sovereign), used as appropriate by 'Your', 'His', 'Her', etc. Compare *Her Majesty*.

Royal Horse Guards /ˌrɔɪəl ˈhɔːs gɑːdz/, **the** (defence) A regiment of the British *Army* raised in 1661, and known as 'The Blues' from the colour of their uniform. In 1969 they joined with the Royal Dragoons to form the *Blues and Royals*.

Royal International Horse Show /ˌrɔɪəl ɪntəˌnæʃnəl ˈhɔːs ʃəʊ/, **the** (sport and leisure) An international show-jumping contest held annually at *White City* Stadium, *London*.

Royal Liverpool Philharmonic Orchestra /ˌrɔɪəl ˌlɪvəpuːl ˌfɪləmɒnɪk ˈɔːkɪstrə/, **the (RLPO, the)** (arts) A well-known symphony orchestra founded in Liverpool in 1840.

Royal Marines /ˌrɔɪəl məˈriːnz/, **the (RM, the)** (defence) *Britain*'s 'sea soldiers', a corps first formed in 1664 and part of the *Royal Navy*. The Royal Marines are best known for their units of *Commandos*.

Royal Mews /ˌrɔɪəl ˈmjuːz/, **the** (London) A building near *Buckingham Palace, London,* where the sovereign's coaches are kept and horses stabled, ready for use on state occasions. The three state coaches are of particular interest to the public, who are admitted to the Mews for two hours twice a week. ['Mews' means 'stables', the word was originally used of

royal stables built on the site of hawks' mews (rooms) at
Charing Cross[1]]

Royal Mile /ˌrɔɪəl 'maɪl/, **the** (history) The central streets of
Edinburgh, Scotland, that run through the historic part of the
city (the 'Old Town') from *Edinburgh Castle* in the west to
Holyrood House in the east. [so named for the many *kings*,
queens and *princes* who have walked or ridden here in
historic times]

Royal Military Academy /ˌrɔɪəl ˌmɪlɪtrɪ ə'kædəmɪ/, **the (RMA,
the)** (education) A military establishment founded in 1799 to
train both officers and new entrants to the British *Army*.
Originally it was at High Wycombe, Buckinghamshire, but
eventually was re-established at *Sandhurst*, Berkshire.
Compare *Cranwell, Dartmouth*.

Royal Mint /ˌrɔɪəl 'mɪnt/, **the** (finance) The state organization
that manufactures British coins (with the *Bank of England*
supplying the bank notes). In its present form, the Royal
Mint was founded on *Tower Hill, London*, in 1811, and moved
to a site near *Cardiff, Wales*, in 1968.

Royal National Institute for the Blind /ˌrɔɪəl ˌnæʃnəl ˌɪnstɪtjuːt
fə ðə 'blaɪnd/, **the (RNIB, the)** (charities) A voluntary
organization that aims to provide specialized services for
blind people as the government provides only limited
services. The RNIB was founded in 1868.

Royal National Institute for the Deaf /ˌrɔɪəl ˌnæʃnəl ˌɪnstɪtjuːt fə
ðə 'def/, **the (RNID, the)** (charities) A voluntary body
founded in 1911 with the aim of making deaf people's lives
easier by providing specialized services (including housing,
employment, social communication and information), as the
government provides only limited services.

Royal National Lifeboat Institution /ˌrɔɪəl ˌnæʃnəl 'laɪfbəʊt
ˌɪnstɪˌtjuːʃn/, **the (RNLI, the)** (charities) A voluntary
organization that operates the round-the-clock lifeboat rescue
service round the coasts of *Britain* and *Ireland*. It was founded
in 1824 and has 2,000 fund-raising branches and 30,000
members.

Royal Naval College /ˌrɔɪəl 'neɪvl ˌkɒlɪdʒ/ see **Britannia Royal
Naval College** (education)

Royal Naval Reserve /ˌrɔɪəl ˌneɪvl rɪ'zɜːv/, **the (RNR, the)**
(defence) A volunteer force of service men and women who
undergo regular training and who can be called upon in time
of war to serve with the *Royal Navy*.

Royal Navy /ˌrɔɪəl 'neɪvɪ/, **the (RN, the)** (defence) The British
navy existed in early historic times but was formally
established by King *Henry VIII* in the 16th century. The total
number of naval service men and women, including the
Royal Marines, is under 72,000, making it *Britain*'s smallest
armed force.

Royal Observer Corps /ˌrɔɪəl əb'zɜːvə kɔː(r)/, **the** (defence) A
uniformed voluntary civilian organization established in

1925, originally to identify and track flying aircraft in wartime. In 1955 the Corps changed its role to the detection of nuclear explosions and to the monitoring of radioactive fallout. The Corps is affiliated to the *RAF*.

Royal National Lifeboat Institution

Royal Opera /ˌrɔɪəl ˈɒprə/, **the** (arts) A leading *London* opera company with its own orchestra. It was founded in 1946 and has its home, together with that of the *Royal Ballet*, at the *Royal Opera House*, London. See also *Covent Garden²*.

Royal Opera House /ˌrɔɪəl ˈɒprə haʊs/, **the** (arts) The leading theatre of opera and ballet in *London*, also known, from its location, as *Covent Garden²*. The first theatre on this site was built in 1732. After this and a later building were burnt down, the present building was opened in 1858 and is now the home of the *Royal Opera* and *Royal Ballet* companies.

royal park /ˌrɔɪəl ˈpɑːk/ (London) Any of the 12 parks in *London* that are maintained by the *Crown²* (ie, the government in the name of the sovereign). Among them are the five great parks that began as royal preserves, later opened to the public — *Green Park*, *Hyde Park*, *Kensington Gardens*, *Regent's Park* and *St James's Park*. Two further royal parks are *Kew Gardens* and the gardens at *Hampton Court*. Most of London's other parks are maintained by the *GLC*.

Royal Pavilion /ˌrɔɪəl pəˈvɪlɪən/, **the** (arts) A famous building in *Brighton*, East Sussex, noted for its many royal connections. It was originally built in the late 18th century for the *Prince Regent* but was rebuilt in the early 19th century in its present oriental style, with onion-shaped domes, spires and minarets. Today it is open to the public as a museum. Part of its interior is in the Chinese style, existing from the original building.

Royal Philharmonic Orchestra /ˌrɔɪəl ˌfɪləmɒnɪk ˈɔːkɪstrə/, **the (RPO, the)** (arts) A leading *London* symphony orchestra, founded as the orchestra of the Royal Philharmonic society (itself founded in 1813) and from 1946 called by its present name. From 1943 it has performed regularly at *Glyndebourne*.

Royal Regiment /ˌrɔɪəl ˈredʒɪmənt/ see *Royal Scots* (defence)

royal salute /ˌrɔɪəl səˈluːt/, **the** (royal family) A ceremonial salute fired on the riverside at the *Tower of London* on a royal occasion. On the sovereign's birthday, and also on the anniversary of his or her accession (see *Accession Day*) and *Coronation*, 62 guns are fired, as they are at present on the birthdays of the *Duke of Edinburgh* and *Queen Elizabeth, the Queen Mother*. When the sovereign opens, prorogues (see *prorogation*) or dissolves parliament, or passes through *London* in procession, 41 guns are fired. When a child is born to a member of the *royal family*, 41 guns are also fired, in *Hyde Park* as well as at the Tower of London.

Royal Scots /ˌrɔɪəl ˈskɒts/, **the** (defence) The senior regiment of the British *Army*, raised in *Scotland* in 1633 and formally known as the *Royal Regiment*.

Royal Shakespeare Company /ˌrɔɪəl ˈʃeɪkspɪə ˌkʌmpənɪ/, **the (RSC, the)** (arts) One of *Britain*'s most important theatre companies working in the *Shakespeare Memorial Theatre* at *Stratford-(up)on-Avon* and called the Shakespeare Memorial Company until 1961. It is now based both in Stratford and in *London*, with its London home at the *Barbican* from 1982.

Royal Smithfield Show /ˌrɔɪəl ˌsmɪθfiːld ˈʃəʊ/, **the** (tradition) An annual exhibition of agricultural machinery and livestock held at *Earls Court, London*. [named for its historic connection with *Smithfield*]

Royal Society /ˌrɔɪəl səˈsaɪətɪ/, **the** (science and technology) The oldest and most important scientific society in *Britain*, originating in 1645 as the Royal Society for Improving Natural Knowledge, and functioning as the equivalent of a national academy of sciences. Election as a *Fellow*[3] of the Society is regarded as one of the greatest honours for an academic. The Society's headquarters are in central *London*.

Royal Society for the Protection of Birds /ˌrɔɪəl səˌsaɪətɪ fə ðə prəˌtekʃn əv ˈbɜːdz/, **the (RSPB, the)** (charities) A voluntary organization founded in 1889 with the aim of conserving and protecting wild birds. The Society has over 200,000 members.

royal standard /ˌrɔɪəl ˈstændəd/**, the** (royal family) A flag
bearing the arms of the sovereign, and flown to show he or
she is present in a particular place.

royal standard

Royal Tournament /ˌrɔɪəl ˈtɔːnəmənt/**, the** (sport and
leisure) An annual display given by teams from the three
armed services (the *Army*, the *Royal Navy* and the *RAF*) at
Earls Court, London. One of the highlights is a contest in
dismantling field guns, transporting them over obstacles and
re-assembling them.

Royal Ulster Constabulary /ˌrɔɪəl ˌʌlstə kənˈstæbjʊlərɪ/ see *RUC*
(law)

Royal Worcester /ˌrɔɪəl ˈwʊstə(r)/ (style) The term used for
Worcester (*china*) made from 1862 by a factory in Worcester
(Royal Worcester Ltd), originally founded in 1751 and known
by a variety of names since then.

Royal Variety Show/Performance /ˌrɔɪəl vəˈraɪətɪ ʃəʊ/
pəˌfɔːməns/**, the** (arts) An annual variety and entertainment
show held at a leading *London* theatre, with top artists and
entertainers performing, in order to raise money for the
Variety Artistes' Federation (part of *Equity*). The performance
is traditionally attended by one or more members of the *royal
family*, and is usually televised.

Royal Yacht /ˌrɔɪəl ˈjɒt/**, the** (royal family) A special ship of
the *Royal Navy*, named *Britannia*[3], used for official visits
overseas by members of the *royal family*. The ship can be
converted into a hospital ship in wartime. It first entered
service in 1954.

Royals /ˈrɔɪəlz/**, the** (1 defence 2 royal family) 1 The nickname
of the Royal Dragoons, now joined with the *Royal Horse
Guards*. See *Blues and Royals*. 2 A colloquial name for the
royal family.

RP /ˌɑː ˈpiː/ **(Received Pronunciation)** (language) A non-
regional accent of standard British English, often regarded as

a prestige form. [traditionally called 'Received' in the sense 'accepted as standard']

RSA /ˌɑːr es 'eɪ/, **the (Royal Society of Arts, the)** (education) A learned society founded in 1754 'for the encouragement of arts, manufactures and commerce'. It arranges series of lectures on a wide range of subjects. The Society also arranges many examinations, in *commercial subjects* and in various languages. These examinations are held both in *Britain* and in other countries.

RSPCA /ˌɑːr es ˌpiː siː 'eɪ/, **the (Royal Society for the Prevention of Cruelty to Animals, the)** (charities) A voluntary organization founded in 1824 to promote kindness in the treatment of animals and to discourage, by *court*[3] prosecution if necessary, cruelty to them. The Society has 70,000 members.

RUC /ˌɑː juː 'siː/, **the (Royal Ulster Constabulary, the)** (law) The police force of *Northern Ireland*, formed as a separate force from the Royal Irish Constabulary, which was disbanded in 1922.

rugby football /ˌrʌgbɪ 'fʊtbɔːl/ (sport and leisure) A form of *football* different from *association football*. See *rugby league* and *rugby union*.

rugby league /ˌrʌgbɪ 'liːg/ (sport and leisure) A form of *rugby football* played by 13 players instead of 15, with professional players allowed. The game originated in 1893, when professionals were still banned, and is traditionally associated with the north of *England*. There are some differences in the rules and in scoring between rugby league and *rugby union*.

rugby union /ˌrʌgbɪ 'juːnɪən/ (sport and leisure) The standard game of *rugby football* (popularly known as 'rugger'), played by teams of 15, always amateurs. The game originated in 1871, when the *FA* banned handling the ball. (This had first happened at Rugby School when, one day in 1823 a player picked up the ball and ran with it.)

rugger /'rʌgə(r)/ see *rugby union* (sport and leisure)

Rule, Britannia /ˌruːl brɪ'tænjə/ (tradition) A patriotic British song, sung traditionally during the *Last Night of the Proms*, as well as on other occasions when strong (or even militaristic) patriotism is expressed. The song was written in 1840, and is well-known for its last two lines: 'Rule, Britannia, Britannia rule the waves; Britons never, never, never shall be slaves'. See also *Britannia*[2].

Ryder Cup /ˌraɪdə 'kʌp/, **the** (sport and leisure) A professional golf contest between *Britain* and the United States held every two years. Compare *Walker Cup*. [first held in the United States in 1927, the trophy presented by a Briton, Samuel Ryder]

'S' level /'es ˌlevl/ **(Scholarship level)** (education) An additional examination paper, at a higher level, taken by a student sitting the *'A' level* examination of the *GCE*. Passing an 'S' level examination will strengthen the student's chances of getting a place at a university.

Saatchi & Saatchi /ˌsɑːtʃɪ ən ˈsɑːtʃɪ/ (commerce) An advertising agency which became famous in the early 1980s for its work in promoting the *Conservative Party*.

Sadler's Wells Theatre /ˌsædləz ˌwelz ˈθɪətə(r)/ (arts) A *London* theatre famous for its presentation of opera and ballet. It was originally the home of the *Royal Ballet* (until 1956 known as the Sadler's Wells Ballet) and that of the Sadler's Wells Opera Company (which in 1968 moved to the *Coliseum*). [original theatre built in 1756 on the site of a medicinal spring (wells) discovered in 1683 by a Mr Sadler]

safari park /səˈfɑːrɪ pɑːk/ (sport and leisure) An enclosed park in which lions and other wild animals are on display to the public, who are usually allowed to drive through the park in cars and coaches. [from the 'safari' (Swahili, 'journey') made by British travellers in East Africa, originally as a hunting expedition, and on foot, in the first half of the 20th century]

safari park

safe seat /ˌseɪf 'siːt/ (politics) A *seat* whose *MP* has been elected by a large majority, and which is therefore unlikely to change its political support in a future *general election* or *by-election*. Many *constituencies*, such as those in the south of *England* held by the *Conservative Party*, and some seats in northern industrial areas held by the *Labour Party*, have long been regarded as safe seats.

Sainsburys /'seɪnzbrɪz/ (commerce) A chain of privately-owned, good quality supermarkets. The stores sell mainly food but some also sell other goods, such as cosmetics and clothing. [the first shop was opened in *London* in 1869 by dairyman John James Sainsbury (1844–1928)]

Saint . . . /snt . . . / see *St* . . .

sale of work /ˌseɪl əv 'wɜːk/ (daily life) A sale of home-made goods such as knitwear, ornaments, furnishings, cakes and sweets, usually organized by a group of women or by a school in aid of a particular charity. Compare *bring-and-buy sale, coffee morning*.

Salisbury Plain /ˌsɔːlzbrɪ 'pleɪn/ (geography) An extensive area of open land to the north of Salisbury, Wiltshire, owned by the *Ministry* of Defence and used by the *Army* for military exercises. The main tourist attraction here is *Stonehenge*.

Sally Army /ˌsælɪ 'ɑːmɪ/, **the** (religion) A colloquial name for the *Salvation Army*. [based on girl's name, Sally]

Sally Lunn /ˌsælɪ 'lʌn/ (food and drink) A flat, round cake made from flour, sugar, yeast, milk, butter and eggs. It is usually eaten hot. [said to be named after a girl who sold them in the streets of Bath, Avon in the 18th century]

saloon bar /sə'luːn bɑː(r)/ (daily life) A *bar¹* in a *pub* which is more comfortable, and has slightly higher prices, than the *public bar*. Compare *lounge bar, private bar, snug*.

Salopian /sə'ləʊpɪən/ (geography) **1** A native or inhabitant of the county of Shropshire. **2** A native or inhabitant of Shrewsbury, the *county town* of Shropshire. [from Salop, the alternative name for Shropshire, in official use from 1974 to 1980 but also used in written addresses and other documents]

Salvation Army /sælˌveɪʃn 'ɑːmɪ/, **the** (religion) A uniformed religious movement organized on semi-military lines to carry out Christian evangelistic work and give practical aid and spiritual comfort to the poor and needy. It was founded in 1865 and is familiar for the plain, dark uniforms of its men and women members, its public prayer meetings and hymn singing and its lively brass bands. The movement, though of British origin, is now international.

Salvationist /sæl'veɪʃənɪst/ (religion) A member of the *Salvation Army*.

Samaritans /sə'mærɪtənz/, **the** (religion) An organization which befriends those in despair, especially anyone thinking of suicide. It is staffed almost entirely by volunteers and usually operates by telephone contact, after which a personal contact may be made. It was founded in 1953 and has 19,000 volunteer members. [from the biblical story of the 'Good Samaritan', Luke 10 : 30–37]

Salvation Army

Sandhurst /'sændhɜ:st/ (education) The short name of the *Royal Military Academy*, at Sandhurst, Berkshire.

Sandown Park /ˌsændaʊn 'pɑ:k/ (sport and leisure) A race course near Esher, Surrey. [named after old house here]

Sandringham /'sændrɪŋəm/ (royal family) A village in Norfolk where the *royal family* has a country residence, Sandringham House.

sandwich course /'sænwɪdʒ kɔ:s/ (education) A course at a university or other place of *further education* in which students alternate periods of full-time study with periods of supervised experience in a particular job. [study and work experience alternate like the layers of a sandwich]

sandwich man /'sænwɪdʒ mæn/ (commerce) A man who wears two advertising boards, one on his chest, the other on his back, joined by straps across the shoulders, and who walks along a pavement in a shopping street to publicize his advertisement. [boards suggest a 'sandwich', with the bearer as the 'filling']

Sanger's Circus /ˌsæŋəz 'sɜ:kəs/ (sport and leisure) A famous travelling circus, one of the oldest in *Britain*, founded in 1871 by the showman George Sanger (1825–1911).

Santa Claus /'sæntə klɔ:z/ (tradition) The legendary patron saint of children, who brings them presents at *Christmas*. He is traditionally represented as a cheery old man, rosy cheeked and with a white beard, dressed in a scarlet robe and hood. In popular folklore he arrives from the North Pole (or some northern country such as Greenland) in a sledge drawn by reindeer and visits each child's house by coming down the chimney on *Christmas Eve* in order to leave his presents. He appears as a character in many *pantomimes*, and, commercially, is an attraction in many large department stores at Christmas, where he usually sits in a fairy-tale setting and runs a *lucky dip* for young children. He is also known as *Father Christmas*. He is not associated with the religious aspect of Christmas. [modification of Dutch dialect, 'Sante Klaas', 'St Nicholas']

Santa Claus

Sarum /'seərəm/ (geography) The historical name of Salisbury, Wiltshire. Today it is most commonly used in the names Old Sarum and New Sarum. Old Sarum is an Iron Age camp site to the north of Salisbury, where the city stood until the 13th century. New Sarum is an official name of the modern city of Salisbury.

SAS /ˌes eɪ 'es/, **the (Special Air Service, the)** (defence) A special force of one regular army regiment (see *Army*) and two *Territorial Army* regiments containing highly trained and experienced troops, whose main task is to cause problems behind enemy lines, usually by means of sabotage, etc. The Service originated in the Special Air Service Brigade formed in the Second World War.

Saturday girl /'sætədɪ gɜːl/ (daily life) A girl, often a schoolgirl or student, who works as a temporary shop assistant on Saturdays, when trade is busiest.

Saturday person /'sætədɪ ˌpɜːsn/ (daily life) A young person, male or female, who carries out the work of a *Saturday girl*.

sausage roll /ˌsɒsɪdʒ 'rəʊl/ (food and drink) A sausage, or filling of sausage meat, in a small roll of light flaky pastry, eaten either hot or cold.

Save the Children Fund /ˌseɪv ðə 'tʃɪldrən fʌnd/, **the** (charities) A voluntary organization founded in 1919 with the aim of rescuing children in disaster areas and working for their welfare. The organization operates internationally, as well as in *Britain*, and its practical objectives change according to the country. In Britain it aims chiefly to provide homes, *clubs* and *playgroups* for children where these are not fully provided by the *local authorities*.

Savings Certificates /'seɪvɪŋz səˌtɪfɪkəts/ see *National Savings Certificates* (finance)

Savoy (Hotel) /sə'vɔɪ (səˌvɔɪ həʊ'tel)/, **the** (London) A luxury hotel with a high-class restaurant, off the *Strand, London*. [named, as are many streets here, after the Savoy Palace built for Peter of Savoy in 13th century]

Savoy (Theatre) /sə'vɔɪ (səˌvɔɪ 'θɪətə(r))/, **the** (arts) A *London* theatre founded in 1881. For many years it was famous for its productions of *Gilbert and Sullivan operas* but now it puts on ordinary stage plays. [located in Savoy Court; see *Savoy Hotel*]

Savoy Operas /səˌvɔɪ 'ɒprəz/, **the** (arts) A name for *Gilbert and Sullivan operas*, which were first staged almost exclusively at the *Savoy (Theatre), London*.

Saxon (architecture) /'sæksn (ˌsæksn 'ɑːkɪtektʃə(r))/ (style) The earliest form of English architecture, also known as Anglo-Saxon, and covering the period 600–1086. It is a simple style and is characterized by small, deep-set windows, rounded arches and alternate long and short angle stones.

SAYE /ˌes eɪ waɪ 'iː/ **(Save As You Earn)** (finance) A government savings scheme operated by the *Post Office*, in which monthly contributions (from £4 to £50) paid over a fixed period, earn interest free of *income tax*. In 1984 the scheme was replaced by a 'Yearly Plan' similar to that for *Savings Certificates*, with monthly contributions of £20 to £200 made to yield an increasing rate of interest (currently from 6% at the end of the first year to 9.75% at the end of the fifth year).

Scargill, Arthur /'skɑːgɪl, 'ɑːθə(r)/ (people) Arthur Scargill (born 1938) became a miner when he was a young man. He joined the Young Communist League, later leaving the *Communist Party* to join the *Labour Party*. He was also taking an increasingly active part in the *NUM* and in 1973 he was elected area president of this trade union. Arthur Scargill was elected president of the NUM in 1982, thus becoming one of the most influential men in *Britain*. In 1984–5 Arthur Scargill's vigorous support for the miners in their prolonged strike (which was a protest against the proposed pit closures announced by the *NCB*) brought him both widespread hatred and widespread admiration from many members of the public.

scholarship /ˈskɒləʃɪp/ (education) A special financial grant given to a clever scholar at a fee-paying school or *college[1]*.

school song /ˌskuːl ˈsɒŋ/ (education) A traditional song sung on special occasions, such as an end-of-term concert, at many schools, especially *public schools[1]*. The words of the song are usually intended to make students proud of their school and to describe the best enduring qualities of a public school education.

school tie /ˌskuːl ˈtaɪ/ (education) The distinctive tie worn as part of the school uniform by members of a school and regarded as symbolic of the particular school and its educational values. School ties are typically designed with a repeated pattern such as a crest or stripe. Compare *old school tie*.

school welfare officer /ˌskuːl ˈwelfeər ˌɒfɪsə(r)/ (education) A *social worker* who aims to ensure that school children, especially those who are 'difficult' or needy, both attend school and receive their rights, such as school *dinners* and transport to and from school.

school year /ˌskuːl ˈjɪə(r)/ (education) The academic year, beginning in September and ending in late June or early July. It is divided into three *terms[1]*.

schooner /ˈskuːnə(r)/ (food and drink) A large, tall wine glass, especially one in which sherry is served in a *bar[1]*.

Science Museum /ˈsaɪəns mjuː: ˌzɪəm/, **the** (science and technology) A famous museum in southwest *London*, housing collections that illustrate the history and development of science, engineering and industry, with many working models. The museum, originally part of the South Kensington Museum that developed after the *Great Exhibition* of 1851, is particularly popular with children, for whom it has a special Children's Gallery. A development of the Science Museum is the *National Railway Museum*, York.

Scilly Isles /ˈsɪlɪ aɪlz/, **the** (geography) A group of islands off the southwest coast of *England*, some 28 miles (45 km) from *Lands End*. There are five sizeable inhabited islands (St Mary's, Tresco, St Martin's, St Agnes and Bryher) and a large number of small islands. The islands are popular with tourists in the spring, when early flowers (especially daffodils) are grown commercially. The unusually mild climate makes the islands additionally attractive to visitors.

scone /skɒn/ (food and drink) A light, plain cake made of flour, milk and very little fat and cooked either in an oven or on a griddle (a flat iron plate). It is usually round in shape and eaten split and buttered. It is popular throughout *Britain*.

Scotch /skɒtʃ/ (food and drink) *Whisky* made in *Scotland*, regarded by many as the only genuine kind. See also *whiskey*.

Scotch broth /ˌskɒtʃ ˈbrɒθ/ (food and drink) A thick soup made from beef stock, chopped vegetables and pearl barley.

Scotch egg /ˌskɒtʃ ˈeg/ (food and drink) A hard-boiled egg enclosed in sausage-meat and covered in fried bread crumbs, eaten either hot or cold.

Scotch mist /ˌskɒtʃ 'mɪst/ (daily life) A misty rain or drizzle, regarded as typical of the weather over moorland in *Scotland*.

Scotch/Scottish terrier /ˌskɒtʃ/ˌskɒtɪʃ 'terɪə(r)/ (animal world) A small breed of terrier with long, black hair and erect ears and tail, noted for its loyalty and companionship. It is familiarly known as a 'Scotty'. [originally bred in the *Highlands* of *Scotland*]

Scotch woodcock /ˌskɒtʃ 'wʊdkɒk/ (food and drink) A savoury dish of hot *toast* with anchovies and creamy scrambled eggs, usually eaten at the end of a meal rather than as an hors-d'oeuvre.

Scotland /'skɒtlənd/ (geography) The northernmost part of mainland *Britain*, bordered on the south by *England*. Although a part of the *United Kingdom*, Scotland has its own legal and educational system, its own banknotes and now its own £1 coin. With its many moors, lochs (ie, lakes), mountains, islands and ancient castles, Scotland is rightly regarded as a beautiful country, and is popular with English tourists, especially those who enjoy sporting facilities such as skiing in winter which is not possible in England. The *Gaelic* language is still spoken by about 82,000 people mainly in the north and west, for example, in the *Highlands and Islands*[1].

Scotland Yard /ˌskɒtlənd 'jɑːd/ (law) The former name of the headquarters of the *Metropolitan Police Force* in *London*, still in use for the present headquarters that are officially known as *New Scotland Yard*.

Scots Greys /ˌskɒts 'greɪz/**, the** (defence) One of the best known Scottish army regiments (in full, the Royal Scots Greys), raised in 1678 and named after the colour of their horses.

Scots Guards /ˌskɒts 'gɑːdz/**, the** (defence) One of the five army regiments that form the *Guards Division*, originally raised in the early 17th century for service in *Ireland*, then reformed under its present name in 1660 as a regiment of the Scottish army.

Scots, wha hae /ˌskɒts wʌ 'heɪ/ (tradition) The opening words of the unofficial Scottish national anthem, taken from a poem by Robert Burns (see *Burns' Night*), published in 1798. [in full, 'Scots, wha hae' wi' Wallace bled' ('Scots, who have with Wallace bled'); the reference is to Sir William Wallace, the 13th-century Scottish patriot, who defeated the English in 1297 but who was later himself defeated and executed]

Scotsman /'skɒtsmən/**, The** (media) One of *Scotland*'s leading daily newspapers, first published in 1817. It is a *quality paper* and has a circulation of over 90,000.

Scouse /skaʊs/ (**1** geography **2** language) **1** The nickname of a native or inhabitant of Liverpool. **2** The characteristic dialect of such a person. [from the dialect word 'scouse', used for a type of Lancashire *hotpot*, itself a shortened form of 'lobscouse', a similar dish once popular with sailors]

Scout/scout /skaʊt/skaʊt/ (**1** sport and leisure **2** education) **1** A boy aged 11 to 16 who is a member of the *Scout Association*. **2** A *college*¹ servant at *Oxford University*.

Scout Association /'skaʊt əsəʊsɪˌeɪʃn/, **the** (sport and leisure) A uniformed organization for boys founded in 1908 by Lord Baden-Powell (as a world-wide movement) to encourage a sense of adventure and of responsibility for others among young people. The Association's British membership is constantly increasing (1974—593,000; 1983—645,000). See *cub (scout)*, *scout*. Compare *Girl Guides Association*.

Scrabble /'skræbl/ (sport and leisure) The trade name of a board game in which small tiles marked with letters of the alphabet, are arranged to form words, such words being arranged as in a crossword puzzle. Each letter has a numerical value; more 'difficult' letters, such as Q and X having higher values. The aim is to use all one's letters and form high-scoring words.

scrip issue /'skrɪp ˌɪʃuː/ (finance) An issue of shares made by a company to its shareholders without charge.

Scrooge /skruːdʒ/ (arts) The miser, Ebenezer Scrooge, is the central character in Charles *Dickens*'s popular story 'A Christmas Carol' (1843). The subject of the story is the conversion of Scrooge from a mean and unpleasant man to a cheerful and loving man. The name 'Scrooge' is now used to describe a very mean person.

Scrubs /skrʌbz/, **the** (law) A colloquial name for *Wormwood Scrubs* prison.

scrumpy /'skrʌmpɪ/ (food and drink) A kind of rough, dry cider brewed in the *West Country* of *England*.

SDLP /ˌes diː el 'piː/, **the (Social Democratic and Labour Party, the)** (politics) A party formed in *Northern Ireland* in 1970 as a reaction to the *Troubles*. Its supporters are largely Catholic and would like *Ireland* (ie, Northern Ireland and the Republic of Ireland) to be reunited as one country.

SDP /ˌes diː 'piː/, **the (Social Democratic Party, the)** (politics) A political party formed in 1981 by a small number of right-wing *Labour Party* politicians, and entering the same year into an alliance with the *Liberal Party* (see *Liberal-SDP Alliance*). The party has gained considerable popular support, largely from voters who are disillusioned with the two major parties (see *Conservative Party* and *Labour Party*). SDP candidates have done well in recent *by-elections* although it does not have many *MPs* in the *House of Commons*.

Sealink /'siː lɪŋk/ (transport) A company (in full Sealink UK Ltd) that, until 1984, was a subsidiary transport company of *BR*. It operates ship and *hovercraft* ferry services across the English Channel and between mainland *England* and the *Isle* *of Wight* and *Channel Islands* (as well as services to the *Isle of Man* and *Ireland*).

Sealyham (terrier) /ˈsiːlɪəm (ˌsiːlɪəm ˈterɪə(r))/ (animal world) A small breed of wire-haired terrier with white coat and short legs. [originally bred in the small village of Sealyham, near Fishguard in *Wales*]

Searchlight Tattoo /ˌsɜːtʃlaɪt təˈtuː/, **the** (sport and leisure) An annual display by the armed forces, with massed military bands, at the *White City* in *London*. Searchlights originally featured in the display when it was held in an army arena at Aldershot, Hampshire, in the 1920s.

season ticket /ˈsiːzn ˌtɪkɪt/ (**1** transport **2** arts) **1** A ticket for a form of public transport (usually train or bus) that allows regular travel over a particular route for a particular period (a week, a month, a quarter or a year) at a reduced rate. **2** A similar ticket giving regular admission to a series of concerts, performances or exhibitions.

Seaspeed /ˈsiːspiːd/ (transport) A transport company that operated cross-Channel ferry services on *hovercraft* until 1981, when it merged with Hoverlloyd to become *Hoverspeed*. Compare *Sealink*.

seat /siːt/ (government) An alternative term for a parliamentary *constituency*, so called because it provides its *MP* with a seat in the *House of Commons*. See also *safe seat*.

second class /ˌsekənd ˈklɑːs/ (**1** transport **2** commerce **3** education) **1** The standard, and most popular, class of seat in a railway train. **2** The lower of two postal rates, providing delivery at a slower rate than *first class*[2] mail. **3** The second and most common class of *honours degree*, indicating high academic competence but not originality or excellence.

second reading /ˌsekənd ˈriːdɪŋ / (government) The second presentation of a *bill* in the *House of Commons* or *House of Lords*, usually followed by a debate on it. Compare *first reading*, *third reading*.

secondary modern (school) /ˌsekəndrɪ ˈmɒdn (skuːl)/ (education) A type of *secondary school* that offers a more general and technical and less academic education than a *grammar school*. Of all school children of secondary school age, only 5% attend such schools.

secondary picketing /ˌsekəndrɪ ˈpɪkɪtɪŋ/ (work) Action taken by *pickets* at the premises of a firm where they are not themselves employed but which has trading links with their own workplace or which produces similar products or goods. Such action, which is legally an offence, is carried out to support pickets from a workplace's own employees.

secondary school /ˈsekəndrɪ skuːl/ (education) A *state school* or *private school* that provides education for school children aged between 11 and 18. Such schools are organized in a number of ways, with the most common type being the *comprehensive school*, attended by over 90% of school children of this age. Other types of secondary schools are *grammar schools*, and *secondary modern schools* and *public schools*[1]. An extension of a state secondary school is the *tertiary college*. Most students leave their state secondary school at the age of 16, usually having passed one or more subjects in either the *CSE* or *GCE*. See also *GCSE*.

Secretary of State /ˌsekrətrɪ əv ˈsteɪt/ (government) The title of the head of certain government *departments*, corresponding to *minister*[2]. At present such departments include the Home Office (see *Home Secretary*), Trade and Industry, Defence, the Environment, *Scotland*, *Wales*, *Northern Ireland* and Education and Science.

Selectapost /sɪˈlektəpəʊst/ (commerce) A special service that is offered to firms and other customers by the *Post Office*, in which, for a fee, the customer's mail is sorted into sub-addresses (eg, a firm's different departments) before delivery. [based on '*select*ive' and '*post*']

Selfridges /ˈselfrɪdʒɪz/ (commerce) *London*'s largest department store after *Harrods*, in *Oxford Street*. It is particularly famous for its food section, and also contains two restaurants and several cafés. [founded in 1909 by an American businessman, H Gordon Selfridge (died 1947)]

Sellafield /ˈseləfiːld/ (science and technology) The industrial installation of *British Nuclear Fuels* at Sellafield, in the north-west of *England*, where a reprocessing plant recovers unused uranium and plutonium from spent nuclear fuel. In 1983 there was public concern at a leakage of nuclear waste from the plant on to the nearby seashore. Until 1981 the site was known as *Windscale*.

semi(-detached house) /ˈsemɪ (ˌsemɪ dɪˌtætʃt ˈhaʊs)/ (style) A house attached on one side only to another, usually very similar house. A house of this kind is less expensive than a *detached house*, but still offers a good standard of privacy and comfort. See also *terraced house*.

semi(-detached house)

SEN /ˌes iː ˈen/ **(state enrolled nurse)** (medicine) A qualified hospital nurse who has satisfactorily completed a two-year course of training. Compare *SRN*.

senior citizen /ˌsiːnɪə ˈsɪtɪzn/ (life and society) A term, regarded by some as patronizing, for a person who has reached *retirement age*, otherwise called an *OAP*.

senior service /ˌsiːnɪə ˈsɜːvɪs/**, the** (defence) A name for the *Royal Navy*, which is the oldest of the three armed services.

sense of humour /ˌsens əv ˈhjuːmə(r)/ **(English/British sense of humour)** (daily life) The humour believed to be characteristic of the British, or specifically of the English (since there are also regional Scottish, Irish and Welsh senses of humour). It includes a love of 'double entendre' (a word or phrase meaning two things at the same time, one 'proper', one 'improper' or vulgar), self-mockery and an enjoyment of what is absurd and eccentric. Much English humour originated in the music-halls, and is seen today in the performances of comedians in *working men's clubs*, *pantomimes* and, most of all, on radio and television.

Sergeant/Serjeant at Arms /ˌsɑːdʒənt/ˌsɑːdʒənt ət ˈɑːmz/ (government) Another title of *Black Rod*, in his capacity as an official in the *House of Lords*. He attends the *Lord Chancellor* and is responsible for security and for accommodation and services in the house.

Serpentine /ˈsɜːpəntaɪn/**, the** (London) A lake in *Hyde Park, London*, artificially made in 1730 to be a centre for boating, fishing and swimming. [from the winding or 'serpentine' course of the former river Westbourne here]

servants /ˈsɜːvənts/ (life and society) Before the First World War and for a short time after it, servants were widely employed in even quite small households in *Britain*, especially as housemaids, cooks and gardeners. Such servants lived in their employer's house. Today some rich families with large houses still employ servants, only they are not usually called as such but are known by their type of employment, for example 'cook', 'nanny' (looking after young children), 'chauffeur', etc.

service area /ˈsɜːvɪs ˌeərɪə/ (transport) A place on a *motorway* where a number of facilities are available for drivers and travellers, usually including a *service station*, restaurant or café and toilets.

service charge /ˈsɜːvɪs tʃɑːdʒ/ (commerce) An amount, usually 10% of the total, that is often added to the bill in a restaurant or hotel as a charge for service. This is instead of the customer deciding how much, if anything, he will leave. Some restaurant menus indicate that no service charge is made, but add that the amount left (the 'tip') is for the customer to decide.

service flat /ˈsɜːvɪs flæt/ (daily life) A flat or apartment in a large residential block, especially in *London*. The rent paid for the flat includes such services as cleaning, laundry and delivery of meals.

service road /ˈsɜːvɪs rəʊd/ (commerce) A fairly narrow road running parallel to a main road and giving access to the rear entrances of shops, offices and factories built along it, so that deliveries and collections can be made without affecting traffic on the main road.

service station /ˈsɜːvɪs ˌsteɪʃn/ (transport) A commercial garage that not only supplies petrol, oil, air, etc but also usually carries out repairs, services vehicles (eg, for the *MOT test*), and sells mechanical parts and other goods.

set book /ˌset ˈbʊk/ (education) A literary work, in English or a foreign language, (set) to be studied for a school-leaving examination such as the *CSE* or *GCE*.

Severn /ˈsevən/, **the** (geography) *Britain*'s longest river (180 miles, or 290 km), which rises in northeast *Wales* and flows east and south into the Bristol Channel. It is famous for its periodic 'bore' (tidal wave) which, for a short time, makes the water flow back up the part of the river nearest the sea. See also *Severn Bridge* and *Severn Tunnel*.

Severn Bridge /ˌsevən ˈbrɪdʒ/, **the** (science and technology) The road bridge across the estuary of the river *Severn*, opened in 1966 and carrying the M4 *motorway*. The bridge, which is 3,240 feet (987 metres) long, frequently has to be closed to vehicles with high sides during strong winds and storms because it would be dangerous for them to cross it. See also *Severn Tunnel*.

Severn Tunnel /ˌsevən ˈtʌnl/, **the** (transport) The longest tunnel in *Britain*, taking the railway under the estuary of the river *Severn* on the main line from *England* to *Wales*. The tunnel is to the southwest of the *Severn Bridge*.

S4C /ˌes fɔː ˈsiː/ **(Sianel Pedwar Cymru)** (media) A mainly Welsh language television channel transmitted and financed by the *IBA* since 1982. The programmes are supplied by *HTV Wales*, the *BBC* and various independent producers, including *Channel Four*. [Welsh for 'Channel Four Wales']

Shadow Cabinet /ˌʃædəʊ ˈkæbɪnɪt/, **the** (government) The team of *ministers*[2] in the *Opposition* (the major political party not currently in power) who would probably form the *Cabinet* if their party won the next *general election*. Meanwhile, they individually deal with the same matters as the Cabinet ministers in the current government.

shadow minister /ˌʃædəʊ ˈmɪnɪstə(r)/ (government) A *minister*[2] in the *Shadow Cabinet*. He will usually be called by his particular area of responsibility, eg, 'Shadow Chancellor', 'Shadow Home Secretary'. See *Chancellor of the Exchequer*, *Home Secretary*. However, the party leader is usually known as the *Leader of the Opposition*, not the 'Shadow *Prime Minister*'.

Shaftesbury Avenue /ˈʃɑːftsbrɪ ˈævənjuː/ (London) A street in central *London*, running northeast from *Piccadilly Circus*, and famous for the many theatres and cinemas on it. The street was built only in the 1850s and is named in honour of the industrial reformer and churchman, Lord Shaftesbury (1801–85).

Shaftesbury Society /ˈʃɑːftsbrɪ səˌsaɪətɪ/, **the** (charities) A voluntary organization founded in 1844 by Lord Shaftesbury (see *Shaftesbury Avenue*) to help physically handicapped, poor and needy children. The Society runs schools, homes, holiday camps and *club*s for the physically handicapped. A tradition has developed that physically able boys in the Home often join the *Royal Navy* or Merchant Navy.

Shakespeare country /ˈʃeɪkspɪə ˌkʌntrɪ/ (geography) The towns, villages and other places connected with William *Shakespeare* (1564–1616), in particular *Stratford-(up)on-Avon*, Warwickshire and the surrounding countryside.

Shakespeare Memorial Theatre /ˌʃeɪkspɪə məˈmɔːrɪəl ˌθɪətə(r)/, **the** (arts) A theatre in *Stratford-(up)on-Avon* that opened in 1879 for annual summer seasons of *Shakespeare*'s plays. It was destroyed by fire in 1926 and the new theatre built in its place in 1932 was renamed the Royal Shakespeare Theatre in 1961. See *Royal Shakespeare Company*.

Shakespeare, William /ˈʃeɪkspɪə(r), ˈwɪljəm/ (people) William Shakespeare (1564–1616) is generally acknowledged to have been *Britain*'s finest playwright and one of her most accomplished poets. His plays show a great understanding of human activities of all kinds. In them, he very skilfully uses many different literary styles to express a wide range of emotions. The plays are usually described as comedies, tragedies and histories but this is an over-simplification as many of them do not fall neatly into any one category. His poems, especially his 'Sonnets', show his extraordinary powers of expression and his depth of emotional understanding. His work has had a great influence on English and many of his expressions have become part of the language, for example, 'a *winter of discontent*'[1,2]. Because the English language has changed so much since Shakespeare's day, many people (including school students obliged to read him for examination purposes) find his works difficult and 'dated'. There have been several recent attempts to present his plays in a more accessible way, either by modernizing the language or by printing the original text with cartoon illustrations. His birthplace at *Stratford-(up)on-Avon* remains a popular tourist attraction.

shamrock /ˈʃæmrɒk/ (tradition) The plant that is the national emblem of *Ireland*, and the equivalent of the English *rose*, the Welsh *leek* and *daffodil* and the Scottish *thistle*. According to legend, it was the plant chosen by St Patrick, patron saint of Ireland, to illustrate the Christian doctrine of the Trinity to the Irish.

shandy /'ʃændɪ/ (food and drink) An alcoholic drink of beer mixed with ginger beer or lemonade.

Shaw's Corner /ˌʃɔːz 'kɔːnə(r)/ (arts) A 19th-century house in the village of Ayot St Lawrence, Hertfordshire, where the dramatist George Bernard Shaw lived for 44 years until his death in 1950. The house is now owned by the *National Trust* and is open to the public.

She /ʃiː/ (media) A monthly magazine for women first published in 1955 and having a circulation of nearly 250,000. The magazine concentrates more on factual information and features of general interest than on feminine subjects.

Sheffield United /ˌʃefiːld juːˈnaɪtɪd/ (sport and leisure) A *football club* founded in 1889 with a stadium in south central Sheffield, South Yorkshire.

Sheffield Wednesday /ˌʃefiːld 'wenzdɪ/ (sport and leisure) A popular *football club* founded in 1867 with a stadium in northwest Sheffield, South Yorkshire. [so named as originally it played matches on a Wednesday]

Sheldonian (Theatre) /ʃelˈdəʊnɪən (ʃelˌdəʊnɪən 'θɪətə(r))/, **the** (education) An historic building in *Oxford*[1] where degrees are conferred on *graduates* of *Oxford University*, special University ceremonies take place, and concerts are held. The building contains the chair of the *vice-chancellor* of the University, and was itself built in the second half of the 17th century by the clergyman Gilbert Sheldon (1598–1677).

Shell Centre /ʃel ˌsentə(r)/, **the** (commerce) A 25-storey building in *London* near the *South Bank* site. It was built over the period 1957–62 as the headquarters of the Shell Transport and Trading Company.

Shelter /'ʃeltə(r)/ (charities) A voluntary organization founded in 1966 to provide homes for poor or needy people who have nowhere to live.

shepherd's pie /ˌʃepədz 'paɪ/ (food and drink) A hot savoury dish, also known as *cottage pie*, containing minced meat usually mixed with onions, carrots and gravy, topped with a layer of mashed potato, and then baked. [said to have been a common dish with shepherds]

Sheraton /'ʃerətən/ (style) A style of furniture popular from the 18th century, when it was invented by the cabinet-maker Thomas Sheraton (1751–1806). It is characterized by a neo-classical design and by its lightness and elegance, as well as the extensive use of inlay. Compare *Chippendale* and *Hepplewhite*.

sheriff /'ʃerɪf/ (1 government 2 law) 1 In *England* and *Wales*, the chief state executive officer in a *county*, having mainly ceremonial duties. 2 In *Scotland*, a judge in a court[3] of law.

Sherlock Holmes /ˌʃɜːlɒk 'həʊmz/ see *Holmes* (1 arts 2 London)

Shetland pony /ˌʃetlənd 'pəʊnɪ/ (animal world) A small, sturdy breed of pony with a long mane and tail, popular for children because of its small size, although in fact the animal is often quite stubborn and can be difficult to control. [originally bred in the *Shetlands* in *Scotland* and used in the 19th century as work ponies]

Shetlands /'ʃetləndz/, **the** (geography) The most northerly group of islands in *Britain*, which are part of *Scotland* and lie to the north of the *Orkneys*. The largest island is Mainland and the most northerly is Unst. For many centuries the islands were ruled by Scandinavia, and both the Shetlands and the Orkneys belonged to Scandinavia until the 15th century. This link is clear in the many Norse archaeological sites and place-names here. From the 1970s, the Shetlands have become an increasingly important centre of the *North Sea oil* industry.

shilling /'ʃɪlɪŋ/ (daily life) A silver coin worth 12 pence (see penny) or one twentieth of a *pound (sterling)*, officially replaced in 1971 by the 5p piece (value 5 pence), which is the same size. The shilling is sometimes still found in use. The term is still sometimes used, especially among older people, for the 5p coin. See also *bob*.

shinty /'ʃɪntɪ/ (sport and leisure) A game like hockey played chiefly in *Scotland*. The stick used is shorter and heavier than a hockey stick, and the game itself more vigorous and faster, since the ball is often hit when still in the air.

shire horse /'ʃaɪə hɔːs/ (animal world) A large, strong, heavy breed of cart-horse formerly used all over *Britain* as a work horse on farms. [originally bred in the *Shires*]

Shires /'ʃaɪəz/, **the** (geography) A traditional name for the *counties* of the *Midlands*, long famous for their *hunts*. Those of Northamptonshire, Leicestershire and the south of Lincolnshire are especially famous. [from 'shire' in meaning of 'county'; the names of many counties still end in '-shire', with the first part of the name usually being that of the *county town*, so that 'Northamptonshire', for example, means 'county of Northampton']

shooting brake /'ʃuːtɪŋ breɪk/ (transport) An alternative name for an *estate car*.

shooting stick /'ʃuːtɪŋ stɪk/ (sport and leisure) A special kind of walking stick that has a point (for digging into the ground) at the lower end, and a folding seat at the top. It is chiefly used as a temporary seat by sportsmen when shooting game (see *gamekeeper*), watching horse racing and attending shows.

shop steward /ˌʃɒp 'stjuːəd/ (work) A trade union leader in a factory or other local work force.

shopping precinct /'ʃɒpɪŋ ˌpriːsɪŋkt/ (commerce) An area in a town or *city* where there are a lot of shops and where traffic is banned to make shopping easier for people on foot.

shortbread /'ʃɔːtbred/ (food and drink) A rich, crumbly biscuit made of flour and butter. It is also known as shortcake. ['short' in sense 'rich in fat' and therefore crumbly]

shorthorn (cattle) /'ʃɔːθɔːn (ˌʃɔːθɔːn 'kætl)/ (animal world) A stocky breed of beef and dairy cattle, in several regional varieties, with short horns.

shove-ha'penny /ˌʃʌv 'heɪpnɪ/ (sport and leisure) A game popular in *pub*s and some *club*s, in which old (pre-1971) *halfpennies* or polished discs are pushed by hand on to marked sections of a smooth wooden board.

Shrewsbury (School) /'ʃrəʊzbrɪ (ˌʃrəʊzbrɪ 'skuːl)/ (education) A leading *public school*[1] in Shrewsbury, Shropshire, founded in 1552 and having over 650 students.

Shrove Tuesday /ˌʃrəʊv 'tjuːzdɪ/ (religion) The day before *Ash Wednesday*, once thought of as a last day of enjoyment before the fasting of Lent in the Christian year. Many people still traditionally eat *pancakes* on Shrove Tuesday, hence its popular name of *Pancake Day*. [named from a rare verb 'shrive', meaning 'to make one's confession': at this time Christians used to confess their sins to a priest before Lent; this is still done by many members of the *Roman Catholic Church* and some *Anglicans*]

sidesman /'saɪdzmən/ (religion) A man appointed to assist the *churchwarden* in the *Church of England*. Among his duties are giving out prayer books and collecting money from the congregation during a church service. [so called as he 'stands beside' the churchwarden]

Silbury Hill /ˌsɪlbərɪ 'hɪl/ see *Avebury* (tradition)

silk /sɪlk/ (law) A term used to refer to the silk gown worn by a *QC*, and so to the QC himself, who is said to 'take silk' on reaching this rank as a *barrister*.

silly season /'sɪlɪ ˌsiːzn/, **the** (media) The summer season, traditionally regarded as a time when journalists, without important news in the holiday period and during the *recess*[1] of *Parliament*, fill their columns with amusing and unimportant reports.

Silverstone /'sɪlvəstən/ (sport and leisure) A racing track near Towcester, Northamptonshire, where the *British Grand Prix*[1] for motor racing is held every second year and where the *British Grand Prix*[2] for motorcycle racing is held every year. Many other important national and international races are also held here.

simnel cake /'sɪmnəl keɪk/ (food and drink) A small fruit cake covered in marzipan, traditionally eaten on *Mothering Sunday*, or in *Lent* or at *Easter*.

Sinclair, Clive /'sɪŋkleə(r), klaɪv/ (people) Clive Sinclair (born 1940) is the inventor and promoter of the personal computer, which he began to sell in 1980 as a 'home-based' instrument that was smaller and cheaper than any other existing computer. Sinclair founded his original firm, Sinclair Radionics, in 1962. He then founded his present company of Sinclair Research, and rapidly gained fame as an electronics pioneer. After the initial success of his home computer, Sinclair went on to sell a flat-screen pocket television in 1983 and at the same time announced his plans to develop a new type of small electric vehicle suitable for driving in cities. In 1984 he announced a much more ambitious project to develop so-called 'fifth generation' (ie, 'thinking') computers. Clive Sinclair was knighted in 1983.

Sinn Féin /ˌʃɪn ˈfeɪn/ (politics) The Irish republican movement that arose before the First World War and which campaigned for the economic and political separation of *Ireland* from *Great Britain*. Today it is the political wing of the PrGisional *IRA*, and wants *Northern Ireland* to become part of the Republic of Ireland, by using force if necessary. In recent years Sinn Féin has gained some successes in political elections (see *Northern Ireland Assembly*), and in the *general election* of 1983 one Provisional Sinn Féin member was elected to the *House of Commons*. He did not, however, take his seat in *Parliament*. [Irish for 'we ourselves']

sir /sɜː(r)/ (life and society) A polite form of address to a man, used most commonly by schoolchildren to their teachers, junior military ranks to senior officers, and assistants, officials, etc in shops, banks, *clubs*, public transport vehicles, to their customers, clients and passengers. The form of address is becoming less common, however, and is more likely when the man so addressed is noticeably older than, or senior to, the speaker.

Sir /sə(r) [unstressed]/ (life and society) The title of honour placed before the name of a knight or baronet, as 'Sir Edward Brown' (or 'Sir Edward', but never 'Sir Brown')

sit-down strike /ˌsɪt daʊn ˈstraɪk/ (work) A strike in which workers refuse to leave their place of work (where they may normally sit or stand while working) until settlement has been reached.

sit-in /ˈsɪt ɪn/ (politics) A form of protest or 'civil disobedience' in which demonstrators occupy areas normally belonging to their management or superiors (as students in a staff common room, workers in a factory boardroom).

sixpence /ˈsɪkspəns/ (daily life) A small silver coin worth six old pence (see *penny*) and two and half (new) pence, not minted since 1970, although in circulation for nearly ten years after that.

sixth form /ˈsɪksθ fɔːm/ (education) The most senior class in a *secondary school*, especially a *public school*[1], often divided into two years as a 'lower sixth' and an 'upper sixth'. The class is usually intended for students preparing for the *'A' level* examination of the *GCE*.

sixth form college /ˌsɪksθ fɔːm ˈkɒlɪdʒ/ (education) A *further education college*[2], often an independent (fee-paying) one, for students who wish to prepare for the *'A' level* examination of the *GCE* or, in some cases, to retake *'O' levels*. Unlike a

tertiary college it takes both *sixth form* students and those
wanting less academic courses.

skillcentre /ˈskɪlˌsentə(r)/ (work) A government training
centre where young people aged 19 and over can receive
professional training (mainly in engineering, and electrical
and electronic trades) under *TOPS*. Until 1974 skillcentres
were known as *government training centres*.

skinheads /ˈskɪnhedz/ (life and society) Gangs of youths
(occasionally also including girls) who cut their hair very
short or even shave their heads, and show, by violence or
vandalism, their dissatisfaction with the life around them.
They are often very right wing and racialist. Such groups first
appeared at the end of the 1960s, and were still active in the
mid-1980s.

skins /skɪnz/ (life and society) A colloquial term for *skinheads*.

Skye terrier /ˌskaɪ ˈterɪə(r)/ (animal world) A short-legged,
long-coated breed of terrier, originally bred as a working dog
on the island of Skye, *Scotland*.

Slade School of (Fine) Art /ˌsleɪd ˌskuːl əv (ˌfaɪn) ˈɑːt/, **the**
(education) A *college²* of *London University* founded in 1871
and providing *higher education* courses in fine art. [named
after art collector and benefactor Felix Slade (1790–1868)]

sleeping partner /ˌsliːpɪŋ ˈpɑːtnə(r)/ (finance) A partner in a
business or company who does not play an active role but
who merely provides the capital.

sleeping policeman /ˌsliːpɪŋ pəˈliːsmən/ (transport) A low
bump built across a road to prevent drivers of vehicles from
travelling too fast, usually in residential areas or, for example,
in a university campus.

sleeping policeman

slip road /ˈslɪp rəʊd/ (transport) A short, narrow road linking
a standard main road, such as an *A-road*, with a *motorway*.

Sloane /sləʊn/ (life and society) A colloquial term for a *Sloane Ranger*.

Sloane Ranger /ˌsləʊn 'reɪndʒə(r)/ (life and society) A semi-humorous name for a fashionable *upper middle class* young man or woman who lives in southwest *London*, near Sloane Square, and who is, supposedly, a trend-setter. Some male Sloane Rangers are also known as *Hooray Henrys* (and their female equivalents as Hooray Henriettas). [the name was made popular by the book 'The Sloane Ranger Official Handbook' (1982), by Peter Yorke and Ann Barr; the name itself is a blend of 'Sloane Square' and 'The Lone Ranger', the latter being the hero of an American TV series]

smallholding /'smɔːlˌhəʊldɪŋ/ (daily life) A small farm, especially one that is leased from a *local authority*.

Smith Square /ˌsmɪθ 'skweə(r)/ (London) A square in central *London* where the headquarters of three major political parties (the *Conservative Party*, the *Labour Party* and the *Liberal Party*) are, those of the Labour Party being in *Transport House*. [the square itself was laid out in 18th century on land belonging to Sir James Smith]

Smithfield (Market) /'smɪθfiːld (ˌsmɪθfiːld 'mɑːkɪt)/ (London) The popular name of the Central Meat Market, *London*. [said to mean 'smooth field'; the site was originally used for fairs, tournaments and public executions]

Smith's /smɪθs/ (commerce) One of a number of chain stores selling newspapers, magazines, stationery, books, records, cassettes, home computers and confectionery. [in full *W H Smith* & Son (Holdings) Ltd; business was established in 19th century by newsagent father and son William Henry Smith]

snakes and ladders /ˌsneɪks ən 'lædəz/ (sport and leisure) A children's board game using dice and a board divided into 100 numbered squares. On the board are pictures of snakes and ladders, the snakes leading down from a higher number to a lower, the ladders leading up from a lower number to a higher. Each player moves a counter according to a throw of the dice: if a counter lands on the head of a snake, it moves down to the lower square where the snake's tail is; if it lands at the foot of a ladder it moves up to the square at the top of the ladder. The first player to reach the 100th square wins.

snap /snæp/ (sport and leisure) A children's card game using either ordinary playing cards or special picture cards. Players lay their cards face up on the table simultaneously: the first player to see two identical cards, or two of the same value, calls 'snap!' and wins his opponent's cards.

snooker /'snuːkə(r)/ (sport and leisure) A game like billiards, played with 15 red balls, worth one point each, six coloured balls (yellow, worth two points; green, three; brown, four; blue, five; pink, six; black, seven) and one white cue ball.

snow pudding /ˌsnəʊ 'pʊdɪŋ/ (food and drink) A light sweet dish containing whipped egg whites and a lemon gelatine mixture.

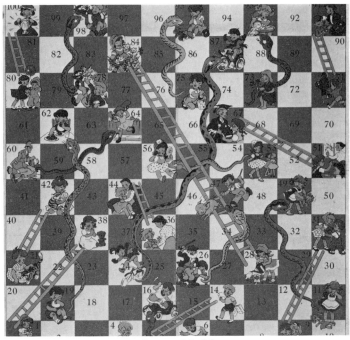

snakes and ladders

Snowdonia /snəʊˈdəʊnɪə/ (geography) A *national park* in northwest *Wales*, famous for its picturesque mountain scenery, and including the highest mountain in Wales, Snowdon (1,085 m).

SNP /ˌes en ˈpiː/, **the (Scottish National Party, the)** (politics) Scotland's largest nationalist party, advocating the separation of *Scotland* from the *United Kingdom* in order to safeguard the country's cultural and economic life. The Party was founded in 1928 and in the 1970s had a rising membership of over 80,000 (1976). In recent years, however, support has decreased, although the Party still contests parliamentary *seats* in *by-elections* and *general elections*.

snug /snʌg/ (daily life) A *private bar* in some *pubs*, offering an intimate ('snug') setting for a small number of people.

soapbox /ˈsəʊpbɒks/ (1 life and society 2 sport and leisure) **1** An improvised platform for a public speaker, once traditionally made from a wooden crate used for packing soap. Such speakers were known as 'soapbox orators'. See *Speakers' Corner*. **2** A child's home-made racing car made from a similar crate or box to which wheels and a steering device are fitted.

soccer /ˈsɒkə(r)/ (sport and leisure) A popular abbreviation for *association football*.

Social Democratic and Labour Party /ˌsəʊʃl deməˌkrætɪk ənd ˈleɪbə ˌpɑːtɪ/ see *SDLP* (politics)

social security /ˌsəʊʃl sɪˈkjʊərətɪ/ (finance) Money given by the government in cases of sickness, old age and unemployment. The money is raised by means of taxation and insurance schemes (notably *national insurance*). See also *welfare state*.

social worker /ˈsəʊʃl ˌwɜːkə(r)/ (life and society) A person employed by a *local authority* or a voluntary organization to give practical aid and advice to people in need, such as the sick, the handicapped, the elderly (especially any of these living alone), and to children at risk of neglect or ill treatment. Many social workers are employed by the *NHS*.

Society of Friends /səˌsaɪətɪ əv ˈfrendz/, **the** (religion) The formal name of the *Quakers*.

SOGAT '82 /ˌsəʊgæt ˌeɪtɪ ˈtuː/ (**Society of Graphical and Allied Trades, the**) (work) An influential trade union having a membership of 213,000, representing a majority of the employees in the printing and allied trades. In 1981 SOGAT merged with another printers' union, NATSOPA (the National Society of Operative Printers, Graphical and Media Personnel), then having a membership of over 54,000, to form SOGAT '82.

solicitor /səˈlɪsɪtə(r)/ (law) A person specially trained in legal matters, and who advises his clients on matters of law, draws up official documents, and acts in many court cases. Most people engage a solicitor for domestic matters, such as buying or selling a house, negotiating a will or bequest, or advising on some apparent legal injustice.

Solicitor General /səˌlɪsɪtə ˈdʒenrəl/, **the** (law) The state legal official who ranks next to the *Attorney General* and in effect acts as his assistant.

Somerset House /ˌsʌməset ˈhaʊs/ (London) A large 18th-century building in the *Strand, London*, which formerly housed the General Register Office (of all births, marriages and deaths in the country), the *Inland Revenue* and other important government offices. [built on the site of palace begun in 16th century for the Duke of Somerset]

Sotheby's /ˈsʌðəbɪz/ (commerce) An important firm of fine art auctioneers in *London*, specializing in rare books and manuscripts. It was founded in 1744 by a bookseller, Samuel Baker, with its present name coming from that of Baker's nephew, John Sotheby (1740–1807), who had become a partner of the firm. Compare *Christie's*.

Sounds /saʊndz/ (media) A weekly magazine devoted to pop music, founded in 1970 and having a circulation of nearly 117,000.

South Bank /ˌsaʊθ ˈbæŋk/, **the** (London) A site on the south bank of the river *Thames* in central *London*, developed mainly for the 1951 *Festival of Britain*. The main complex here, called the South Bank Arts Centre, contains several famous concert halls, theatres and galleries, among them the *Royal Festival Hall*, the *Queen Elizabeth Hall*, the *National Theatre¹*, the *National Film Theatre* and the *Hayward Gallery*.

South Downs /ˌsaʊθ ˈdaʊnz/, **the** (geography) A range of chalk hills in southern *England*, extending from Hampshire (near Petersfield) in the west to East Sussex (near Eastbourne) in the east. [by contrast with the North Downs that run roughly parallel through Surrey and Kent]

Southdown (sheep) /ˈsaʊθdaʊn (ˌsaʊθdaʊn ˈʃiːp)/ (animal world) A breed of sheep with short wool and dark faces and legs. The breed is one of the oldest in *Britain* and is still found mainly on the *South Downs*.

Spaghetti Junction /spəˈɡetɪ ˌdʒʌŋkʃn/ (transport) The nickname of a complex *motorway* intersection on the M6 in north Birmingham, properly known as the Gravelly Hill Interchange. [from the air the complex of roads and flyovers looks like spaghetti]

Spaghetti Junction

SPCK /ˌes piː siː ˈkeɪ/, **the (Society for Promoting Christian Knowledge, the)** (charities) A society founded in 1698, originally with the aim of providing children with a religious education and generally promoting religion in the English colonies. Later, the society started to publish religious works, which it continues today, selling its publications, as well as general books, through a number of bookshops in *Britain*. Its missionary activity is today chiefly concentrated in developing countries in Africa and Asia.

Speaker /ˈspiːkə(r)/, **the** (government) The chief officer of the *House of Commons*, who is elected by *MP*s to preside over proceedings and keep order. [in the *House of Lords*, the *Lord Chancellor* acts as speaker]

Speakers' Corner /ˌspiːkəz ˈkɔːnə(r)/, **the** (London) The northeast corner of *Hyde Park, London*, where at weekends individuals or representatives of various organizations and causes, which vary from the ordinary to the eccentric, make public speeches from improvised stands (*soapboxes¹*). The area was set aside for such use in 1872 after Hyde Park itself became a popular centre for orators.

Speaking Clock /ˌspiːkɪŋ ˈklɒk/, **the** (commerce) A service (officially called *Timeline*) operated by *British Telecom* by which people can dial a special telephone number (in London, 123) to hear the exact time (given every ten seconds on a continuous recorded announcement).

Special Branch /ˈspeʃl brɑːntʃ/, **the** (law) The department of the police force that deals with political security.

special constable /ˌspeʃl ˈkʌstəbl/ (law) A person who volunteers to carry out police duties in his spare time under the guidance of a particular police force. He receives no pay, but wears a standard police uniform with the letters 'SC' on the shoulder.

special development area /ˌspeʃl dɪˈveləpmənt ˌeəriə/ (work) A former type of *assisted area* where the need for financial aid was regarded as the most urgent. This type of area was abolished in 1984 when the government reorganized assisted areas. Compare *development area, intermediate area*.

special school /ˈspeʃl skuːl/ (education) A school catering for children with physical or mental handicap, or emotional or behavioural disorders. Such schools can be either state (non-fee-paying) or private (fee-paying, or run by a voluntary organization).

Spectator /spekˈteɪtə(r)/, **the** (media) A weekly magazine containing features and articles of political and general cultural interest, including news commentaries, readers' letters and book reviews. It was first published in 1828 (taking the title of an earlier periodical) and is generally regarded as supporting the *Conservative Party*. Its circulation in 1982 was over 18,000. Compare the *New Statesman*, its 'opposite number'.

speech day /ˈspiːtʃ deɪ/ (education) An annual day in many schools, usually at the end of the school year (in July), when prizes are presented and a special speech is made by a distinguished visitor (who may be a former student of the school).

Speech from the Throne /ˌspiːtʃ frəm ðə ˈθrəʊn/, **the** (government) A name for the *Queen's Speech* made at the opening of each session of *Parliament*.

Spitalfields /ˈspɪtlfiːldz/ (London) A permanent wholesale market for fruit, vegetables and flowers in *London*'s *East End*. [name can be understood as 'hospital fields': there was a 12th-century priory on this site]

Spithead Review /ˌspɪthed rɪˈvjuː/, **the** (defence) A ceremonial review of *Royal Navy* ships anchored in the Spithead channel between Portsmouth and the *Isle of Wight*. Before the Second World War this review was held each year; since then it has been held only on special occasions such as the 1977 Silver Jubilee (25-year anniversary) of the reign of *Queen Elizabeth*.

Speech from the Throne

Spode (china) /spəʊd ('tʃaɪnə)/ (style) Fine porcelain manufactured by the pottery established in 1770 at Stoke-on-Trent, Staffordshire (see *Potteries*) by Joseph Spode (1733–97).

sponsored walk /ˌspɒnsəd 'wɔːk/ (charities) A walk undertaken to collect funds for a particular charity or cause. Beforehand, each walker draws up a list of people who agree to give a certain amount of money for each mile covered (or for completion of the walk). The walker collects the money after the walk. So similarly 'sponsored jog', 'sponsored run', 'sponsored climb', 'sponsored swim', etc. See also *fun run*.

sporran /'spɒrən/ (clothing) Part of the traditional costume of a *highlander*[1] or other Scot. It is a large leather or fur pouch worn in front of the *kilt*. It hangs from a narrow belt worn round the hips.

Sporting Life /ˌspɔːtɪŋ 'laɪf/, **the** (media) A daily newspaper mainly concerned with publishing racing results and forecasting the performance of horses in future races. The newspaper was first published in 1859 and has a circulation of over 73,000.

sports jacket /'spɔːtsˌdʒækɪt/ (clothing) A man's informal jacket, often made of tweed, for both indoor and outdoor wear, usually worn with trousers of a contrasting colour and material. [as originally worn for some outdoor sports, hiking, etc.]

spotted dick /ˌspɒtɪd 'dɪk/ (food and drink) Another name for *spotted dog*.

spotted dog /ˌspɒtɪd 'dɒg/ (food and drink) A colloquial name for a steamed or boiled pudding in the shape of a roll. The pudding contains fruit such as raisins or sultanas, some of which can be seen on the outside of the roll and give it a 'spotty' appearance. [the roll is thought to look like the body of a Dalmatian, also nicknamed 'spotted dog' from the black or brown spots on its white coat]

spring bank holiday /ˌsprɪŋ bæŋk 'hɒlədeɪ/, **the** (daily life) A name often used (or 'late spring bank holiday') for the *bank holiday* that falls on the last Monday in May.

spring double /ˌsprɪŋ 'dʌbl/ (sport and leisure) A bet placed simultaneously on the results of two annual horse races: the Lincoln Handicap, run at Doncaster, South Yorkshire (formerly run at Lincoln) and the *Grand National*. Compare *autumn double*.

Spurs /spɜːz/ (sport and leisure) The nickname of the *football club Tottenham Hotspur*.

Square Mile /ˌskweə 'maɪl/ (London) A term for the *City (of London)*, whose area is approximately one square mile.

squash (rackets) /'skwɒʃ (ˌrækɪts)/ (sport and leisure) A game for two or, more rarely, four players in an enclosed court. It is played with a small rubber ball and rackets like tennis rackets but with a smaller head and a longer, lighter handle. The ball is hit off any wall but must strike the front wall above a line painted above the floor in order to count. Compare *rackets*, from which it evolved (probably at *Harrow School*) in the 19th century. [so named as the ball is soft and 'squashy' (easily pressed)]

squash (rackets)

SRN /ˌes ɑː 'en/ **(state registered nurse)** (medicine) A qualified hospital nurse who has satisfactorily completed the standard three-year course of training. Compare *SEN*.

St Andrews /snt 'ændruːz/ (geography) An ancient town and seaside resort in Fife, *Scotland*, where Scotland's oldest university (founded in 1411) is situated. Also at St Andrews is the famous *Royal and Ancient* golf *club*. [named after a holy shrine here to St Andrew; see *St Andrew's cross*]

St Andrew's cross /snt ˌændruːz ˈkrɒs/ (tradition) The national flag of *Scotland*, consisting of two diagonal white stripes crossing on a blue background. The flag forms part of the *Union Jack*, together with *St George's cross* and *St Patrick's cross*. St Andrew is the patron saint of Scotland. See also *St Andrew's Day*.

St Andrew's Day /snt ˈændruːz deɪ/ (tradition) 30 November, the church festival of St Andrew, regarded as *Scotland*'s national day (although not an official *bank holiday*). On this day some Scotsmen wear a *thistle* in their buttonhole. See also *St Andrew's cross*.

St Bartholomew's Hospital /snt bɑːˌθɒləmjuːz ˈhɒspɪtl/ (medicine) An important *teaching hospital* in *London*, and the oldest hospital in *England*. [named after a church here dedicated to St Bartholomew]

St Clement Danes /snt ˌklemənt ˈdeɪnz/ (London) A famous *London church* designed by Sir Christopher Wren and built in the 17th century on the site of a much older church believed to date back to a 9th-century Danish settlement. Although seriously damaged in the Second World War, the church, which is the central church of the *RAF*, was fully restored in the 1950s. The bells of the church play the melody of the song sung in the children's game *oranges and lemons*. (The song begins with the words 'Oranges and lemons, Say the bells of St Clement's'.)

St David's Day /snt ˈdeɪvɪdz deɪ/ (tradition) 1 March, the *church* festival of St David, a 6th-century monk and bishop, the patron saint of *Wales*. The day is regarded as the national holiday of Wales, although it is not an official *bank holiday*. On this day, however, many Welshmen wear either a *daffodil* or a *leek* pinned to their jackets, as both plants are traditionally regarded as national emblems of Wales.

St George's Chapel, (Windsor) /snt ˌdʒɔːdʒɪz ˈtʃæpl (snt ˌdʒɔːdʒɪz ˌtʃæpl ˈwɪnsə(r))/ (history) The main *chapel*² of *Windsor Castle*, built in the 15th and 16th centuries in the *Perpendicular* (*style*). The *Garter ceremony* is held in the Chapel, which also contains the tombs of many sovereigns and famous men and women. Together with the Castle, it is one of *Britain*'s most popular tourist attractions, and with its royal connections and dedication to St George (see *St George's cross*) is regarded as uniquely symbolic of *England*. Officially it is a *chapel royal*.

St George's cross /snt ˌdʒɔːdʒɪz ˈkrɒs/ (tradition) The national flag of *England*, consisting of a red cross on a white background. The flag is part of the *Union Jack*, together with *St Andrew's cross* and *St Patrick's cross*. St George is the patron saint of England. See also *St George's Day*.

St George's Day /snt ˈdʒɔːdʒɪz deɪ/ (tradition) 23 April, the *church* festival of St George, regarded as *England*'s national day (although not an official *bank holiday*). On this day some patriotic Englishmen wear a *rose* pinned to their jackets. See also *St George's cross*.

St James's Palace /snt ˌdʒeɪmzɪz ˈpælɪs/ (London) A famous palace in *Pall Mall*, *London*, built in 1532 by King *Henry VIII* on the site of a former leper hospital dedicted to St James, and the residence of British sovereigns from 1697 to 1837. Foreign ambassadors are still 'accredited to the Court of St James'.

St James's Park /snt ˌdʒeɪmzɪz ˈpɑːk/ (London) The oldest of London's *royal parks*, originally laid out as pleasure grounds for King Charles II on the site of a deer park adjoining *St James's Palace*. Many regard it as *London*'s most attractive park, with its lake (containing an island with a bird sanctuary), walks, lawns and flowerbeds.

St John Ambulance (Brigade) /snt ˌdʒɒn ˈæmbjʊləns (brɪˌgeɪd)/ (medicine) A voluntary organization providing first aid and nursing services in hospitals and residential homes, and also, when required, at public and sporting events and in theatres and concert halls. [name of religious nursing order, the Knights Hospitallers of St John of Jerusalem]

St John's, Smith Square /snt ˌdʒɒnz ˌsmɪθ ˈskweə(r)/ (London) A *church* in *Smith Square*, *London*, whose interior was destroyed in the Second World War and which was restored in the 1960s to be an arts centre for concerts, exhibitions and lectures.

St Martin-in-the-Fields /snt ˌmɑːtɪn ɪn ðə ˈfiːldz/ (London) A famous *church* in *Trafalgar Square*, *London*, built in a neo-classical style in the early 18th century. The catacombs under the church were used as a bomb shelter in the Second World War, and have now been used for some years as a shelter for the poor and homeless. The main church itself is frequently used for musical performances. See *Academy of St Martin-in-the-Fields*. [original church on this site stood on open land]

St Mary-le-Bow /snt ˌmeəri lə ˈbəʊ/ (London) A well-known *church* in the *City (of London)*, famous for its *Bow Bells*. See also *cockney*[2]. [church was built over 11th-century crypt, thus was constructed on arches (bows) of stone]

St Michael /snt ˈmaɪkl/ (commerce) The trade name of goods sold by the chain stores of *Marks & Spencer*. [derived from name of Michael Marks, original founder of firm]

St Mirren /snt ˈmɪrən/ (sport and leisure) A Scottish *football club* founded in 1876 with a stadium in Paisley, southwest *Scotland*. [named after location of stadium at St Mirren Park]

St Pancras /snt ˈpæŋkrəs/ (transport) A *London* main line railway station near *King's Cross*[1,2], and a terminus of the London Midland Region of *BR*. It is famous for its *Victorian*

Gothic architecture. [named after district here, from *church* dedicated to St Pancras]

St Patrick's cross /snt ˌpætrɪks ˈkrɒs/ (tradition) The national flag of *Northern Ireland* (and earlier, the national flag of *Ireland* before the establishment of the Irish Republic). It consists of two diagonal red stripes crossing on a white background, and is part of the *Union Jack*, together with *St Andrew's cross* and *St George's cross*. St Patrick is the patron saint of Ireland. See *Paddy*, *St Patrick's Day*.

St Patrick's Day /snt ˈpætrɪks deɪ/ (tradition) 17 March, the church festival of St Patrick, regarded as a national day in *Northern Ireland* and an official *bank holiday* there.

St Paul's (Cathedral) /snt ˈpɔːlz (snt ˌpɔːlz kəˈθiːdrəl)/ (London) One of *London*'s most famous landmarks, regarded as the 'parish *church* of the British *Commonwealth*[1]'. The present cathedral, built in the latter part of the 17th century and early part of the 18th, is the third on the site, the previous one having been destroyed by the *Great Fire of London*. The cathedral contains a number of famous tombs and memorials, including that of its architect, Sir Christopher Wren (1632–1723). One of its most popular features is the *Whispering Gallery*.

St Paul's (School) /snt ˈpɔːlz (snt ˌpɔːlz ˈskuːl)/ (education) A well-known *London public school*[1], founded in 1509 by the *dean*[3] of *St Paul's (Cathedral)*, and having 750 students.

St Thomas's Hospital /snt ˌtɒməsɪz ˈhɒspɪtl/ (medicine) A *London teaching hospital*, founded in 1552.

St Trinian's /snt ˈtrɪnɪənz/ (arts) The name of a fictitious girls' school invented in 1941 by the cartoonist Ronald Searle (born 1920). In his cartoons, and in the subsequent books and films that evolved, the girls of St Trinian's school became comically famous for their scruffy uniforms, riotous behaviour and generally rebellious attitude to life and authority. [random name chosen to suggest a typical private girls' school; Searle's daughters had actually attended St Trinnean's school in *Edinburgh*]

Standard /ˈstændəd/, **The** (media) A daily *London* evening newspaper noted for its lively, up-to-the-minute reporting, popular features and profiles of people in the news, and large advertising section. It is at present London's only evening paper. It was founded in 1827 under its present name (changed some years later to the 'Evening Standard') and joined with the 'St James's Gazette' in 1905. In 1923 it absorbed the 'Pall Mall Gazette' and the *Glasgow* 'Evening Citizen'. In 1980 it merged with the 'Evening News' to form the 'New Standard', and in 1981 returned to its original name of 'The Standard'. Its circulation was about 480,000 in 1984.

standing order /ˌstændɪŋ ˈɔːdə(r)/ (finance) An order from a customer to his bank requesting that regular payments should be made from his account, usually monthly or annually, to the account of a named individual or organization. The amount of the payment is decided by the customer. It is a convenient way to pay regular subscriptions. Compare *direct debit*.

Stanley Gibbons /ˌstænlɪ ˈgɪbənz/ (commerce) A well-known *London* firm of stamp dealers, who hold important philatelic auctions and publish annually a range of authoritative stamp catalogues. [firm founded by Stanley Gibbons in 1856]

Stansted (Airport) /ˈstænstɪd (ˌstænstɪd ˈeəpɔːt)/ (transport) An international airport near Stansted, Essex. It is *Britain*'s third largest airport (after *Heathrow* and *Gatwick*) and the government intends to make it *London*'s third airport.

starting price /ˈstɑːtɪŋ praɪs/ (sport and leisure) The odds on a horse in a race as quoted by *bookmakers* as the horse is about to start the race.

State Opening of Parliament /ˌsteɪt ˌəʊpənɪŋ əv ˈpɑːləmənt/, **the** (government) The official opening of a new session of *Parliament*, usually at the end of October or beginning of November, or after a *general election*. The sovereign travels in procession to the *Houses of Parliament* for the occasion, and there makes the *Speech from the Throne*.

state school /ˈsteɪt skuːl/ (education) A school, usually a *primary school* or a *secondary school*, that is run by the state through a *LEA*, and so is non-fee-paying, as distinct from an *independent school*. Nearly 94% of British schools are state schools.

stately home /ˌsteɪtlɪ ˈhəʊm/ (life and society) A term for a *country house*, especially one open to the public. [term comes from opening lines of a poem by Felicia Hemans (1793–1835): 'The stately homes of *England*, How beautiful they stand!']

STD /ˌes tiː ˈdiː/ **(subscriber trunk dialling)** (commerce) A telephone system operated by *British Telecom* by which one caller can dial another direct (ie, without contacting the operator) both in *Britain* and to most countries abroad.

steak and kidney pie /ˌsteɪk ən ˌkɪdnɪ ˈpaɪ/ (food and drink) A savoury pie, usually eaten hot, made of meat and kidney in gravy baked in pastry.

steak and kidney pudding /ˌsteɪk ən ˌkɪdnɪ ˈpʊdɪŋ/ (food and drink) A savoury dish eaten hot, made of meat and kidney in gravy cooked in a suet case.

Steel, David /stiːl, ˈdeɪvɪd/ (people) David Steel (born 1938) first became an *MP* for the *Liberal Party* in 1965. He was elected leader of the party in 1976. Since he became leader, the Liberal Party has co-operated with the *Labour Party* in 1977 (the 'Lib-Lab pact') and, in 1981 formed the *Liberal-SDP Alliance*. David Steel is well-known for his strong opposition to apartheid.

Stewards' Cup /ˌstjuːədz ˈkʌp/, **the** (sport and leisure) **1** An annual horse race run at *Goodwood*, and also the prize awarded to its winner. **2** An annual race for rowing fours at *Henley Regatta*, and also the prize awarded to the winners.

stiff upper lip /ˌstɪf ˈʌpə ˈlɪp/ (tradition) The characteristic ability of the English to stay calm and unemotional in a crisis, especially when in pain or distress. [alluding to the concealing of emotion by compressing the lips]

Stilton (cheese) /ˈstɪltən (ˌstɪltən ˈtʃiːz)/ (food and drink) A type of rich blue-veined cheese with a strong flavour. [originally sold, but not made, in the village of Stilton, Cambridgeshire]

Stock Exchange /ˈstɒk ɪksˌtʃeɪndʒ/, **the** (finance) The *London* financial centre, founded in 1801, where stocks and shares are bought and sold by *stockbrokers* and *stock-jobbers*. Until recently only men could be members of the Exchange; now women are also accepted. In 1973 the Exchange moved to a tower block, and members of the public are admitted to a gallery over the trading floor in working hours.

stockbroker /ˈstɒkˌbrəʊkə(r)/ (finance) A member of the *Stock Exchange* who buys and sells stocks and shares for clients. Compare *stock-jobber*.

stockbroker belt /ˈstɒkbrəʊkə belt/, **the** (geography) A colloquial name for the outer suburbs of *London*, or some other large city, where rich *stockbrokers* and other wealthy people live.

stock-jobber /ˈstɒk ˌdʒɒbə(r)/ (finance) A member of the *Stock Exchange* who buys and sells stocks and shares on his own account, not for clients, and who thus deals only with *stockbroker* members of the Exchange, who approach him on behalf of their clients. Stock-jobbers do not deal in all stocks and shares but in a specialized range, such as *gilt-edged securities*, mining shares or bank shares. Compare *stockbroker*.

Stoke Mandeville /ˌstəʊk ˈmændəvɪl/ (medicine) A village near Aylesbury, Buckinghamshire, well-known for the hospital here in which there is a department that specializes in the treatment of spinal diseases and injuries (officially the National Spinal Injuries Unit).

Stone of Scone /ˌstəʊn əv ˈskuːn/, **the** (tradition) The ancient stone coronation seat of the kings of *Scotland*, at present lying below the Coronation chair in *Westminster Abbey*, *London* to where it was taken from Scone, east Scotland, by King Edward I in 1296. The Stone has been removed more than once by Scottish Nationalists trying to return it to Scotland. See *SNP*.

Stonehenge /ˌstəʊn ˈhendʒ/ (tradition) A prehistoric (megalithic) complex on *Salisbury Plain*, Wiltshire, regarded as one of the most important monuments of its kind in Europe, and very popular with visitors. The great circle of standing stones (many now fallen) is believed to have had some religious or astronomical purpose. The complex has become well-known in recent years for the annual assembly there of *Druids*[2] at sunrise on *Midsummer Day* (since on this day the sun rises above a certain stone), and also for the summer camp nearby of hippie-style visitors. [the name is said by some to mean 'stone hanger', referring to the horizontal stone 'hanging' or lying across two vertical stones]

Stormont /'stɔːmɒnt/ (government) The large house on the outskirts of *Belfast*, Northern Ireland, where the *Northern Ireland* parliament was held from 1921 to 1972, when *direct rule* was introduced. The parliament buildings now form the administrative centre of Northern Ireland.

stout /staʊt/ (food and drink) A strong dark beer brewed with roasted malt.

Strand /strænd/**, the** (London) One of the main streets of central *London*, linking the *West End* with the *City (of London)* and containing several theatres and high-class shops and hotels. [from the 'strand' or bank of the river Thames, where it formerly ran as a riverside walk]

Strangers' Gallery /'streɪndʒəz ˌgælərɪ/**, the** (government) The galleries in the *House of Commons* and *House of Lords* to which members of the public are admitted, usually by invitation. ['stranger' in the sense of 'non-member']

strap-hanger /'stræp ˌhæŋə(r)/ (daily life) A colloquial term for a passenger in a public transport vehicle, especially an *Underground* train, who has to travel standing, holding on to an overhead strap.

Stratford-(up)on-Avon /ˌstrætfəd (əp)ɒn 'eɪvn/ (geography) A town in Warwickshire, famous as the birthplace of William *Shakespeare* (1564–1616) and for this reason visited by thousands of tourists annually. Some buildings in or near the town connected with Shakespeare are: his birthplace, Holy Trinity Church, where he was buried, *Anne Hathaway's Cottage* and the *Shakespeare Memorial Theatre*. See also *Royal Shakespeare Company*.

strathspey /ˌstræθ'speɪ/ (sport and leisure) A slow Scottish dance. [originating in Strathspey, the valley of the river Spey]

strawberries and cream /ˌstrɔːbrɪz ən 'kriːm/ (food and drink) A traditional English summer dish, often eaten during some special outdoor occasion or event, for example, at *Wimbledon*.

streaming /'striːmɪŋ/ (education) The division of schoolchildren into groups either according to ability or by subject.

Street /striːt/**, the** (media) A colloquial nickname for the television programme series *Coronation Street*.

strike pay /'straɪk peɪ/ (work) Money paid to strikers from the funds of their trade union.

striker /'straɪkə(r)/ (sport and leisure) An attacking player in *football*, especially one who stays near the opponents' goal in the hope of scoring.

Sturmer /ˈstɜːmə(r)/ (food and drink) A variety of eating apple with yellow-green skin and sweet, juicy flesh. [originating from the village of Sturmer, Essex]

STV /ˌes tiː ˈviː/ (**Scottish TV**) (media) One of the 15 television companies of the *IBA*, transmitting programmes to central *Scotland*.

suburbia /səˈbɜːbɪə/ (life and society) A suburban or outer residential district of a town or *city*, and thought of with regard to its residents and their social standing (sometimes said to be typically *middle class* and conservative).

suet pudding /ˌsuːɪt ˈpʊdɪŋ/ (food and drink) A name used for different kinds of boiled or steamed pudding made with suet, whether savoury (such as *steak and kidney pudding*) or sweet (such as *spotted dog*).

Suffolk (sheep) /ˈsʌfək (ˌsʌfək ˈʃiːp)/ (animal world) A breed of black-faced sheep. [originally bred in Suffolk]

Suffolk punch /ˌsʌfək ˈpʌntʃ/ (animal world) A breed of draught horse with powerful body, relatively short legs and chestnut-coloured coat. [originally bred in Suffolk: 'punch' is the dialect word for a thick-set person or animal]

suffragan bishop /ˌsʌfrəgən ˈbɪʃəp/ (religion) A bishop who assists a senior bishop or an archbishop by being responsible for a certain district within his superior's area.

Sullom Voe /ˌsʌləm ˈvəʊ/ (geography) *Britain*'s largest *North Sea oil* terminal and oil exporting port, in the *Shetlands*, *Scotland*. [named after inlet (*voe*) here]

summer pudding /ˌsʌmə ˈpʊdɪŋ/ (food and drink) A sweet dish made from fruit, usually strawberries or raspberries, and red and black currants (sometimes with apples or blackberries) and bread. The fruit is boiled and then put in a bowl lined with bread. All the juice soaks into the bread, and the pudding is served chilled, usually with cream.

summer school /ˈsʌmə skuːl/ (education) A school or academic course such as a language course held in the summer months, often on the premises of a school or university whose regular students are on holiday. Many students of the *Open University* go on week-long summer schools as part of their courses.

summer time /ˈsʌmə taɪm/ (daily life) A colloquial term for *BST*.

summons /ˈsʌmənz/ (law) An official order, often served by a *bailiff*, to a person to attend a *court*[3] of law, either to answer a charge or to give evidence.

Sun /sʌn/, **The** (media) A daily *popular paper* with a circulation of just over 4.1 million. The newspaper was first published in 1964 and is noted for its sensational stories, many photographs and *page three* model. In 1984 it had the largest circulation of all daily newspapers in *Britain*, having taken over from the *Mirror*.

Sunday /'sʌndeɪ/ (media) The colour magazine published (from 1981) to accompany the *News of the World* newspaper.

Sunday /'sʌndɪ/ (life and society) A distinctive day of the week in *Britain*, when most people are at home. Many people spend the whole day at home, although visits to friends and relatives are also popular, as are outings to a place of interest or leisure. Most people sleep later on Sunday than on any other day. Some people go to a religious service. Most shops and stores are closed for the day (except in *Scotland*, where legal regulations are different). However, many newsagents open in the morning to sell newspapers and magazines, and many *corner shops* are open all day. *Licensing hours* are shorter (*pubs* cannot open in the evening before 7.0, for example), public transport services are less frequent, and entertainment facilities are restricted. Cinemas open, although later than on other days of the week, but it is still rare for theatres to be open on Sunday. Post offices (see *Post Office*) and banks are closed. Sport is now more commonly played on Sunday than previously. The British Sunday still retains much of its 19th-century atmosphere of solemnity and respectability, and many young people find Sunday boring. There is, however, a general slow move towards a more lively and varied day, and strong support for the opening of some kinds of shop that at present remain closed. See also *Sunday roast*.

Sunday Express /ˌsʌndɪ ɪk'spres/, **the** (media) A weekly (*Sunday*) *popular paper* with a circulation of 2.6 million. It was first published in 1918 and, like the *Daily Express* is conservative in political outlook (see *Conservative Party*). It is noted for its contributions from leading national and international figures. It is accompanied by a colour magazine.

Sunday Mirror /ˌsʌndɪ 'mɪrə(r)/, **the** (media) A weekly (*Sunday*) *popular paper* with a circulation of 3.5 million. It was first published in 1915 (as the 'Sunday Pictorial', until 1964) and, like the weekday *Mirror*, is politically left of centre.

Sunday People /ˌsʌndɪ 'piːpl/, **the** (media) A weekly (*Sunday*) *popular paper* with a circulation of over 3.5 million. It was first published in 1881 (as the 'People', until 1973) and is specially noted for its 'true life' stories and features.

Sunday roast/joint /ˌsʌndɪ 'rəʊst/'dʒɔɪnt/, **the** (life and society) The main ingredient of a traditional English family lunch on *Sunday*—hot roast beef (or other meat) with vegetables and gravy. The tradition of having meat on Sunday is a survival of a religious custom, when Sunday was a feastday and followed the austerity of Friday, when only fish was eaten (as it still is by devout Roman Catholics).

Sunday school /'sʌndɪ skuːl/ (religion) Religious instruction for children on *Sunday*s which is usually organized by the priest in a particular *church* or *chapel*[3]. Instruction is voluntary and is usually given in the church or chapel building itself, either by the priest or pastor or by a regular member of the congregation. Sunday schools are often held at the same time as the main Sunday morning service, so that parents can attend the service while their children attend the instruction.

Sunday Telegraph /ˌsʌndɪ ˈtelɪɡrɑːf/, **the** (media) A weekly (*Sunday*) *quality paper* with a circulation of under 740,000. It was first published in 1961 and, like the *Daily Telegraph*, is politically right of centre. In common with other Sunday quality papers, it has a section for reviews of books and the arts, a detailed financial and industrial survey and an extensive sports coverage. A colour magazine ('Telegraph Sunday Magazine') accompanies the newspaper.

Sunday Times /ˈsʌndɪ ˈtaɪmz/, **the** (media) A weekly (*Sunday*) *quality paper* with a circulation of just over 1.3 million. It was first published in 1822. It is noted for the high standard of its literary and arts reviews, and for its sections on finance and the business world, women's interests and sport and leisure. Its regular articles on foreign affairs, politics and economics are also a special feature of the newspaper. It was the first newspaper in *Britain* to be printed in separate sections and also the first (in 1962) to publish an accompanying colour magazine.

supplementary benefit /ˌsʌplɪmentrɪ ˈbenɪfɪt/ (finance) A weekly payment made by the state to certain groups of people (in particular those not working full time) to bring their incomes up to the minimum levels required by law. See also *social security*.

supply teacher /səˈplaɪ ˌtiːtʃə(r)/ (education) A teacher appointed temporarily by an *LEA* in place of another, regular teacher who is absent through illness or for some other reason.

Supreme Court (of Judicature) /suːˌpriːm ˈkɔːt (suːˌpriːm ˌkɔːt əv ˈdʒuːdɪkətʃə(r))/, **the** (law) The highest *court*[3] of law in *England* and *Wales*, formed in 1873 by the amalgamation of several courts[3] into two divisions, the Court of Appeal and the *High Court of Justice* (which consists of the *Chancery* Division, the *Queen's Bench Division* and the Family Division). The central office of the Supreme Court of Judicature (officially the Royal Courts of Justice, but popularly known as the Law Courts) is in the *Strand, London*.

Sussex (hen) /ˈsʌsɪks (ˌsʌsɪks ˈhen)/ (animal world) A heavy breed of domestic fowl used mainly for its meat, but also for its eggs. There are several varieties, all originally bred in Sussex, among them Light Sussex, Red Sussex, Brown Sussex and Speckled Sussex (all named for the colour of its feathers).

swan-upping /ˈswɒn ˌʌpɪŋ/ (tradition) An annual ceremony held on the river *Thames*, near Windsor, Berkshire, when swans are driven upstream and marked (with small cuts on the beak) to show who owns them. Those belonging to the *Crown*[1] (ie, the royal Swans) are marked with five cuts; those belonging to two *livery companies* (the Dyers' and the Vintners' Companies) are marked with two cuts.

sweepstake /ˈswiːpsteɪk/ (sport and leisure) **1** A term loosely used for any horse race with a money prize for the winner. **2** A type of horse race in which the winner (and sometimes near-winner) receives a money prize from the combined entrance fees, forfeit payments (eg, for horses withdrawn from the race), etc. The first such race was held at Doncaster, South Yorkshire, in 1714. **3** A method of gambling on a horse race, in which the prize is the combined stakes (bets) of all who have taken part in the sweepstake, each person usually buying a ticket with the name of an individual horse. The winner is the person who has drawn the name of the winning horse.

Swiss roll /ˌswɪs ˈrəʊl/ (food and drink) A thin sponge cake spread with jam, cream or some other filling, and then rolled up while still hot. [said to be of Swiss origin, but perhaps simply an alteration of 'sweet roll']

sword dance /ˈsɔːd dɑːns/ (sport and leisure) A traditional Scottish dance in which a dancer performs fast dance steps over two crossed swords on the ground. It is usually performed by one dancer but occasionally two dancers dance together over the same pair of swords. Sometimes the swords are waved in the air while the dance continues.

sword dance

Synod /ˈsɪnəd/**, the** (religion) The *General Synod* of the *Church of England*.

T and G /ˌtiː ən ˈdʒiː/ see **TGWU** (work)

Tablet /ˈtæblɪt/**, the** (media) A weekly Roman Catholic newspaper, containing current affairs in the world of politics, the arts and religion. It was first published in 1840 and had a circulation in 1981 of just over 9,000.

tabloid /ˈtæblɔɪd/ (media) A term for a newspaper with small-size pages (conventionally about 30 cm by 40 cm). Almost all *popular papers* are of tabloid size, and the term, therefore, usually implies the popular press. [derived from an earlier trade name, Tabloid, used for a medicinal tablet]

Taffy /ˈtæfɪ/ (tradition) A nickname for a Welshman, deriving from the supposed Welsh pronunciation of Dafydd, a common Welsh forename. [Dafydd is the Welsh form of the English name, David]

take-home pay /ˌteɪk ˈhəʊm peɪ/ (finance) An employee's net pay after the deduction from his gross pay of *income tax* (see *PAYE, National Insurance*) and any other contributions. [reference to the pay that a worker takes home weekly in a pay packet]

Talk of the Town /ˌtɔːk əv ðə ˈtaʊn/**, the** (London) A fashionable restaurant in *Leicester Square, London*, famous for its nightly floor show and for its international stars.

tam-o'-shanter /ˌtæm ə ˈʃæntə(r)/ (clothing) A Scottish flat wool cap without a brim but with a bobble on top, traditionally worn pulled down at one side. [named after Tam o'Shanter, the hero of Burns' (see *Burns' Night*) poem of this name, published in 1790]

Tannoy /ˈtænɔɪ/ (daily life) The trade name of a loudspeaker amplification and relay system. The name is often popularly used for any such system.

tartan /ˈtɑːtn/ (**1, 3** style **2** clothing) **1** The special checked design, of contrasting colours, used in Highland dress in *Scotland*. By long tradition, each Scottish *clan* has its own distinctive tartan. **2** Highland dress itself. **3** A similar design reproduced on Scottish souvenirs or other items such as postcards, badges and bookmarks.

Tate (Gallery) /teɪt (ˈgælərɪ)/**, the** (arts) One of *London*'s best-known art galleries, opened in 1897 with the financial support of Sir Henry Tate, who also gave a collection of 65 paintings. The Gallery contains a unique collection of British paintings from the 16th century to the present day (with Turner and Blake particularly well represented), as well as modern foreign paintings and modern sculpture. The Gallery also regularly holds special exhibitions.

Tattenham Corner /ˌtætnəm ˈkɔːnə(r)/ (sport and leisure) A notorious sharp bend before the final straight on the race course at *Epsom*, regarded as a major obstacle in the *Derby*. [named after historic house here, Tottenham Lodge]

Tattersall's /ˈtætəslz/ (commerce) A famous firm of racehorse auctioneers, founded in 1766 by Richard Tattersall as a horse market in *London*, but today holding its annual auctions at Newmarket, Suffolk.

tax disc /ˈtæks dɪsk/ (transport) A small, round, paper document showing that a motor vehicle has been officially licensed by the Department of Transport (see *department*) to travel on the road. The disc is usually stuck to the bottom left-hand corner of the windscreen inside the vehicle. Drivers buy their tax discs (the fee varying with the type of vehicle) at either a post office or a local office (known as a Local Vehicle Licensing Office) of the Driver and Vehicle Licensing Centre in Swansea, South *Wales*.

tax disc

tea /tiː/ (food and drink) **1** The traditional popular British drink, usually taken with milk and sometimes sugar. It is drunk at all hours of the day. It is especially popular on awakening (when still in bed), at breakfast, during a working morning (either for *elevenses* or as a 'tea break'), after *lunch* (or *dinner*), for tea[2] and during the evening. Coffee is now more popular for breakfast and in the middle of the morning. See also *cuppa*. **2** A light, usually uncooked meal, taken between four and five o'clock, and traditionally consisting of bread and butter and jam (or some other spread), cakes or biscuits, and tea[1] to drink. Instead of plain bread, various kinds of pastries or cakes are often preferred, such as *scones, crumpets, muffins* and *teacakes,* the last three eaten toasted (see also *toast*). In towns, tea is served in hotels and *tea-shops* as well as in restaurants and snack-bars. **3** A light supper (sometimes called *high tea*), usually with a single cooked dish and with tea[1] to drink.

teacake /'ti:keɪk/ (food and drink) A light, flat, usually slightly sweet kind of bun, sliced horizontally into two halves and eaten toasted, with butter, for *tea*[2].

teaching hospital /'ti:tʃɪŋ ˌhɒspɪtl/ (medicine) A hospital in which medical students train to become doctors and nurses.

tea-shop /'ti:ʃɒp/ (daily life) A type of restaurant serving *tea*[2] and occasionally light evening meals. Such shops, which also usually serve coffee in the morning, are often old or 'quaint' in character with corresponding furnishings and furniture that are typical of the age of the building. See also *ye olde tea shoppe*.

tech /tek/ (education) A colloquial abbreviation for a *technical college*.

technical college /'teknɪkl ˌkɒlɪdʒ/ (education) A *college*[2] of *further education* that provides courses in technical subjects such as industrial skills, secretarial work, technology, art and agriculture.

technical school /'teknɪkl sku:l/ (education) A state *secondary school* that provides an integrated academic and technical course. Such schools are attended by only 1% of all students of secondary school age.

Telecom Tower /ˌtelɪkɒm 'taʊə(r)/, **the** (London) The official name since 1982 of the Post Office Tower, *London,* a tall tower 620 feet (176 metres) high. It was built by the *Post Office* in 1965 to transmit and receive radio, television and telephone communications in and out of London without interference from other tall London buildings. The Tower has two viewing galleries and a revolving restaurant at the top, usually open to the public.

Telegraph /'telɪɡrɑ:f/, **the** (media) The short name of the *Daily Telegraph* newspaper.

telemessage /'telɪˌmesɪdʒ/ (commerce) A form of telegram introduced by the *Post Office* in 1982 to replace conventional telegrams. It enables a message to be sent anywhere in *Britain* by telephone or telex so that it can be delivered the following day (although not on a *Sunday*). Telemessages can also be sent to some countries abroad.

Television South /ˌtelɪvɪʒn 'saʊθ/ (**TVS**) (media) One of the 15 television companies of the *IBA* transmitting programmes to south and southeast *England*.

Television South West /ˌtelɪvɪʒn ˌsaʊθ ˈwest/ (**TSW**) (media)
One of the 15 television companies of the *IBA* transmitting
programmes to southwest *England* (*Cornwall* and Devon).

Temple /ˈtempl/, **the** (**1** London **2** transport) **1** The historic
buildings in the *City* (*of London*) that house two *Inns of
Court*—the *Inner Temple* and the *Middle Temple*. [built on site
of buildings owned by the Knights Templars in the 13th
century] **2** An Underground railway station just west of here.
See *London Underground*.

Temple Bar /ˌtempl ˈbɑː(r)/ (London) The historic western
entrance to the *City* (*of London*), where a gate built after the
Great Fire of London (1666) stood until 1878 and where now a
memorial (the Temple Bar Memorial) stands to mark the site.
When the sovereign visits the City he or she is met at this
point by the *Lord Mayor*. [understood as 'Temple Gate']

Temple Church /ˌtempl ˈtʃɜːtʃ/, **the** (London) An ancient
church in the *City* (*of London*) near the *Temple*, built in the
12th century for the Knights Templars.

10 pence (piece) /ˌten ˈpens (ˌtenpens ˈpiːs)/ (finance) A coin
made from a mixture of copper and nickel that looks like silver.
It is worth one-tenth of the value of a *pound* (*sterling*) and
replaces the old *two-shilling piece* which was similar in
appearance and had the same value. See p 376.

tenner /ˈtenə(r)/ (daily life) A colloquial term for a £10 note.
Compare *fiver*.

term /tɜːm/ (**1** education **2** law) **1** A division of the academic
year in a school, *college*[1,2] or other educational establishment.
Most schools and colleges have three terms in a year, with
school terms extending from September to December
(autumn term or *Christmas* term), January to March (winter
term or *Easter* term) and April to July (summer term). College
(university) terms are shorter and often have religious names
(*Michaelmas*, Hilary, *Lent*, Trinity). **2** A similar division when
law *courts*[3] are in session; January–March (Hilary Term),
April–May (Easter Term), June–July (Trinity Term),
October–December (Michaelmas Term).

terraced house /ˌterəst ˈhaʊs/ (style) A (usually small) house
that is one of a continuous row in one block in a street. Many
rows of terraced houses were originally built for workers in
nearby factories or coalmines. A terraced house usually costs
less than a *semi-detached* or *detached house* of similar size.
['terrace' in sense 'connected row of houses'; originally such a
row overlooked a slope]

Territorial Army /ˌterɪtɔːrɪəl ˈɑːmɪ/, **the (TA, the)** (defence) A
reserve force of approximately 75,000 (expected to be 86,000
by 1990) trained and equipped volunteers, both men and
women, who can be called on in time of national emergency
to reinforce the regular army.

tertiary college /ˈtɜːʃərɪ ˌkɒlɪdʒ/ (education) A state
educational *college*[2] that provides a range of specialized

courses for students over 16 at *sixth form* or *further education*
level. Compare *sixth-form college* and see also *secondary
school*. ['tertiary' as the third level of education after primary
and secondary]

terraced house

Tesco /ˈteskəʊ/ (commerce) A food supermarket chain, with
stores in many towns through *Britain*. [name based on initials
of original tea supplier, *TE S*tockwell, to firm's founder Sir
John Cohen (1898–1979)]

test match /ˈtest mætʃ/ (sport and leisure) An international
commercially sponsored series of five-day *cricket* matches
played in summer between the *England* team and a visiting
team from Australia, New Zealand, India, Pakistan, Sri Lanka
or the West Indies. The *England* team usually tours one or
more of these countries in the winter to play similar matches.
The first test match was played in 1877, between England and
Australia. [matches are a *test* of which is the better team]

TGWU /ˌtiː ˌdʒiː ˌdʌbljuː ˈjuː/, **the (Transport and General
Workers' Union, the)** (work) A powerful trade union
comprising a range of industrial groups, including busmen,
lorry (truck) drivers, engineers, dockers, clerical workers and
technicians, formed in 1922 and having a membership of
nearly 1.6 million, making it the largest trade union in
Britain.

Thames /temz/, **the** (geography) *Britain*'s best known river,
on which *London* stands. It rises in the Cotswolds, southwest
England, and flows east for a distance of 210 miles (338 km) to
London and out into the North Sea. Ocean-going vessels can
sail up it as far as London, and smaller craft can sail up it for a

further 86 miles (138 km). *Oxford* and Henley-on-Thames (see *Henley Regatta*) are also on the Thames.

Thames Barrier /ˌtemz ˈbærɪə(r)/, **the** (science and technology) A specially constructed flood barrier built across the river *Thames* in *London*. The barrier, which was officially opened in 1984, consists of ten gates which, when not in use, lie horizontally on the river bed, allowing ships to travel normally up and down the river. When the barrier is raised, the gates stand vertically so that the top of the barrier is more than 50 ft (15 m) above the river bed. The barrier was constructed to protect London from the serious flooding that has sometimes occurred in the past.

Thames Barrier

Thames Television /ˈtemz ˈtelɪvɪʒn/ (media) One of the major companies of the 15 that make up the *IBA*, transmitting programmes in and around *London* from Monday morning to Friday afternoon. Compare *LWT*.

Thatcher, Margaret /ˈθætʃə(r), ˈmɑːɡrɪt/ (people) Margaret Thatcher (born 1925) began her career in politics in 1959, when she became a Conservative *MP*. Her shrewdness and political insight brought her rapid advancement within the *Conservative Party* so that in 1975 she became its leader. In 1979 she was elected as *Britain*'s first woman *Prime Minister*. From the start, her autocratic style earned her the nickname of the 'Iron Lady', and she soon acquired a reputation for speaking her mind boldly and even brusquely. Her abrasive manner has attacted some criticism. During the Falklands War of 1982, however, Margaret Thatcher's militant patriotism found her many new supporters, and she became something of a popular hero-figure, much as Winston *Churchill* had done in the Second World War. Mrs Thatcher was re-elected prime minister in the general election of 1983, and her noticeably right-wing policies became known by the name of *Thatcherism*.

Thatcherism /ˈθætʃərɪzəm/ (politics) The political and economic policies pursued by Margaret *Thatcher, Prime Minister* and leader of the *Conservative Party* from 1979. The underlying aim of Thatcherism is to shift the economic emphasis back to private enterprise which is directly contrary to *Labour Party* policy. This involves cutting public expenditure, returning state-owned enterprise to private ownership wherever possible, curbing the power of the trade unions and reducing inflation by 'monetarist' financial policies (ie, by controlling the supply of money in *Britain*). In the early 1980s this 'hard-line' right-wing doctrine was moderated slightly, partly because of opposition within the Conservative Party from the *wets*, and partly because most Conservative voters seemed to prefer less extreme policies.

Theatre Royal /ˌθɪətə ˈrɔɪəl/, **the** (arts) The official name of the *Drury Lane* theatre in *London*.

Theatre Upstairs /ˌθɪətər ʌpˈsteəz/, **the** (arts) A *London* theatre on the *first floor* of the *Royal Court Theatre*, staging mainly modern and experimental or 'avant-garde' plays.

theme park /ˈθiːm pɑːk/ (sport and leisure) A large park or leisure complex whose layout and exhibits are devoted to a particular theme, for example, maritime history. Such parks, which usually include restaurants, amusement facilities and special attractions for children, are mostly privately owned and became popular from the early 1980s.

Think Tank /ˈθɪŋk tæŋk/, **the** (government) The colloquial name of the Central Policy Review Staff, a government body of senior *ministers*[2] established in 1970 to advise ministers collectively on major issues of policy. It was abolished in 1983.

third leader /ˌθɜːd ˈliːdə(r)/, **the** (media) In The *Times*, the third editorial leading article which, traditionally, sometimes deals with a relatively unimportant topic, but is written in a witty style.

third reading /ˌθɜːd ˈriːdɪŋ/ (government) The final review of a *bill* in the *House of Commons* and *House of Lords*, after which, if agreement is reached between the two Houses, it is sent to the sovereign for the *royal assent*. On receiving this it becomes an *Act of Parliament* and part of the law of the land.

third-party insurance /ˌθɜːdˌpɑːtɪ ɪnˈʃɔːrəns/ (finance) A type of insurance that all drivers of motor vehicles must have. A person is insured against damage or injury caused to someone who is not party to the insurance policy. [the policy is agreed between two parties, the insured and the insurer, and any one outside this agreement is thus a 'third party']

Thirty-Nine Articles /ˌθɜːtɪ naɪn ˈɑːtɪklz/, **the** (religion) A set of doctrines accepted by the *Church of England* in 1563. Since 1865 the clergy have been required to agree to them in general outline. [in full, the 'Articles agreed upon by the Archbishops and Bishops of both Provinces, and the whole Clergy, in the Convocation holden at London in the Year 1562, for the avoiding of Diversities of Opinions, and for the establishing of Consent touching true Religion']

This Is Your Life /ˌðɪs ɪz jɔː ˈlaɪf/ (media) A series of programmes shown on *ITV* in which, in each programme, the life story of a famous person is retold with the help of specially invited former colleagues, friends and members of his family. The guest himself, although the star in the programme, is told nothing in advance about it, and so it is a complete surprise. At the end of the programme he is presented with his 'biography' in a special book. The programmes are among the most popular on British television.

thistle /ˈθɪsl/ (tradition) The national emblem of *Scotland*, apparently first used in the 15th century as a symbol of defence. Some Scotsmen wear a thistle pinned to their jackets on *St Andrew's Day*. See also *Order of the Thistle*.

Thompson, Daley /ˈtɒmpsn, ˈdeɪlɪ/ (people) By the early 1980s Daley Thompson (born 1958) had clearly become not only *Britain*'s finest all-round athlete but one of the best athletes of his generation in the world. Thompson's excellence in the decathlon was shown when he won the gold medal in the Olympic Games of 1980 and again in the Olympic Games of 1984.

Threadneedle Street /θredˈniːdl striːt/ (finance) A street in the *City (of London)* on which there are several large banks including the *Bank of England*. See *Old Lady of Threadneedle Street*.

Three As /ˌθriː ˈeɪz/, **the** (sport and leisure) A colloquial name for the *Amateur Athletics Association* and for the championship contest organized by it.

Three Choirs Festival /ˌθriː ˌkwaɪəz ˈfestɪvl/, **the** (arts) A music festival, first held in 1724, held annually (in turn) in the cathedrals of Gloucester, Hereford and Worcester. The music consists of both choral and orchestral religious works (church music), and is performed by each cathedral choir, as well as special festival choirs and outside orchestras.

three-card trick /ˌθriː ˈkɑːd trɪk/ (sport and leisure) A gambling game occasionally played in the street. A man with a pack of cards invites members of the public to bet on which of three cards, laid face down, is the queen. The man with the cards always wins.

three-cornered fight /ˌθriː kɔːnəd ˈfaɪt/ (politics) A term for an election (either a *by-election* or a *general election*) in which the contest is between candidates from three political parties, usually *Conservative, Labour,* and *Liberal-SDP Alliance.* In certain areas of *Scotland, Wales* and *Northern Ireland,* the third party may be a local nationalist one, such as the *SNP, Plaid Cymru, Sinn Féin* or one of the Unionist parties in *Northern Ireland.*

three-day event /ˌθriː deɪ ɪˈvent/ (sport and leisure) A horse riding contest held over three days, usually comprising dressage (the control of horses in obedience) on the first day, cross-country riding on the second day and show jumping (in the ring) on the third. The event originated at *Badminton* in 1949. See also *eventing.*

three-legged race /ˌθriː ˈlegɪd reɪs/ (sport and leisure) A race popular with children, in which two competitors run together, with the right leg of one tied to the left leg of the other.

three-legged race

three-line whip /ˌθriː laɪn ˈwɪp/ (**1** government **2** daily life) **1** An urgent request by a *whip¹* to an *MP* to attend a particular debate or to vote. **2** A similar request to a person to attend a particular function or take part in a particular event. ['three-line' with reference to the triple underlining of the written request, indicating its extreme urgency]

Throgmorton Street /θrɒgˈmɔːtn striːt/ (finance) A street in the *City (of London)* where the *Stock Exchange* is, and so also a name for the Stock Exchange itself. [the street is named after a 16th-century diplomat]

tick-tack man /ˈtɪk tæk ˌmæn/ (sport and leisure) A *bookmaker* at a race course who sends betting information to other bookmakers by means of a special sign language, using his hands and arms.

tied cottage /ˌtaɪd ˈkɒtɪdʒ/ (life and society) A cottage or house whose occupant, such as a farmworker, can live in it only as long as he works for the employer who owns it. In a few cases, however, people who live in tied cottages can continue to live there after they retire.

tied house /ˌtaɪd ˈhaʊs/ (daily life) A *pub* under contract ('tied') to a particular brewery for its supplies of beer and other alcoholic drinks. Compare *free house*.

Time Out /ˌtaɪm ˈaʊt/ (media) A weekly magazine giving information and reviews of current plays, films, concerts, exhibitions, meetings and restaurants, etc in *London*. The magazine, first published in 1968, and with a circulation of over 72,000, is noted for its 'progressive' style and its radical political and social views.

Timeline /ˈtaɪmlaɪn/ (commerce) The commercial name for the *Speaking Clock* telephone service.

Times /taɪmz/, **The** (media) A daily *quality paper* with a circulation (1984) of over 380,000 (1970 — 437,000). It was first published in 1785 (as the 'Daily Universal Register') and is generally regarded as the major *Establishment* newspaper. Its views and interests appeal to the *upper middle class* Englishman. It is particularly noted for its regular features, such as its editorial leaders (and its *third leader*), readers' letters, advertisements (including its *personal column*) and its crossword. As a quality paper it covers home and overseas news, finance, sports, and more recently, features and book and arts reviews. Politically it is officially independent but it is actually inclined towards the *Conservative Party*.

Times Educational Supplement /ˌtaɪmz edʒʊˌkeɪʃənl ˈsʌplɪmənt/, **the (TES, the)** (education) A weekly supplement to The *Times*, published and sold separately with a circulation of over 87,000. It specializes in reports and features on education in schools, and is aimed almost exclusively at school teachers. It has an extensive advertising section of teaching posts, and for many teachers is regarded as the best journal for seeking a teaching job. It first appeared in 1910 as a monthly insert in 'The Times'. From 1972 'The Times' has also published a 'Higher Education Supplement', concerned chiefly with university education.

Times Literary Supplement /ˌtaɪmz ˌlɪtərərɪ ˈsʌplɪmənt/, **the (TLS, the)** (education) A weekly supplement to The *Times*, published and sold separately, with a circulation of over 29,000. It is one of *Britain*'s leading literary weekly magazines, noted for its scholarly reviews and its comprehensive coverage of the literary and publishing world. It is also noted for its readers' letters to the editor, mostly from authors who want to correct what they regard as an unfair or unbalanced review.

tip and run /ˌtɪp ən ˈrʌn/ (sport and leisure) A form of *cricket*, popular with children, in which the batsman must run to the opposite wicket every time his bat hits or touches ('tips') the ball. This rule speeds up the game considerably.

tipsy cake /ˈtɪpsɪ keɪk/ (food and drink) A kind of *trifle* made from sponge cake soaked with wine or sherry and usually decorated with nuts and crystallized fruit. [from colloquial 'tipsy', meaning 'slightly drunk'].

Titanic /taɪ'tænɪk/**, the** (history) A British passenger liner, at the time the largest vessel afloat, which collided with an iceberg on her maiden voyage to New York in 1912, and sank with the loss of all but 703 of her 2,206 passengers. Attempts to locate and raise the sunken liner have so far failed.

Titbits /'tɪtbɪts/ (media) A weekly magazine that contained a wide range of popular articles, features, stories and pictures, with an emphasis on personalities in the news and items of homely interest. The magazine was first published in 1881 and ceased publication in June 1984.

toad-in-the-hole /ˌtəʊd ɪn ðə 'həʊl/ (food and drink) A savoury dish, usually eaten hot, consisting of sausages cooked in batter. [the sausage buried in batter is thought to look like a toad hidden in a hole]

toast /təʊst/ (food and drink) A traditional part of an *English breakfast*—slices of bread that have been lightly cooked and browned by exposure to heat, in an electric toaster, under a grill or by a fire. Toast is also eaten at *tea*[2] or supper (similar to *high tea*); in the latter meal often with a savoury covering, such as eggs or cheese.

toby jug /'təʊbɪ dʒʌg/ (style) A mug or jug in the shape of a squat, seated man wearing a three-cornered hat and smoking a pipe. The spout is formed from one of the corners of the hat. Some people collect toby jugs and the old ones are valuable. [said to be derived from an 18th-century poem about a man called 'Toby Philpot']

toby jug

Toc H /ˌtɒk 'eɪtʃ/ (charities) A Christian organization founded after the First World War to encourage comradeship and social service in the place of hatred and loneliness. The name comes from the former telegraphic sign for the letters 'T' and 'H', which stood for 'Talbot House'. The original Talbot House was opened in the small town of Poperinghe, west Belgium, in 1915, as a *chapel²* and *club* for soldiers and as a memorial to Gilbert Talbot, the brother of the organization's founder, Neville Talbot.

toffee apple /'tɒfɪ ˌæpl/ (food and drink) An apple on a stick covered with a layer of brittle toffee. It is traditionally sold at *fêtes* or made for *Hallowe'en* parties.

Tommy /'tɒmɪ/ (tradition) A rather dated nickname for a British soldier. [said to derive from Thomas Atkins, a random name for a soldier used in instruction manuals giving directions for completing certain army forms]

Tony Benn /ˌtəʊnɪ 'ben/ see *Benn* (people)

top hat /ˌtɒp 'hæt/ (clothing) A man's or boy's tall, black or grey hat with a cylindrical crown and narrow brim, worn on some formal occasions (eg, at *Ascot*) or, in the case of boys, as part of the uniform at some schools such as *Eton* or *Harrow*.

Top of the Pops /ˌtɒp əv ðə 'pɒps/ (media) A weekly television programme on *BBC 1* in which a selection of recently released pop and rock hits is performed, including those in the *top ten*, either live or recorded, often with an accompanying video film. The programme was first transmitted in 1964.

top ten /ˌtɒp 'ten/, **the** (media) The top-selling pop and rock records released in a particular week, as established by market research and sales figures. The records are played frequently on *Radio 1* and several *local radio* stations. A selection, including the 'number one' best-seller, is performed weekly on *Top of the Pops*.

TOPS /tɒps/ (**Training Opportunities Scheme, the**) (education) A state scheme providing practical training in industry and commerce for adults over the age of 19, with training carried out at special centres called *skillcentres*, as well as at *colleges²* and employers' own establishments. The scheme, which was first operated in 1973, is intended mainly for people wanting to change to a different kind of job or returning to work after a break (eg, women with children).

torpids /'tɔːpɪdz/ (sport and leisure) The annual spring boat races between teams of eight oarsmen from each of the *colleges¹* of *Oxford University*, held on the river *Thames* at *Oxford¹*. [from 'torpid' in sense 'slow', 'sluggish'; the races were originally between the second eights of the colleges, which were slower than the main crews]

Torvill and Dean /ˌtɔːvɪl ən 'diːn/ (**Jayne Torvill and Christopher Dean**) (people) Jayne Torvill and Christopher Dean (born in 1957 and 1958 respectively) are a young British ice-skating couple who set exceptionally high standards in ice dancing, winning their third world title in a row in 1983 with a free-dance performance that gained maximum marks from all nine judges. Their total dedication to their art, their technical skill and originality made them very popular in the early 1980s. Both dancers come from Nottingham, and this fact, combined with a knowledge of their previous careers (Torvill worked for an insurance company and Dean was a policeman), has helped to give them the reputation of fulfilling the popular British ideal of 'local boy/girl makes good'.

Tory /ˈtɔːrɪ/ (politics) An alternative term for Conservative, used either critically, as applied to an extreme Conservative, or simply as a convenient shorter word (eg, in newspaper headlines). See *Conservative Party*. [name was inherited from the former English right-wing political party in existence from the 17th century to the 1830s when the Conservative party was formed]

tossing the caber /ˌtɒsɪŋ ðə ˈkeɪbə(r)/ (sport and leisure) A contest popular in Scottish *Highland games*, in which a heavy wooden pole ('caber') is thrown through the air as a test of strength. The winner is the competitor whose caber is thrown the furthest.

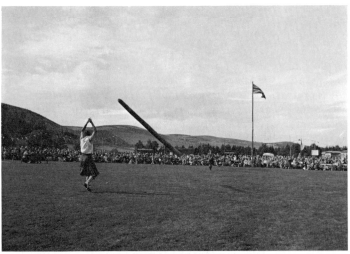

tossing the caber

tossing the pancake /ˌtɒsɪŋ ðə ˈpæŋkeɪk/ (tradition) A tradition marked on *Shrove Tuesday*, when either in a race (see *pancake race*) or among a group of standing participants, *pancakes* are tossed in the air out of a frying pan so that they turn over and are caught again in the pan. The custom developed from the days when Shrove Tuesday was a final day of feasting and enjoyment before the start of *Lent*.

Tottenham Court Road /ˌtɒtnəm kɔːt ˈrəʊd/ (London) A street in central *London* well-known for its shops selling radio, television and video equipment and home computers, as well as for its furniture dealers.

Tottenham Hotspur /ˌtɒtnəm ˈhɒtspɜː(r)/ (sport and leisure) A popular *London football club* with a stadium at *White Hart Lane*. The club was founded in 1882, originally as Hotspur Football Club. [named after district in north London where stadium is; 'Hotspur', meaning 'person of fiery temper', was the nickname of Sir Henry Percy (1364–1403), who led the English into battle against the Scots]

Tower Bridge /ˌtaʊə ˈbrɪdʒ/ (London) One of *London*'s best-known landmarks—the distinctive twin drawbridges with *Gothic* towers over the river *Thames* near the *Tower of London*. The Bridge was built in the late 19th century and is the farthest downstream of all London's bridges.

Tower Hill /ˌtaʊə ˈhɪl/ (London) The historic open space near the *Tower of London*, which was the main place where traitors imprisoned in the Tower were executed.

Tower of London /ˌtaʊər əv ˈlʌndən/**, the** (London) One of the oldest, best-known, and most imposing fortresses in *England*, on the north bank of the river *Thames* in *London*. The Tower was begun in the 11th century by William the *Conqueror*, and was added to and altered by later sovereigns. In the course of its history it has been a royal palace, a state prison, a citadel and an arsenal. Its many associations with English history make it a popular tourist attraction. Two important parts of it are the *Bloody Tower* and the *White Tower*. Here also the *Crown Jewels* are on public display, and *Yeomen Warders* are on guard.

town and gown /ˌtaʊn ən ˈgaʊn/ (life and society) The term used for the native inhabitants ('town') and students (and sometimes academic staff) ('gown') of some university cities, especially the older ones such as *Oxford*[2] and *Cambridge*[2]. The phrase also implies a culture clash between the two groups. See also *gown*[1,2].

town clerk /ˌtaʊn ˈklɑːk/ (government) Until 1974, the secretary and chief administrative officer of a town or *city*. He is now often called the Chief Executive.

town council /ˌtaʊn ˈkaʊnsl/ (government) The *local authority* in a town (usually within a *district council*) that is headed by a *mayor* or *mayoress* and that has certain legislative powers, for example, to make *by-laws*. The secretary and chief administrative officer of a town council is usually called the *town clerk*. Larger towns usually have a local authority that is a *borough council* or a district council.

town crier /ˌtaʊn ˈkraɪə(r)/ (tradition) **1** A person formerly employed to make public announcements in a town. **2** In modern times, a person who plays this role on special occasions, usually for publicity or when sponsored by a particular commercial promoter. See also *oyez*.

town hall /ˌtaʊn ˈhɔːl/ (government) The chief building in a town or *city* (where it may be called a city hall and be a more important building) in which local government business is carried out, and which usually has a public hall, which may be available for concerts or meetings.

town house /ˈtaʊn haʊs/ (style) A house in a town or *city*, either a fashionable one or (in *estate agents'* language) simply a *terraced house*.

Trade Descriptions Act /ˌtreɪd dɪˈskrɪpʃnz ækt/**, the** (law) An *Act* (*of Parliament*), passed in 1968 and later, according to which goods and services must be honestly and correctly described and not exaggerated through advertising or promotion.

trading estate /ˈtreɪdɪŋ ɪˌsteɪt/ (commerce) A district of a town, often on the outskirts, where several commercial or trading firms have their premises. Compare *industrial estate*.

trading stamps /ˈtreɪdɪŋ stæmps/ (commerce) Stamps with a specific stated value, which are given by some shops and stores to their customers when they buy goods. The stamps can then either be exchanged for articles offered in a catalogue or else used to pay for further goods.

Trafalgar /trəˈfælgə(r)/ **(Battle of Trafalgar, the)** (history) A decisive naval battle of 1805 in the Napoleonic Wars, in which the allied French and Spanish fleets were defeated by the British under the command of Admiral Nelson, who was mortally wounded in it. [The battle was fought off Cape Trafalgar, southwest Spain]

Trafalgar Square /trəˌfælgə ˈskweə(r)/ (London) The main square of central *London*, where there are a number of famous buildings and monuments, including the *National Gallery, St Martin-in-the-Fields* and *Nelson's Column*. The Square is popular with visitors, who come to relax by the fountains here or to feed the pigeons. Trafalgar Square is also a popular meeting place for political and other demonstrations. [named in commemoration of Nelson's victory at the Battle of *Trafalgar*]

traffic warden /ˈtræfɪk ˌwɔːdn/ (transport) A person whose job is to make sure drivers obey parking regulations. Wardens have the authority to issue *parking tickets*, and may also help to direct traffic. They wear a special black uniform with yellow cap bands.

Transcash /ˈtrænzkæʃ/ (finance) A money transfer system operated by the *Post Office*, by which payment made in cash at the counter is transferred to a named individual or organization provided they have a *National Girobank* account. The system is useful for people who do not have a bank account and so cannot send cheques or make payment by *direct debit* or *standing order*.

transport café /ˈtrænspɔːt ˌkæfeɪ/ (daily life) A cafe on a main road, such as a *motorway*, that provides good, inexpensive food, mainly for long-distance lorry (truck) drivers.

Transport House /ˌtrænspɔːt ˈhaʊs/ (politics) The building in *Smith Square, London* that houses the headquarters of the *Labour Party* and the *TGWU*.

treasure trove /ˈtreʒə trəʊv/ (law) Precious goods such as money, jewels, gold or silver found buried in the ground and of unknown ownership. Such treasure belongs to the state and must be declared by the finder. [from Old French 'tresor trové', 'found treasure']

Treasury /ˈtreʒərɪ/**, the** (government) The state *department* responsible for the management of *Britain*'s finances and economy, officially headed by the *Prime Minister* (as First Lord of the Treasury) but actually the responsibility of the *Chancellor of the Exchequer*.

treble chance /ˌtrebl ˈtʃɑːns/ (sport and leisure) A method of betting in football *pools* in which the main aim is to pick the draws, which count more than wins. [from original three different possible results: a win away, a win at home, or a draw]

Trent Bridge /ˌtrent ˈbrɪdʒ/ (sport and leisure) A *cricket* ground in Nottingham where *test matches* take place. [ground is near bridge over river Trent]

Tribune /ˈtrɪbjuːn/ (media) A weekly political and literary magazine that gives the viewpoint of the left wing of the *Labour Party*. Its circulation is under 40,000. It was first published in 1937.

trick or treat /ˌtrɪk ɔː ˈtriːt/ (tradition) A tradition popular on the night of *Hallowe'en*, when children visit houses and ask the residents if they want a 'trick' or 'treat'. If the people in the house give the children a 'treat' (usually money or sweets), then the children will not play a 'trick' on them. The custom was imported to *Britain* from America in the early 1980s.

Trident /ˈtraɪdnt/ (**1** transport **2** defence) **1** A jet passenger aircraft manufactured by Hawker Siddeley in various modifications (Trident One, Trident Two, Trident Three). They are operated by *British Airways*. **2** A long-range missile, fired from a submarine, that can carry a nuclear warhead. Trident I has been carried by suitable submarines since 1979 and a more sophisticated model, Trident II, will become available in the late 1980s.

trifle /ˈtraɪfl/ (food and drink) A sweet dish consisting of a sponge cake (sometimes soaked in wine) spread with jam or fruit, then covered with a layer of *custard*, and topped with cream. It is often decorated with nuts and more fruit.

trilby (hat) /ˈtrɪlbɪ (ˌtrɪlbɪ ˈhæt)/ (clothing) A type of man's soft felt hat with an indented crown. [named after the heroine of a dramatized novel (1893) by George du Maurier]

Trinity House /ˌtrɪnətɪ ˈhaʊs/ (transport) The authority (in full, Corporation of Trinity House) that controls light-houses and buoys, and some lightships, around the coasts of *England* and *Wales*. It is the largest English pilot authority and is a charitable organization providing homes and financial support for retired mariners and their families. The Corporation was founded in 1514.

Trinity Sunday /ˌtrɪnətɪ ˈsʌndɪ/ (religion) The *Sunday* after *Whit Sunday*, and is one of the major festivals of the Christian year.

Triple Crown /ˌtrɪpl ˈkraʊn/, **the** (sport and leisure) **1** The title awarded to the *rugby football* team of *England, Scotland, Wales* or *Ireland* that in one season defeats all three of its opponents. **2** The title awarded to a horse that has won the three races, Two Thousand Guineas, *Derby* and *St Leger*.

Triple Event /ˌtrɪpl ɪˈvent/, **the** (sport and leisure) The three horse races whose winner is awarded the *Triple Crown*[2].

tripos /ˈtraɪpɒs/ (education) At *Cambridge University*, the final *honours degree* examination in certain subjects. [said to derive from the nickname of 'Mr Tripos' given to an examination candidate who sat on a three-legged stool]

Trooping the Colour /ˌtruːpɪŋ ðə ˈkʌlə(r)/ (tradition) An annual ceremony held on the *Official Birthday* of the sovereign on *Horse Guards Parade, London,* when regiments of the *Guards Division,* and the *Household Cavalry,* parade ('troop') the regimental flag ('colour') before the sovereign. The ceremony dates from the 18th century and was originally a guard-mounting ceremony.

Troubles /ˈtrʌblz/, **the** (politics) The name used for the sectarian divisions (between Roman Catholics and Protestants) and terrorism in *Northern Ireland* from 1969. By the end of 1983 the Troubles had claimed over 2,000 lives, including those of members of the British *Army* and innocent civilians.

trunk call /ˈtrʌŋk kɔːl/ (commerce) A long-distance telephone call.

trunk road /ˈtrʌŋk rəʊd/ (transport) A main road, especially one used by lorries (trucks) and other heavy vehicles. Trunk roads are usually *A-roads*.

Trustcard /ˈtrʌstkɑːd/ (finance) The credit card issued by the *Trustee Savings Bank*.

Trustee Savings Bank /ˌtrʌstiː ˈseɪvɪŋz bæŋk/, **the (TSB, the)** (finance) A government-sponsored savings bank directed in a number of branches on a regional basis by local voluntary trustees (managers) and also providing a full range of banking services including cheque accounts and credit services. See also *Trustcard*.

TT /ˌtiː ˈtiː/, **the (Tourist Trophy, the)** (sport and leisure) An important annual series of motorcycle races held on the *Isle of Man*. The races were first held in 1907, originally for tourists visiting the Isle of Man, and currently comprise the Senior TT

Race, for riders of 500cc machines, and the Classic Race for less powerful motorcycles.

tube /tjuːb/, **the** (transport) A colloquial term for the *London Underground* railway. [from its tube-shaped tunnels]

TUC /ˌtiː juː ˈsiː/, **the (Trades Union Congress, the)** (work) The major association of British trade unions, founded in 1868 and each year meeting as an assembly of delegates to discuss common problems. Its main object is to promote the interests of its members and improve the social and economic conditions of working people. It represents 90% of all trade union members in *Britain*, ie, 10.5 million people.

Tudor (style) /ˈtjuːdə(r) (staɪl)/ (style) An architectural style of the late *Perpendicular* period, characterized in particular by half-timbered houses. [named after the 16th-century royal house of Tudor]

turf /tɜːf/, **the** (sport and leisure) Horse-racing as a sport or industry. [from the turf of the race-course]

turf accountant /ˈtɜːf əˌkaʊntənt/ (sport and leisure) A formal name for a *bookmaker*.

tutor /ˈtjuːtə(r)/ (education) **1** A member of staff at a university responsible for the teaching and supervision of a fixed number of students in a particular subject or subjects. **2** A teacher who usually works with individual students or pupils and who is usually employed privately.

TV Times /ˌtiː viː ˈtaɪmz/ (media) A weekly magazine containing all the week's television programmes (from one Friday evening to the following Friday evening) broadcast by the *IBA* and also including popular features and articles on television personalities and subjects of family interest. The magazine was first published in 1968 and has a circulation (1984) of about 3.3 million. Compare *Radio Times*.

TV-am /ˌtiː viː eɪ ˈem/ (media) A television company established by the *IBA* in 1983 to transmit early morning programmes (so-called *breakfast television*) nationwide.

Twelfth Night /ˌtwelfθ ˈnaɪt/ (tradition) 6 January, the twelfth day after *Christmas Day* and the traditional end of the celebrations of *Christmas* and the *New Year* (see *New Year's Day*). On this day Christmas decorations are usually taken down, as are Christmas cards that have been on display since Christmas Day or earlier. Twelfth Night coincides with the *church* festival of the Epiphany.

20 pence (piece) /ˌtwentɪ ˈpens (ˌtwentɪ pens ˈpiːs)/ (finance) A seven-sided coin made from a mixture of copper and nickel that looks like silver. It is worth one-fifth of the value of a *pound (sterling)*. See p 376.

Twickenham /ˈtwɪkənəm/ (sport and leisure) A district of Richmond-upon-Thames (southwest *Greater London*) where international matches are played on the famous *rugby football* ground here. See also *University Match*.

2 pence (piece) /ˌtuː ˈpens (ˌtuː pens ˈpiːs)/ (finance) A bronze coin that is worth one-fiftieth of the value of a *pound (sterling)*. See p 376.

two-minute silence /ˌtuː mɪnɪt ˈsaɪləns/, **the** (tradition) A silence observed at the *Cenotaph, London,* and elsewhere in *Britain,* at 11.00 am on *Remembrance Sunday,* in order to remember the dead of both world wars.

two-shilling piece /ˌtuː ʃɪlɪŋ ˈpiːs/ see *10 pence (piece)* (finance).

Tyne Tees TV /ˌtaɪn ˌtiːz ˌtiː ˈviː/ (media) One of the 15 television companies of the *IBA,* transmitting programmes to northeast *England.* [named after the rivers Tyne and Tees]

Tynwald /ˈtɪnwɔːld/, **the** (government) The parliament of the *Isle of Man.* It has two houses: the Legislative Council and the House of Keys. After *bills* are passed through both houses they are sent for the *royal assent.*

U /juː/ (life and society) A somewhat dated term used half-humorously for a word or action that is socially acceptable, for example, saying 'sofa' instead of the *non-U* equivalent 'settee', or having plain carpets in one's house as distinct from non-U wall-to-wall patterned ones. [initial of '*upper class*']

U certificate /ˈjuː səˌtɪfɪkət/ (arts) A category in which a cinema film is placed by the *British Board of Film Censors*, indicating that it is suitable for anyone, including children, to see. Compare *15* (listed under letter F), *18* (listed under letter E) and *PG*. ['U' for 'universal']

UCCA /ˈʌkə/ **(Universities Central Council on Admissions, the)** (education) The organization through which students in their final year at school apply for admission to a degree course at a university. All universities in *Britain* belong to the scheme except the *Open University*. The organization was formed in 1961.

UDR /ˌjuː diː ˈɑː(r)/, **the (Ulster Defence Regiment, the)** (law) A locally recruited and mainly part-time reserve force which supports the police and the *Army* in *Northern Ireland*.

UK /ˌjuː ˈkeɪ/ see *United Kingdom* (geography)

Ullswater /ˈʌlzˌwɔːtə(r)/ (geography) The second largest lake (after *Windermere*) in the *Lake District*. It is 7½ miles long and half a mile wide, and is generally regarded as the most spectacular of the lakes.

Ulster /ˈʌlstə(r)/ (geography) A name for *Northern Ireland*, originally the name of a former kingdom here.

Ulster Defence Association /ˌʌlstə dɪˈfens əˌsəʊsɪˌeɪʃn/, **the (UDA, the)** (politics) A Protestant paramilitary organization founded in 1972 to oppose the *IRA* by using force if necessary in *Northern Ireland*.

Ulster Defence Regiment /ˌʌlstə dɪˈfens ˌredʒɪmənt/ see *UDR* (defence)

Ulster Democratic Unionist Party /ˌʌlstə deməˌkrætɪk ˈjuːnɪənɪst ˌpɑːtɪ/ (politics) A political party formed in *Northern Ireland* in 1971. The founders (who include Ian *Paisley*) disagree with many of the policies of the official Unionist Party (see *Ulster Unionist Party*). The Democratic Unionist Party is strongly Protestant and insists that *Ulster* should remain part of the *United Kingdom*. Ian Paisley is the current leader of the party and an *MP* in the *House of Commons*.

Ulster Unionist Party /ˌʌlstə ˈjuːnɪənɪst ˌpɑːtɪ/ (politics) A political party which has been active in *Northern Ireland* for very many years. Most of its supporters are Protestants who wish *Ulster* to remain part of the *United Kingdom*. After 1920, when Ulster and the Republic of *Ireland* became separate countries, the Unionists were the ruling party in the Northern Ireland Parliament until *direct rule* began in 1972. The party has regularly been well represented among the Northern Ireland *MPs* in the *House of Commons*.

unadopted road /ˌʌnədɒptɪd ˈrəʊd/ (geography) A public road not maintained by a *local authority*.

undergraduate /ˌʌndəˈɡrædʒʊət/ (education) A university student studying for a first degree at any university. The word 'student' is probably more widely used in everyday speech. Compare *postgraduate*.

Underground /ˈʌndəɡraʊnd/, **the** (transport) An electric passenger railway operated largely underground in a city, especially the one in *London*. See *London Underground*. There are also underground railways in *Glasgow* and Liverpool. See also *Metro*.

underwriter /ˈʌndəˌraɪtə(r)/ (finance) **1** An insurance agent who decides how much a person should pay to insure something, taking into account the degree of risk involved and charging more for the insurance when risks are high. **2** An official who undertakes (by 'underwriting' or subscribing his name) to accept responsibility for any losses that result from another person's insurance policy. **3** A person who accepts financial responsibility for any shares in a company that are offered to the public but not bought by them.

unicorn /ˈjuːnɪkɔːn/ (tradition) A mythical animal that looks like a horse with a long straight horn growing from its forehead. It has appeared on the Scottish and British royal coats of arms for many centuries and is a symbol of purity.

Union Flag /ˌjuːnɪən ˈflæɡ/, **the** (tradition) The formal name of the British national flag, more commonly known as the *Union Jack*.

Union Jack /ˌjuːnɪən ˈdʒæk/, **the** (tradition) The national flag of the *United Kingdom*, combining the *St George's cross* of *England*, *St Andrew's cross* of *Scotland* and *St Patrick's cross* of *Ireland* (now representing *Northern Ireland*). [properly the *Union Flag*; 'Union' for the union of England and Scotland in 1606, 'jack' as flown on the jack staff (a small flagstaff) of ships to show their nationality]

Unionist Party /'juːnɪənɪst ˌpɑːtɪ/ see *Ulster Democratic Unionist Party* (politics) and *Ulster Unionist Party* (politics)

unit trust /'juːnɪt trʌst/ (finance) An *investment trust* that issues units for public sale. The unit holders are not shareholders but creditors, and their interests are represented by a trust company operating independently from the agency that issued the units.

United /juːˈnaɪtɪd/ (sport and leisure) The colloquial name of any *football club* having 'United' in its name, especially *Manchester United*.

United Kingdom /juːˌnaɪtɪd ˈkɪŋdəm/, **the (UK, the)** (geography) The short name of the United Kingdom of *Great Britain* and *Northern Ireland*, that is, *England, Scotland, Wales* and Northern Ireland. Compare the *British Isles*. See map on p 380.

United Kingdom Atomic Energy Authority /juːˌnaɪtɪd ˌkɪŋdəm əˌtɒmɪk ˈenədʒɪ ɔːˌθɒrətɪ/, **the (UKAEA, the)** (science and technology) The United Kingdom Atomic Energy Authority was set up in 1954, with the aim of developing nuclear power from a basic science to an essential part of the *United Kingdom*'s energy supply. It conducts research into all types of nuclear reactor, and also provides skill and expertise for other organizations. Its principal research establishments include Harwell, Oxfordshire, Risley, Cheshire and Winfrith, Dorset in *England* and Dounreay in *Scotland*.

United Reformed Church /juːˌnaɪtɪd rɪˌfɔːmd ˈtʃɜːtʃ/, **the** (religion) A leading Protestant, non-*Anglican church* in *Britain*, formed in 1972 by the union of the Presbyterian *Church of England* and the Congregational Church. It is particularly strong in *Wales*.

Universal Aunts /ˌjuːnɪvɜːsl ˈɑːnts/ (commerce) A long-established *London* firm providing private and domestic services especially for non-Londoners, such as finding accommodation, doing shopping and escorting children across London.

Universe /'juːnɪvɜːs/, **The** (media) A leading weekly newspaper and review for Roman Catholics, with features and articles on a wide range of subjects of interest to Catholics. It was founded in 1860 and had a circulation in 1980 of over 151,000.

University College Hospital /juːnɪˌvɜːsətɪ ˌkɒlɪdʒ ˈhɒspɪtl/, **the (UCH, the)** (medicine) A London *teaching hospital* founded by University College, *London* in 1833.

University Match /juːnɪˈvɜːsətɪ mætʃ/, **the** (sport and leisure) The traditional annual *rugby football* match at *Twickenham* between teams from *Oxford University* and *Cambridge University*.

Unknown Warrior /ˌʌnnəʊn ˈwɒrɪə(r)/, **the** (history) The grave in *Westminster Abbey*, *London*, where the remains of an unknown British serviceman killed in France in the First

World War are buried. [full title: Tomb of the Unknown Warrior]

unofficial strike /ˌʌnəfɪʃl ˈstraɪk/ (work) A strike not officially supported or called by a trade union.

upper class /ˌʌpə ˈklɑːs/ (life and society) The class that occupies the highest position in the social scale, usually members of the aristocracy (such as the *royal family* or the *peerage*) with their wealth, breeding and air of exclusivity. See also *U*.

upper middle class /ˌʌpə ˈmɪdl klɑːs/ (life and society) The social class that is higher than the *middle class* but not as high as *upper class*, usually regarded as including professional people such as politicians, surgeons, university lecturers, company directors and senior *civil servants*.

upper school /ˈʌpə skuːl/ (education) The senior classes in a *secondary school* or *public school*[1,2], usually including the *sixth form*.

USDAW /ˈʌzdɔː/, **the (Union of Shop, Distributive and Allied Workers, the)** (work) A trade union whose members are mainly in retail and wholesale distribution, but also in food manufacturing, chemical processing, catering and other service trades. It was formed as the result of a merger in 1947, and has a membership of 403,000.

V and A /ˌviː ən ˈeɪ/ see *Victoria and Albert Museum* (arts)

Valentine's Brook /ˌvæləntaɪnz ˈbrʊk/ (sport and leisure) One of the major jumps in the *Grand National* horse race, consisting of a thorn fence with a brook on the far side. [named after horse who fell here]

Variety Club /vəˈraɪətɪ klʌb/**, the** (charities) A theatrical organization founded to raise money for children's charities. Its president is the Chief Barker. [in full, Variety Club of *Great Britain*]

VAT /ˌviː eɪ ˈtiː/ **(value added tax)** (finance) A tax charged on most goods and services paid for by the customer. VAT is not charged on books, newspapers and magazines, heating and lighting fuels, public transport fares, postal services and food bought in a shop for cooking at home (meals in restaurants and hot take-away meals, like *fish and chips*, include a VAT charge in the price). The current rate is 15% of the basic cost and this is added to the price at time of payment.

Vaughan Williams, Ralph /ˌvɔːn ˈwɪljəmz, reɪf/ (people) Probably more than any other British composer, Ralph Vaughan Williams (1872–1958) was the true founder of a nationalist movement in English music. His great interest was English folksong, and this, combined with his interest in early English music, enabled him to develop a style that was both typically 'English' and very original (eg, his 'Sinfonia Antartica' of 1952). Many of his short pieces are very popular, such as the early song 'Linden Lea' (1902) and the stirring hymn-tune 'For All the Saints'. He was awarded the *Order of Merit* for his services to English music.

VC /ˌviː ˈsiː/**, the (Victoria Cross, the)** (defence) The highest British decoration, awarded for 'conspicuous bravery or devotion to the country in the presence of the enemy'. It was founded by Queen Victoria in 1856 and has been awarded fewer than 1,400 times since then (over 600 of these in the First World War). It shows the royal crown with a lion above it. Under the crown are the words, 'For Valour'.

verger /ˈvɜːdʒə(r)/ (religion) **1** An official in the *Church of*

England who acts as a general caretaker in a *church* and often also looks after the vestments (priests' robes) and church furnishings. **2** A similar official who carries a verge (rod) of office in front of a bishop or other important person in church services and ceremonies, usually in a cathedral.

Very Reverend /ˌverɪ ˈrevərənd/**, the (Very Rev, the)** (religion) The title given to a *dean*[3] in the *Church of England* (eg, 'The Very Reverend the Dean of Ely').

veteran car /ˌvetərən ˌkɑː(r)/ (transport) An old, usually carefully preserved, motor-car, technically one built before 1905. Compare *vintage car*, and see also *Veteran Car Run*.

veteran car

Veteran Car Run /ˌvetərən ˈkɑː rʌn/**, the** (transport) An annual race of *veteran cars* from *London* to *Brighton*, organized by the *RAC* and usually held on the first *Sunday* in November.

vicar /ˈvɪkə(r)/ (religion) A clergyman appointed to be the priest of a parish in the *Church of England*. Compare *rector*[1].

vicarage /ˈvɪkərɪdʒ/ (religion) The house provided by the *Church Commissioners* for a vicar in the *Church of England*. Compare *rectory*.

Vice Squad /'vaɪs skwɒd/, **the** (law) A police department dealing with prostitution, gambling, pornography and similar offences.

vice-chancellor /ˌvaɪs 'tʃɑːnsələ(r)/ (education) The executive and administrative head of a university, usually elected or appointed for a fixed number of years from among the senior members of the university, in particular the heads of *colleges¹*. Compare *chancellor*.

Victoria /vɪk'tɔːrɪə/ (transport) **1** A main line railway station in central *London*, and a Southern Region terminus of *BR*. **2** An Underground railway station here. See *London Underground*. [main line station was opened in 1860 and named in honour of *Queen Victoria*]

Victoria and Albert Museum /vɪkˌtɔːrɪə ənd ˌælbət mjuːˈzɪəm/, **the (V and A, the)** (arts) A famous museum in south central *London*, housing a national collection of fine and applied art of all countries and periods, especially collections of sculpture, water-colours, miniatures and a large art library. It grew out of the Museum of Manufactures established at *Marlborough House* in 1852, and was given its present name (in honour of *Queen Victoria* and her husband, Prince Albert) when founded in its present form, in 1899.

Victoria Cross /vɪkˌtɔːrɪə 'krɒs/ see *VC* (defence)

Victoria plum /vɪkˌtɔːrɪə 'plʌm/ (food and drink) A late-ripening dessert plum with round, dark red or yellow fruit and a delicious flavour. [named after *Queen Victoria*]

Victorian /vɪk'tɔːrɪən/ (history) A term used to refer to the times of *Queen Victoria* (reigned 1837–1901), who was considered to be, somewhat mistakenly, narrow-minded, hypocritical and humourless.

Victoriana /ˌvɪktɔːrɪ'ɑːnə/ (style) Objects manufactured in the reign of *Queen Victoria* (reigned 1837–1901), in particular ornaments, furnishings and household items. Such objects are sought after by many collectors and have, therefore, come to acquire a value and rarity much greater than their true worth.

Victory /'vɪktərɪ/, **the** (history) The flagship of Admiral Nelson at the Battle of *Trafalgar*, now preserved at Portsmouth, Hampshire, and open to the public.

village college /ˌvɪlɪdʒ 'kɒlɪdʒ/ (education) A centre, serving one or more villages, that provides educational and sports facilities, the former usually at post-school level. Such colleges grew up in the 1930s and currently only five still exist, all in Cambridgeshire.

village green /ˌvɪlɪdʒ 'griːn/ (daily life) A grass area of common land found in or near the centre of many villages and often serving as a recreational area or as a site for *fêtes* and other public gatherings.

village hall /ˌvɪlɪdʒ 'hɔːl/ (daily life) A kind of *community centre* in a village, often a smallish hall hired out for dances, *jumble sales*, public meetings, etc.

village idiot /ˌvɪlɪdʒ 'ɪdɪət/**, the** (tradition) A colloquial, somewhat dated, term for an eccentric or perhaps mentally disturbed person. The term was originally used for such a person who lived in a particular village and was well-known to the other inhabitants.

vintage car /ˌvɪntɪdʒ 'kɑ:(r)/ (transport) An old, usually carefully preserved, motor-car, technically one built between 1919 and 1930. Compare *veteran car*.

VISA (card) /'vi:zə (kɑ:d)/ (finance) One of the two main credit cards issued by British banks, the other being the *Access card*. The main banks issuing VISA cards are *Barclays* (as a *Barclaycard*), the *Bank of Scotland*, the *Trustee Savings Bank* and the Co-operative (Co-op) Bank (operated by the *Co-operative Wholesale Society*). VISA is an international system, and is currently one of the largest consumer payments organizations in the world.

Vogue /vəʊg/ (media) A monthly fashion magazine, with features and articles on a wide range of cultural and other subjects of interest to women. It was first published in 1916 and had a circulation in 1984 of nearly 166,000.

voluntary school /'vɒləntrɪ sku:l/ (education) A school maintained by an *LEA* but founded by a voluntary body, usually a religious denomination such as the *Church of England* or the *Roman Catholic Church*. In 1982 almost 22% of all students in *state schools* attended a voluntary school. (The majority of other state schools are known as *county schools*.) See *church school*.

voting system /'vəʊtɪŋ ˌsɪstəm/ (government) In a *general election* or a local election, each voter casts one vote in a secret ballot for the candidate he or she wishes to support. The vote is normally made in person at a *polling station*. Voting is not compulsory, and in the general election of 1983 just under 73% of the electorate voted. The candidate who polls the most votes is elected (see *'first past the post'*), and in political elections there is no *proportional representation*, as in some countries.

V-sign /'vi: saɪn/ (daily life) **1** A sign formed with the forefinger and middle finger of the hand (forming a 'V') with the palm turned outwards and the thumb holding down the third and fourth fingers, indicating victory (as in war, a match or an election). **2** A similar sign but with the palm turned inwards, and usually accompanied by an abrupt upward thrust of the arm, indicating contempt, defiance or general frustration. [in second sense, sign has sexual symbolism]

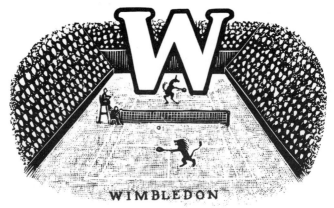

WIMBLEDON

W H Smith /ˌdʌblju: ˌeɪtʃ 'smɪθ/ (commerce) The full name of the chain-store stationery and record shops known more popularly as *Smith's*.

wakes week /'weɪks wi:k/ (tradition) An annual holiday in certain towns of the north of *England*, when factories and schools close for a week (occasionally two weeks).

Waldorf (Hotel) /'wɔ:ldɔ:f (ˌwɔ:ldɔ:f həu'tel)/**, the** (London) A luxury hotel in central *London*. [named after William Waldorf Astor, 1st Viscount Astor, Anglo-American financier (1848–1919)]

Walker Cup /ˌwɔ:kə 'kʌp/**, the** (sport and leisure) A biennial golf tournament between amateur players of *Britain* and the United States, held since 1922 alternately in Britain and the United States. Compare *Ryder Cup*. [named after George H Walker, the American golfer who organized the event]

Wales /weɪlz/ (geography) The most westerly part of mainland *Britain*, bordered on the east by *England*. Wales (properly the 'Principality of Wales') is the smallest land of the *United Kingdom*, but has considerable variety, from the picturesque mountains of the north (including *Snowdonia*) to the mining and industrial areas of the south. Wales now has its own £1 coin with a picture of a *leek* on one side of it. Welsh is still spoken in some parts of the country and in recent years there has been increasing interest in encouraging the use of this Celtic language, especially in schools and by radio and television. See *S4C, eisteddfod*.

Wallace Collection /'wɒlɪs kəˌlekʃn/**, the** (arts) A collection of paintings, furniture and armour in central *London*, bequeathed to the nation by the widow of the art collector Sir Richard Wallace in 1897. A distinctive feature of the Collection is the French furniture and paintings of the 18th century.

Wandsworth (Prison) /'wɒndzwəθ (ˌwɒndzwəθ 'prɪzn)/ (law) The largest prison in *Britain*, founded in 1851 in the village (now *London borough²*) of Wandsworth.

War on Want /ˌwɔ:r ɒn 'wɒnt/ (charities) A charitable organization collecting funds for the aid of poor and underprivileged people in many countries of the world.

ward /wɔːd/ (government) A district of a *city*, town or other area, used chiefly as an administrative unit in a political election such as a *by-election* or *general election*, with each ward having its own *polling station*.

warden /'wɔːdn/ (**1** education **2** daily life) **1** The head of certain *colleges*[1,2] and higher or specialized educational establishments (eg, All Souls College at *Oxford University* or Lincoln Theological College). **2** The short title of a *churchwarden* or *traffic warden*.

Wardour Street /'wɔːdə striːt/ (London) A central street in *London*, famous for its many offices connected with the film industry. [street named after family who built it in 17th century]

Wars of the Roses /ˌwɔːz əv ðə 'rəʊzɪz/, **the** (history) The wars in the second half of the 15th century between the house of York (whose symbol was a white rose) and the house of Lancaster (symbolized by a red rose). The aim of each side was to win the throne of *England* and each was sometimes successful. The Wars ended in 1485 when Henry *Tudor* (house of Lancaster) defeated Richard III (house of York) and became *Henry VIII*. Henry's marriage to Elizabeth of York united the two sides and ended the fighting. See *rose*.

Wash /wɒʃ/, **the** (geography) A large but shallow inlet of the North Sea (15 miles long, 12 miles wide) between Lincolnshire and Norfolk. Much of the agricultural land round the Wash has been reclaimed from the sea over a period of many years.

watch night service /'wɒtʃ naɪt ˌsɜːvɪs/ (religion) A service held in some *church*es, or in a public place such as a square, on the night of 31 December (*New Year's Eve*), to mark the passing of the old year and to pray for what the New Year will bring.

Waterloo /ˌwɔːtə'luː/ (transport) **1** A main line railway station in *London*, south of the *Thames*, and a terminus of the Southern Region of *BR*. **2** An Underground railway station here. See *London Underground*. [main line station named after Waterloo Bridge, built here over the Thames in 1817 to mark the victory of the Battle of *Waterloo*]

Waterloo /ˌwɔːtə'luː/ (**Battle of Waterloo, the**) (history) The final battle of the Napoleonic Wars, in which in 1815 near the village of Waterloo, Belgium, the English forces under the Duke of Wellington, with the support of Prussian forces under Field Marshal Blücher, gained a victory over the French army of Napoleon.

Waterloo and City Line /ˌwɔːtəluː ən 'sɪtɪ laɪn/, **the** (transport) One of the oldest Underground railway lines, *London*, linking *Waterloo*[1,2] with the *City (of London)*. It is mainly used by businessmen who live in the southern *Home Counties* and who travel to and from London via Waterloo main line station. The Line is operated by the Southern

Region of *BR*, not by *London Regional Transport*, and is closed on *Sundays*. See *London Underground*.

Watling Street /'wɒtlɪŋ striːt/ (history) One of the main *Roman roads* in *Britain*, running from Dover, Kent, through *Canterbury* to *London* and then north to St Albans, Hertfordshire and Wroxeter, Shropshire. [said to come from an old name of St Albans]

wedding breakfast /'wedɪŋ ˌbrekfəst/ (food and drink) A meal (not breakfast) served to guests at the reception that follows a wedding ceremony.

Wedgwood /'wedʒwʊd/ (style) A famous make of pottery and china. The most famous Wedgwood design has raised classical-style decorations in white on a pale blue background. [named after the potter Josiah Wedgwood (1730–95), who established a pottery near Stoke-on-Trent, Staffordshire in the late 18th century; see also *Potteries*]

weekend /ˌwiːk'end/ (daily life) Traditionally, the period of relaxation and holiday between one working week and the next, extending from early Friday evening to *Sunday* night.

welfare officer /'welfeər ˌɒfɪsə(r)/ (law) An alternative term for a *social worker* or *probation officer* who supervises the well-being and behaviour of a former juvenile criminal.

welfare state /ˌwelfeə 'steɪt/, **the** (government) A system by which the government provides the economic and social security of the population through its organization of health services, pensions and other facilities. In *Britain* the term applies mainly to the *NHS*, *national insurance* and *social security*.

welfare worker /'welfeə ˌwɜːkə(r)/ (charities) A person who helps the underprivileged, poor or needy, especially the sick, elderly and handicapped, usually through a voluntary (charity) organization.

wellies /'welɪz/ (clothing) A colloquial name for *wellington boots*, especially those worn by children.

wellington boots /ˌwelɪŋtən 'buːts/ **(wellingtons)** (clothing) Knee-length (less often, calf-length) rubber boots, worn in wet weather or over wet ground. [they look like the leather boots worn by the Duke of Wellington (1769-1852)]

Welsh Guards /ˌwelʃ 'gɑːdz/, **the** (defence) The most recently formed *Army* regiment of the *Guards Division*, established in 1915 from a group of Welshmen in the *Grenadier Guards*.

Welsh pony /ˌwelʃ 'pəʊnɪ/ (animal world) A small, sturdy breed of pony, used mainly for *pony-trekking* but also for leisure riding. [originally bred in *Wales*]

Welsh rarebit /ˌwelʃ 'ræbɪt/ **(Welsh rabbit)** (food and drink) A savoury dish consisting of melted cheese, sometimes with milk added, on hot *toast*. [originally 'Welsh rabbit', although never containing rabbit's meat]

Wembley /'wemblɪ/ (sport and leisure) A large sports stadium in northwest *Greater London*, where several important *football*, *rugby football* and hockey matches are held, including the *FA Cup* (see also *Cup Final*). In the large arena here matches and contests are held at international level in many other sports, such as badminton, basketball, boxing, cycling, ice hockey, show-jumping, tennis and table tennis.

wellington boots

Wendy house /ˈwendɪ haʊs/ (sport and leisure) A toy house that young children can play inside. [named after the house built for Wendy, the young heroine of the play *'Peter Pan*[1]*'* (1904) by J M Barrie]

Wensleydale (cheese) /ˈwenzlɪdeɪl (ˌwenzlɪdeɪl ˈtʃiːz)/ (food and drink) A white, crumbly cheese with a mild taste, originally produced in Wensleydale (a valley in North Yorkshire where the village of Wensley is located).

Wentworth /ˈwentwəθ/ (sport and leisure) A famous golf *club* and course in Virginia Water, Surrey. [on land formerly owned by a Mrs Wentworth (died 1816)]

West Brom /ˌwest ˈbrɒm/ (sport and leisure) The colloquial abbreviation for the West Midlands town of West Bromwich, especially when speaking of its *football club*, *West Bromwich Albion*.

West Bromwich Albion /ˌwest brɒmɪdʒ ˈælbɪən/ (sport and leisure) A popular *football club* founded in 1879, with a stadium (The Hawthorns) in West Bromwich, West Midlands. ['Albion' is a poetic name for *Britain* or *England*]

West Country /ˈwest ˌkʌntrɪ/, **the** (geography) The southwest of *England*, especially the *counties* of *Cornwall*, Devon and Somerset.

West End /ˌwest ˈend/, **the** (London) The area of west central *London* that contains the main fashionable shopping streets, *clubs*, high-class hotels, cinemas and theatres. Compare *East End*.

West Ham (United) /ˌwest ˈhæm (ˌwest hæm juːˈnaɪtɪd)/ (sport and leisure) A well-known *football club* founded in 1900, with a stadium in West Ham, east *London*.

Western Approaches /ˌwestən əˈprəʊtʃɪz/, **the** (geography) The western shipping lanes of the English Channel, south of *Cornwall* and Devon.

Westminster /ˈwestmɪnstə(r)/ (1 London 2 government) **1** A *borough*[2] of central *London*, on the river *Thames*, containing several important buildings, including the *Houses of Parliament* and *Buckingham Palace*. **2** An alternative term for the Houses of Parliament, especially in the sense of the government of the day.

Westminster Abbey /ˌwestmɪnstər ˈæbɪ/ (religion) One of the leading landmarks of *London*: a fine *Early English church* in *Westminster*[1] where almost all the English sovereigns have been crowned since the 11th century, and where many famous Englishmen and women are buried. (See also *Poets' Corner*, *Unknown Warrior*, *Stone of Scone*.)

Westminster Cathedral /ˌwestmɪnstə kəˈθiːdrəl/ (religion) The principal *Roman Catholic Church* in *England*, in *Westminster*[1], *London*. The large church was built in neo-Byzantine style in the late 19th century.

Westminster Hall /ˌwestmɪnstə ˈhɔːl/ (London) A large hall in *Westminster*[1], *London*, the only surviving part of the old *Palace of Westminster*[1], and one of the finest medieval halls in western Europe. The Hall was formerly a royal residence and in recent times the bodies of many sovereigns have lain in state here.

Westminster School /ˌwestmɪnstə ˈskuːl/ (education) One of the best known *public schools*[1], founded in 1560 in *Westminster*[1], *London*, and having nearly 600 students.

wet /wet/ (politics) A colloquial term for a *Conservative Party* politician who in the 1980s opposed the aggressive or 'hard line' policies of the *Prime Minister* (Margaret *Thatcher*, from 1975). [from slang 'wet' in sense 'favouring easy or conventional approach', 'ineffective']

wheel clamp /ˈwiːl klæmp/ (law) A device introduced by the *Metropolitan Police Force* in *London* in 1983 to prevent illegally parked cars from being driven away by their owners. It consists of a heavy lock or clamp that is fitted to one wheel of the vehicle. The clamp can only be removed by a policeman using a special key.

Which? /wɪtʃ/ (media) The monthly magazine of the *Consumers Association*, containing factual reports and details of the quality, content and performance of a range of consumer products and services. The magazine usually recommends a 'best buy' for each of the products it examines. 'Which?' is available only to members of the Consumers

Association. It was first published in 1957, and now has several related supplements, eg, 'Motoring Which?', 'Money Which?' and 'Handyman Which?' (the last for *DIY* enthusiasts). Its average circulation is 650,000.

wheel clamp

whip /wɪp/ (politics) **1** An *MP* in the *House of Commons*, or a *peer* in the *House of Lords*, appointed to organize the members of his party in parliamentary procedures, and in particular to ensure their participation in votes and debates. See also *Chief Whip*. **2** A schedule of parliamentary business sent out from time to time by a whip[1] to members of his party. See also *three-line whip[1]*. [term derives from 'whips' or 'whippers-in' employed by a *hunt* to control and discipline the hounds]

whippet /'wɪpɪt/ (animal world) A breed of thin, short-haired racing dog resembling (and probably originating from) a small *greyhound*. The dog is especially popular in the north of *England*.

Whipsnade (Zoo) /'wɪpsneɪd (ˌwɪpsneɪd 'zu:)/ (animal world) A large open-air zoo for over 2,000 animals near Dunstable, Bedfordshire, opened by the Zoological Society of London (see *London Zoo*) in 1931. The zoo occupies a park of 500 acres (200 hectares) in area. There are few cages at the zoo and most animals are kept in open enclosures. [named after nearby village of Whipsnade]

whiskey /'wɪskɪ/ (food and drink) The usual spelling for *whisky* made in *Ireland* or the United States.

whisky /'wɪskɪ/ (food and drink) The traditional spirit drink of *Scotland*, made by distilling fermented cereals, especially malted barley. It is usually taken mixed with another drink, either alcoholic (eg, ginger wine, to make a *whisky mac*) or non-alcoholic (eg, soda water), although some whisky drinkers prefer the drink 'neat' (undiluted). Its country of origin gives it the popular alternative name of *Scotch*. Compare *whiskey*.

whisky mac /ˌwɪskɪ 'mæk/ (food and drink) A drink consisting of a mixture of *whisky* and ginger wine. ['mac' for the characteristic Scottish surname beginning 'Mac-' or 'Mc-' (as 'Macdonald' or 'McDonald')]

Whispering Gallery /'wɪspərɪŋ ˌgælərɪ/, **the** (London) A famous gallery in *St Paul's (Cathedral), London*. It runs right round the inside of the lower section of the dome. If someone who is standing near the wall on one side whispers some words, those words can be heard near the wall on the opposite side, 107 feet (32 m) away.

Whit Monday /ˌwɪt 'mʌndɪ/ (tradition) The day following *Whit Sunday*, for many years (until the 1960s) one of the most popular *bank holidays* of the year. The name is still used unofficially for the *spring bank holiday* (which sometimes coincides with Whit Monday in the *church* calendar).

Whit Sunday /ˌwɪt 'sʌndɪ/ (religion) A major festival in the Christian *church* that falls on the seventh *Sunday* after *Easter*. The day is named after the white robes formerly worn by converts to the church admitted at this time. The festival is still a popular occasion in some churches for the christening (baptism) of babies, also dressed in white.

Whitaker's Almanack /ˌwɪtəkəz 'ɔːlmənæk/ (media) A well-known annual reference book, containing a wide range of information, facts and figures about *Britain* and all the countries of the world. The Almanack also includes detailed astronomical data. It was first published by Joseph Whitaker in 1868 and is still issued by the publishing house he founded (today, J Whitaker & Sons).

White City /ˌwaɪt 'sɪtɪ/, **the** (sport and leisure) A large open-air complex for sports and shows in west *London*, opened in 1908. It is particularly noted for the athletics, *greyhound racing* and show-jumping contests held here. [properly, White City Stadium; named after the colour of the buildings when first built]

White Ensign /ˌwaɪt 'ensən/, **the** (defence) The official ensign (flag) of the *Royal Navy*, consisting of a *St George's cross* on a white background with the *Union Jack* in the top left quarter (nearest the flagstaff). It is flown at the stern of all Royal Navy ships in daylight hours. It is also flown on the flagstaff of land naval establishments.

White Hart Lane /ˌwaɪt hɑːt 'leɪn/ (sport and leisure) The stadium of *Tottenham Hotspur football club* in north *London*. [named after street where it is; street named after *inn* here]

white horse /ˌwaɪt 'hɔːs/ (history) One of a number of large figures of horses carved out of the chalk hills at several points in the south of *England*, especially in the Vale of the White Horse, Berkshire and in Wiltshire. Many of the figures were made in prehistoric times.

white paper /ˌwaɪt 'peɪpə(r)/ (government) An official report setting out the government's policy on a matter being discussed, or about to be discussed, in *Parliament*.

white tie /ˌwaɪt 'taɪ/ (clothing) A conventional indication on an invitation card that formal men's *evening dress* is to be worn.

White Tower /ˌwaɪt 'taʊə(r)/, **the** (history) The oldest part of the *Tower of London*, built in the 11th century and one of the largest *Norman* keeps in western Europe. The Tower, which is built in white stone imported from Normandy, is in the centre of the whole fortress and contains a fine collection of arms and armour. It is believed by some that the White Tower was the site of the murder of the *Princes in the Tower*, since the bones of two children were found here in the 17th century.

white-collar worker /ˌwaɪt 'kɒlə ˌwɜːkə(r)/ (work) A person who does clerical or professional work, not manual work. Such people used to wear white shirts in contrast to the overalls (often blue) of a manual or *blue-collar worker*.

Whitehall /'waɪthɔːl/ (1 London 2 government) 1 A street in central *London* running from *Trafalgar Square* to the *Houses of Parliament* and containing many important buildings and government offices. 2 A term used for the government itself. [street named after former Whitehall Palace here, of which only the *Banqueting House* survives]

Whitehouse, Mary /'waɪthaʊs, 'meərɪ/ (people) Mary Whitehouse (born 1910) became well-known in the 1960s and 1970s for her crusading campaign against what she believed to be sexual permissiveness on television. She also criticized violence and bad language. In 1965 she founded the National Viewers' and Listeners' Association, with an initial membership of 31,000. Mrs Whitehouse believed in matching deeds with words, and accordingly she took several cases to the law courts. Although she did not win all the cases, she did succeed in overturning a proposal to abolish film censorship in *London* (in 1975), and also brought a successful conviction of blasphemous libel against the magazine 'Gay News' in 1977.

Whitley Council /ˌwɪtlɪ 'kaʊnsl/ (work) An industrial council, at national or local level, that meets regularly to discuss and settle conditions of employment in the workplace. It is composed of representatives of employers and employees at all levels of a particular work force. [established as the result of a report made in 1917 by J H Whitley, an *MP*]

Who's Who /ˌhuːz 'huː/ (media) An annual biographical reference book of distinguished or titled (aristocratic) British people, giving (in the person's own words) details of his or her birth, family, career, posts held, special interests and current address and *club*. The work was first published in 1848, and today includes some entries for distinguished non-British people. However, few popular personalities are included. The interests ('recreations') given by some of the people are deliberately not serious, such as those of the writer Patricia Highsmith (snail-watching) or the pianist John Lill (avoiding the media).

WI /ˌdʌblju: 'aɪ/, **the (Women's Institute, the)** (life and society) A local branch of the National Federation of Women's Institutes, an organization founded in 1915 with the aim of improving and developing the lives of women who live in rural areas. The Federation, through its many local branches, offers a wide range of social and cultural activities and courses. It also runs a number of country markets as part of the weekly markets held in *market towns* and cities. It has its own *further education* establishment. In 1982 there were 384,000 members in over 9,000 local branches thoughout *England* and *Wales*.

Wightman Cup /ˌwaɪtmən 'kʌp/, **the** (sport and leisure) An annual contest between women tennis players of *Britain* and the United States, and also the prize awarded to the winning team. The contest was begun in 1923 by the American tennis champion Hazel Wightman. The matches are played alternately in Britain and the United States (in Britain, at *Wimbledon* regularly until the early 1970s).

Wigmore Hall /ˌwɪgmɔ: 'hɔ:l/, **the** (arts) A *London* concert hall opened in 1901 and used mainly for recitals of chamber music and songs. [in Wigmore Street]

William and Mary (style) /ˌwɪljəm ən 'meərɪ (staɪl)/ (style) A furniture style of the end of the 17th century, characterized by finely carved wooden chairs with upholstered seats, elegant tables and cabinets and a fashion for tallboys (high chests of drawers), with much use of walnut and exotic woods. [named after King William and Queen Mary who ruled together over the period 1688–94]

William Shakespeare /ˌwɪljəm 'ʃeɪkspɪə(r)/ see *Shakespeare* (people)

willow pattern /'wɪləʊ ˌpætn/ (style) A popular pattern on pottery and porcelain, usually in blue on a white background, and showing a stylized oriental scene of figures by a willow tree and a bridge over a river. [designed in the late 18th century by the potter Thomas Turner]

Wilton (carpet) /'wɪltən (ˌwɪltən 'kɑ:pɪt)/ (style) A type of thick wool carpet. Most are plain and of just one colour, but some have an oriental pattern. They were first made at Wilton, Wiltshire.

Wimbledon /'wɪmbldən/ (sport and leisure) The short name of the *All England Club*, in the district of Wimbledon, southwest

Greater London, where annual international tennis championships are held.

willow pattern

Winchester (College) /ˈwɪntʃɪstə(r) (ˌwɪntʃɪstə ˈkɒlɪdʒ/ (education) A well-known *public school*[1] in Winchester, Hampshire, founded in 1382 by the bishop of Winchester, William of Wykeham. It has 630 students.

Windermere /ˈwɪndəmɪə(r)/ (geography) The largest natural lake in *England*, in the *Lake District*. It is $10\frac{1}{2}$ miles long and 1 mile wide. It is a popular tourist centre with many hotels and facilities for yachting, boating and fishing, and during the summer there is a regular boat service from one end to the other.

Windmill Theatre /ˌwɪndmɪl ˈθɪətə(r)/, **the** (London) A *London* theatre once famous for its non-stop variety shows with nearly nude girls, and for its slogan 'We never close', referring to the fact that it was the only London theatre to remain open throughout the Second World War. Many well-known comedians began their career here. After a period as a cinema in the 1960s it reopened in the early 1970s, also as a variety theatre but with sex revues that today lack the former element of comedy.

Windscale /ˈwɪndskeɪl/ see *Sellafield* (science and technology)

Windsor Castle /ˌwɪnzə ˈkɑːsl/ (royal family) An official residence of the sovereign, in Windsor, Berkshire. William the *Conqueror* began to build the Castle in the 11th century and it is now one of the most famous royal palaces in Europe. Some of the interior apartments are open to the public when the sovereign is not in residence, but the Albert Memorial Chapel is open throughout the year, being closed only on

Sundays. *St George's Chapel*, however, is the better known of the two chapels, both because many members of the *royal family* go to a service there on *Christmas Day* and because the *Order of the Garter* holds its special services there.

Windsor chair /ˌwɪnzə ˈtʃeə(r)/ (style) A style of strong wooden chair popular from the late 18th century, with a shaped seat, a back containing slender, rod-shaped uprights and straight arm-rests. [originally made in Windsor, Berkshire, but later also in *Wales*]

Winnie the Pooh /ˌwɪnɪ ðə ˈpuː/ (arts) The toy bear ('of very little brain') who is the constant companion of the child hero, Christopher Robin, in the children's books by A A Milne (1882–1956), 'Winnie the Pooh' (1926) and 'The House at Pooh Corner' (1928). As with Lewis *Carroll*'s children's books, A A Milne's 'Pooh' books have come to be widely loved by adults. Christopher Robin was the author's young son, and Winnie the Pooh represents the boy's teddy bear that accompanied him everywhere.

Winston Churchill /ˌwɪnstən ˈtʃɜːtʃɪl/ see *Churchill* (people)

winter of discontent /ˌwɪntər əv dɪskənˈtent/ (1 work 2 life and society) 1 The winter of 1978–9, when severe industrial unrest, including strikes by car production workers, lorry drivers and local government and hospital workers, forced the Labour government (see *Labour Party*) to hold a general election (which was won by the *Conservative Party*). The political and economic troubles were accompanied by the worst winter weather experienced in *Britain* for 15 years. 2 A colloquial or journalistic term for any winter more recent that has been marked by political or industrial unrest, especially when accompanied by bad weather. [quotation from *Shakespeare*'s Richard III: 'Now is the winter of our discontent']

Wisden /ˈwɪzdən/ (sport and leisure) A well-known *cricket* reference book. A new edition is published each year, giving full details of professional cricket matches and the performance of well-known cricketers. The book was first published in 1864 by the cricketer John Wisden. [full title, 'Wisden Cricketers' Almanack']

Woburn Abbey /ˌwuːbən ˈæbɪ/ (arts) An 18th-century *country house* near Luton, Bedfordshire, the home of the Duke of Bedford. The house and grounds are open to the public, who come to see the valuable collection of paintings and furniture in the house and the large deer park and bird sanctuary in the grounds. There is also an antiques market.

Wodehouse, P G /ˈwʊdhaʊs, ˌpiː ˈdʒiː/ (people) P G Wodehouse (1881–1975) is best known for his comic novels of *upper class* life about the young bachelor, Bertie Wooster, and his manservant, Jeeves. The novels are set either in elegant flats in *Mayfair*, *London*, or in grand baronial castles in the country, and the same characters feature over and over again, presenting a humorously exaggerated picture of English aristocratic social life in the early part of the 20th century. Wodehouse wrote more than 90 novels, and about a third of these involve Bertie Wooster and Jeeves. Wodehouse also wrote plays, musical comedy lyrics and film scripts, and in 1955 became an American citizen.

Wolverhampton Wanderers /ˌwʊlvəhæmptən 'wɒndərəz/ (sport and leisure) A famous *football club*, founded in 1877, with a stadium in Wolverhampton, West Midlands.

Wolves /wʊlvz/ (sport and leisure) The nickname of *Wolverhampton Wanderers football club*.

Woman /'wʊmən/ (media) A popular illustrated weekly magazine for women, containing fashion details, short stories and serial stories, often on romantic themes. It also has practical advice and hints for housewives, and a variety of articles of general interest. It was first published in 1937 and has a circulation of over 1.3 million.

Woman's Hour /'wʊmənz aʊə(r)/ (media) A daily hour-long radio programme of topical and general interest to women, broadcast each weekday afternoon on *Radio 4* since 1946.

Woman's Own /ˌwʊmənz 'əʊn/ (media) A popular illustrated weekly magazine for women, containing short stories and serial stories, often with a strong romantic theme, as well as practical advice and hints for housewives. It also has articles on home decoration, furnishing, fashion and features of general interest. The magazine was first published in 1932 and had a circulation in 1984 of over 1.2 million.

Woman's Realm /ˌwʊmənz 'relm/ (media) An illustrated weekly magazine for women, particularly young housewives with growing families, containing a wide range of articles and features on topical subjects and popular personalities. It also has short stories and serials and regular items of general interest to women in the home. The magazine was first published in 1958 and has a circulation of over 618,000.

Woman's Weekly /ˌwʊmənz 'wiːklɪ/ (media) A popular illustrated weekly magazine for women for all ages and their families, containing short stories and serials of strong romantic interest, as well as features on personalities and their autobiographical memoirs. It also has articles of general interest. The magazine was first published in 1911 and has a circulation of over 1.4 million.

Woman's World /ˌwʊmənz 'wɜːld/ (media) An illustrated monthly magazine for women, containing profiles of personalities in the news, articles on subjects of topical interest and factual articles on family and romantic relationships. It also has items of practical interest to the young housewife as well as short stories. The magazine was first published in 1977 and has a circulation of over 277,000.

woolsack /'wʊlsæk/, **the** (tradition) The seat on which the *Lord Chancellor* (as *Speaker*²) sits in the *House of Lords*. At present this is a large square cushion of wool, without back or arms, covered with red cloth. Originally there were four sacks of wool on which the sovereign's counsellor sat in medieval times.

Woolworth's /'wʊlwəθs/ (commerce) One of a large chain of stores, found in most towns in *Britain*, and developing in 1909 from the equivalent stores in the United States founded by Frank Winfield Woolworth in 1879. For many years the Woolworth stores sold goods at two cheap prices only (threepence and sixpence). Today, the stores stock a large range of goods, from confectionery to home computers, and some of the bigger branches also have a restaurant. [in full, F W Woolworth & Co]

Worcester (china) /'wʊstə(r) (ˌwʊstə 'tʃaɪnə)/ (style) A type of superior porcelain made in Worcester since 1751, and particularly popular as table-ware.

Worcester sauce /ˌwʊstə 'sɔːs/ (food and drink) A strong-flavoured sauce made with vinegar and spices, originally produced in Worcester.

work-in /'wɜːkɪn/ (work) A form of strike in which workers occupy a factory that is due to close down and attempt to continue working in it.

working class /'wɜːkɪŋ klɑːs/ (life and society) A social class of low status, made up almost entirely of manual workers but ranking above *lower class*. Some class-conscious manual workers are proud to be regarded as working class, seeing this as the productive base on which all the other social classes depend. Similarly, working class people who have risen to a higher class are often proud of their former status.

working men's club /ˌwɜːkɪŋ menz 'klʌb/ (sport and leisure) A local *club* in a town or *city* for *working class* men, who meet their work mates there to enjoy games such as *darts* and cards, to drink, or to watch an entertainment of some kind (often a comedy show, with or without a strip-tease act). The working men's club is thus a blend of a modern *pub* and an old-style music hall.

work-to-rule /ˌwɜːk tə 'ruːl/ (work) A form of strike or industrial protest in which workers or employees keep strictly to all the rules, thus slowing the rate of working or production.

World Service /ˌwɜːld 'sɜːvɪs/ see *BBC World Service* (media)

Wormwood Scrubs /ˌwɜːmwʊd 'skrʌbz/ (law) A large prison for first-time male offenders, in northwest *London*. It was opened in 1874. [name of original site here, with 'scrubs' meaning 'woods']

Worship /'wɜːʃɪp/ (life and society) A title (preceded by 'Your', 'His' or 'Her') used to refer to a number of people of high rank, in particular a *mayor* and a *magistrate*.

WRAC /ˌdʌbljuː ɑːr eɪ 'siː/, **the (Women's Royal Army Corps, the)** (defence) The women's branch of the British *Army*, begun as the Auxiliary Territorial Service (ATS) in 1938 and renamed in 1949. Women can be employed in many of the trade groups available to men. In the Second World War many women in the ATS, for example, worked as members of gun crews in anti-aircraft installations in *Britain*. Some women went overseas to be drivers for senior Army officers or work at coding and deciphering secret messages.

WRAF /ˌdʌblju: ɑːr eɪ 'ef/, **the (Women's Royal Air Force, the)** (defence) The women's branch of the *RAF*, originally formed in the First World War and known as the Women's Auxiliary Air Force (WAAF) from 1939 to 1949. Women can be employed in many of the trade groups available to men, but do not fly in any kind of aircraft.

Wren /ren/ (defence) A name for a member of the *WRNS*. [name based on initials WRNS, but influenced by the name of the bird, noted for its small size, chattering and alertness]

writ /rɪt/ (law) A legal document requiring the person to whom it is addressed to do some specific act, or not to do it. It may be served by a *bailiff*.

WRNS /ˌdʌblju: ɑːr en 'es/, **the (Women's Royal Naval Service, the)** (defence) The women's section of the *Royal Navy*, first formed in 1917. It was disbanded in 1919 but was re-formed in 1939. Women can work in many of the branches available to men, but usually serve only in shore bases. Only rarely do women go to sea. See *Wrens*.

WRVS /ˌdʌblju: a: vi: 'es/, **the (Women's Royal Voluntary Service, the)** (defence) An organization formed in 1938 to enable women not in the armed services to engage in war work, in particular in the Air Raid Precaution Services. After the Second World War, the WRVS changed its activities to cover welfare work for the armed services, the elderly (delivering *meals on wheels*), children (running holiday schemes and play centres) and the disabled. It also carries out welfare work in prisons. Another of its functions is to collect clothing and furniture and to distribute them to people in need, and to help out in any local emergency such as a flood.

X certificate /ˈeks səˌtɪfɪkət/ (arts) A certificate awarded until 1982 by the *British Board of Film Censors* to a cinema film that was regarded as unsuitable, because of its subject or because of particular scenes, for showing to people aged under 18. The title of the category was changed to *18* (listed under letter E).

Xmas /ˈkrɪsməs/ (tradition) A conventional and commercial abbreviation of *Christmas*. [from the Greek letter 'X' that was used as a symbol for 'Christ' by early Christians]

Yard /jɑːd/, **the** (law) A colloquial term for *Scotland Yard* or *New Scotland Yard*.

ye olde tea shoppe /jiː ˌəʊld 'tiː ʃɒp/ (daily life) A mock Old English spelling of 'the old tea shop', used to refer to a *tea shop* in a historic building. The name is actually used by some tea shops in real or imitation historic buildings. ['ye', meaning 'the', originates from a mistranscription (as 'y') of an old letter representing 'th'; the spellings of 'olde' and 'shoppe' are regarded as typical of medieval English words]

yellow lines /ˌjeləʊ 'laɪnz/ (law) Yellow lines painted along the side of a road or street to indicate waiting restrictions for vehicles. A single yellow line means that no vehicle may wait (park) during the working day (usually from 8.0 am to 6.30 pm) except to load and unload. Two yellow lines close together normally mean that no vehicles may park there at any time.

Yellow Pages /ˌjeləʊ 'peɪdʒɪz/, **the** (commerce) A classified commercial telephone directory that lists subscribers according to their trade or business. It is printed on yellow paper and published by *British Telecom*.

Yeoman Warder /ˌjəʊmən 'wɔːdə(r)/ (tradition) One of the guardians at the *Tower of London*, who wears a similar uniform to that worn by the *Yeomen of the Guard*. Yeomen Warders have apparently existed since the 11th century, when the *White Tower* was built. A Yeoman Warder is popularly nicknamed a *Beefeater* (and this name is also sometimes used for a member of the Yeomen of the Guard).

Yeomen of the Guard /ˌjəʊmən əv ðə 'gɑːd/, **the** (tradition) The men who form the bodyguard of the sovereign on state occasions. The bodyguard was first formed in the late 15th century, and the men still wear the red uniform of that period. Compare *Yeoman Warder*.

YHA /ˌwaɪ eɪtʃ 'eɪ/ see *Youth Hostels Association* (sport and leisure)

YMCA /ˌwaɪ em siː 'eɪ/, **the (Young Men's Christian Association, the)** (charities) A Christian organization offering a wide range of religious, educational, sports and social activities to young men of all races, religions and social backgrounds. It was founded in *Britain* in 1844 but now operates internationally. It is well-known for its regional centres and hostels.

Yeoman Warder

Yorkshire Post /ˌjɔːkʃə ˈpəʊst/, **the** (media) A daily *quality paper* published in Leeds and covering a wide part of West Yorkshire and nearby areas. Although it is a regional newspaper, the Yorkshire Post is noted for its influential views and its support of the *Conservative Party*. It was first published in 1754 (as the 'Leeds Intelligencer') and has a circulation of over 92,000.

Yorkshire pudding /ˌjɔːkʃə ˈpʊdɪŋ/ (food and drink) A light savoury dish baked from a batter of flour, eggs and milk, and traditionally served with roast beef (usually for the main course of the midday meal on *Sunday*). See also *Sunday roast*.

Yorkshire Ripper /ˌjɔːkʃə ˈrɪpə(r)/, **the** (law) The nickname, widely used by the media, of the criminal Peter Sutcliffe (born 1946), from Bradford, West Yorkshire. He was convicted in 1981 of the murder of thirteen women. [so named from similarity of the crimes to those committed by *Jack the Ripper*]

Yorkshire Terrier /ˌjɔːkʃə ˈterɪə(r)/ (animal world) A small breed of terrier with a long, silky, steel-blue coat. [originally bred in the 19th century in West Yorkshire]

Yorkshire TV /ˌjɔːkʃə tiːˈviː/ (YTV) (media) One of the 15 television companies of the *IBA*, transmitting programmes to the whole of Yorkshire (the three *counties* of North, South and West Yorkshire) and nearby areas. The company is one of the largest and is noted for the high standard of its plays, documentaries and comedy programmes.

Young Pretender /ˌjʌŋ prɪˈtendə(r)/, **the** (history) The nickname of Charles Edward Stuart, the Scottish prince (also known as *Bonnie Prince Charlie*) who was the pretender to (claimant for) the British throne in 1745. See the *Forty-Five*. [named by contrast with his father, James Francis Edward Stuart, nicknamed the Old Pretender]

Young Vic /ˌjʌŋ ˈvɪk/, **the** (arts) A theatre for young playgoers in *London*, founded in 1970 as part of the *National Theatre*. It was built in 1971 opposite the *Old Vic*.

youth club /ˈjuːθ klʌb/ (sport and leisure) A *club* for young people, usually one belonging to the National Association of Youth Clubs. Such a club offers a wide range of sporting and social activities for young people aged mainly between 14 and 21. They are run mainly by voluntary leaders and helpers, and they are frequently associated with a particular *church* or *community centre*.

youth custody centre /ˌjuːθ ˈkʌstədɪ ˌsentə(r)/ (law) An establishment for young offenders of either sex between the ages of 17 and 20 (16 and 21 in *Scotland*). The youth custody centre aims both to be a place of punishment for the offences committed and to provide training which will be useful to the young people later. At present there are 27 such centres. Until the early 1980s they were called *borstals*. Compare *attendance centre*, *community home*, *detention centre*, *remand home*.

youth hostel /ˈjuːθ ˌhɒstl/ (sport and leisure) A hostel run by the *Youth Hostels Association*.

Youth Hostels Association /ˈjuːθ ˌhɒstlz əsəʊsɪˌeɪʃn/, **the (YHA)** (sport and leisure) An organization first formed in *Britain* in 1930 (as a development of the movement founded in Germany in 1910) to provide cheap residential hostels for young travellers, in particular hikers (walkers) and cyclists. The Association is now operated internationally, and in Britain, as in many other countries, membership is not restricted to young people.

Youth Opportunities Programme /ˌjuːθ ɒpəˈtjuːnətɪz ˌprəʊɡræm/, **the (YOP)** (work) A measure introduced by the government in 1981 to provide unemployed school-leavers with work experience and training opportunities for a period of up to two years (until the age of 18). In 1983 it was replaced by the *Youth Training Scheme*.

Youth Training Scheme /ˌjuːθ ˈtreɪnɪŋ skiːm/, **the (YTS)** (education) A comprehensive state-sponsored scheme to provide all 16-year-old school-leavers with either continuing full-time education to the age of 18, or a period of planned work experience for the same length of time. The scheme was introduced in 1983 to replace the *Youth Opportunities Programme*.

Yule/yule log /ˈjuːl/ˈjuːl lɒɡ/ (tradition) A large log of wood traditionally used as the basis of a fire in a hearth at *Christmas*. Such fires are found in some *country houses*, hotels, and *pubs*, as well as larger private homes. [from 'yule', an old pagan festival held in mid-winter and later replaced by the Christian festival of Christmas]

YWCA /ˌwaɪ dʌbljuː siː ˈeɪ/, **the (Young Women's Christian Association, the)** (charities) The sister organization of the *YMCA*, founded in 1855, and now operating internationally. It is well-known for its hostels and flatlets, offering accommodation to young single women living or working away from home.

zebra crossing /ˌziːbrə ˈkrɒsɪŋ/ (transport) A pedestrian crossing over a road, marked with alternating black and white stripes. Such crossings are indicated by *Belisha beacons* and are often operated as a *pelican crossing*. [from black and white stripes like those of a zebra]

Index

Edinburgh Festival
18
eisteddfod
Elgin Marbles
English Chamber Orchestra
English National Opera
15
Fitzwilliam Museum
Fringe
G and S
Geffrye Museum
Georgian poets
Gilbert and Sullivan operas
Globe (Theatre)
Glyndebourne
Gothic novel
Gray's Elegy
Greensleeves
Hallé (Orchestra)
Haymarket (Theatre)
Hayward Gallery
Her Majesty's Theatre
Holmes, Sherlock
Lake Poets
Lake School
Last Night of the Proms
Lilliburlero/Lillibullero
London Festival Ballet
London Library
London Mozart Players
London Philharmonic
  Orchestra
London Symphony
  Orchestra
Londonderry Air
Magic Circle
Malvern Festival
Mermaid Theatre
Mersey sound
mod
National Film Theatre
National Gallery
National Portrait Gallery
National Theatre
National Youth Orchestra
National Youth Theatre
New Sadler's Wells Opera
Norwich School
Old Vic
Palladium

Penguin
Peter Pan
PG
Philharmonia Orchestra
Pinewood Studios
Poet Laureate
Poets' Corner
Pre-Raphaelites
Promenade Concerts
promenader
Proms
Purcell Room
Queen Elizabeth Hall
Queen's Gallery
Ronnie Scott's
Round House
Royal Academy (of Arts)
Royal Ballet
Royal Court (Theare)
Royal Festival Hall
Royal Liverpool
  Philharmonic Orchestra
Royal Opera
Royal Opera House
Royal Pavilion
Royal Philharmonic
  Orchestra
Royal Shakespeare
  Company
Royal Variety
  Show/Performance
Sadler's Wells Theatre
Savoy (Theatre)
Savoy Operas
Scrooge
season ticket
Shakespeare Memorial
  Theatre
Shaw's Corner
Sherlock Holmes
St Trinian's
Tate (Gallery)
Theatre Royal
Theatre Upstairs
Three Choirs Festival
Times Literary Supplement
U certificate
V and A
Victoria and Albert
  Museum

Wallace Collection
Wigmore Hall
Winnie the Pooh
Woburn Abbey
X certificate
Young Vic

Variety Club
War on Want
welfare worker
WRVS
YMCA
YWCA

charities
Al-Anon
Alcoholics Anonymous
almshouse
Amnesty International
ASH
Barnardo's
British Legion
Charity Commission
Cheshire Homes
Christian Aid
Church Army
Civic Trust
Darby and Joan club
Dr Barnardo's (Homes)
flag day
Grand Order of Water Rats
Help the Aged
Lions Club
MIND
National Marriage
  Guidance Council
NSPCA
NSPCC
Oxfam/OXFAM
PDSA
Royal British Legion
Royal National Institute for
  the Blind
Royal National Institute for
  the Deaf
Royal National Lifeboat
  Institution
Royal Society for the
  Protection of Birds
RSPCA
Samaritans
Save the Children Fund
Shaftesbury Society
Shelter
SPCK
sponsored walk
Toc H

clothing
black tie
blazer
boater
bowler
brogues
Burberry
busby
cap
cavalry twill
cloth cap
deerstalker (hat)
dinner jacket
dog-collar
donkey jacket
duffle-coat
Eton suit
evening dress
Fair Isle
glengarry
gown
guernsey
gum boots
Harris tweed
heather mixture
jersey
kilt
morning coat
morning dress
Moss Bros
paisley shawl
Peter Pan collar
pinstripe suit
plaid
plus-fours
pork-pie hat
sporran
sports jacket
tam-o'-shanter
tartan
top hat
trilby (hat)
wellies

wellington boots
white tie

commerce
bargain basement
Blackwell's
book token
Boots
British Telecom
Britoil
broker
BTA
Bull Ring
chamber of commerce
Christie's
Consumers Association
Co-op
Co-operative Movement
Co-operative Wholesale
  Society
corner shop
Datapost
Datel
Dictaphone
Discline
door-to-door salesman
estate agent
F W Woolworth
first class
Fortnum and Mason
Foyle's
Freefone
Freepost
garden centre
gazumping
gift token
good will
GPO
Harrods
Heals
HMV
Homelink
Ideal Home Exhibition
Intelpost
Liberty's
Littlewoods
Luncheon Voucher
market garden
Marks & Spencer
Mercury

Milk Marketing Board
Muzak
National Exhibition Centre
nationalized industries
NCP
off-licence
Olympia
Payphone
Penguin Books
Post Office
recorded delivery
registered post
restrictive practice
Saatchi & Saatchi
Sainsburys
sandwich man
second class
Selectapost
Selfridges
service charge
service road
Shell Centre
shopping precinct
Smith's
Sotheby's
Speaking Clock
St Michael
Stanley Gibbons
STD
telemessage
Tesco
Timeline
trading estate
trading stamps
trunk call
Universal Aunts
W H Smith
Woolworth's
Yellow Pages

daily life
A to Z
ADC call
Advertising Standards
  Authority
allotment
A-1
August Bank Holiday
avoirdupois
bank holiday

bed and breakfast
bedsit(ter)
beer garden
Biro
bob
bring-and-buy (sale)
BST
CAB
Cambridge blue
CAMRA
chapel of rest
Chubb (lock)
coffee morning
community centre
copper
council estate
council house
court
Dinky Toy
DIY
dress circle
Easter Monday
ex-directory
fête
first floor
fiver
foolscap
foot
free house
front room
gallon
gill
granny flat
Green Cross Code
ground floor
guest house
happy hour
Harvey Smith
hatches, matches and
  dispatches
Heath Robinson
High Street
home help
housing estate
inch
inn
inn sign
Jiffybag
jumble sale
kitemark

knees-up
landlady
licensing hours
living room
local
lodge
lollipop lady/man
lounge bar
market day
meals on wheels
Meccano
milkman
naughty postcard
999
office party
open day
Oxford blue
paperboy/girl
pavement artist
paying guest
piggy bank
pint
play street
postcode
postman
private bar
private hotel
pub
public bar
quid
sale of work
saloon bar
Saturday girl
Saturday person
Scotch mist
sense of humour
service flat
shilling
sixpence
smallholding
snug
spring bank holiday
strap-hanger
summer time
Tannoy
teashop
tenner
three-line whip
tied house
transport café

village green
village hall
V-sign
warden
weekend
ye olde tea shoppe

defence
Admiralty
Aldermaston
Army
BAOR
Black Watch
Blue Ensign
Blues and Royals
CND
Coldstream Guards
Commandos
D-notice
Edinburgh Military Tattoo
Fleet Air Arm
Fylingdales
GCHQ
Gordon Highlanders
Green Jackets
Greenham Common
Grenadier Guards
Guards
Guards Division
guardsman
highlander
HMS
Holy Loch
Horse Guards
Household Cavalry
Household Troops
Imperial War Museum
Irish Guards
Life Guards
MI5
MI6
NAAFI
Naffy
NATO
RAF
Red Arrows
Red Devils
Royal Aircraft
  Establishment
Royal Highland Regiment

Royal Horse Guards
Royal Marines
Royal Naval Reserve
Royal Navy
Royal Observer Corps
Royal Regiment
Royal Scots
Royals
SAS
Scots Greys
Scots Guards
senior service
Spithead Review
Territorial Army
Trident
Ulster Defence Regiment
VC
Victoria Cross
Welsh Guards
White Ensign
WRAC
WRAF
Wren
WRNS

education
'A' level
academic year
academy
approved school
assisted place
Aston (University)
BA
Backs
Billy Bunter
Birkbeck (College)
Britannia Royal Naval
  College
British Council
BSc
Burnham scale
Cambridge
Cambridge University
cap
cathedral school
CFE
chancellor
Charterhouse (School)
choir school
Christ's Hospital

church school
Clifton (College)
college
college of education
commercial subjects
Common Entrance
commoner
comprehensive school
correspondence college
correspondence course
county school
crammer
Cranwell
CSE
Dartington Hall
Dartmouth
day release
day-boy
day-girl
dean
dinner lady
direct grant school
don
Duke of Edinburgh's
  Award Scheme
Dulwich (College)
Edinburgh Academy
eleven-plus
Encyclopaedia Britannica
Eton (College)
fellow
fifth form/year
finishing school
first class
first degree
first school
fresher
further education
GCE
GCSE
general degree
general science
Gordonstoun (School)
governor
gown
graduand
graduate
graduate student
grammar school
Greats

Greyfriars
Guildhall School of Music
  (and Drama)
hall
hall of residence
Harrovian
Harrow (School)
Heriot-Watt University
high school
higher degree
higher education
honours degree
house
housefather/housemother
housemaster
housemistress
independent school
infant school
kindergarten
King's School
LEA
lodge
London University
long vacation
lower school
LSE
MA
Marlborough (College)
master
mature student
Mays
middle school
mortarboard
Natural History Museum
nursery school
NUS
NUT
'O' level
old boy
old girl
old school tie
Open University
Outward Bound (Trust)
Oxbridge
Oxford
Oxford University
pass (degree)
playgroup
playschool
polytechnic

postgraduate
prefect
prep school
preparatory school
pre-preparatory school
pre-school playgroup
primary school
private school
proctor
progressive school
provost
PTA
public school
Queen's University
RADA
Radcliffe Camera
rag (week)
reader
rector
redbrick university
Regius professor
Roedean (School)
Royal Academy of Music
Royal Ballet School
Royal College of Art
Royal College of Music
Royal Military Academy
Royal Naval College
RSA
'S' level
Sandhurst
sandwich course
scholarship
school song
school tie
school welfare officer
school year
Scout/scout
second class
secondary modern (school)
secondary school
set book
Sheldonian (Theatre)
Shrewsbury (School)
sixth form
sixth form college
Slade School of (Fine) Art
special school
speech day
St Paul's (School)

state school
streaming
summer school
supply teacher
tech
technical college
technical school
term
tertiary college
Times Educational
  Supplement
TOPS
tripos
tutor
UCCA
undergraduate
upper school
vice-chancellor
village college
voluntary school
warden
Westminster School
Winchester (College)

finance
Access (card)
Baltic (Exchange)
Bank of England
Bank of Scotland
bank rate
Barclaycard
Barclays (Bank)
base lending rate
bear
big four
black
blue chip
broker
building society
bull
bursar
capital gains tax
capital transfer tax
Cashpoint
chartered accountant
clearing bank
closing price
Clydesdale Bank
corporation tax
credit union

direct debit
dividend
divvy
Ernie
50 pence (piece)
finance house
financial year
5 pence (piece)
Footsie
friendly society
FT Index
gilt-edged securities
giro
Giro (bank)
granny bonds
ground rent
guinea
halfpenny
Handybank
holding company
House
housing association
income tax
Inland Revenue
insurance broker
investment trust
IOU
jobber
limited company
Lloyd's
Lloyds (Bank)
Lombard Street
Ltd
merchant bank
Midland (Bank)
MIRAS
mortgage
National Girobank
national insurance
National Savings Bank
National Savings
  Certificates
National Westminster
  (Bank)
NatWest
old age pension
Old Lady of Threadneedle
  Street
ordinary shares
PAYE

penny
PLC/Plc/plc
postal order
pound (sterling)
preference shares
Premium (Savings) Bonds
private company
private income
private limited company
private means
provident society
PSBR
public limited company
rates
red
Royal Bank of Scotland
Royal Mint
Savings Certificates
SAYE
scrip issue
sleeping partner
social security
standing order
Stock Exchange
stockbroker
stock-jobber
supplementary benefit
take-home pay
10 pence (piece)
third-party insurance
Threadneedle Street
Throgmorton Street
Transcash
Trustcard
Trustee Savings Bank
20 pence (piece)
2 pence (piece)
two-shilling piece
underwriter
unit trust
VAT
VISA (card)

food and drink
bacon and eggs
Bakewell tart
Banbury cake
bangers and mash
bannock
bap

bar
bar snacks
Bath bun
Bath Oliver
bitter
black pudding
Blenheim Orange
Bloody Mary
Bramley's (Seedling)
bread and butter pudding
Bristol Cream
Bristol Milk
bubble and squeak
Buck's fizz
bullseye
butterscotch
butty
Caerphilly
Cheddar (cheese)
Chelsea bun
Cheshire (cheese)
chippy
Christmas dinner
Christmas pudding
clotted cream
cock-a-leekie
Conference (pear)
continental breakfast
Cornish pasty
cottage loaf
cottage pie
Cox's (Orange Pippin)
cream cracker
crumpet
cuppa
custard
Devonshire cream
dinner
dog's nose
doorstep
double
double Gloucester (cheese)
draught beer
drop scone
Dundee cake
Dunlop
Eccles cake
Edinburgh rock
elevenses
English breakfast

fish and chips
Gaelic coffee
gin
gin and it
gin and tonic
ginger biscuit
gobstopper
gooseberry fool
griddle cake
Guinness
haggis
high tea
horse's neck
hot cross bun
hotpot
hundreds and thousands
Irish coffee
Irish stew
jugged hare
Lancashire (cheese)
lardy cake
Laxton's Superb
Leicester (cheese)
light ale
liquorice allsorts
lollipop
lunch
luncheon
Madeira cake
magnum
maid of honour
marmalade
Melba toast
Melton Mowbray pie
mild
mince pie
mincemeat
mock turtle soup
Mrs Beeton
muffin
oatcake
Ovaltine
pancakes
pease pudding
pinta
ploughman's lunch
plum pudding
porridge
pudding
real ale

red biddy
rock
rock cake
roly-poly
Sally Lunn
sausage roll
schooner
scone
Scotch
Scotch broth
Scotch eggs
Scotch woodcock
scrumpy
shandy
shepherd's pie
shortbread
simnel cake
snow pudding
spotted dick
spotted dog
steak and kidney pie
steak and kidney pudding
Stilton (cheese)
stout
strawberries and cream
Sturmer
suet pudding
summer pudding
Swiss roll
tea
teacake
tipsy cake
toad-in-the-hole
toast
toffee apple
trifle
Victoria plum
wedding breakfast
Welsh rarebit
Wensleydale (cheese)
whiskey
whisky
whisky mac
Worcester sauce
Yorkshire pudding

geography
Aberdonian
Anglesey
area of outstanding natural

beauty
Belfast
Ben Nevis
benchmark
B'ham
Black Country
Blackpool
Borders
Boston Stump
Bournemouth
Brecon Beacons
bridleway
Brighton
Brit
Britain
British Isles
Briton
Broads
Brum
Brummie
Caernarfon
Cairngorms
Caledonia
Caledonian Canal
Cambria
Cambridge
Canterbury
Cardiff
Celtic fringe
Cerne Giant
Channel Islands
Cheltenham
Chilterns
Cinque Ports
city
Clyde
conservation area
Constable country
Cornwall
Countryside Commission
county
county town
dalesman
Dartmoor
Derwentwater
dewpond
Downs
East Anglia
Edinburgh
England

Fens
Fingal's Cave
forest park
Forth
garden city
Garden of England
garden suburb
garden village
Geographical Magazine
Geordie
Giant's Causeway
Glasgow
Glaswegian
Gloucester
GMT
Gog Magog Hills
Goodwin Sands
Gorbals
Grampians
Granite City
Granta
Grasmere
Great Britain
Great Glen
green belt
Greenwich
Greenwich Park
Harrogate
Hastings
Hebrides
heritage coast
highlander
Highlands
Highlands and Islands
Holy Island
Home Counties
Inverness
Iona
Ireland
Isis
Isle of Man
Isle of Wight
John o'Groats
Kentish Man
Lake District
Land's End
Liverpudlian
Loch Lomond
Loch Ness
Lough Neagh

Lowlands
Man of Kent
Mancunian
market town
metropolitan county
Midlands
national grid
national park
New Commonwealth
new town
Norfolk Broads
North (Country)
Northern Ireland
Ordnance Survey
Orkneys
Oxford
Peak District
Pennine Way
Pennines
Pilgrims' Way
postal district
Potteries
Princes Street
Salisbury Plain
Salopian
Sarum
Scilly Isles
Scotland
Scouse
Severn
Shakespeare country
Shetlands
Shires
Snowdonia
South Downs
St Andrews
stockbroker belt
Stratford-up(on)-Avon
Sullom Voe
Thames
UK.
Ullswater
Ulster
unadopted road
United Kingdom
Wales
Wash
West Country
Western Approaches
Windermere

government
Admiralty
alderman
another place
backbencher
ballot paper
bill
Black Rod
borough
borough council
Budget
budget leak
burgh
Cabinet
Chancellor of the Duchy of
  Lancaster
Chancellor of the Exchequer
Chancery
Chequers
Chiltern Hundreds
civic centre
civil servant
Civil Service
Clerk of the House (of
  Commons)
COI
Common Market
Commons
community council
constituency
constitutional monarchy
councillor
county council
County Hall
crossbencher
Crown
Crown Agent
Customs and Excise
department
Deputy Lieutenant
devolution
Diplomatic Service
direct rule
district council
division
Downing Street
EEC
Euro-MP
Father of the House
first reading

Foreign and
  Commonwealth Office
Foreign Secretary
Forestry Commission
front bench
frontbencher
gangway
GLC
Great Seal
green paper
guillotine
Hansard
HMG
HMSO
Home Office
Home Secretary
House
House of Commons
House of Lords
Houses of Parliament
Lancaster House
Leader of the House
Leader of the Opposition
Little Neddy
local authority
London Gazette
lord
Lord Chancellor
Lord High Chancellor
Lord Lieutenant
Lord Mayor
Lord President of the
  Council
Lord Privy Seal
Lord Provost
Lords Spiritual
Lords Temporal
maiden speech
mayor
mini-budget
minister
ministry
Monopolies Commission
MP
Northern Ireland Assembly
Number Ten/No 10
ombudsman
Opposition
order in council
order paper

Palace of Westminster
parish council
Parliament
Parliamentary
  Commissioner
parliamentary private
  secretary
parliamentary secretary
parliamentary
  under-secretary of state
Patent Office
Paymaster General
positive vetting
Prime Minister
private bill
private member
private member's bill
Privy Council
Privy
  Councillor/Counsellor
Privy Seal
prorogation
public bill
Public Record Office
quango
Queen's Speech
recess
registry office
returning officer
seat
second reading
Secretary of State
Sergeant/Serjeant at Arms
Shadow Cabinet
shadow minister
sheriff
Speaker
Speech from the Throne
State Opening of
  Parliament
Stormont
Strangers' Gallery
Think Tank
third reading
three-line whip
town clerk
town council
town hall
Treasury
Tynwald

voting system
ward
welfare state
Westminster
white paper
Whitehall

history

Abdication
Accession Day
Act of Supremacy
Act of Union
ancient monument
Ann Hathaway's Cottage
Antonine Wall
Armada
Armistice Day
Battle of Britain
Battle of Britain Day
Black Prince
Blenheim
Blenheim Palace
Blitz
Bloody Mary
Bloody Tower
Boer War
Bonnie Prince Charlie
Boyne
Britannia
British Empire
Briton
Chartwell
Commonwealth
Conqueror
Conquest
Coronation
Coronation Chair
Culloden
Cutty Sark
D-day
Depression
Discovery
Domesday Book
Druids
Duchy of Cornwall
Duchy of Lancaster
Dunkirk
Edgehill
Edinburgh Castle
English Civil War

Ermine Street
Festival of Britain
Fifth of November
Forty-Five
Fosse Way
Gaiety Girls
General Strike
Georgian
Glencoe Massacre
Globe (Theatre)
Glorious Twelfth
Golden Age
Golden Hind
Great Exhibition
Great Fire (of London)
Great Plague (of London)
Great Train Robbery
guinea
Gunpowder Plot
Hadrian's Wall
Hampton Court
Hastings
Home Guard
hundred
Industrial Revolution
Jack the Ripper
listed building
Long Man of Wilmington
Magna Carta
Martello tower
Mary Rose
Merry Monarch
national service
Norman Conquest
Offa's Dyke
Old Contemptibles
Penny Black
Prince Regent
Princes in the Tower
Roman road
Royal Mile
St George's Chapel
  (Windsor)
Titanic
Trafalgar
Unknown Warrior
Victorian
Victory
Wars of the Roses
Waterloo

Watling Street
white horse
White Tower
Young Pretender

language
A N Other
Anglo-Saxon
Basic English
BBC English
Brewer
clerihew
four-letter word
Fowler
Gaelic
ITA
limerick
Manx
Oxford accent
Piccadilly Circus
pidgin English
Queen's English
rhyming slang
Roget
RP
Scouse

law
Act (of Parliament)
act of God
age of consent
age of discretion
attendance centre
attorney
Attorney General
bailiff
bar
barrister
Black Maria
bobby
borstal
Bow Street
Broadmoor
by-law
capital punishment
Central Criminal Court
chambers
Chancery
Chief Constable
CID

citizen's arrest
coming of age
common law
common law husband/wife
community home
constable
copper
coroner
court
crown court
Dartmoor
death penalty
decree absolute
decree nisi
detention centre
DPP
Flying Squad
Fraud Squad
governor
Gray's Inn
habeas corpus
H-blocks
High Court (of Justice)
Holloway (Prison)
Inner Temple
Inns of Court
JP
jury
juvenile court
Law Lords
Law Society
Lincoln's Inn
lord
Lord Chief Justice
magistrate
Master of the Rolls
Maze (Prison)
McNaughten Rules
Metropolitan Police Force
Middle Temple
minor
M'Lud
Moor
Murder Squad
New Scotland Yard
not proven
Old Bailey
panda car
Parkhurst (prison)
patrial

penal system
Pentonville (prison)
planning permission
police
private treaty
probate
probation
probation officer
probationer
procurator fiscal
Public Lending Right
QC
quarter day
Queen's Bench Division
receiver
recorder
Regina
remand centre
remand home
royal assent
Royal Ulster Constabulary
RUC
Scotland Yard
Scrubs
sheriff
silk
solicitor
Solicitor General
Special Branch
special constable
summons
Supreme Court (of
  Judicature)
term
Trade Descriptions Act
treasure trove
Vice Squad
Wandsworth (Prison)
welfare officer
wheel clamp
Wormwood Scrubs
writ
Yard
yellow lines
Yorkshire Ripper
youth custody centre

life and society
BEM
Birthday Honours

bluestocking
bottle party
brother
Burke('s Peerage)
chieftain
child care
clan
club
College of Arms
Commission for Racial
  Equality
commoner
Companion of Honour
constable
corporal punishment
Country Code
crofter
Dame
Debrett
Druids
duchy
Earl Marshal
English-Speaking Union
Equal Opportunities
  Commission
Establishment
eventide home
fellow
freedom (of the city)
garden party
Garter
Garter ceremony
gaudy
Gay Liberation Front
GC
gentleman
gentleman farmer
gentleman-at-arms
gentleman's gentleman
Gentlemen-at-Arms
gentry
George Cross
George Medal
ginger group
glue-sniffing
God Save the Queen
Gold Stick
governor
Grace and Favour residence
Grand Old Man

greetings card
hall
Hell's Angels
hereditary peer
Honourable
Hooray Henry
in-laws
Joneses
lady
laird
latchkey child
life peer
lifemanship
Lord Chamberlain
Lord's Day Observance
  Society
lower class
lower middle class
ma'am
madam
Master
mayoress
Men of the Trees
Mensa
Messrs
middle class
Miss
Mods
MORI
Mr
Mrs
Ms
My Lady
My Lord
national anthem
National Council for Civil
  Liberties
National Trust
National Trust for Scotland
NBL
New Year Honours
non-U
Notting Hill Carnival
OAP
old boy network
one-upmanship
Order of Merit
Order of the Bath
Order of the Garter
Order of the Thistle

Oxford Group
peer
peerage
peeress
Peter Pan
punks
race relations
rest home
Right Honourable
Rockers
Rotary Club
Round Table
senior citizen
servants
sir
Sir
skinheads
skins
Sloane
Sloane Ranger
soapbox
social worker
stately home
suburbia
Sunday
Sunday roast/joint
tied cottage
town and gown
U
upper class
upper middle class
WI
winter of discontent
working class
Worship

London
Admiralty Arch
Albert Hall
Albert Memorial
Alexandra Palace
Ally Pally
Baker Street
Banqueting House
Belgravia
Big Ben
Bond Street
Bow Bells
Brown's Hotel
Burlington House

Caledonian Market
Carnaby Street
Cenotaph
Centre Point
Chamber of Horrors
Changing of the Guard
Charing Cross
Chelsea
Chelsea Flower Show
Chelsea Hospital
City (of London)
Cleopatra's Needle
Clubland
cockney
Covent Garden
Crystal Palace
Dorchester
Earls Court
East End
Embankment
Eros
Festival Gardens
Fleet Street
Goldsmiths' Hall
Great Paul
Greater London
Green Park
Grosvenor House
Grosvenor Square
Guildhall
Hampstead
Hilton
Holmes, Sherlock
Horse Guards
Horse Guards Parade
Hyde Park
Hyde Park Corner
Kensington
Kensington Gardens
Kensington Palace
Kenwood
Kew Gardens
Knightsbridge
Leicester Square
Little America
London
London Museum
London Tourist Board
London Zoo
Lord Mayor's Banquet

Lord Mayor's Show
Madame Tussaud's
Mansion House
Marble Arch
Marlborough House
Mayfair
Millbank
Millbank Tower
Millionaires' Row
Monument
Museum of London
Nelson's Column
New Covent Garden
  (Market)
Notting Hill
Oxford Street
Palace of Westminster
Pall Mall
Park Lane
pearly king/queen
Peter Pan
Petticoat Lane
Piccadilly
Portobello Road
Post Office Tower
Queen Victoria Memorial
Regent Street
Regent's Park
Ritz
Rotten Row
Round Pond
Row
Royal Albert Hall
Royal Mews
royal park
Savoy (Hotel)
Serpentine
Shaftesbury Avenue
Sherlock Holmes
Smith Square
Smithfield (Market)
Somerset House
South Bank
Speakers' Corner
Spitalfields
Square Mile
St Clement Danes
St James's Palace
St James's Park
St John's, Smith Square

St Martin-in-the-Fields
St Mary-le-Bow
Strand
Talk of the Town
Tattersall's
Telecom Tower
Temple
Temple Bar
Temple Church
Tottenham Court Road
Tower Bridge
Tower Hill
Tower of London
Trafalgar Square
Waldorf (Hotel)
Wardour Street
West End
Westminster
Westminster Hall
Whispering Gallery
Whitehall
Windmill Theatre

media
  Alf Garnett
  Andy Capp
  Anglia TV
  annual
  Archers
  Auntie
  BBC
  BBC 1
  BBC Television Centre
  BBC 2
  BBC World Service
  Beano
  Beeb
  Birmingham Post
  Blue Peter
  Border Television
  Brain of Britain
  breakfast TV
  British Broadcasting
    Corporation
  Broadcasting House
  Bunty
  Bush House
  Capital Radio
  Ceefax
  Central TV

Channel Four
comic
commercial radio
commercial television
Coronation Street
Cosmopolitan
Country Life
Crossroads
Daily Express
Daily Mail
Daily Mirror
Daily Star
Daily Telegraph
Dandy
Desert Island Discs
Doctor Who
Economist
Evening News
Evening Standard
Exchange and Mart
Exchange Telegraph
  Company
Express
Extel
Field
Financial Times
Financial Weekly
Fleet Street
fourth estate
FT
Garnett, Alf
Giles cartoons
Goons
gossip column
Gramophone
Grampian Television
Granada Television
Grandstand
Guardian
Guinness Book of Records
gutter press
heavies
HTV
IBA
Illustrated London News
ILR
IRN
ITN
ITV
Jackie

Judy
Kelly's (Directories)
LBC
Listener
local radio
LWT
Mail
Mail on Sunday
Man Alive
Mandy
Marplan
Mastermind
Melody Maker
Mirror
Morning Star
Motor
Muppets
Nature
New Musical Express
New Scientist
New Society
New Statesman
News At Ten
News of the World
Nine O'Clock News
Observer
Old Moore's Almanack
Oracle
page three
Panorama
People
personal column
pips
popular paper
Press Association
Press Council
Prestel
Printing House Square
Private Eye
Punch
quality paper
Radio 4
Radio 1
Radio 3
Radio Times
Radio 2
Record Mirror
red book
Reith lectures
Reuters

Scotsman
S4C
She
silly season
Sounds
Spectator
Sporting Life
Standard
Street
STV
Sun
Sunday
Sunday Express
Sunday Mirror
Sunday People
Sunday Telegraph
Sunday Times
Tablet
tabloid
Telegraph
Television South
Television South West
Thames Television
third leader
This Is Your Life
Time Out
Times
Titbits
Top of the Pops
top ten
Tribune
TV Times
TV-am
Tyne Tees TV
Universe
Vogue
Which?
Whitaker's Almanack
Who's Who
Woman
Woman's Hour
Woman's Own
Woman's Realm
Woman's Weekly
Woman's World
World Service
Yorkshire Post
Yorkshire TV

medicine
Bart's
BUPA
Charing Cross Hospital
cottage hospital
Disprin
district nurse
Durex
Elastoplast
Epsom salts
general hospital
General Medical Council
general practitioner
government health warning
GP
Great Ormond Street
group practice
Guy's Hospital
Harley Street
health centre
health visitor
hospice
King's College Hospital
Lancet
locum
matron
Medical Research Council
Middlesex Hospital
NHS
nursing home
PPP
prescription
private patient
private practice
SEN
SRN
St Bartholomew's Hospital
St John Ambulance
   (Brigade)
St Thomas's Hospital
Stoke Mandeville
teaching hospital
University College Hospital

people
Arthur
Arthur Scargill
Austen, Jane
Beatles
Benjamin Britten

Benn, Tony
Bernard Levin
Britten, Benjamin
Carroll, Lewis
Charles Dickens
Churchill, Winston
Clive Sinclair
Daley Thompson
David Owen
David Steel
Dickens, Charles
Edward Elgar
Elgar, Edward
Fonteyn, Margot
Gielgud, John
Hartnell, Norman
Henry VIII
Ian Paisley
Jane Austen
Jayne Torvill and
  Christopher Dean
John Gielgud
John Milton
King Arthur
Kinnock, Neil
Levin, Bernard
Lewis Carroll
Margaret Thatcher
Margot Fonteyn
Mary Quant
Mary Whitehouse
Milton, John
Neil Kinnock
Norman Hartnell
Owen, David
P G Wodehouse
Paisley, Ian
Quant, Mary
Ralph Vaughan Williams
Rolling Stones
Scargill, Arthur
Shakespeare, William
Sinclair, Clive
Steel, David
Thatcher, Margaret
Thompson, Daley
Tony Benn
Torvill and Dean
Vaughan Williams, Ralph
Whitehouse, Mary

William Shakespeare
Winston Churchill
Wodehouse, P G

politics

Alliance
Alliance Party (of Northern
  Ireland)
Bennism
blue
Bow Group
by-election
Chief Whip
coalition
cod war
Commonwealth
Communist Party (of Great
  Britain)
Conservative Party
dry
Fabian Society
first past the post
Friends of the Earth
general election
Home Rule
IRA
Irish Republican Army
Labour Party
landslide (victory)
Liberal Party
Liberal-SDP Alliance
Loyalists
marginal constituency
marginal seat
Militant Tendency
National Front
Orangemen
Paisleyites
Plaid Cymru
polling booth
polling day
polling station
polls
postal vote
presiding officer
Primrose League
proportional representation
Provisionals
proxy vote
Red Flag

safe seat
SDLP
SDP
Sinn Féin
sit-in
SNP
Social Democratic and
  Labour Party
Thatcherism
three-cornered fight
Tory
Transport House
Troubles
UDR
Ulster Defence Association
Ulster Democratic Unionist
  Party
Ulster Unionist Party
Unionist Party
wet
whip

religion
Advent
Anglican
Anglo-Catholic
Archbishop of Canterbury
Archbishop of York
Ascension Day
Ash Wednesday
Authorized Version
Baptists
Book of Common Prayer
carol service
chapel
chapel royal
Christmas
church
Church Commissioners
Church House
Church of England
Church of Scotland
churchwarden
close
Crockford
curate
deacon
dean
district visitor
Easter

Free Churches
General Assembly of the
  Church of Scotland
General Synod
Good Friday
grace
harvest festival
High Church
Hymns Ancient and
  Modern
Jersusalem Bible
King James Bible
kirk
Lady Chapel
Lady Day
Lambeth Conference
Lambeth Palace
lay reader
Lent
lord
Low Church
Low Sunday
Methodist
Methodist Church
minister
minster
Nonconformists
Oxford Movement
Palm Sunday
parish church
parish magazine
parish register
parson
Passion Sunday
PCC
Plymouth Brethren
presbytery
primate
Primate of All England
Primate of England
provost
Quakers
rector
rectory
registry
Reverend
Revised Version
Right Reverend
Rogation Days
Roman Catholic Church

Sally Army
Salvation Army
Salvationist
Shrove Tuesday
sidesman
Society of Friends
St Paul's (Cathedral)
suffragan bishop
Sunday school
Synod
Thirty-Nine Articles
Trinity Sunday
United Reformed Church
verger
Very Reverend
vicar
vicarage
watch night service
Westminster Abbey
Westminster Cathedral
Whit Sunday

royal family
Balmoral
Britannia
Buck House
Buckingham Palace
Civil List
court circular
Duke of Cornwall
Duke of Edinburgh
Duke of Windsor
Glamis Castle
Her Majesty
Holyrood House
king
lady-in-waiting
Lord Mountbatten
Master of the Horse
Master of the Queen's
  Music
Mountbatten
Official Birthday
Palace
prince
Prince of Wales
princess
Princess of Wales
queen
Queen Elizabeth

Queen Elizabeth, the
  Queen Mother
queen mother
Queen Victoria
Queen's Birthday
royal duke
royal family
Royal Highness
royal salute
royal standard
Royal Yacht
Royals
Sandringham
Windsor Castle

science and technology
Astronomer Royal
BNOC
BP
British Aerospace
British Association
British Gas Corporation
British Nuclear Fuels (Plc)
British Technology Group
BSI
CEGB
Electricity Council
Forth Bridge
Geological Museum
Goonhilly
Harwell
ICI
Jodrell Bank
National Physical
  Laboratory
North Sea gas
North Sea oil
nuclear power
Porton Down
Royal Greenwich
  Observatory
Royal Society
Science Museum
Sellafield
Severn Bridge
Thames Barrier
United Kingdom Atomic
  Energy Authority
Windscale

sport and leisure
accumulator
Admiral's Cup
Aintree
Alexandra Park
All England Club
Amateur Athletics
  Association
Arsenal
Ascot
association football
Aston Villa
autumn double
Badminton (Horse Trials)
ball boy/girl
bar billiards
Barbarians
Becher's Brook
betting shop
bingo
Bisley
blood sports
blue
Bluebird
Boat Race
Boat Show
bookie
bookmaker
bowl
bowling
bowls
boy scout
Braemar Gathering
Brands Hatch
British Grand Prix
British Lions
British Open
  (Championship)
Brownie (Guide)
Butlin's
Cambridge blue
cap
Cardiff City
CB (radio)
CBer
Celtic
Chelsea
Cheltenham Gold Cup
Chief Scout
clock golf

colours
conkers
county cricket
Cowes (Week)
cricket
Crystal Palace
cub (scout)
Cup
Cup Final
cup tie
curling
darts
Derby
Devizes–Westminster race
Diamond Sculls
dinner dance
division
Dodgem
dogs
donkey derby
Dons
double
drive
each way bet
Edgbaston
egg-and-spoon race
Eights
eleven
Epsom
eventing
Everton
FA
FA Cup
Fastnet (Race)
field sports
fives
Flat
fly-fishing
Fontwell Park
football
Football League
French cricket
Fulham
fun run
gala
gamekeeper
gamesmanship
Gang Show
Gay Gordons
gillie

Gipsy Moth
Girl Guide
Girl Guides Association
Glorious Goodwood
Glorious Twelfth
Gold Cup Day
Goldie crew
Goodison Park
Goodwood
Grand National
Greyhound Derby
greyhound racing
groundsman
grouse shooting
Guide
Guides
gun-dog
gymkhana
Hampden Park
Hampden roar
hare and hounds
hat trick
Head of the River Race
Heart of Midlothian
Hearts
Henley Regatta
Hibernian
Highland fling
Highland games
Highland gathering
hopscotch
hornpipe
Horse of the Year Show
Hoylake
hunt
hunt-the-thimble
Ibrox park
Isis
I-spy
jamboree
Jockey Club
jodhpurs
Kempton Park
League Against Cruel
  Sports
long distance footpath
Lonsdale Belt
Lord's
Lord's Taverners
lucky dip

ludo
Mallory Park
Manchester City
Manchester United
master of foxhounds
master of hounds
Mays
MCC
Milk Cup
Milk Race
Moor Park
morris dance
Murrayfield
musical chairs
National
nineteenth hole
Ninian Park
Norwich City
nursery stakes
Old Trafford
Oulton Park
Oval
Oxford blue
Paul Jones
pig in the middle
point-to-point
Pony Club
pony-trekking
pools
postman's knock
punt
punter
putting
Pytchley (Hunt)
QPR
Queen of the South
Queen's Club
Queen's Park Rangers
Queen's Prize
Queensberry Rules
Quorn
race meeting
rackets
raffle
Rangers
real tennis
redcoat
rounders
Royal and Ancient
Royal Ascot

Royal Enclosure
Royal International Horse
  Show
Royal Tournament
rugby football
rugby league
rugby union
rugger
Ryder Cup
safari park
Sandown Park
Sanger's Circus
Scout/scout
Scout Association
Scrabble
Searchlight Tattoo
Sheffield United
Sheffield Wednesday
shinty
shooting stick
shove-ha'penny
Silverstone
snakes and ladders
snap
snooker
soapbox
soccer
spring double
Spurs
squash (rackets)
St Mirren
starting price
Stewards' Cup
strathspey
striker
sweepstake
sword dance
Tattenham Corner
test match
theme park
Three As
three-card trick
three-day event
three-legged race
tick-tack man
tip and run
torpids
tossing the caber
Tottenham Hotspur
treble chance

Trent Bridge
Triple Crown
Triple Event
TT
turf
turf accountant
Twickenham
United
University Match
Valentine's Brook
Walker Cup
Wembley
Wendy house
Wentworth
West Brom
West Bromwich Albion
West Ham (United)
White City
White Hart Lane
Wightman Cup
Wimbledon
Wisden
Wolverhampton Wanderers
Wolves
working men's club
YHA
youth club
youth hotel
Youth Hostels Association

style
Adam (style)
Bridge of Sighs
but and ben
Chippendale
close
Coalport
cottage
country house
court
Crown Derby
Decorated (style)
detached house
Doulton (pottery)
drive
Dutch barn
Early English
Elizabethan
folly
gate-leg(ged) table

Georgian (style)
gnome
Gothic Revival
Gothic (style)
Hepplewhite
Jacobean
Kidderminster (carpet)
Minton
Norman
paisley pattern
pebble dash
Perpendicular (style)
quadrangle
Queen Anne (style)
Regency (style)
Royal Worcester
Saxon (architecture)
semi(-detached house)
Sheraton
Spode (china)
tartan
terraced house
toby jug
town house
Tudor (style)
Victoriana
Wedgwood
William and Mary (style)
willow pattern
Wilton (carpet)
Windsor chair
Worcester (china)

tradition
Apprentice Boys' Parade
April Fools' Day
Auld Lang Syne
Aunt Sally
Avebury
Bampton fair
Bath and West
beating the bounds
Beefeater
bell ringing
best man
Blighty
Boxing Day
Britannia
Burns' Night
busker

Canterbury bell
ceilidh
Ceremony of the Keys
change ringing
Chelsea Pensioners
Cheshire Cat
Christmas Day
Christmas Eve
Christmas tree
corn exchange
cracker
Crown Jewels
daffodil
dame
Easter egg
farthing
Father Christmas
Father's Day
folk museum
Furry Dance
Goldsmiths' Company
Good King Wenceslas
Goose Fair
grace cup
Great Tom
Gretna Green
guildhall
guy
Guy Fawkes' Day
Guy Fawkes' Night
gyp
Hallowe'en
Heart of Oak
Hogmanay
holly
Home, Sweet Home
Humpty Dumpty
It's a Long Way to
    Tipperary
Jack the Giant-Killer
Jack-in-the-box
Jerusalem
Jock
John Bull
Knights of the Round Table
Lambeth Walk
Land of Hope and Glory
Land of My Fathers
leap year
leek

lion
Liver bird
livery company
Loch Ness Monster
loyal toast
Lutine bell
Lyonesse
Maundy money
Maundy Thursday
May Day
May Queen
maypole
Men of Harlech
Merlin
Merry England
Michaelmas
Midsummer Day
Moonraker
Mothering Sunday
Mother's Day
nativity play
Nessie
New Year's Day
New Year's Eve
nursery rhyme
O Come, All Ye Faithful
Old woman who lived in a
  shoe
oranges and lemons
oyez
Paddy
Pancake Day
pancake race
pantomime
Poppy Day
principal boy
Punch and Judy
Red Hand of Ulster
Remembrance Sunday
Robin Hood
rose
Round Table
Royal Smithfield Show
Rule, Britannia
Santa Claus
Scots, wha hae
shamrock
Silbury Hill
St Andrew's cross
St Andrew's Day

St David's Day
St George's cross
St George's Day
St Patrick's cross
St Patrick's Day
stiff upper lip
Stone of Scone
Stonehenge
swan-upping
Taffy
thistle
Tommy
tossing the pancake
town crier
trick or treat
Trooping the Colour
Twelfth Night
two-minute silence
unicorn
Union Flag
Union Jack
village idiot
wakes week
Whit Monday
woolsack
Xmas
Yeoman Warder
Yeomen of the Guard
Yule/yule log

transport
AA
A-1
APT
A-road
Beaulieu
Belisha beacon
Bentley
BL
Bluebell Line
box junction
BR
Bradshaw
British Airways
British Caledonian
  (Airways)
British Leyland
British Shipbuilders
B-road
bucket shop

CAA
cat's-eyes
Channel Tunnel
Charing Cross
Chunnel
Clansman
Clapham Junction
clearway
Clifton Suspension Bridge
Concorde
Cornish Riviera
Cunard
Daimler
derv
disc parking
double decker
estate car
E-type
Euston
Farnborough Air Show
first class
freightliner
Gatwick
Golden Hind
Grand Union Canal
Great North Road
Green Line coach
GT
hackney carriage
Heathrow
HGV
Highway Code
hovercraft
hoverport
Hoverspeed
InterCity train
Jaguar
juggernaut
King's Cross
L-driver
Liverpool Street
Lloyd's Register
London Airport
London Bridge
London Regional Transport
London Transport
London Underground
L-plates
Mansion House
Marylebone

Metro
MG
Mini
Montagu Motor Museum
MOT (test)
Motor Show
Motorail
motorway
mystery tour
National Bus Company
National Railway Museum
Nightrider
P & O
Paddington
parking ticket
pelican crossing
penny-farthing
Piccadilly Circus
Port of London Authority
Postbus
Prestwick
private road
provisional licence
Pullman (train)
QE2
Queen Elizabeth 2
RAC
Railcard
Red Arrow (bus)
Red Bus Rover
Red Ensign
registration number
Rolls(-Royce)
Sealink
season ticket
Seaspeed
second class
service area
service station
Severn Tunnel
shooting brake
sleeping policeman
slip road
Spaghetti Junction
St Pancras
Stansted (Airport)
tax disc
Temple
traffic warden
Trident

Trinity House
trunk road
tube
Underground
veteran car
Veteran Car Run
Victoria
vintage car
Waterloo
Waterloo and City Line
zebra crossing

work
ACAS
APEX
Aslef
assisted area
ASTMS
AUEW
blacking
blackleg
block vote
blue-collar worker
BSC
CBI
chapel
clerk of works
closed shop
COHSE
collective bargaining
Congress House
development area
Durham Miners' Gala
employment office
enterprise zone
Equity
father of the chapel
flying pickets
fringe benefits
G and M
ganger
General Council
girl Friday
GMBATU
GMWU
golden bowler
golden handshake
go-slow
government training centre
grey area

industrial action
industrial council
industrial estate
Institute of Directors
intermediate area
job release scheme
Jobcentre
jobs for the boys
lockout
lump
NALGO
National Coal Board
NCB
NEB
NEDC
Neddy
nine-to-five job
NUJ
NUM
NUPE
NUR
open shop
PA
Parkinson's law
pickets
probationer
Remploy
restrictive practice
retirement age
secondary picketing
shop steward
sit-down strike
skillcentre
SOGAT '82
special development area
strike pay
T and G
TGWU
TUC
unofficial strike
USDAW
white-collar worker
Whitley Council
winter of discontent
work-in
work-to-rule
Youth Opportunities
  Programme
Youth Training Scheme

Coins

penny

2 pence (piece)

5 pence (piece)

10 pence (piece)

20 pence (piece)

50 pence (piece)

pound (sterling)

Festivals

(of the United Kingdom)

Aldeburgh Festival of Music and Arts, 6–22 June 1986

Bath International Festival of Music and the Arts, 22 May–8 June 1986

Belfast Festival at Queen's, 12–29 November 1986

Brighton Festival, 4–27 May 1986

Cambridge Festival, 18 July–2 August 1986

Camden Festival (London), 15–29 March 1986

Cardiff Festival of Music, 22 November–6 December 1986

Cheltenham International Festival of Music, 5–20 July 1986

Chester Summer Music Festival, 16–26 July 1986

Chichester 910 Festivities, 5–19 July 1986

City of London Festival, 6–19 July 1986

Edinburgh International Festival, 10–30 August 1986

Fishguard Festival (Wales), 19–26 July 1986

Greenwich Festival (London), 1–15 June 1986

Harrogate International Festival, 29 July–10 August 1986

King's Lynn Festival (Norfolk), 25 July–2 August 1986

Ludlow Festival, 21 June–6 July 1986

Newbury Spring Festival, 7–17 May 1986

Royal National Eisteddfod of Wales, 2–9 August 1986

Salisbury Festival, 6–20 September 1986

Sidmouth International Folklore Festival, 1–8 August 1986

St Asaph — North Wales Music Festival, 21–27 September 1986

Swansea Festival of Music and the Arts, 26 September–18 October 1986

Three Choirs Festival (Hereford, Gloucester and Worcester), 17–23 August 1986 (Gloucester)

Windsor Festival, 21 September–2 October 1986

These are the major festivals in the United Kingdom, and dates may be subject to change.

Relative ranks of the armed forces (officers)

Royal Navy

Admiral of the Fleet
Admiral
Vice-Admiral
Rear-Admiral
Commodore
Captain
Commander
Lieutenant-Commander
Lieutenant
Sub-Lieutenant
Acting Sub-Lieutenant

Army

Field Marshal
General
Lieutenant-General
Major-General
Brigadier
Colonel
Lieutenant-Colonel
Major
Captain
Lieutenant
Second Lieutenant

Royal Air Force

Marshal of the Royal Air Force
Air Chief Marshal
Air Marshal
Air Vice-Marshal
Air Commodore
Group Captain
Wing Commander
Squadron Leader
Flight-Lieutenant
Flying Officer
Pilot Officer

Peers in order of rank

(and current number of each)

Peers
royal duke (4)
duke (26)
marquess (36)
earl (192)
viscount (126)
baron (482)

Peeresses
countess (5)
baroness (13)

Order of succession to the throne

(first nine only)

1 Prince Charles, Prince of Wales (eldest son of the Queen), born 1948
2 Prince William (first son of Prince Charles), born 1982
3 Prince Henry (second son of Prince Charles), born 1984
4 Prince Andrew (second son of the Queen), born 1960
5 Prince Edward (third son of the Queen), born 1964
6 Princess Anne (only daughter of the Queen), born 1950
7 Peter Phillips (only son of Princess Anne), born 1977
8 Zara Phillips (only daughter of Princess Anne), born 1981
9 Princess Margaret (only sister of the Queen), born 1930

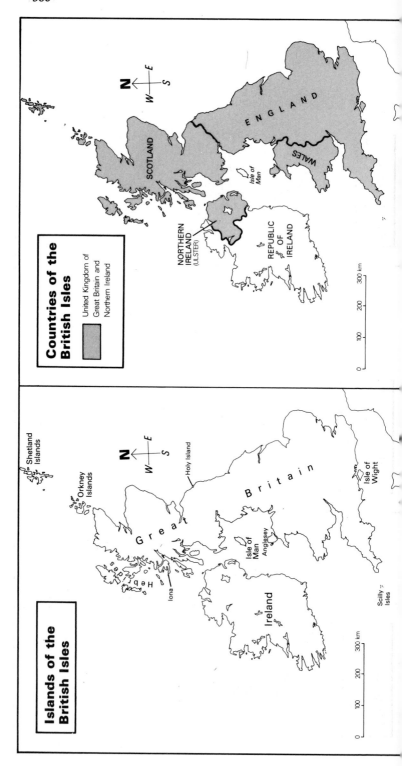

Countries of the British Isles

United Kingdom of Great Britain and Northern Ireland

ENGLAND

SCOTLAND

WALES

Isle of Man

NORTHERN IRELAND (ULSTER)

REPUBLIC OF IRELAND

N
E
S
W

0 100 200 300 km

Islands of the British Isles

Shetland Islands

Orkney Islands

Great Britain

Hebrides

Iona

Holy Island

Isle of Man

Anglesey

Ireland

Isle of Wight

Scilly Isles

N
E
S
W

0 100 200 300 km

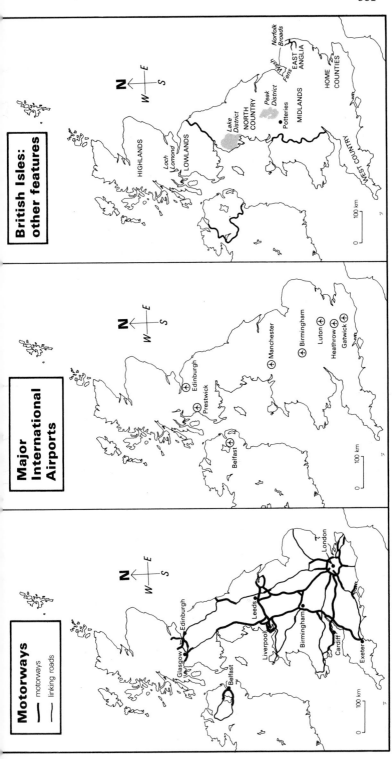

Motorways

motorways
linking roads

Glasgow
Edinburgh
Belfast
Leeds
Liverpool
Birmingham
Cardiff
Exeter
London

N
W E
S

0   100 km

Major International Airports

Edinburgh
Prestwick
Belfast
Manchester
Birmingham
Luton
Heathrow
Gatwick

N
W E
S

0   100 km

British Isles: other features

HIGHLANDS
Loch Lomond
LOWLANDS
Lake District
NORTH COUNTRY
Peak District
Potteries
MIDLANDS
Fens
Norfolk Broads
EAST ANGLIA
HOME COUNTIES
WEST COUNTRY

N
W E
S

0   100 km

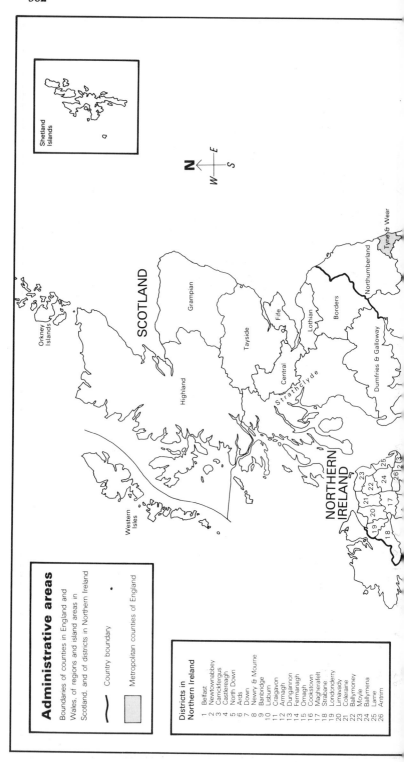

Administrative areas

Boundaries of counties in England and
Wales, of regions and island areas in
Scotland, and of districts in Northern Ireland

— Country boundary

▪ Metropolitan counties of England

Districts in Northern Ireland

1 Belfast
2 Newtownabbey
3 Carrickfergus
4 Castlereagh
5 North Down
6 Ards
7 Down
8 Newry & Mourne
9 Banbridge
10 Lisburn
11 Craigavon
12 Armagh
13 Dungannon
14 Fermanagh
15 Omagh
16 Cookstown
17 Magherafelt
18 Strabane
19 Londonderry
20 Limavady
21 Coleraine
22 Ballymoney
23 Moyle
24 Ballymena
25 Larne
26 Antrim

Shetland
Islands

N

SCOTLAND

Orkney
Islands

Western
Isles

Highland

Grampian

Tayside

Central

Strathclyde

Fife

Lothian

Borders

Dumfries & Galloway

Northumberland

Tyne & Wear

NORTHERN
IRELAND

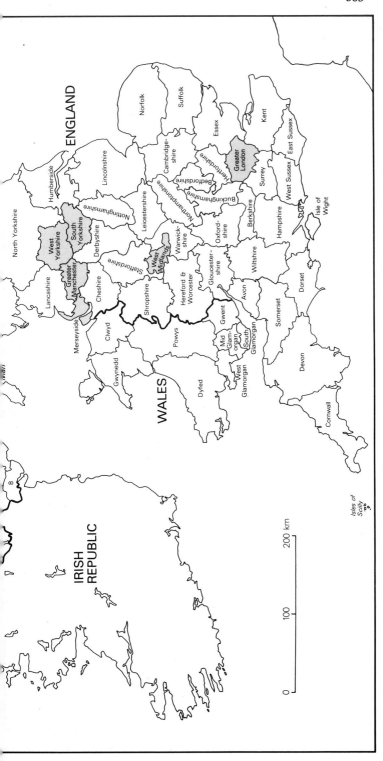